# THE SOCIALIST PHENOMENON

*Igor Shafarevich*

# THE SOCIALIST
# PHENOMENON

TRANSLATED FROM THE RUSSIAN BY *William Tjalsma*

*Foreword by Aleksandr I. Solzhenitsyn*

1817

HARPER & ROW, PUBLISHERS, New York
Cambridge, Hagerstown, Philadelphia, San Francisco
London, Mexico City, São Paulo, Sydney

This work was first published in Russian in France under the title *Sotsializm kak iavlenie mirovoi istorii*, 1975, by YMCA Press.

FIRST EDITION

*Designer: Sidney Feinberg*

Library of Congress Cataloging in Publication Data

Shafarevich, Igor̓ Rostislavovich.
    The socialist phenomenon.
    Includes index.
    1. Socialism—History.  2. Communism—History.
I.  Solzhenitsyn, Aleksandr Isaevich, 1918–
II.  Title.
HX21.S51313  1980        335′.009        79–1684
ISBN (U.S.A. and Canada) 0–06–014017–8
        (except U.S.A. and Canada) 0–06–337014–X

80 81 82 83 84 10 9 8 7 6 5 4 3 2 1

# Contents

# Foreword

It seems that certain things in this world simply cannot be discovered without extensive *experience,* be it personal or collective. This applies to the present book with its fresh and revealing perspective on the millennia-old trends of socialism. While it makes use of a voluminous literature familiar to specialists throughout the world, there is an undeniable logic in the fact that it emerged from the country that has undergone (and is undergoing) the harshest and most prolonged socialist experience in modern history. Nor is it at all incongruous that within that country this book should not have been produced by a humanist, for scholars in the humanities have been the most methodically crushed of all social strata in the Soviet Union ever since the October Revolution. It was written by a mathematician of world renown: in the Communist world, practitioners of the exact sciences must stand in for their annihilated brethren.

But this circumstance has its compensations. It provides us with a rare opportunity of receiving a systematic analysis of the theory and practice of socialism from the pen of an outstanding mathematical thinker versed in the rigorous methodology of his science. (One can attach particular weight, for instance, to his judgment that Marxism lacks even the *climate* of scientific inquiry.)

World socialism as a whole, and all the figures associated with it, are shrouded in legend; its contradictions are forgotten or concealed; it does not respond to arguments but continually ignores them—all this stems from the mist of irrationality that surrounds socialism and from its *instinctive* aversion to scientific analysis, features which the author of this volume points out repeatedly and in many contexts. The doctrines of socialism seethe with contradictions, its theories are at constant odds with its practice, yet due to a powerful *instinct*—also laid bare by Shafarevich—these contradictions do not in the least hinder the unending propaganda of socialism. Indeed, no precise, distinct socialism even exists; instead there is only a vague, rosy notion of something noble and good, of equality, communal ownership, and justice: the advent of these things will bring instant euphoria and a social order beyond reproach.

The twentieth century marks one of the greatest upsurges in the success of socialism, and concomitantly of its repulsive practical manifestations. Yet due to the same passionate irrationality, attempts to examine these results are repelled: they are either ignored completely, or implausibly explained away in terms of certain "Asiatic" or "Russian" aberrations or the personality of a particular dictator, or else they are ascribed to "state capitalism." The present book encompasses vast stretches of time and space. By carefully describing and analyzing dozens of socialist doctrines and numerous states built on socialist principles, the author leaves no room for evasive arguments based on so-called "insignificant exceptions" (allegedly bearing no resemblance to the glorious future). Whether it is the centralization of China in the first millennium B.C., the bloody European experiments of the time of the Reformation, the chilling (though universally esteemed) utopias of European thinkers, the intrigues of Marx and Engels, or the radical Communist measures of the Lenin period (no wit more humane than Stalin's heavy-handed methods)—the author in all his dozens of examples demonstrates the undeviating consistency of the phenomenon under consideration.

Shafarevich has singled out the invariants of socialism, its fundamental and unchanging elements, which depend neither on time nor place, and which, alas, are looming ominously over today's tottering world. If one considers human history in its entirety, socialism can boast of a greater longevity and durability, of wider diffusion and of control over larger masses of people, than can contemporary Western civilization. It is therefore difficult to shake off gloomy presentiments when contemplating that maw into which—before the century is out—we may all plunge: that "Asiatic formation" which Marx hastened to circumvent in his classification, and before which contemporary Marxist thought stands baffled, having discerned its own hideous countenance in the mirror of the millennia. It could probably be said that the majority of states in the history of mankind have been "socialist." But it is also true that these were in no sense periods or places of human happiness or creativity.

Shafarevich points out with great precision both the cause and the genesis of the first socialist doctrines, which he characterizes as *reactions:* Plato as a reaction to Greek culture, and the Gnostics as a reaction to Christianity. They sought to counteract the endeavor of the human spirit to stand erect, and strove to return to the earthbound existence of the primitive states of antiquity. The author also convincingly demonstrates the diametrical opposition between the concepts of man held by religion and by socialism. Socialism seeks to reduce human personality to its most primitive levels and to extinguish the highest, most complex, and "God-like" aspects of human individuality. And even *equality* itself, that powerful appeal and great promise of socialists throughout the ages, turns out to signify not equality of rights, of opportunities, and of external conditions, but equality *qua* identity, equality seen as the movement of variety toward uniformity.

Even though, as this book shows, socialism has always successfully avoided truly scientific analyses of its essence, Shafarevich's study challenges present-day theoreticians of socialism to demonstrate their arguments in a businesslike public discussion.

ALEKSANDR I. SOLZHENITSYN

# Preface

This book is inspired by the conviction that the cataclysms which humanity has experienced in the twentieth century are only the beginning of a much more profound crisis—of a radical shift in the course of history. To characterize the scope of this crisis, I had thought of comparing it to the end of ancient civilization or to the transition from the Middle Ages to the modern period. But later I became acquainted with a bolder and, it seems to me, more penetrating approach. For example, F. Heichelheim in his fascinating *An Ancient Economic History* expresses the supposition that the present period of history, which has lasted over three thousand years, is coming to an end. It had its beginnings in the Iron Age, when tendencies rooted in the free development of personality led to the creation of the spiritual and cultural values upon which contemporary life is based:

> It is quite possible that the economic state controls of the last decades, produced by immanent trends of our Late Capitalist Age of the twentieth century, mean the end and conclusion of the long development in the direction of economic individualism, and the beginnings of a novel organization of labor which is closer to the Ancient Oriental models of five thousand years ago than to the ideals for which the foundations were laid at the beginning of the Iron Age. (90: pp. 115–116)*

It is hardly necessary to demonstrate that one of the basic forces influencing the developing crisis of mankind is socialism. It both pro-

* Throughout this work, Arabic numbers within parentheses refer to entries in the bibliography beginning on page 301. Roman numerals indicate volume numbers.

motes this crisis, as a force destroying the "old world," and undertakes to show a way out. Therefore the attempt to comprehend socialism—its origins, its driving forces, the goal toward which it leads—is dictated quite simply by the instinct for self-preservation. We fear the possibility of finding ourselves at the crossroads with blinders on, at a time when choosing which road to take may determine the whole of mankind's future.

But it is precisely such attempts to understand which seem to curtail all discussion. The fact that the adherents of socialism themselves have expressed so many contradictory views ought to put us on guard. In addition, notions about the nature of socialism are as a rule strikingly vague, and yet they do not elicit doubt and are perceived as truth needing no verification. This is especially apparent in attempts to make critical evaluations of socialism. Pointing out the tragic facts that so frequently have accompanied the socialist experiments of the twentieth century usually evokes the objection that an idea cannot be judged by the unsuccessful attempts at its implementation. The task of rebuilding society is so immeasurably complicated, it is said, that in the initial stages errors are inevitable; they are, however, due to the shortcomings of certain individuals or the heritage of the past; in no sense do they follow from the fine principles enunciated by the founders of the doctrine. The fact that even in the earliest declarations of socialist doctrine there are schemes which in their cruelty far exceed any real system is dismissed as insignificant. It is argued that the determining factor is real life and hardly the constructions of theoreticians or the fantasy of utopian thinkers. Life, it is said, has its own laws. It will temper and smooth out the extremes of the fanatics and create a social structure which, even if it does not quite correspond to their original plans, will be at least viable, and in any case closer to perfection than that which now exists.

In attempting to break out of this vicious circle, it is useful to compare socialism to some other phenomenon which has had an influence of similar magnitude on life; for example, religion. Religion may have a social function, supporting or destroying social institutions; it may have an economic function (as the temples of the ancient East did with their landholdings, or as in the case of the Catholic Church in the Middle Ages); or it may have a political role, and so on. But this is possible only because there are people who believe in God and because there is a striving for a union with God which religion creates.

Without taking this fundamental function of religion into account, it is impossible to understand how it influences life generally. It is this aspect that must be clarified before one can examine the question of how it interacts with other spheres of life.

It is natural to suppose that socialism, too, contains a fundamental tendency which makes possible its phenomenal influence on life. But it is unlikely to be identified by studying, for example, the Western socialist parties, in which basic socialist tendencies are hopelessly entangled with practical politics. It is necessary, first, to study this phenomenon over a sufficiently long time span in order to ascertain its basic characteristics and, second, to examine its most striking and consistent manifestations.

In pursuing this method we shall be astonished to find that socialism (at least at first sight) turns out to be a glaring contradiction. Proceeding from a critique of a given society, accusing it of injustice, inequality and lack of freedom, socialism proclaims—in the systems where it is expressed with the greatest consistency—a far greater injustice, inequality and slavery! Noble Utopias and golden dreams about the City of the Sun usually evoke nothing more than a reproach for their "utopian" nature, for their ideals that are too high for mankind at present. But it is enough merely to open these books to be astonished by the scene: disobedient citizens turned into slaves; informers; work and life in paramilitary detachments and under close supervision; passes that are needed even for a simple stroll, and especially the details of general leveling, depicted as they are with great relish (identical clothing, identical houses, even identical cities). A work entitled "The Law of *Freedom*" describes an ideal society where in each small commune there is a hangman and anyone who has been remiss or disobedient is flogged or turned into a slave and where each citizen is considered a soldier. The revolutionaries who drew up the "Conspiracy of *Equals*" understood equality in such a way that they alone formed the government, while others were to obey implicitly—and those who did not were to be exiled to certain islands for forced labor. In the most popular work of Marxism, the *Communist Manifesto,* one of the first measures of the new socialist system to be proposed is the introduction of *compulsory labor.* And it is predicted that this will lead to a society in which "the free development of each will be the condition of the free development of all"!

Attempts to establish the happy society of the future by means of executions may perhaps be explained by the discrepancy between vision and reality, by the distortion that the idea undergoes in being put into practice. But how to understand a teaching which in its *ideal* version includes both an appeal to freedom and a program for the establishment of slavery?

Or how to reconcile the impassioned condemnation of the old order and quite justified indignation at the suffering of the poor and the oppressed with the fact that the same teachings envisage no less suffering for these oppressed masses as the lot of whole generations prior to the triumph of social justice? Thus Marx foresees fifteen, perhaps even *fifty* years of civil war for the proletariat, and Mao Tse-tung is ready to accept the loss of *half* of humanity in a nuclear war for the sake of establishing a socialist structure in the world. A call for sacrifices on this scale might sound convincing on the lips of a religious leader appealing to a truth beyond this world. But not from convinced atheists.

It would seem that socialism lacks that feature which, in mathematics, for example, is considered the minimal condition for the existence of a concept: *a definition free of contradictions.* Perhaps socialism is only a means of propaganda, a set of several contradictory conceptions, each of which appeals to a given group? The entire history of socialism speaks against such a view. The monumental influence it has had on mankind proves that socialism is in essence an internally consistent view of the world. One needs only to uncover the true logic of socialism and to find that vantage point from which it can be seen as a phenomenon without contradiction. The present book is an attempt to accomplish such a task.

In the search for this vantage point, I propose to treat the works of socialist ideology not as the writings of supermen to whom the past and the future of mankind are known, nor as mere journalistic propaganda. One ought not accept all their pretensions as truth, but on the other hand, one need not deny the accuracy of their views in areas where they may well be competent—first of all, in pronouncements bearing on themselves. If, for example, Marx repeatedly expresses the thought that man exists only as a representative of the interests of a definite class and has no existence as an individual, of course we are not obliged to believe that the essence of man was revealed to Marx. But why not accept that he is describing a view of the world inherent in certain people, himself in particular, who regard man not as a personality having an independent significance in the world but merely as a *tool* of forces outside his control? If we read that society (and the world) must be destroyed, "razed to the ground," that life cannot be improved or corrected and that history may be assisted only by its midwife Violence, it would be incautious to trust the prophetic gift of the authors of such predictions. But it is quite possible that they are conveying a view of life in which the entire world evokes malevolence, loathing and nausea (as in Sartre's first novel, *Nausea*). Life reeks of death and by force of a strange dualism is just as loathsome as death and decay under normal circumstances.

The perception of the world that may be inferred in this way from the study of socialist ideology appears to be accurate and true to life. And it is natural to assume that this is precisely what moves the adherents of socialist ideology. Furthermore, since socialism is capable of inspiring mass movements, it follows that many are subject to the influence of such a world view, perhaps even all people are to a greater or lesser degree. If socialism is viewed as the ultimate truth about man, then it unquestionably disintegrates into contradictory elements. But if we consider it to be a manifestation of only one of the tendencies in man and mankind, then it appears possible to remove the contradictions and to understand socialism as a basically cohesive and consistent phenomenon. Only then may the question be raised as to the role of socialism in history. The considerations set forth in the last paragraphs of this book do not constitute a definitive answer to this question. Rather, they indicate the direction in which, so it seems to me, the answer should be sought.

In the present work, the problem is considered in its most abstract form: What are those basic features of socialism which, interwoven as in each case they are with the individual peculiarities of various countries and epochs, engender the multiplicity of its manifestations? Therefore, although a considerable number of facts and concrete historical situations are examined, we shall abstract from the specific nature of these situations in order to delineate basic features common to all of them. As a result, the conclusions to which this discussion leads are not directly applicable to any concrete situation—not until socialist ideals find their absolute and unconstrained realization. In all existing historical realizations of the socialist ideal, we are dealing not with a pure phenomenon but with a fusion of socialist and many other tendencies. Therefore, in order to apply our views to a specific historical situation, it would be necessary to take the opposite approach: to elucidate how the general tendencies of socialism singled out by us are reflected in the peculiarities of historical epochs and national traditions. Such is not the purpose of this book. However, it seems to me that without making a distinction between the phenomenon in its general aspect and the specifics generated by concrete historical conditions, all attempts at understanding are hopeless.

Parts One and Two of the book are an exposition of concrete facts from the history of socialist teachings and socialist states. Only in Part Three is there an attempt to analyze these facts and to draw certain conclusions. This structure entails a number of difficulties for the reader. If he does not wish to go into the details of the various historical epochs, he may simply skim Parts One and Two and move quickly into Part Three. For the convenience of such a reader, several summaries review those conclusions from the historical sections which are of special importance for the subsequent discussion.

Working on this book without official permission, under the conditions prevailing in our country, I encountered constant difficulties in obtaining the necessary literature. Given this situation, I am aware of the likelihood (and perhaps even the inevitability) of error in certain specific questions and of the shortcomings of my arguments, which may have been presented earlier and more effectively by others. My only justification is the urgency of the theme and the special historical experience of our country.

The latter circumstance was the basic stimulus for my work, inspiring me with a certain hope of success. Russia's experience in the twentieth century has been unique among modern nations; perhaps there are few precedents in the whole of world history. We became witnesses to events and changes which we would hardly have thought possible before this time. A new field of phenomena, formerly attainable only through artistic or mystical intuition, now became open to rational investigation, based on a study of facts and their logical analysis. We have had the opportunity of seeing history in a new aspect—an advantage that can outweigh many difficulties.

This book would never have been written were it not for the assistance rendered me by numerous people. At the moment, it is not possible for me to name them all and to express to each my debt of gratitude. But I can thank two of them here: A. I. Solzhenitsyn, under whose influence I undertook to write this book, and V. M. Borisov, whose criticism was invaluable.

# PART ONE

# CHILIASTIC SOCIALISM

# Introduction

The word "socialism" often implies two quite different phenomena:

1. A doctrine and an appeal based on it, a program for changing life, and

2. A social structure that exists in time and space. The most obvious examples include Marxism as contained in the "classic" writings of Marx and others and the social structure that exists in the U.S.S.R. and the People's Republic of China. Among the fundamental principles of the state doctrine in these countries is the assertion that the connection between the two phenomena is very simple. On the one hand, it is asserted, there is a scientific theory which proves that after achieving a definite level in the development of productive forces, mankind will pass over to a new historic formation; this theory points the way to the most rational paths for such a transition. And on the other hand, we are assured, there is the embodiment of this scientific prognosis, its confirmation. As an example of quite a different point of view we cite H. G. Wells, who visited Russia in 1920 and, though infected by the worship of socialism, fashionable then as now, nevertheless almost instinctively refused to accept Marxism, in this sense reflecting the antipathy toward all scholastic theories typical of an Englishman. In his book *Russia in the Shadows*, Wells writes: "Marxist Communism has always been a theory of revolution, a theory not merely lacking in creative and constructive ideas but hostile to creative and constructive ideas." (1: p. 60) He describes the communism that governed Russia as ". . . in so many matters like a conjurer who has left his

pigeon and his rabbit behind him and can produce nothing whatever from the hat." (1: p. 64)

From this point of view, Marxism does not set itself any goal other than that of preparing for the seizure of power. The state system established as a result is therefore defined and shaped by the necessity of holding power. Since these tasks are entirely different, the official theory and the actual implementation have nothing in common.

It would be incautious to take either of these assertions on faith. On the contrary, it would be desirable, first, to study both "socialisms" independently, without any a priori hypotheses, and only then attempt to come to conclusions about the connections that exist between them.

We shall begin with socialism understood as a doctrine, as an appeal.

All such doctrines (and as we shall see, there were many of them) have a common core—they are based on the complete rejection of the existing social structure. They call for its destruction and paint a picture of a more just and happy society in which the solution to all the fundamental problems of the times would be found. Furthermore, they propose concrete ways of achieving this goal. In religious literature such a system of views is referred to as belief in the thousand-year Kingdom of God on earth—chiliasm. Borrowing this terminology, we shall designate the socialist doctrines of this type as "chiliastic socialism."

In order to give some sense of the scale of this phenomenon and of the place it occupies in the history of mankind, we shall examine two doctrines that fit the category of chiliastic socialism, as they are described by their contemporaries. In doing so, we shall attempt to extract a picture of the future society envisaged, leaving to one side for the moment the motivation as well as the concrete means recommended for achieving the ideal.

The first example takes us to Athens in 392 B.C. during the great urban Dionysia, when Aristophanes presented his comedy *Ecclesiazusae* or *The Congresswomen*. Here he depicts a teaching fashionable in the Athens of the time. The plot is as follows: The women of the city, wearing beards and dressed in men's clothing, come to the assembly and by a majority vote pass a resolution transferring all power in the state to women. They use this power to introduce a series of measures, which are expounded in a dialogue between Praxagora, the leader of the women, and her husband, Blepyros. Here are several quotations.

PRAXAGORA: Compulsory Universal Community Property is what I propose to propose; across-the-board Economic Equality, to fill those fissures that scar our society's face. No more the division between Rich and Poor. . . .

. . . We'll wear the same clothes, and share the same food. . . .

. . . My initial move will be to communalize land, and money, and all other property, personal and real.

BLEPYROS: But take the landless man who's invisibly wealthy . . . because he hides his silver and gold in his pockets. What about him?

PRAXAGORA: He'll deposit it all in the Fund. . . .

. . . I'll knock out walls and remodel the City into one big happy household, where all can come and go as they choose. . . .

. . . I'm pooling the women, creating a public hoard for the use of every man who wishes to take them to bed and make babies.

BLEPYROS: A system like this requires a pretty wise father to know his own children.

PRAXAGORA: But why does he need to? Age is the new criterion: Children will henceforth trace their descent from all men who *might* have begot them. . . .

BLEPYROS: Who's going to work the land and produce the food?

PRAXAGORA: The slaves. This leaves you just one civic function: When the shades of night draw on, slip sleekly down to dinner. . . .

. . . The State's not going to stint. Its hand is full and open, its heart is large, it'll stuff its menfolk free of charge, then issue them torches when dinner's done and send them out to hunt for fun.

(2: pp. 43–51)

The reader will of course already have noticed many of the features of a familiar doctrine. Let us attempt to specify the associations that arise by considering a second example—the classic statement of the Marxist program contained in the *Communist Manifesto*. Here are some quotations characterizing the future society as the authors imagine it: ". . . the theory of the Communists may be summed up in the single sentence: Abolition of private property. . . ." (3: V: p. 496) "Abolition of the family! Even the most radical flare up at this infamous proposal of the Communists. . . . On what foundation is the present family, the bourgeois family based? On capital, on private gain. In its completely developed form, this family exists only among the bourgeoisie. But this state of things finds its complement in the practical absence of the family among the proletarians, and in public prostitution.

"The bourgeois family will vanish as a matter of course when its complement vanishes, and both will vanish with the vanishing of capital.

"But, you will say, we destroy the most hallowed of relations when we replace home education by social.

"And your education! Is not that also social, and determined by the social conditions under which you educate? . . ." (3: V: p. 499)

That last thought is somewhat clarified in "Principles of Communism," a document written by Engels in the course of preparing the *Communist Manifesto.*

Among the first measures to be taken after the revolution, we find:

"8. The education of all children, from the moment that they can get along without a mother's care, shall be at state institutions and at state expense." (3: V: p. 475)

The *Communist Manifesto* again:

"But you Communists would introduce communality of women, screams the whole bourgeoisie in chorus." (3: V: p. 499)

Answered by: "The Communists have no need of introducing communality of women; it has existed almost from time immemorial.

"Our bourgeois, not content with having the wives and daughters of proletarians at his disposal, not to speak of common prostitutes, takes the greatest pleasure in seducing each other's wives.

"Bourgeois marriage is in reality a system of wives in common and thus, at the worst, what the Communists might possibly be reproached with is that they desire to introduce, in the place of a hypocritically concealed, an openly legalized communality of women." (3: V: p. 500)

In the *Communist Manifesto* there is no reference to the other material aspects of life. In "Principles of Communism" we find:

"9. The building of large palaces in the national estates as common dwellings for the communes, whose citizens will be busy in industry, agriculture; these structures will combine the merits of urban and rural life and avoid their defects." (3: V: p. 475)

We see concealed in Marx's Hegelian phraseology and Aristophanes' buffoonery almost the same program:

1. Abolition of private property.
2. Abolition of the family—i.e., communality of wives and disruption of the bonds between parents and children.
3. Purely material prosperity.

It would even be possible to say that both programs coincide perfectly, were it not for one place in the *Ecclesiazusae*. In answer to Blepyros's question as to who will do the plowing, Praxagora replies: "Slaves!" Here she proclaims the fourth point of the program, and a most significant one—liberation from the necessity of work. Interestingly enough, on this point Herbert Marcuse, the best-known of the neo-Marxists and one of the leaders of the New Left in the U.S.A., differs from Marx.

For instance, in his essay "The End of Utopia," Marcuse says that "it is no accident that for modern avant garde left intellectuals the works of Fourier have become relevant again. Fourier did not flinch where Marx was insufficiently bold. He spoke of a society where work would become play." And elsewhere in the same essay: "New technical potentialities lead to oppression unless there develops a vital need for the abolition of alienating work." (4: pp. 75, 77)

Supplementing the program of the *Communist Manifesto* in this fashion, we obtain a description of the ideal which fully coincides with what had been the object of Aristophanes' derision on the stage of the Athenian theater in 392 B.C.

We are confronted by a set of ideas with certain strikingly durable features which have remained almost unchanged from antiquity to our day. The term "chiliastic socialism" will be applied to such ideas. Below, we shall attempt to outline this concept more precisely, to point out the main stages of its historical development and to take note of the broader ideological framework within which the doctrines of chiliastic socialism came into being.

# I The Socialism of Antiquity

In classical Greece we encounter the concept of chiliastic socialism in its full-fledged, one might even say ideal, form. Plato's enunciation of this concept in itself had an enormous influence on the subsequent history of chiliastic socialism. Two of Plato's dialogues are devoted to this theme: *The Republic* and *Laws.* In the former, Plato depicts what he considers an ideal state structure, while the latter shows the best practical approximation of this ideal. *The Republic* was written during the middle years of Plato's life, *Laws* in his old age. It seems possible that the failures Plato experienced trying to put his views into practice are reflected in these works.

We begin with an overview of the picture of the ideal society that is given in *The Republic,* a work that Sergius Bulgakov calls "wondrous and perplexing." Indeed, the ten books of this dialogue reflect almost all aspects of Plato's philosophy—his conception of being (the world of ideas), cognition (the visual world, the world accessible to the mind), the soul, justice, art and society. *The Republic* may at first sight seem too narrow a title for such a work. Nevertheless, it is fully justified, since the question of the structure of society is the center around which Plato's many-sided philosophy revolves, as well as serving as the principal illustration of his teaching. Understanding the concepts of Good and Beauty is essential for ruling a state. The doctrines of the immortality of the soul and of retribution after death promote the development of the spiritual qualities essential for rulers, the state must be founded on justice, and art is one of the major instruments for the education of citizens.

Plato expounds on the possible forms of a state (he names five structures) and speaks about the corresponding spiritual qualities. All the
states that existed contemporary to him he classifies as belonging to
four *corrupt* types. Division, hostility, discord, willfulness and striving
for riches reign in these states.

". . . such a city should of necessity be not one, but two, a city
of the rich and a city of the poor, dwelling together, and always plotting
against one another." (5:551d)*

The fifth form of state structure is, according to Plato, the *perfect
state*. Its basic quality is justice, which permits it to partake of virtue.
In answer to the question what constitutes justice in a state, Plato
says:

". . . what we laid down in the beginning as a universal requirement when we were founding our city, this I think, or some form of
this, is justice. And what we did lay down, and often said, if you recall,
was that each one man must perform one social service in the state
for which his nature was best adapted." (433a)

On the basis of this proposition, the population of the state is divided
into three social groups; we may even call them castes. They are:
philosophers, guardians or soldiers, artisans and peasants. The children
of artisans and peasants belong to the same group as their parents
and may never become guardians. The children of guardians as a rule
inherit their fathers' occupation, but if they show negative inclinations
they are made into either artisans or peasants. But the philosophers
may supplement their numbers from the best of the guardians, but
not until the latter reach the age of fifty.

Plato's conception is not at all materialistic: his concern is not with
the manner in which production is organized in his state. Thus he
speaks very little about the daily life of the artisans and peasants. He
believes that the life of the state is determined by its laws, hence he
is concerned above all with the life of those castes that create and
guard the law.

The philosophers have unlimited power in the state. (Bulgakov even
suggests that the word "philosophers" should be translated "the righteous men" or "saints.")

They are the people ". . . enamored of the kind of knowledge
which reveals to them something of that essence which is eternal,
and is not wandering between the two poles of generation and decay."

---

* In subsequent references to Plato's *Republic,* only the marginal sigla will be quoted.

(485b) A philosopher possesses ". . . a mind habituated to thoughts of grandeur and the contemplation of all time and all existence. . . . such a man will not suppose death to be terrible." (486b)

Once the philosophers have understood their high mission, they will structure their lives in accordance with it, ". . . devoting the greater part of their time to the study of philosophy, but when the turn comes for each, toiling in the service of the state and holding office for the city's sake, regarding the task not as a fine thing but a necessity. And so, when each generation has educated others like themselves to take their place as guardians of the state, they shall depart to the Islands of the Blessed and there dwell." (540a, b)

The guardians are under the philosophers' command. Plato's favorite image in describing the guardians is that of the dog. Thus, as with pure-bred canines, the guardians' ". . . natural disposition is to be most gentle to their familiars and those whom they recognize, but the contrary to those whom they do not know." (375e) Their children should be taken on campaigns in order to accustom them to war . . . "give them a taste of blood as we do with whelps." (537a) Youthful guardians possess the qualities of pure-bred pups: ". . . each of them must be keen of perception, quick in pursuit of what it has apprehended, and strong too if it has to fight it out with its captive." (375a) Women are to enjoy equal rights with men and are to have the same obligations, allowing only for the fact that they have less physical strength than men. Plato argues by analogy: "Do we expect the females of watchdogs to join in guarding what the males guard and to hunt with them and share all their pursuits, or do we expect the females to stay indoors. . . . ?" (451d) The whole of the guardian caste is compared with a pack of hard and wiry hounds. (422d)

But a guardian should also possess other, higher qualities: "And does it seem to you that our guardian-to-be will also need, in addition to being high-spirited, the further quality of having the love of wisdom in his nature?" (375e) And: ". . . never by sorcery nor by force can be brought to expel from their souls . . . this conviction that they must do what is best for the state." (412e)

These qualities are attained by means of a carefully thought-out system of education guided by the philosophers and lasting until age thirty-five. A fundamental role in education is reserved for art, which, for the benefit of the state, is subjected to strict censorship. "We must begin, then, it seems, by a censorship over our story-makers, and what they do well we must pass and what not, reject." (377c) "What they do well" applies here not to the esthetic qualities of stories and myths but to their educational function. Bad stories are those "that Hesiod and Homer and the other poets relate to us." (377d) Furthermore, "Shall we, then, thus lightly suffer our children to listen to any chance stories fashioned by any chance teachers and so to take into their minds opinions for the most part contrary to those that we shall think it desirable for them to hold when they are grown up?" (377b)

All stories that might inspire a false impression of divinity are forbidden, as well as those that describe the cruelty of the gods, their quarrels or love adventures, and stories which suggest that gods may be the cause of misfortune. ". . . we must contend in every way that neither should anyone assert this in his own city if it is to be well governed, nor anyone hear it, neither younger nor older, neither telling a story in meter or without meter." (380b) All poetic works that speak about the horrors of the nether world and of death are to be eliminated, as well as those that involve any manifestation of fear or sorrow—all that hinders the development of courage. Guardians should see nothing frightening about death. It is forbidden to speak about the injustice of fate—that righteous people can suffer misfortune and unrighteous ones can lead happy lives. It is forbidden to criticize the leaders or to write about any manifestation of fear, grief, famine or death. "We will beg Homer and the other poets not to be angry if we cancel those and all similar passages, not that they are not poetic and pleasing to most hearers, but because the more poetic they are, the less are they suited to the ears." (387b)

Other arts are also to be kept under surveillance. "It is here, then, I said, in music, as it seems, that our guardians must build their guardhouse and post a watch." (424d) Polyphony and the combining of various scales are forbidden. There are to be no flutes or makers of flutes in the state; only the lyre and the kithara are permitted. Plato expands on these principles: "Is it, then, only the poets that we must supervise and compel to embody in their poems the semblance of the good character or else not write poetry among us, or must we keep watch over the other craftsmen, and forbid them to represent the evil disposition, the licentious, the illiberal, the graceless, either in the likeness of living creatures or in buildings or in any other product of their art, on penalty, if unable to obey, of being forbidden to practice their art among us? . . ." (401b) The answer is obvious for Plato.

On the other hand, new myths are created, with the purpose of instilling in the guardians a spirit necessary to the state. For instance, to inculcate in them love for one another and the state, they are told that they are all brothers, sons of the single mother earth of their land. But to reinforce the idea of castes, it is stressed that in the process philosophers received an admixture of gold, guardians of silver, peasants and artisans of iron.

The entire education of the guardians, beginning with children's games, is supervised by the philosophers, who subject them to various tests, checking their memory, endurance, moderation and courage. Adults, as well as children, are severely punished for lying. But lying is permitted the philosophers. "It seems likely that our rulers will have to make considerable use of falsehood and deception for the benefit of their subjects." (459d)

It has already been noted that Plato perceives the major defect of faulty states in the absence of unity among citizens, in animosity and discord. He seeks to find the cause of these phenomena.

"And the chief cause of this is when the citizens do not utter in unison such words as 'mine' and 'not mine,' and similarly with regard to the word 'alien'?

"Precisely so."

"That city, then, is best ordered in which the greatest number use the expression 'mine' and 'not mine' of the same things in the same way." (462c)

The guardians' life is regulated accordingly. They possess "nothing in private possession but their bodies, but all else in common." (464e)

"Secondly, none must have any habitation or treasure house which is not open for all to enter at will. Their food, in such quantities as are needful for athletes of war sober and brave, they must receive as an agreed stipend from the other citizens as the wages of their guardianship, so measured that there shall be neither superfluity at the end of the year nor any lack. And resorting to a common mess like soldiers on campaign they will live together." (416d)

". . . for these only of all the dwellers in the city it is not lawful to handle gold and silver and to touch them nor yet to come under the same roof with them, nor to hang them as ornaments on their limbs nor to drink from silver and gold." (417a)

Guardians live in their own state as hired guard detachments. ". . . and what is more, they serve for board wages and do not even receive pay in addition to their food as others do, so that they will not even be able to take a journey on their own account, if they wish to, or make presents to their mistresses, or spend money in other directions according to their desires like the men who are thought to be happy." (420a)

Property, however, is only one of the things by which private interests may distract the guardians from their duty. Another factor that could set them apart is the family; therefore it is also eliminated.

"These women shall all be common to all these men, and that none shall cohabit with any privately, and that the children shall be common, and that no parent shall know its own offspring nor any child its parent." (457d) Marriage is replaced by a temporary union of sexes for purely physiological satisfaction and propagation of the species. This aspect of life is carefully regulated by the philosophers, which permits the introduction of a perfect system of sex selection. The union of couples is conducted solemnly and is performed to the accompaniment of songs composed by poets especially for these occasions. Who is to be joined to whom is decided by lot so that no one can blame anyone but fate. But the leaders of the state carefully manipulate the process to achieve the desired results.

As could be expected, the education of children is in the hands of the state. ". . . the children . . . will be taken over by the officials appointed for this. . . ." (460b) ". . . but the offspring of the inferior, and any of those of the other sort who are born defective, they will properly dispose of in secret, so that no one will know what has become of them." (460c) As for a child born of unregulated sexual union, the following is indicated: ". . . to dispose of it on the understanding that we cannot rear such an offspring." (461c) Parents ought not know their children: ". . . conducting the mothers to the pen when their breasts are full, but employing every device to prevent anyone from recognizing her own infant." (460c) As to the question how parents and children shall recognize one another, the answer is as follows: "They won't . . . except that a man will call all male offspring born between the seventh and the tenth month after he became a bridegroom his sons, and all female, daughters, and they will call him father." (461d)

Deprived of family, children and all property, the guardians live exclusively for the benefit of the state. Any violation of the interests of the state is punished. Soldiers who show cowardice are turned into artisans or peasants; prisoners taken are not to be ransomed out of slavery. Medicine is also used as a means of control. Physicians and judges ". . . will care for the bodies and souls of such of your citizens as are truly well-born, but those who are not, such as are defective in body, they will suffer to die, and those who are evil-natured and incurable in soul they will themselves put to death." (410a)

Why would the guardians undertake such a life? One of the participants in the dialogue says: "What will be your defense, Socrates, if anyone objects that you are not making these men very happy, and that through their own fault? For the city really belongs to them and yet they get no enjoyment out of it as ordinary men do." (419a)

However, from Plato's point of view happiness is not determined by material well-being. In discharging their duties, the guardians will achieve the respect and love of other citizens, as well as the hope for reward after death. He says:

". . . they will live a happier life than that men count most happy, the life of the victors at Olympia.

"How so?

"The things for which those are felicitated are a small part of what is secured for these. Their victory is fairer and their public support more complete. For the prize of victory that they win is the salvation of the entire state, the fillet that binds their brows is the public support of themselves and their children—they receive honor from the city while they live and when they die a worthy burial.

"A fair guerdon, indeed, he said." (465e)

Though giving a detailed account of the life of the philosophers and guardians, Plato says almost nothing about the rest of the population—the artisans and peasants. Laws for them are determined by the philosophers in accordance with the basic principles expressed in the dialogue: "Nay, 'twould not be fitting . . . to dictate to good and honorable men. For most of the enactments that are needed about these things they will easily, I presume, discover." (425d)

Clearly, the entire population is subjected to the philosophers and the guardians. The guardians set up their camp in the city: ". . . a position from which they could best hold down rebellion against the laws from within." (415e)

Everyone is bound to his profession:

". . . we were at pains to prevent the cobbler from attempting to be at the same time a farmer, a weaver, or a builder instead of just a cobbler, to the end that we might have the cobbler's business well done, and similarly assigned to each and every one man one occupation, for which he was fit and naturally adapted and at which he was to work all his days." (374c) The life of the artisans and the peasants is regulated on the basis of a greater or lesser degree of leveling, since for them both poverty and riches lead to degradation, and "the work that he turns out will be worse, and he will also make inferior workmen of his sons or any others whom he teaches." (421e) But it is not clear to what extent the socialist principles that govern the life of the two other groups extend to artisan and peasant.

In conclusion, it is interesting to note that religious problems are given a good deal of space in the dialogue, and are clearly connected with the question of the ideal state. However, this linkage is treated in a quite rationalistic fashion—religion does not set the state any goals, but rather plays a protective and educational role. Myths, many of which are specially invented, as Plato says, with this purpose in mind, facilitate the development of characteristics useful to the state.

Almost everyone who has written on Plato's *Republic* has remarked on the ambiguous impression produced by this dialogue. Plato's scheme for the destruction of the subtlest and most profound features of human personality and the reduction of human society to the level of an ant hill evokes revulsion. And at the same time one cannot help being impressed by the almost religious impulse to sacrifice personal interests to a higher goal. Plato's entire program is founded on the denial of personality—but on the denial of egoism as well. He understood that the future of mankind is not dependent on the victory of this or that contending group in the struggle for material interests, but rather on the changes within people and on the development of new human qualities.

It is difficult to deny that Plato's *Republic* is morally, ethically and in purely aesthetic terms far superior to other systems of chiliastic socialism. If we can suppose that Aristophanes' *Ecclesiazusae* is a parody of ideas such as Plato's—presumably widely discussed in Athens at the time—then modern systems like that of Marcuse seem much nearer to the caricature than to the original. Marcuse's "turning work into play," his "socio-sexual protest," the struggle against the "necessity of suppressing one's instincts," are shockingly primitive in comparison with the lofty asceticism described by Plato.

In spite of their unique role in the history of socialist ideas, Plato's

*Republic* and his *Laws* are but one of many expressions of ancient chiliastic socialism. Attic comedy abounds with references to ideas of this kind. For example, out of the eleven surviving comedies of Aristophanes, two (*Ecclesiazusae* and *Plutus*) are devoted to socialist themes.

During the Hellenistic epoch there came into being an extensive utopian socialist literature, partially serious, in part meant as entertainment, where the ascetic ideal of the Platonic *Republic* was replaced by "the land of milk and honey" and by the happy state of free love. The plots of a number of these works are known to us from the *Historical Library* by the first century B.C. writer Diodorus.

One of the most vivid descriptions tells of a traveler to a state situated on "sunny islands" (apparently in the Indian Ocean). This state consists of socialist communes of four hundred people each. Labor is obligatory for all members of society, moreover, with "all serving the others in turn, fishing, engaging in crafts, arts or public service." (6: p. 323) Food is regimented in a similar manner; the menu for each day is regulated by law. "Marriage is unknown to them; instead they enjoy communal wives; children are brought up in common as they belong to the whole of the community and are equally loved by all. Frequently, it so happens that nurses exchange babies they are suckling so that even mothers do not recognize their children." (6: p. 63) Due to the excellent climate, the inhabitants of the islands were much taller than ordinary mortals. They lived to the age of 150. All who were incurably ill or suffered from some physical defect were supposed to commit suicide. Those who reached a certain age were also to kill themselves.

Socialist ideas in one or another form frequently played a role in the movements and sects that arose around emerging Christianity. Even in the first century A.D., the sect of the Nicolaites preached the communality of property and wives. The Christian writer Epiphanes considers the sect's founder to be Nicolas—one of the seven deacons chosen by the community of the disciples of the Apostles in Jerusalem (as recounted in Acts of the Apostles 6: 5).

Irenaeus of Lyons and Clement of Alexandria describe the gnostic sect of Carpocratians which appeared in Alexandria in the second century A.D. The founder of this sect, Carpocrates, taught that faith and love bring salvation and place man above good and evil. These ideas were elaborated by his son Epiphanes, who died at the age of seventeen, having written a work "On Justice." According to Clement of

Alexandria, he was later worshiped as a god in Samos, where a sanctuary was erected to him.

Some quotations from Epiphanes follow:

"God's justice consists in community and equality."

"The Creator and Father of all gave everyone equally eyes to see and established laws in accordance with his justice without distinguishing female from male, wise from humble and in general one thing from any other."

"The private character of laws cuts and gnaws the community established by God's law. Do you not understand the words of the Apostle: 'Through law I knew sin' (Romans 7: 7)? 'Mine' and 'thine' were spread to the detriment of community by virtue of the law."

"Thus, God made everything common for man; according to the principles of communality, he joins man and woman. In the same way, he links all living beings; in this he has revealed justice demanding communality in conjunction with equality. But those begotten in this way deny the community that has created them, saying: 'He who takes a wife, let him possess her.' But they can possess all in common as the animals do."

"It is therefore laughable to hear the giver of laws saying: 'Do not covet' and more laughable still the addition: 'that which is your neighbor's.' For he himself invested us with desires, which moreover must be safeguarded as they are necessary for procreation. But even more laughable is the phrase 'your neighbor's wife,' for in this way that which is common is forcibly turned into private property." (7: p. 117)

The members of this sect, which extended as far as Rome, followed principles of complete communality, including communality of wives.

The appearance of Manicheism gave rise to a great number of sects that professed doctrines of a socialist character. St. Augustine informs us of the existence of such sects at the end of the third and the beginning of the fourth centuries A.D.

The movement inspired by Mazdak, which was widespread at the beginning of the fifth century in Persia, was also of Manichean origin. Mazdak taught that contradictions, anger and violence are all related to women and material things. "Therefore," in the words of the Persian historian Mohammed Ibn Harun, "he made all women accessible and all material wealth common and prescribed that everyone had an equal share, just as each has an equal share of water, fire and pastures." (8:

p. 20) This movement spread over the entire country, and for a time even King Kawadh I supported it. Another historian, Tabari, writes: "Frequently, a man did not know his son nor the son his own father, and no one possessed enough to be guaranteed life and livelihood." (8: p. 35) In the disturbance which subsequently arose, the followers of Mazdak were defeated.

The extent of social dislocation caused by this movement can be appreciated from the information (8: pp. 32–33) that Kawadh's heir issued a law ensuring the welfare of fatherless children and legislating the return of abducted women to their families.

We encounter here the phenomenon of broad masses of people affected by a socialist doctrine. This was unknown in antiquity, although it is typical of the Middle Ages, to which Mazdak's movement brings us chronologically.

# II   The Socialism
of the Heresies

During the Middle Ages and the period of the Reformation, doctrines of chiliastic socialism often fomented broad popular movements in Western Europe. Such a situation did not obtain in antiquity, when these ideas were expressed by individual thinkers or within narrow groups. As a result of this evolution, the socialist doctrines, in turn, acquired new and extremely important traits, which they have preserved to this day.

The survey below provides a very general and schematic overview of the development of socialist ideas in this epoch. In order to compensate somewhat for the abstract character of the presentation and to help make more concrete the atmosphere in which these ideas arose, we introduce (in the Appendix following the General Survey) three biographies of eminent representatives of the chiliastic socialism of the period. In the subsequent section, an attempt is made to delineate the ideological framework within which the doctrines of chiliastic socialism developed.

## 1. General Survey

Beginning with the Middle Ages and the Reformation, doctrines of chiliastic socialism in Western Europe appeared under religious guise. As varied as they were, all these doctrines had in common a characteristic trait—the rejection of numerous aspects of the teachings of the Catholic Church and a fierce hatred for the Church itself. As a result, they developed largely within the framework of the heretical movements. Below we shall review several characteristic Medieval heresies.

18

*Cathars.* The movement of the Cathars (Greek for "the pure") spread in Western and Central Europe in the eleventh century. It seems to have originated in the East, arriving from Bulgaria, the home of Bogomil heresy in the preceding century. The ultimate origins of both, however, are more ancient.

Among the Cathars there were many different groups. Pope Innocent III counted as many as forty Cathar sects. In addition, there existed other sects that had many doctrinal points in common with the Cathars; among the best known were the Albigenses. They are all usually categorized as gnostic or Manichean heresies. In order to avoid unnecessary complexity, we shall describe the beliefs and notions common to all groups, without specifying the relative importance that a particular view might have in a given sect. (For a more detailed account, see 9 [Vol. I], 10, and 11.)

The basic contention in all branches of the movement was the belief in the irreconcilable contradiction between the physical world, seen as the source of evil, and the spiritual world, seen as the essence of good. The so-called dualistic Cathars believed this to be caused by the existence of two Gods—one good, the other evil. It was the God of evil who had created the physical world—the earth with everything that grows upon it, the sky, the sun and the stars, and human bodies as well. The good God, on the other hand, was seen as the creator of the spiritual world, in which there is another, spiritual sky, other stars and another sun. Other Cathars, called monarchian Cathars, believed in one beneficent God, the creator of the universe, but assumed that the physical world was the creation of his eldest, fallen son— Satan or Lucifer. All the Cathars held that the mutual hostility of the realms of matter and spirit allowed for no intermingling. They therefore denied the bodily incarnation of Christ (asserting that his body was a spiritual one, which had only the appearance of physicality) and the resurrection of the flesh. They saw a reflection of their dualism in the division of the Holy Scriptures into Old and New Testaments. They identified the God of the Old Testament, the creator of the physical world, with the evil God or with Lucifer. They professed the New Testament as the teaching of the good God.

The Cathars did not believe that God had created the world from nothing; they held that matter was eternal and that the world would have no end. So far as people were concerned, they considered their bodies to be the creation of the evil force. Their souls, though, did not have a single source. The souls of the majority of men, just like their bodies, were begotten by evil—such people had no hope for salvation and were doomed to perish when the entire material world returned to a state of primeval chaos. But the souls of some men had been created by the good God; these were the angels led into temptation by Lucifer and thus imprisoned in earthly bodies. As a result of changing into a series of bodies (Cathars believed in the transmigration of souls), they were destined to end up in their sect so as to receive liberation from the prison of matter. The ultimate goal and the ideal of all mankind was in principle universal suicide. This was conceived either as in the most direct sense (we shall encounter the practical realization of this view later) or through ceasing to bear children.

These views determined the attitude toward both sin and salvation. The Cathars denied the existence of freedom of will. The doomed children of evil could not avoid their fate. But those who were initiated into the highest rank of the sect could no longer sin. The stringent rules to which members had to subject themselves were justified by the danger of being defiled by sinful matter. Nonobservance of these rules merely indicated that the initiation had been invalid, since either the initiates or those who had initiated them did not possess angelic souls. Before initiation, no restrictions of any kind were placed on behavior: the only real sin was the fall of the angels in heaven; everything else was considered to be an inevitable consequence. After initiation, neither repentance for sins committed nor their expiation was considered necessary.

The Cathars' attitude toward life followed consistently from their view that evil permeated the physical world. Propagation of the species was considered Satan's work. Cathars believed that a pregnant woman was under the influence of demons and that every child born was accompanied by a demon. Hence the prohibition against eating meat and against anything that came from sexual union. The same tendency led to a complete avoidance of social involvement. Secular power was considered to be the creation of the evil God and hence not to be submitted to, nor were they to become involved in legal proceedings, the taking of oaths, or the carrying of arms. Anyone using force was considered a murderer, be he soldier or judge. It follows that participation in many areas of life was completely closed to the Cathars. Moreover, many considered that any contact whatever with people outside the sect was a sin, with the exception of attempts to proselytize. (12: p. 654)

All Cathars were united in their hatred of the Catholic Church. They regarded it not as the Church of Jesus Christ but as the church of sinners, the Whore of Babylon. The Pope was held to be the source of all error and priests considered sophists and pharisees. In the opinion of the Cathars, the fall of the Church had taken place in the time of Constantine the Great and Pope Sylvester, when the Church had violated the commandments of Christ by encroaching upon secular power. They denied the sacraments, particularly the baptism of children (since they were too young to believe), but matrimony and Communion as well. Some branches of the movement systematically plundered and defiled churches. In 1225, Cathars burned down a Catholic Chruch in Brescia; in 1235, they killed the Bishop of Mantua. A certain Eon de l'Étoile, head of a Manichean sect (1143–1148), proclaimed himself the son of God and the Lord of everything on earth. In this capacity, he called upon his followers to plunder churches.

The Cathars hated the cross in particular, considering it to be a symbol of the evil God. As early as about 1000 A.D., a certain Leutard, preaching near Châlons, called for the smashing of crosses and religious images. In the twelfth century, Pierre de Bruys made bonfires of broken crosses, until finally he himself was burned by an angry mob. The Cathars considered churches to be heaps of stones and divine services mere pagan rites. They rejected religious images, denied the intercession of the saints and the efficacy of prayer for the departed. A book by the Dominican inquisitor Rainier Sacconi, himself a heretic for seventeen years, states that the Cathars were not forbidden to plunder churches.

Although the Cathars rejected the Catholic hierarchy and the sacraments, they had a hierarchy and sacraments of their own. The basic division of the sect was into two groups—the "perfect" (perfecti) and the "faithful" (credenti). The former were few in number (Rainier counted only four thousand in all), but they constituted the select group of the sect leaders. The clergy was drawn from the perfecti, and only they were privy to all the doctrines of the sect; many extreme views that were radically opposed to Christianity were unknown to the ordinary faithful. Only the perfecti were obliged to observe the many prohibitions. In particular, they were not allowed to deny their faith under any circumstances. In case of persecution, they were to accept a martyr's death. The faithful, on the other hand, were allowed to go to regular church for form's sake and, when persecuted, to disavow the faith.

In compensation for the rigors imposed on the *perfecti*, their position was far higher than that occupied by Catholic priests. In certain respects, the *perfecti* were as gods themselves, and the faithful worshiped them accordingly. The faithful were obliged to support the *perfecti*. One of the important rites of the sect was that of "submission," in which the faithful performed a threefold prostration before the *perfecti*. The *perfecti* had to renounce marriage, and they literally did not have the right to touch a woman. They could not possess any property and were obliged to devote their whole lives to service of the sect. They were forbidden to keep a permanent dwelling of any kind and were required to spend their lives in constant travel or to stay in special secret sanctuaries. The consecration of the *perfecti*, the "consolation" *(consolamentum)*, was the central sacrament of the sect. This rite cannot be compared to anything in the Catholic Church. It combined baptism (or confirmation), ordination, confession, absolution and sometimes supreme unction as well. Only those who received it could count on being freed from the captivity of the body and having their souls returned to their celestial abode.

The majority of the Cathars had no hope of fulfilling the strict commandments that were obligatory for the *perfecti* and intended, rather, to receive "consolation" on their deathbed. This was called "the good end." The prayer to grant "the good end" under the care of "the good people" (the *perfecti*) was recited together with the Lord's Prayer.

Sometimes, having received "consolation," a sick person recovered. He was then usually advised to commit suicide (called "endura"). In many cases, "endura" was in fact a condition for receiving "consolation." Not infrequently, the aged or the very young who had received "consolation" were subjected to "endura"—i.e., in effect, murdered. There were various forms of "endura." Most frequently it was by starvation (especially for children, whom the mothers simply stopped suckling); bleeding, hot baths followed by sudden chilling, drinking of liquid mixed with ground glass and strangulation were also used. I. Döllinger, who studied the extant archives of the Inquisition in Toulouse and Carcassonne, writes: "Whoever examines the records of the above-mentioned courts attentively will have no doubt that far more people perished from the 'endura' (some voluntarily, some forcibly) than as a result of the Inquisition's verdicts." (10: p. 226)

These basic notions were the source of the socialist doctrines disseminated among the Cathars. They rejected property as belonging to the material world. The *perfecti* were forbidden to have any personal belongings, but as a group they controlled the holdings of the sect, which often were considerable.

Cathars enjoyed influence in various segments of society, including the highest strata. Thus it is said that Count Raymond VI of Toulouse always kept in his retinue Cathars disguised in ordinary attire, so they could bless him in case of impending death. For the most part, however, the preaching of the Cathars apparently was directed to the urban lower classes, as indicated in particular by the names of various sects: *populicani* (i.e., populists, although certain historians see this name as a corruption of "Paulicians"), *piphlers* (derived from "plebs"), *texerants* (weavers), etc. In their sermons, the Cathars preached that a true Christian life was possible only on the condition that property was held in common. (12: p. 656) In 1023, a group of Cathars were put on trial in Monteforte, charged with promulgating celibacy and communality of property and with attacking the accepted religious traditions.

It seems that the appeal for communality of property was rather widespread among the Cathars, since it is mentioned in certain Catholic works directed against them. In one of these, for instance, Cathars are accused of demagogically proclaiming this principle while not adhering to it themselves: "You do not have everything in common. Some have more, others less." (13: p. 176)

Celibacy among the *perfecti* and the general condemnation of marriage are common to all Cathars. But in a number of cases, only marriage is considered sinful—not promiscuity outside marriage. It should be recalled that "Thou shalt not commit adultery" was considered to be a commandment of the God of evil. By the same token, these prohibitions had as their aim not so much mortification of the flesh as destruction of the family. In the writings of contemporaries, the Cathars are constantly accused of "free" or "holy" love, and of having wives in common.

Saint Bernard of Clairvaux, between 1130 and 1150, accused the Cathars of preaching against marriage while cohabiting with women who had abandoned their families. (10: p. 16) Rainier supports this contention. (9: pp. 72–73) The same accusation against a Manichean sect that was making inroads into Brittany around 1145 can be found in the Chronicle of Hugo d'Amiens, Archbishop of Rouen. A book against heresies by Alain de Lille, which was published in the twelfth century, ascribed the following view to the Cathars: "Marital bonds are contrary to the laws of nature, since these laws demand that everything be held in common." (13: p. 176)

The Cathar heresy swept over Europe with extraordinary swiftness. In 1012, a sect of Cathars is recorded in Mainz, in 1018 and again in 1028 in Aquitaine, in 1022 in Orléans, in 1025 in Arras, in 1028 in Monteforte (near Turin), in 1030 in Burgundy, in 1051 in Goslar, etc. Around 1190, Bonacursus, who had previously been a bishop with the Cathars, wrote of the situation in Italy: "Are not all townships, cities and castles overrun with these pseudo-prophets?" (12: p. 651) And in 1166, the Bishop of Milan asserted that there were more heretics than faithful in his diocese. One work from the thirteenth century enumerates seventy-two Cathar bishops. Rainier Sacconi speaks of sixteen Churches of Cathars. They were all closely associated and apparently headed up by a Cathar Pope, who was located in Bulgaria. Councils were called, which were attended by representatives from numerous countries. For example, in 1167, a council was openly held in St. Felix near Toulouse; it was summoned by the heretical Pope Nicetas and was attended by a host of heretics, including some from Bulgaria and Constantinople.

The heresy was particularly successful in the south of France, in Languedoc and Provence. Missions for conversion of the heretics were repeatedly sent there, one of which included St. Bernard of Clairvaux, who reported that churches were deserted and that no one took communion or was baptized. The missionaries and the local Catholic clergy were assaulted and subjected to threats and insults.

The nobles of southern France supported the sect actively, seeing an opportunity to acquire church lands. For more than fifty years Languedoc was under the control of the Cathars and seemed lost to Rome forever. A papal legate, Pierre de Castelnau, was killed by heretics. The Pope announced several crusades against the Cathars. The first of these failed because of support given to the heretics by the local nobility. It was only in the thirteenth century, after more than thirty years of the *guerres albigeoises,* that the heresy was suppressed. However, the influence of these sects continued to be felt for several centuries.

*Brethren of the Free Spirit and the Apostolic Brethren.* In the creation of the doctrines of these sects a special role was played by two thinkers whose ideas were destined to exert a continuous influence on the heretical movements of the Middle Ages and the Reformation: Joachim of Flore and Amalric of Bena. They both lived in the twelfth century and died soon after 1200.

Joachim was a monk and an abbot. His doctrine, as he claimed, was based partly on the study of the Holy Scriptures and partly on revelation. It is based on the view that the history of mankind involves the progressively greater comprehension of God. Joachim divided history into three epochs: the Kingdom of the Father, from Adam to Christ; the Kingdom of the Son, from Christ until 1260; and the Kingdom of the Spirit, which was to begin in 1260. The first was an age of slavish submission; the second, an age of filial obedience; while the third was to be an age of freedom. For in the words of the Apostle: "Where the Spirit of the Lord is, there is freedom." In this last epoch, God's people would abide in peace, freed from labor and suffering. This would be an age of the humble and the poor; people would not know the words "thine" and "mine." Monasteries would embrace the whole of mankind, and the Eternal Gospel would be read and understood in its mystical dimension. An era of perfection would be attained within the framework of earthly life and human history—and by the hand of mortal human beings. This epoch was to be preceded by terrible wars, and the Antichrist would appear. Joachim saw proof of this in the decay of the Church in his time. The Last Judgment would begin with the Church, and the Antichrist would become Pope. The elect of God, reverting to apostolic poverty, would make up the host of Christ in this struggle. They would defeat the Antichrist and unite the whole of mankind in Christianity.

A characteristic feature of Joachim's doctrine is the view of history as a predetermined process whose course can be foreseen and calculated. He calculates, for example, that the first epoch in his scheme lasted forty-two generations, the second would last fifty. . . .

During his life, Joachim was a faithful son of the Church; he founded a monastery and wrote against the Cathars. But a collection of excerpts from his works was later condemned as heretical, probably because of his influence on the heretical sects.

Amalric taught theology in Paris. He did not expound his system in full, only its more inoffensive propositions. Nevertheless, a complaint was lodged against him in Rome and the Pope condemned his system and, in 1204, dismissed him from his chair. Amalric died soon thereafter.

Amalric was ideologically linked to Joachim of Flore. He also saw history as a series of stages in divine revelation. In the beginning, there was Moses' law, then Christ's which superseded it. Now the time of the third revelation had come. This was embodied in Amalric and his followers, as previously revelation had been embodied in Christ. They had now become as Christ. Three basic theses of this new Christianity have been preserved. First of all: "God is all." Second: "Everything is One, for everything that is is God." And third: "Whoever observes the law of love is above sin." These theses were interpreted in such a way that those who followed the teachings of Amalric could attain identity with God through ecstasy. In them, the Holy Spirit became flesh, just as in Christ. Man in this state is incapable of sin, for his deeds coincide with the will of God. He rises above the law.

Thus the followers of Amalric perceived the Kingdom of the Spirit more in terms of a spiritual state of the members of the sect than in terms of a world to be actively transformed. The second interpretation was not entirely foreign to them, however.

In the thirteenth and fourteenth centuries, a sect with views very similar to those of Amalric spread over France, Germany, Switzerland and Austria. Its members called themselves the Brothers and Sisters of the Free Spirit or simply the "Free Spirits."

The key doctrine of this sect was belief in the possibility of "transfiguration into God." Since the soul of each man consists of divine substance, any man in principle can achieve a state of "Godliness." To attain this end he must pass through many years of novitiate in the sect, renounce all property, family, will, and live by begging. Only then does he attain the state of Godliness and become one of the "Free Spirits." Numerous descriptions of the sect's world view have been preserved. There are accounts by Free Spirits or by Free Spirits who later repented, as well as those in the archives of the Inquisition. (See 14: p. 56; 15: p. 136; 16: pp. 110, 119; 17: p. 160; etc.) All sources agree on one point—that Godliness is not a temporary state but a continuous one. Johann Hartmann from a town near Erfurt characterized this ecstasy as "a complete disappearance of the painful sting of conscience." (15: p. 136) In other words, the Free Spirit was liberated from all moral constraints. He was higher than Christ, who was a mortal man who attained Godliness only on the cross. The Free Spirit was the complete equal of God, "without distinctions." Hence his will is the will of God, and to him the notion of sin becomes meaningless.

This sinlessness and freedom from moral restrictions was characterized in a number of ways. The Free Spirit is the king and sovereign of all that is. Everything belongs to him, and he may dispose of it at will. And whoever interferes with this may be killed by him, even if it is the emperor himself. Nothing performed by the flesh of such a man can either decrease or increase his divinity. Therefore, he may give it complete freedom. "Let the whole state perish rather than he abstain from the demands of his nature," says Hartmann. (15: p. 141) Intimacy with any woman, even with a sister or his mother, cannot stain him and will only increase her holiness. Numerous sources dating from the fourteenth and fifteenth centuries report on rituals of the sects, which included indiscriminate sexual union. In Italy, such "masses" were called *barilotto*. In Germany, there were reports of special sanctuaries called "paradises" for this purpose.

The contemporary scholar H. Grundmann (18) points out in this regard that in the late Middle Ages there was no need to belong to a sect in order to adhere to any sort of free views in sexual matters. The basis of the "orgiastic mass" was strictly ideological. The Free Spirit, who had attained "Godliness," broke completely with his former life. What had been blasphemy for him in the past (and remained so for "rude" folk) now became a sign of the end of one historical epoch and the beginning of another—the new Eon. In this way he was able to comprehend and to express his new birth and the break with the old Eon.

It is clear that the Free Spirits had no use for the path of salvation proposed by the Catholic Church—penance, confession, absolution of sins, communion. Moreover, they saw the Church as a hostile organization, since it had usurped the right to examine and to decide, which they considered solely their own prerogative. A bitterly anti-ecclesiastical sentiment pervades the views of the Free Spirits and finds expression in their frequent worship of Lucifer.

In the center of the sect's ideology stood not God but man made divine, freed from the notion of his own sinfulness and made the center of the universe. As a result, Adam played a central role in their teaching, not Adam the sinner depicted in the Old Testament, but Adam the perfect man. Many of the Free Spirits referred to themselves as the "New Adams," and Konrad Kanler even called himself Antichrist ("but not in the bad sense"). It seems possible to argue that here, within the confines of this relatively small sect, we encounter the first prototype of the humanist ideology which would later attain worldwide significance.

The uprising against the Pope in Umbria, in the 1320s, serves as a vivid example of the influence the sect had on social life. The teachings of the Free Spirits were widespread among the nobility of this region and became the ideology of the anti-papal party. In the struggle against the Pope and the urban communes, the doctrine justified the application of all means and the rejection of mercy of any kind. The entire populations of captured towns were slaughtered, including women and children. The head of the uprising, Count Montefeltro, and his followers prided themselves on plundering churches and violating nuns. Their supreme deity was Satan. (17: p. 130)

But the most far-reaching influence that the sect had was among the poor, especially among the Beghards and the Beguines—unions of celibate men and women who engaged in crafts or begging. The external, exoteric circle of participants in the sect was made up from these social elements, while the Free Spirits, those who had attained "Godliness," formed a narrow, esoteric circle. The division into two categories recalls the Cathars with their chosen circle of the *perfecti*.

The broad masses that formed the exoteric circle of the sect were poorly informed about the radical nature of the doctrine, as numerous surviving records of the proceedings of the Inquisition make clear. The ordinary followers felt that the divinity of the Free Spirits justified their right to be spiritual guides. For this group, the most significant aspects of the doctrine were those that proclaimed the idea of communality in its most extreme form and rejected the fundamental institutions of society: private property, the family, the church and the state. It is here that we can see the sect's socialist aspects. The assertion that "all property ought to be held in common" is cited frequently as one of the elements of the doctrine (e.g., 15: p. 53). Appeals for sexual freedom were often directed against marriage—indeed, sexual union in marriage was considered sinful. Such views were expressed, for example, by the "Homines Intelligentia" group, which was active in Brussels in 1410–1411. (9: II: p. 528) The equality proclaimed between Free Spirits and Christ had the aim of destroying hierarchy, not only on earth but in heaven as well. All of these ideas were common mainly among the mendicant Beghards, whom their "divine" leaders called to a complete liberation from this world. For instance, Aegidius Cantoris of Brussels taught: "I am the liberator of mankind. Through

me you will know Christ, as through Christ you know the Father."
(9: II: p. 527)

The Brethren of the Free Spirit exerted an influence on a sect
that emerged in Italy in the second half of the thirteenth century.
The members of this Italian movement called each other "Apostolic
Brethren." This sect taught that the coming of the Antichrist foretold
by Joachim was drawing near. The Catholic Church had fallen away
from Christ's commandments and had become the Whore of Babylon,
the beast of seven heads and ten horns of the Apocalypse. Its fall
dated from the time of Emperor Constantine and Pope Sylvester, who
had been possessed by the Devil. The times of trouble were coming,
which would end in victory for a new, spiritual Church—that of the
Apostolic Brethren, a community of saints. The world would be governed by a saint, a Pope elevated by God and not elected by cardinals
(all the cardinals would have been killed by then, in any case). And
the sect was already thought to be headed by a God-appointed leader.
Implicit obedience was due him. Everything was permitted in defense
of the faith, any violence against enemies, while, at the same time,
the persecution inflicted by the Catholic Church on the Apostolic
Brethren was considered to be the gravest of crimes. The sect preached
communality of property and of wives.

The doctrine was spread among the people by itinerant "apostles."
The letters of the leader of the sect, Dolcino, were disseminated by
way of proclamations. Finally in 1404, an attempt was made to put
the teaching into practice. Gathering some five thousand members
of the sect, Dolcino fortified himself and his army in a mountainous
area of northern Italy, from where he sallied forth to plunder the
surrounding villages and destroy the churches and monasteries. War
went on for three years, until Dolcino's camp was taken and he was
executed.

This episode is described at greater length in the biography of
Dolcino in the Appendix.

Taborites. The burning of Jan Hus in 1415 gave the impetus to the
anti-Catholic Hussite movement in Bohemia. The more radical faction
of the Hussites was concentrated in a well-protected town near Prague.
They called the place Tabor. Preachers from heretical sects gravitated
there from all over Europe: Joachimites (followers of Joachim of Flore),
Waldensians, Beghards. Chiliastic and socialist theories were prevalent

among the Taborites, and there were numerous attempts to bring theory into practice. We shall give a brief outline of the views of the Taborites based on the writings of their contemporaries (the future Pope Aeneas Sylvius Piccolomini, Pržíbram, Vavřinec, Laurence of Březin).

The end of the world—the *consumatio saeculi*—was to occur in 1420. The term, however, covers only the end of the old world and of the "dominion of evil." All the "wicked" would be removed forthwith. "The day of vengeance and the year of retribution" were drawing near. "The lofty and powerful must be bent down like tree branches and cut off and burned in furnaces like straw, leaving neither root nor branch, they must be thrashed like sheaves of grain, their blood drained to the last drop, they are to be exterminated with scorpions, serpents and wild beasts, and put to death everywhere." (19: p. 78)

Christ's law of mercy was to be abolished, since "its interpretation and written tenets contradict in much the opinion cited above." (20: p. 235) On the contrary, one was to act "resolutely and with zeal and with just retribution." Furthermore: "It is necessary for each of the faithful to wash his hands in the blood of the enemies of Christ." (20: p. 231) Moreover: "Anyone who protests against the shedding of the blood of Christ's enemies shall be cursed and punished just as these enemies are. All peasants who refuse to join the Taborites shall be destroyed together with their property." (19: p. 81)

God's Kingdom on earth will be established, but not for all—only for the "elect." "Evil" will not be eliminated from the world but will be subjected to the control of those who are "good." All the faithful were to congregate in five cities; those who remained outside would not be spared the Last Judgment. From these cities the faithful were to rule the world, and those cities and towns opposing them were to be "destroyed and burnt like Sodom." (20: p. 236) In particular: "In this year of retribution, Prague must be destroyed and burnt by the faithful like Babylon." (19: p. 82)

The period was to culminate in the coming of Christ. Then the chosen of God would "reign with the Lord visibly and physically for a thousand years." (19: p. 94) When Christ had descended to earth with his angels, pious souls who had died for Christ were to be resurrected in order to judge the sinners with Him. Wives would conceive without knowing a man and give birth without pain. No one would sow or reap. "The fruit of the earth shall no longer be consumed." (19: pp. 85)

The call went out from the preachers "to do no work, to pull down trees and destroy houses, churches and monasteries." (19: p. 85) "All human institutions and human laws must be abolished, for none of them were created by the Heavenly Father." (19: p. 110) It was taught that the Church was "heretical and unrighteous and that all its wealth must be taken away and given to laymen." And: "The houses of priests and all church property must be demolished, and the churches, altars and monasteries destroyed." (19: p. 83) "Church bells were taken down and broken to pieces and then sold away to foreign lands. Church objects, candlesticks, gold and silver were smashed." (19: p. 84) "Everywhere altars were smashed, the sacraments cast out, God's temples defiled and turned into stalls and stables." (19: p. 127) "The sacrament was trodden underfoot. . . . The Blood of Christ was poured out, chalices stolen and sold." (19: p. 139) One of the Taborite preachers stated that he "would sooner pray to the Devil than bend his knee before the Holy Eucharist." (19: p. 153) "A great multitude of priests were killed, burned and slaughtered, and the greatest joy for them was to seize somebody and murder him." (19: p. 84) The favorite song of the Taborites was: "Come on, monks, let's see you dance for us!" (18: p. 84) It was said that when the Kingdom of the Righteous came there would be "no need for anyone to teach another. There would be no need for books or scriptures, and all worldly wisdom will perish." (19: p. 159) In monasteries the Taborites invariably destroyed the libraries. "All belongings must be taken away from God's enemies and burned or otherwise destroyed." (19: p. 81)

"This winter and summer the preachers and elder headmen have been persistently duping the peasants to pour money into their barrels." (19: p. 101) In this manner all money in the community was socialized. Supervisors of the barrels were appointed to oversee the strict delivery of money and to distribute the communal fund. "In the town of Tabor there is nothing which is mine or thine, but all possess everything in common and no one is to have anything apart, and whoever does is a sinner." (19: pp. 99–100) One point of the Taborite program stated: "No one shall possess anything, but everything must be communal." (19: p. 106) The preachers taught: "Everything will be common, including wives: there will be free sons and daughters of God and there will be no marriage as union of two—husband and wife." (19: p. 113)

Among the Taborites, a Beghard from Belgium founded a sect of Adamites who established themselves on a small island in the Lužnice river. He pronounced himself Adam and the Son of God, called upon to resurrect the dead and to carry out what was foreordained in the Apocalypse. The Adamites considered themselves to be the incarnation of the omnipresent God. They expected the world soon to be flooded with blood as high as a horse's bridle. On this earth they saw themselves as God's scythe sent to take vengeance and to destroy all that is vile in the world. Forgiveness was a sin. They killed and they burned towns and villages at night, citing the phrase from the Bible: "At midnight there was a cry made." In the town of Prčic they "killed people, young and old, and burned the town." (19: p. 464) At their gatherings they wore no clothing, believing that only in this way would they become pure. They had no marriage; every man could choose women at will. It was enough to say about a woman "She inflames my spirit" for Adam to give his blessing: "Go and give fruit and multiply and populate the earth." According to certain sources, their sexual relations were completely indiscriminate. "The sky they call a roof and say there is no God on earth as there are no devils in hell." (19: p. 478) On orders from Jan Žižka, Adamites were exterminated by more moderate Taborites.

For a long time, the stories about the Adamites (as well as many reports about the Taborites) were thought to be the inventions of their enemies. Such a view was first posited by the French Huguenot Isaac de Beausobre, a representative of the Age of Enlightenment, and in its most extreme form it finds expression in the works of the Czech Marxist historian J. Macek. The question of the Adamites has recently been subjected to thorough critical review by the Marxist historians E. Werner and M. Erbstösser. (15, 16, 17) They demonstrate the existence of an earlier "Adamite" tradition, a cult of Adam, within the Brethren of the Free Spirit. If we take into account certain unavoidable distortions due to the hermetic nature of the teaching, information about the Bohemian "Adamites" is in full accord with the picture of the European movement of "Free Spirits" which we have drawn in the preceding section.

For example, Macek considers the passage "All shall be in common, wives as well" (from the Old Chronicle) to be "the height of filthy slander." (19: p. 113) In his opinion, this passage is contradicted by another in Pržíbram, who asserts that in Tabor intimacy between husband and wife was prohibited: "If husband and wife were seen together or their meeting became known, they were beaten to death; others were thrown into the river." However, these two passages actually are in full accord with the tradition of the Free Spirits, who preached unlimited sexual liberty and the sinfulness of marriage at one and the same time. This was also the position of the "Homines Intelligentia" group in Brussels at about the same period. We note in this connection that Engels had pointed out: "It is a curious fact that in every large revolutionary movement the question of 'free love' comes to the foreground." (3: XVI: p. 160)

The emperor and the Pope appealed for a crusade against the Taborites. But the latter not only crushed the crusaders but carried war over into neighboring countries. These raids, which received the name "The Splendid Campaigns" in the Hussite tradition, were undertaken on a yearly basis between 1427 and 1434. Some countries were devastated and looted; in others—for example, Silesia—garrisons were established. A song of the time runs: "Meissen and Saxony are destroyed, Silesia and Lauschwitz lie in ruins, Bavaria has been turned into a desert, Austria is devastated, Moravia stripped, Bohemia turned upside down."

Detachments of Taborites went as far as the Baltic Sea, the walls of Vienna, Leipzig and Berlin; Nuremberg paid tribute. Czechia was ravaged. In the *Old Collegiate Chronicle* it is said: "In these campaigns the majority of soldiers were foreigners who felt no love for the Kingdom." And: "Fires, robberies, murders and acts of violence are on their conscience." (21: p. 161) The whole of Central Europe was subjected to terrible devastation. The Pope was forced to make concessions. At the Basel Council of 1433, an agreement with the Hussites was reached, as a result of which they returned to the Catholic Church. But the more radical, Taborite, faction of Hussites did not recognize the agreement and was annihilated in the battle at Lipany, in 1434.

During the wars of 1419–1434, the impact of the Hussites went beyond the devastation of neighboring countries. They also carried their chiliastic and socialist ideas abroad. Their manifestoes were read in Barcelona, Paris, Cambridge. In 1423 and 1430, there were disturbances by Hussite adherents in Flanders. In Germany and Austria, Hussite influence was still felt a century later, during the period of the Reformation. Inside Bohemia itself, the defeated Taborites gave rise to the sect of "Bohemian Brethren" or "Unitas Fratrum," who combined the previous intolerant attitude toward the Catholic Church and secular authority with a complete renunciation of violence—even for self-defense. We shall have occasion to speak of this sect, which is still in existence, later in this work.

*Anabaptists.* The Reformation called forth a new upsurge of socialist movements. Even in pre-Reformation times, Germany was full of chiliastic sentiment. Wandering preachers exposed the sins of the world and foretold the forthcoming vengeance. Astrological predictions of calamity were common—famine, rebellion, "when the rivers will flow with blood." There was a saying: "Who does not die in 1523, is not drowned in 1524, is not killed in 1525, shall say that a miracle has happened to him."

The invention of printing enormously magnified the effect of these ideas. Any peasant or artisan could be exposed to leaflets showing a peasant army marching toward the future revolution, with a frightened Pope, princes and prelates fleeing before it.

This sentiment was given especially strong expression in the Anabaptist movement, which spread to Germany, Switzerland, Austria, Czechia, Denmark and Holland and which, in the following century, spilled over into England. The sect's name, as so often happened, was given to it by its enemies. It seems that the term was coined by Zwingli. The movement as such had existed long before, its members calling each other "Brother." The designation Anabaptist ("the rebaptized") is to be explained by the fact that the sect refused to recognize the baptism of children and often performed a second baptism of adults. In later times, members of this sect came to call themselves Baptists.

Basically, the doctrine of the Anabaptists (see 22, 23, 24, 25, 26) derived from the notion, already familiar to us, of the falling away of the Catholic Church, in Emperor Constantine's time, from the true teachings of Christ. These sectarians considered themselves direct successors of the Christianity of Apostolic times. They denied the entire tradition of the Catholic Church—that is, every aspect of its doctrine and organization not specifically identified in the Gospels. They refused to recognize the supreme authority of the Pope, believed that salvation of the soul was possible outside the Church and professed a universal priesthood. Of the Scriptures, they recognized only the Gospels as sacred and only the words spoken by Christ himself, at that. The Sermon on the Mount had particular significance for them, and they believed that its commandments should be observed to the letter. According to their doctrine, the meaning of the Gospels is revealed through inspiration to anyone worthy of it, now just as in Apostolic times.

Anabaptists believed murder to be a cardinal sin under any circumstances and rejected oaths of any kind. For this reason, they refused to participate in many aspects of life. In general, the opposition of "true Christians" to the "world of false Christians" played a large role in their teachings. This led at critical periods to militant appeals for "extermination of the impious."

In organization the Anabaptists largely resembled the Cathars. The movement was guided entirely by a society of "Apostles" who, having renounced marriage and property, led the life of pilgrims. They wandered in pairs, the older Apostle devoting himself to matters of faith and the sect's organization, with the younger Apostle helping him with practical matters. The Apostles elected bishops from among their own ranks, the latter guiding the activity of the sect in various regions. Councils of bishops, "synods" or *capituli,* were convened to discuss questions of principle. For example, in his invitation to the synod at Waldshut in 1524, Balthazar Humbayer wrote: "The ancient custom of Apostolic times is such that, in circumstances hard for the faith, those to whom God's word is entrusted gather to take a Christian decision." (24: p. 376)

Often bishops from the whole of Europe came together. For instance, the *capituli* in Basel between 1521 and 1523 were attended by Brethren from Switzerland, Flanders (Beltin), Saxony (Heinrich von Eppendorf), Franconia (Stumpf), Frankfurt-am-Main (the Knight Hartmut von Kronberg), Holland (Rode), England (Richard Crock, Thomas Lipset), and other places. (24: p. 378 f.) At the Augsburg synod of 1526, more than sixty "elder Brethren" were present.

The social views of the Anabaptists were not uniform throughout. The *Chronicle* by Sebastian Franck (sixteenth century) says about them: "Some believe themselves to be holy and pure; they have everything in common. . . . Others practice communality only to the extent that they do not permit need to arise among themselves. . . . Among them a sect appeared which wished to make wives, as well as belongings, communal." (25: p. 306)

There is much data on Anabaptists to be found in the book by Bullinger, also written in the sixteenth century. In describing the sect of "Free Brethren" that appeared in the vicinity of Zürich, he writes: "The Free Brethren, whom many Anabaptists called 'crude Brethren,' were quite widespread in the early days of the movement. They understood Christian freedom in a carnal sense. For they wished to be free of all laws, presuming that Christ had liberated them. Therefore, they regarded themselves as free of tithe, of the corvée and of serfdom. Some of them, desperate libertines, seduced silly women into believing that they could not become spiritual without breaking wedlock. Others believed that if all things must be in common, then also wives. Still others said that after the new baptism they had been born anew and could not sin: only flesh sins. These false teachings were the source of shame and obscenity. And yet they dared to teach that such was the will of the Father." (40: p. 129)

Elsewhere Bullinger reports: "And they say in earnest that no one should have property and that all wealth and patrimony should be in common, as it is impossible to be Christian and wealthy at the same time. . . . They set forth as a new monastic order rules regarding clothing as to the fabric, shape and style, length and size. . . . They set forth rules as to eating, drinking, sleeping, leisure, standing and walking about." (25: p. 284)

In the early 1520s, the Anabaptists renounced the conspiratorial character of their activities and entered into an open struggle with the "world" and the Catholic Church. In 1524, a large-scale secret conference was held in Nuremberg and attended by Denck, one of the most influential Anabaptist writers, by the "Picard" Hetzer, by Hut of the old Waldensian Brethren, and by other Brethren. Many were seized, but Denck fled to Switzerland. Here a new assembly of Brethren from various countries took place. It was decided to begin to practice the second baptism openly. This decision was put into effect in Zürich and St. Gall. This was apparently symbolic of the shift to outright struggle—precisely the course taken by the Czech Brethren in the village of Lota, in 1457, when they decided to demonstrate openly their split with Catholicism.

In St. Gall in 1525, a uniform of coarse gray fabric and a broad gray hat were introduced as obligatory for all members of the community. All forms of participation in public life and entertainment were forbidden. Anabaptists were called "monks without hoods." The leaders of the Anabaptist community in Zürich preached that "all property must be held in common and together." These events were accompanied by strange happenings. Members of some of the groups went naked at their gatherings and, to be like children, crept around on the ground, playing. Others burned the Bible, and with shouts of "Here!

Here!" beat themselves on the breast to show the place where the life-giving spirit dwells. One of them, on orders from his father, killed his brother in imitation of Christ's sacrifice. (23: p. 701)

The Anabaptists did not succeed in taking control of the Reformation movement in Switzerland (thanks in large part to Zwingli's opposition to them). Exiled Swiss Anabaptists fled to Bohemia and joined the Bohemian Brethren there. Large combined communities were founded on collectivist principles.

Communal property was introduced. Everything earned by the Brethren was handed over to the common treasury, which was supervised by a special "distributor." The "good police" controlled the whole of the life of the community—clothing, lodging, upbringing of children, marriage and work.

The type of men's and women's clothing, the hour for going to bed, the time for work and rest were all strictly prescribed. The life of the Brethren took place before the eyes of others. It was forbidden to cook anything for oneself; meals had to be taken in common. The unmarried slept in common bedrooms, men and women separately. Children (from the age of two) were separated from their parents and brought up in common "children's houses." Marriages were arranged by the elders. They also assigned to everyone his or her occupation. Members of the community refused to have any contact with the state; they did not serve in the army, never went to court. They did, however, retain a passively hostile attitude while rejecting violence of any kind. (See 27, 39.)

In Germany, Anabaptism began to take on an increasingly revolutionary character. In Thuringia, near the Bohemian border, the city of Zwickau became the center of the movement. The so-called Zwickau Prophets, headed by the Anabaptist Apostle Klaus Storch, believed that the elect of the Lord could communicate with Him directly, as the Apostles of old could, and denied that the Church was capable of giving salvation. Their teaching considered science and the arts unnecessary for man, for everything essential to his salvation was already given to him by God.

In imitation of Christ, Storch surrounded himself with twelve Apostles and seventy disciples. The "Prophets" predicted an invasion by the Turks, the reign of the Antichrist, destruction of the impious and finally the arrival of the thousand-year Kingdom of God, when there would be one baptism and one faith.

An exposition of Storch's teachings has been preserved in a work by Wagner published in the late sixteenth century in Erfurt. It is titled "How Niklaus Storch Instigated Sedition in Thuringia and the Neighboring Regions" and was written on the basis of eyewitness accounts. It cites the following points of his doctrine:

1. That no matrimonial union, whether secret or open, should be observed. . . .

3. That on the contrary, each may take wives whenever his flesh demands it and his passion rises, and may live with them in intimacy at his will.

4. That everything ought to be held in common, for God has sent all men equally naked into the world. And likewise, He has given them equally everything that is on the earth: the birds of the air and the fish of the water.

5. Therefore it ought to be that all authorities, secular and clerical, be deprived of their offices once and for all or killed by the sword, for they alone live as they will and suck the blood and sweat of the poor, glutting themselves and drinking day and night.

"Hence everyone must rise up, the sooner the better, arm himself and attack the priests in their cozy nests, massacre and exterminate them. For once the sheep are deprived of a leader, it will go easy with the sheep. Next it will be necessary to attack also those who fleece others, to seize their houses, plunder their property, and raze their castles to the ground." (28: p. 53)

This first surge of the Anabaptist movement coincided with the 1525 Peasant War in Germany. The socialist teachings of the time are most vividly mirrored in the activity of Thomas Müntzer. His biography is presented at greater length in the Appendix; we shall therefore limit ourselves to a brief comment on his doctrine here. Müntzer taught that the only Lord and King of the earth is Christ. He assigned to princes a function very like that of hangmen and even this prerogative was to be exercised only on direct orders from the elect of the Lord. If the princes refused to obey, they were to be executed. The authority of Christ was seen as truly embodied in the society of the elect, a narrow union sharply separated from the rest of the population. Müntzer did indeed attempt to organize such a union.

He seized power in the town of Mühlhausen, where rebellious inhabitants had driven out the municipal council. In the city and the surrounding area, monasteries were laid waste, sacred images destroyed, monks and priests killed. Müntzer taught that all property was to be held in common. An identical demand was part of the program of his union. A chronicle written at the time relates that a practical attempt at implementing these principles was undertaken at Mühlhausen. However, an army gathered by the local princes soon approached the town. Müntzer and his followers were overwhelmingly defeated; he was executed. (See the more detailed account in 28 and in 39: pp. 199–253.)

The Anabaptists' participation in the Peasant War called forth the particular ire of the authorities. A violent and extremely cruel wave of persecution of Anabaptists swept across south and central Germany. This temporarily weakened militant and socialist sentiments, but around 1530 they surfaced again. In his *Chronicle*, Sebastian Franck reports that about 1530 (in Switzerland), Brethren who believed in the possibility of self-defense and war under certain circumstances began to gain the upper hand in the organization. "Such Brethren were in the majority."

At the Anabaptist synods, the influence of the more moderate "Apostle" Denck waned, while a former associate of Müntzer's, Hut, who preached complete communality of worldly goods, came to the forefront. He proclaimed: "The saints must be joyful and must take up double-edged swords in order to wreak vengeance in the nations." (23: p. 703) Hut created a new union whose goal was "slaughter of all overlords and powers that be." He also proposed "establishing the rule of Hans Hut on earth" and making Mühlhausen the capital. A majority of the members of the union knew nothing of his radical plans. Only a narrow circle of members, called the "knowers," was initiated into these secrets.

In 1535, counselors to Emperor Charles V submitted a report stating that "Anabaptists, who call themselves true Christians, wish to divide all property. . . ." (24: p. 395) The increasingly explosive situation found expression in some preposterous incidents which were, however, destined to be outstripped by later events. For example, the furrier Augustin Bader proclaimed himself king of the New Israel and made himself a crown and kingly garments. He was tried in Stuttgart. (23: p. 703)

In 1534–1535, this rise of Anabaptist militancy led to an outbreak of violence which can be seen as an attempt to bring about an Anabaptist revolution in northern Europe. The main events were played out in northern Germany; Anabaptists had gravitated there earlier, having

been driven out of southern and central Germany. The town of Münster became the center of these events.

Taking advantage of the struggle going on between Catholics and
Lutherans, the Anabaptists gained control in the municipal council
and then completely subjugated the town. All who refused to accept
a second baptism were expelled after being stripped of their possessions. Thereafter all property in the city was appropriated for the common lot, everyone being obliged to deliver his possessions under the
supervision of special deacons. Next polygamy was introduced, and
women of a certain age were forbidden to stay unmarried.

Anabaptist Apostles fanned out from Münster across Germany, Denmark and Holland, preaching the second baptism and calling the faithful to come to the aid of the city. Revolt gripped a number of towns,
and Anabaptists gathered by land and by sea to support Münster. Terrified by developments Bishop Waldeck, whose diocese included Münster, called up an army together with the neighboring princes and
surrounded the town. The siege lasted for over a year. Within the
town in the meantime, one of the Anabaptists, Jan Bokelson, also called
Johann of Leyden, was proclaimed the king of Münster and of the
whole world. He surrounded himself with a luxurious court and a multitude of wives, and he personally beheaded recalcitrants in the town
square. At the same time, uprisings of Anabaptists broke out all over
northern Germany and in Holland, where they even succeeded in
seizing the Amsterdam town hall for a short time.

The authorities finally began to regain control. In 1535, Münster
was taken by assault and Bokelson and other Anabaptist leaders were
executed. A more detailed description of this episode is given in the
Appendix.

*Sects in the English Revolution of 1648.* After the fall of Münster, a
schism again appeared between the more peaceable and the more
belligerent tendencies of the Anabaptist movement. In 1536, a synod
took place in the vicinity of the town of Buchholz in Westphalia. Batenburg, a leader of the militant faction, supported the views of the
Münster Anabaptists on armed struggle, on the approaching Kingdom
of God, and so on. The followers of Ubbo Phillips took the opposite
position. This latter group gained the upper hand, although its adherents did not condemn their opponents in principle, saying only that
even if Batenburg was right, the time of the "Kingdom of the Elect"
had not yet arrived, and that it was therefore not yet time to attempt

to wrest power from the godless. This episode marks the beginning of decreased political involvement of Anabaptists on the Continent. Its more extreme representatives, the Familists, emigrated (via Holland) to England. It is worth noting that some Englishmen had attended the Buchholz synod. One of them, Henry by name, took an active part in organizing the synod and paid traveling expenses for the delegates. (30: pp. 76–77)

At the beginning of the seventeenth century, the Anabaptists who had migrated to England began to merge with the movement of the Lollards, which had existed there for a long time. The English revolution of 1648 coincided with a flurry of activity by all these sects. The example of Münster and Johann Bokelson gripped the popular imagination once again. A book originating in Quaker circles stated the following, for example: "No Friend has reason to be ashamed of his Anabaptist origins. Even in Münster they rebelled merely against the cruelty of the German tyrants, who literally like devils oppressed the souls and the bodies of the common folk. They were defeated and therefore declared mutineers. Their uprising was violent because their oppressors were still more violent." (33: p. 25) Among the apologists for the Münster rebellion was Lilburne, a highly popular leader of the radical wing in the Puritan army (see his pamphlet "The Basic Laws of Liberty").

In another pamphlet of the day (entitled "Heresiography"), the following Anabaptist doctrine is cited: "A Christian may not with a safe conscience possess anything proper to himself but whatsoever he hath he must make common." (31: p. 99)

In the middle of the seventeenth century, the sect of Ranters appeared in England; its doctrine is strikingly akin to that of the Brethren of the Free Spirit. The Ranters believed that all which exists was divine and that the division between Good and Evil was a man-made concept. In mystical terms this was perceived as an identity: "The Devil is God, Hell is Heaven, Sin Holiness, Damnation Salvation." (32: p. 77)

This led to a denial of morals and to ostentatious amorality. Thus Clarkson says of the period when he was a Ranter: "The very motion of my heart was to all manner of theft, cheat, wrong or injury that privately could be acted, though in tongue I professed the contrary, not considering I brake the law in all points (murder excepted) and the ground of this my judgment was, God made all things good, so nothing evil but as man judged it." (32: p. 78)

In the social field, the Ranters rejected property and marriage.

In the pamphlet "The Ranters' Last Sermon," we find the teaching "that it was quite contrary to the end of Creation to Appropriate anything to any Man or Woman; but that there ought to be a Community of all things. . . . They say that for one man to be tied to one woman, or one woman to be tied to one man, is a fruit of the curse; but they say we are freed from the curse; therefore it is our liberty to make use of whom we please." (32: p. 90)

In his pamphlet "A Wonder," Edward Hide ascribes to the Ranters the following view: "That all the women in the world are but one man's wife in unity and all the men in the world are but one woman's husband in unity; so that one man may lie with all the women in the world in unity, and one woman may lie with all men in the world, for they are all her husband in unity." (32: p. 90)

Ranters were accused of performing rituals which involved a parody of Communion and indiscriminate sexual union, similar to the *barilotto* and the "paradise" of the Brethren of the Free Spirit.

An act of Parliament was directed against the Ranters. It condemned those who preached "that such men and women are most perfect or like to God or Eternity which do commit the greatest sins with least remorse or sense." (32: p. 103)

In the 1650s, the majority of Ranters joined the Quakers, so that it became difficult to draw a distinct line between the two currents. Religious upheavals of the day were exacerbated by the indignation aroused by Cromwell's foreign policy—the conclusion of peace in the Netherlands, which frustrated the hope of spreading the reign of the "saints" throughout Europe.

James Nayler, a Quaker preacher, acquired a considerable following even within Cromwell's retinue. It was rumored that he was a second Christ. People wrote to him, saying: "Henceforeward your name is not James but Jesus." When a visit by him was announced in Bristol, such excitement was aroused that contemporaries considered it likely that Bristol would become a "New Jerusalem," a second Münster. When Nayler rode into town on horseback, thousands followed him. But he was met by Cromwell's soldiers, seasoned by their service in the Civil War, and they dispersed the crowd, seized Nayler and took him to jail. His case was debated in Parliament for several months. It seems to have had political implications: it is possible that an uprising of Anabaptists was feared. Nayler's execution seemed imminent, but there were disturbances and an outpouring of pleas for mercy. Cromwell spoke in favor of mitigating the sentence. Nayler was publicly flogged and branded. A crowd of adherents surrounded the scaffold, kissing his feet, hands and hair. (33: pp. 264–274, 34: pp. 256–263)

Interestingly, the name Ranters reappears 150 years later, in the 1820s, when the term was applied to a certain group of Methodists. From their midst came the first organizers of the English trade union movement, men who had acquired the skills of popular orators in the sect. (31: p. 167)

The movement whose members became known as Diggers had sharply defined socialist characteristics. Externally, it expressed itself (beginning in 1649) in the seizure of communal land by small groups of people for joint tillage. This attempt at organizing communes, however, was a mere gesture, which led to no practical consequences, and it was the Diggers' literary activity that proved to have lasting significance.

Gerrard Winstanley was the most important figure among them. In several pamphlets he proclaimed his basic idea—the illegitimacy of private ownership of land. He reported that he had had a vision, "a voice and a revelation," and was preaching what had been revealed to him: "And so long as we or any other maintain this civil property, we consent still to hold the creation down under that bondage it groans under, and so we should hinder the work of restoration and sin against light that is given unto us, and so through the fear of the flesh (man) lose our peace. And that this civil property is the curse is manifest thus: those that buy and sell land, and are landlords, have got it either by oppression or murder or theft; and all landlords live in the breach of the seventh and eighth commandments, *Thou shalt not steal nor kill.*" ("The True Levellers' Standard Advanced: or, The State of Community opened, and Presented to the Sons of Men.") (35: p. 85)

Winstanley viewed trade and money in equally negative terms: "For buying and selling is the great cheat that robs and steals the earth one from another. . . . We hope," he says, "that people shall live freely in the enjoyment of the earth, without bringing the mark of the Beast in their hands or in their promise; and that they shall buy wine and milk without money or without price, as Isaiah speaks." ("A Declaration from the Poor Oppressed People of England.") (35: p. 101)

The socialist demands of Winstanley were confined to the denial of private property, trade and money. He was explicitly opposed to more extreme views: "Likewise they report that we diggers hold women to be common, and live in that bestialness. For my part I declare against it. I own this to be a truth, that the earth ought to be a common treasury to all; but as for women, Let every man have his own wife, and every woman her own husband; and I know none of the diggers that act in such an unrational excess of female community. If any should, I profess to have nothing to do with such people, but leave them to their own master, who will pay them with torment of mind and diseases in their bodies." ("A New-year's Gift for the Parliament and Army.") (35: p. 177) Winstanley constantly declared himself an enemy of violence as well, persuading his readers that the Diggers would seek their ends only by peaceable means. But the emotional thrust of his message sometimes carried him beyond the point, and he raised his voice against any kind of private property: "the cursed thing, called private property, which is the cause of all wars, bloodshed, theft and enslaving wars, that hold the people under misery." (32: p. 108) He says to his opponents: "But now the time of deliverance is come, and thou proud Esau and stout-hearted covetousness, thou must come down and be lord of the creation no longer. For now the King of righteousness is rising to rule in and over the earth. Therefore, if thou wilt find mercy, *Let Israel go free;* break in pieces quickly the bond of particular property." ("The True Levellers' Standard Advanced . . .") (35: p. 93)

The Diggers comprise only a single group in a wider movement during the period of the English revolution. Supporters of the general movement were called Levellers. One of them, the London merchant William Walwyn, asked "that throughout the country there be no fences, nor hedges, nor moats." A contemporary pamphlet ascribes to Walwyn the following views: "It would never be well until all things were common; and it being replied, will that be ever? answered, we must endeavor it; it being said, that this would destroy all Government, answered, that then there would be no thieves, no covetous persons, no deceiving and abusing of one another, and so no need of Government." (32: pp. 185–186) The author informs us that Walwyn never disproved these assertions. "A few diligent spirits may turn the world upside down if they observe the seasons and shall with life and courage engage accordingly," Walwyn proposes. (32: p. 185)

*The Moderate,* a newspaper espousing the views of the Levellers, wrote on the occasion of the execution of certain robbers: "Many an honest man tries to prove that it is only private property which governs the lives of people of such condition and forces them to violate the law in order to sustain life. Further, they explain with much conviction that property is the prime cause of all clashes between parties." (36: p. 62)

A pamphlet of the day says: "Let us establish in regard to those who are called Levellers the following: They wish that no one call anything whatsoever his own, and, in their words, the power of man over land is tyranny, and, in their opinion, private property is the work of the devil." (33: pp. 168–169)

Unlike Winstanley, who preached renunciation of violence, the extreme Leveller groups agitated for terror. One of their pamphlets is entitled "Removal Is Not Murder." Their effort to foment rebellion was, however, easily crushed by Cromwell's troops.

In almost all Leveller groups, socialist aspirations were combined with some form of atheism. Even Winstanley, who referred to voices and revelation and was fond of quoting the prophets, wrote of Christianity: "This divine teaching that you call 'spiritual and celestial' is in truth the thief who comes and plunders the vineyards of human peace. . . . Those who preach this divine teaching are the murderers of many poor souls." Overton published a book entitled: "Man is wholly mortal, or a treatise wherein 'tis proved both theologically and philosophically that as whole man sinned, so whole man dies contrary to that common disinclination of soul and body." (31: p. 94) His followers formed the sect of the "Sleeping Souls." They believed that the soul falls into the sleep of death along with the body.

The period of the English revolution represents the last great surge in the fortunes of the sectarian movement. In later years, the characteristic figure of the prophet-cum-apostle* disappears from the historical scene. The sects themselves also vanish, after having so persistently preserved all their typical traits for more than six hundred years.

The socialist currents of this period reflect the characteristics of a time of transition. On the one hand, they retain clear traces of their sectarian origin. This is exemplified by Winstanley's references to visions, revelation and voices and his attempts to derive his views from

* The last representative of this type may be seen in Wilhelm Weitling, who had such a great influence on Marx. In Weitling's career we encounter the characteristically endless journeys all over Europe (and to America) to preach his doctrine, and the phenomenon of a Christian vocabulary employed to propound socialism and violence, including a project for arming forty thousand brigands.

the Scriptures. Direct ties with the sectarian movement on the Continent can also be demonstrated. Some of the routes by which Anabaptism came to England have been mentioned above. These direct contacts were maintained throughout the period preceding the revolution. For example, it was at this time that a bishop of the Bohemian Brethren, Jan Komensky (Comenius), settled in England. He was expelled from England in 1642, but his influence lingered for a long time afterward. The works of Komensky were translated into English by the influential Leveller pamphleteer Samuel Hartlib.

On the other hand, many works produced by the Levellers exhibit a purely rationalist spirit and show no trace of any religious consideration. Certain of these writings belong to the new literary genre of socialist utopias. Such was Hartlib's "Kingdom of Macaria," which presents a picture of life wholly subordinated to the state. The most important of Winstanley's works, "The Law of Freedom," is also written in this style. For this reason it will be more properly discussed in the next chapter.

## Appendix
## Three Biographies

*Dolcino and the Apostolic Brethren.* The sect of Apostolic Brethren was founded by a young peasant from near Parma, Gerard Segarelli. Contemporaries portray him as combining the features of a crafty peasant and a simpleton, but judging by his success, he possessed other qualities as well. In any case he was in 1248 refused admittance to the Franciscan order because of his "simplicity." He thereupon entered a neighboring church and remained for a long time contemplating pictures of the Apostles. From then on, he stopped shaving and let his hair grow long, so as to resemble the Apostles in the depictions of the time, and dressed accordingly. He sold his house, went out into the town square and threw the money from the sale on the ground, saying, "Take it, whoever wants to." He left the town and began to live on alms, gathering around him a small band of followers, who dressed and lived as he did.

The times were favorable for the birth of new sects. The year 1260 was approaching, the time Joachim of Flore had predicted would bring world cataclysms and the appearance of the Antichrist. Furthermore, in 1259, a terrible plague had befallen Italy, strengthening the belief in Joachim's prophecy. Crowds of penitents led by monks and priests moved half-naked along the roads, scourging themselves and leaving a bloody trail behind. Singing hymns, the penitents would enter a town and a ceremony of purging would begin. Everyone was to repent, to make peace with his enemies and to give back anything gained by unjust means. Amnesty for all exiles would generally be announced. (38: pp. 288–289)

Segarelli's sect emerged from this troubled period with added strength and influence. It was supported by many rich and powerful men. Segarelli even submitted a request to the Pope to recognize his order, in the manner of the Franciscans. The Curia refused, but in an extremely benevolent tone. At this point, Segarelli sent his Apostles to remote corners of Italy and into France. It seems that the teaching of the Apostolic Brethren at the time differed little from that of numerous other religious groups. The Pope was forced to tolerate most of these sects, and Segarelli himself came under the protection of the Bishop of Parma, in whose palace he resided for twelve years, playing the role, as his opponents asserted, of parasite, almost of a jester.

Little by little, the sect's relations with the Curia began to sour. The sect insisted on exposing corruption among priests and enumerating the ways in which they had strayed from Apostolic ideals. Meanwhile the Curia pointed to the heretical trends of the sect. This seems to have coincided with an increased influence of the views of the Brethren of the Free Spirit upon the Apostolic Brethren. The importance the sect attained can be judged by the fact that it was condemned in England by the Chichester Synod in 1286, and again in Würzburg, in 1289. (38: p. 310) The Inquisition finally took up the matter. In 1294, Segarelli was arrested; after six years of imprisonment, he was condemned and burned at the stake in 1300.

But by this time, the sect was headed by a leader of an entirely different type. His name was Dolcino. He was the illegitimate son of a priest and was studying for the priesthood when he was caught stealing money from his teacher and forced to flee. He was admitted to a Franciscan monastery as a novice, and it was here that he apparently became acquainted with the teachings of the Apostolic Brethren. He left the monastery and met Margaret, a novice in the St. Catherine convent in Trento. Entering the convent as a workman, Dolcino persuaded her to run away with him. The two became wandering preachers of the Apostolic Brethren. A contemporary says that Dolcino taught that "in love everything must be common—property and wives." Mosheim writes: "They called one another brothers and sisters, in the manner of the first Christians. They lived in poverty and could have neither houses nor provisions for tomorrow or anything that could serve as a convenience. When they experienced hunger, they asked for food of the first person they met and ate whatever was offered. Well-off people who joined them were obliged to give their property over to be used by the sect. . . . Brothers who went into the world to preach penitence were allowed to take with them a sister, as the Apostles did. But not as a wife, only as an assistant. They called their female companions 'sisters in Christ' and denied that they lived with them in marital or impure intimacy, even though they slept together in one bed." (Quoted in 37)

Krone, who wrote a history of the Apostolic Brethren using contemporary sources, denies the accusations of sacrilegious violations of the cross and of sexual excesses, but he believes that Dolcino's preaching did include an appeal for communality of property and of wives. (37: p. 224)

A description of the ceremony for admission to the rank of Apostle has been preserved. As a token of his renunciation of his previous life, the initiate would throw off his clothes and take an oath that he would always live in evangelic poverty. He was forbidden to touch money and was to live exclusively on alms—bread from heaven. Any work, any subordination to others, was likewise forbidden. Like the first Apostles, he was to pay heed only to God.

The new Apostle was then sent out into the world to spread the sect's teachings, which by this time had become vehemently hostile to the Church. The falling away of the Church from the commandments of Christ and of the first Apostles had rendered invalid what had been prophesied for it. The Roman Church, with its Pope and cardinals, its abbots and monks, was no longer the Church of God but had become the Whore of Babylon. The power that Christ had given to the Church had now passed over to the Apostolic Brethren. The validity of Church rituals was denied. A consecrated church was no better for communion with God than a stable or a pigsty. Oaths taken in church or sworn on the Gospel need not be binding. A man might hide his beliefs or renounce them, if in his heart he remained faithful to them.

It is not surprising that such tenets provoked a fierce persecution on the part of the Inquisition. During his wanderings, Dolcino fell into the hands of the Inquisition on more than one occasion, but he always denied his ties with the sect and was released. He finally fled from Italy and took refuge in Dalmatia. There he wrote letters which his followers disseminated in Italy. Three of these letters have come down to us in detailed citations. (37: p. 32 f., 38: p. 342 f.)

The letters can be summarized as follows: Dolcino and his followers are called to proclaim the coming of the final days and to urge repentance. In this they are opposed by the host of the Antichrist—the Pope, the bishops, Dominicans and Franciscans, all of them servants of Satan. But the day of vengeance is at hand. The Pope and the prelates will be killed. No monk, nun or priest will survive except those who join the Brethren. The Church will be deprived of all its riches. The whole land will be converted to the new faith by the Apostolic Brethren, upon whom the Lord will lavish his grace. God Himself will give to the world a new and holy Pope in place of Boniface VIII, who will surely be killed. In his third letter, Dolcino states that he himself will be this new Pope.

Victory in the wars with the Antichrist Pope, Dolcino foretells, will be won thanks to the interference of a foreign monarch. He pins his hope on Frederick, the King of Aragon and Sicily, who at the time was engaging in a fierce conflict with the Pope. (He had just strung up all the monks in Sicily who were suspected of supporting the papacy.)

Dolcino derived all this from his interpretation of the Biblical prophets and of the Apocalypse, where, he claimed, the past and the future were revealed. He applied to his time, for instance, texts such as these:

"What hast thou here? and whom hast thou here, that thou hast hewed thee out a sepulchre here? . . .

"Behold, the Lord will carry thee away with a mighty captivity, and will surely cover thee.

"He will surely violently turn and toss thee like a ball into a large country." (Isaiah 22: 16, 17, 18)

"For thy violence against thy brother Jacob shame shall cover thee, and thou shalt be cut off for ever." (Obadiah 1: 10)

"And I will punish Bel in Babylon, and I will bring forth out of his mouth that which he hath swallowed up: and the nations shall not flow together any more unto him: yea, the well of Babylon shall fall." (Jeremiah 51: 44)

From these prophecies Dolcino also extracted the dates for their fulfillment: in 1304, Frederick of Aragon would kill the Pope and the cardinals, and the common priests would be exterminated in 1305. This prediction was based on the text: "But now the Lord hath spoken, saying, Within three years, as the years of an hireling, and the glory of Moab shall be contemned, with all that great multitude; and the remnant shall be very small and feeble." (Isaiah 16: 14)

In 1303 or early 1304, Dolcino and his followers entered Italy. Fresh adherents came flocking to him from all sides—rich and poor, noble opponents of the Pope, villagers and townfolk. Apart from Italy, they came from France and Austria as well. Several thousand gathered in his camp. Contemporaries called Dolcino "the father of a new people," and it was rumored that he worked miracles. The members of the sect decided to establish a new settlement; they sold their property and gathered around Dolcino.

A camp was established in a mountain valley. Provisions were obtained from the neighboring villages, more and more by means of force. Soon the nearby regions were in panic. The citizens of one town wrote: "The godless heretics, the Gazars [Cathars?], have seized the upper reaches of the valley of the river, fortified themselves there and are godlessly plundering the neighboring regions, devastating the land with fire and sword, committing all kinds of impieties." (38: p. 364) The forces of the citizens were far from sufficient for defense against Dolcino's army of some five thousand men, a large force for that time. Soon the area was plundered and burned for dozens of miles around.

The townfolk raised an army and collected funds to hire soldiers for protection against Dolcino's troops. When planning their campaign, they brought in a local priest whose nose, ears and hands had been cut off: Dolcino had punished him in this way on suspicion of treason. Finally, the army was ready, but Dolcino's forces defeated it overwhelmingly. They fell upon the neighboring towns, plundering them and carrying away the inhabitants. The prisoners were exchanged later for provisions, but tortured if no one agreed to ransom them (according to one contemporary, even children were treated in this fashion). (38: p. 374)

At last, the Pope called for a campaign against the heretics. But this, too, ended in failure. The river on the banks of which the Pope's army was annihilated flowed red with blood. Other campaigns followed and the war went on for three years. Dolcino armed women, who fought side by side with men. He nurtured the faith of his supporters by ever new prophecies that victory was at hand. In camp he was revered as a saint and as the Pope, and the custom of kissing his slipper was introduced.

Contemporary accounts tell of the ferocity with which Dolcino's men persecuted priests and monks. His soldiers viewed themselves as the "avenging angels" mentioned in the Apocalypse. They believed that they had been called to exterminate the priesthood in its entirety. Churches were defiled, sacred vessels and vestments stolen, sacred images smashed, priests' houses set on fire, bell towers pulled down and bells destroyed. An eyewitness reported: "Nowhere could you see a Madonna whose hands had not been broken off or a picture not besoiled." (38: p. 374)

After a prolonged struggle, in which Dolcino repeatedly eluded his pursuers, he was finally surrounded. Famine set in in his camp. Dante hints at this episode in the *Inferno* (Canto 28, 55–60). Among the "sowers of discord" Dante meets Mohammed, who, wishing to perpetuate dissent on earth, passes this advice to Dolcino: "Tell Fra Dolcino, then, you who perhaps will see the sun before long, if he would not soon follow me here, so to arm himself with victuals that stress of snow may not bring victory to the Novarese, which otherwise would not be easy to attain."*

In 1307, Dolcino's camp was overrun and a majority of the defenders massacred. Dolcino was subjected to horrible torture. Margaret was burned before his eyes, but he was paraded around town, scourged with a red-hot iron at every crossroad and finally burned.

*Thomas Müntzer.* Müntzer was born in 1488 or 1489 of fairly well-to-do parents and received a theological education. He led a restless life, changing work several times a year; he was at various times teacher, preacher and chaplain. Finally in 1520, he was appointed preacher in Zwickau, where he met the "Zwickau Prophets." The sermons of Storch had a lifelong impact on him. The notion of the possibility of direct communication with God, which was held to be far more important than the letter of the Scriptures; the condemnation of priests and monks, of the rich and the noble; the belief in the coming of the Kingdom of God on earth and in the imminent reign of the elect—these subjects formed the basis of Müntzer's world outlook. In his sermons he supported Storch and attacked the monks and other preachers. Disorders began in the town, and the authorities banished the "Prophets" and Müntzer.

Müntzer then transferred his activities to Prague. We note that he

* Translation by Charles S. Singleton.

gravitated to the traditional seats of the chiliastic movement—first to Zwickau and then to the homeland of the Taborites. A sermon delivered by Müntzer in Prague has been preserved. In it he asserts that after the death of the disciples of the Apostles, the Church, which had been pure, became a lecherous whore. The priests teach the external forms of the Scriptures, which they steal from the Bible "like thieves and murderers." (28: p. 59) He then proceeds to the core of his teaching—his concept of the Church of the Chosen. "Never will it happen, and for this glory to God, that priestlings and apes should represent God's Church, but the Chosen of God shall preach His word. . . . To preach this doctrine I am ready to sacrifice my life. . . . God has wrought miracles for His Chosen, especially in this country. For here a new Church will arise, and this people will be the mirror of the whole world. Therefore, I appeal to everyone to protect the word of God. . . . If you fail to do this, God will give the Turks the force to annihilate you even in this year." (28: p. 61)

Müntzer's teaching did not meet with success in Prague, however, and he again took up a vagrant and hungry life. At last, in 1523, he was appointed preacher in the small town of Allstedt, and here he entered upon the first memorable phase of his career.

Müntzer rapidly gained influence in the town. He introduced the German language in the religious service (one of the first to do so in Germany) and he preached not only from the Gospel but from the Old Testament. Crowds of people flocked to his sermons, from Allstedt and from the neighboring towns and villages. The municipal official Zeiss wrote in a report: "Some of the local nobles have forbidden their subjects to attend the sermons here but the folk do not comply. They are thrown into jail and, when released, run hither again." Müntzer grew ever bolder, calling the lords who had forbidden their people to attend his sermons "big geese." He wrote to Zeiss: "The power of the princes will come to an end and soon it will pass to the common folk." (28: p. 66) His attitude is characterized by the phrase: "Whoever wants to become a building block in the new Church ought to risk his neck or the builders will throw him away." (28: p. 67)

Soon matters were out of hand. Instigated by Müntzer, a mob burned down a chapel at Müllerbach (near Allstedt) which housed a miracle-working image of the Virgin. When one of the participants in the riot was arrested, armed crowds of people appeared on the streets. More supporters arrived from the neighboring towns. Zeiss, who represented the Duke of Saxony, reported to the duke that Müntzer's preaching was at fault. He suggested that Müntzer be summoned to court and banished if found guilty. "Otherwise, his preaching, so popular with the simple folk, will cause us much toil and trouble."

At this point, Luther, who had been disturbed by the actions and preaching of Müntzer for some time, spoke out against him. He reproached Müntzer for using the success of the Reformation to attack it. He concluded by challenging Müntzer to a debate in Wittenberg. Müntzer agreed to take part in the dispute only if the witnesses would be "Turks, Romans and Pagans." At the same time, he printed two works in the neighboring town of Eilenburg, where he had his own print shop: "Protestation of Thomas Müntzer" and "Exposure of the Contrived Faith." These tracts bitterly attacked numerous aspects of Luther's teaching, as well as that of "scholars and erudites" who concoct false faith.

Strangely, we still hear nothing about measures on the part of the authorities against Müntzer, despite writings in which, for example, he characterized the Kurfürst of Saxony as "a bearded fellow with less brains in his head than I've got in my behind." He also calls upon the inhabitants of the neighboring town of Sangerhausen to rise up against the authorities. In spite of such actions, Kurfürst Frederick of Saxony and his brother Johann themselves decided to listen to the renowned preacher on a trip through Allstedt.

Müntzer took this to be a sign of readiness on the part of the princes to become a tool in his hands and in their presence delivered a sermon in which he expounded his views openly. He attacked Luther, whom he called "Brother Swine" and "Brother Sluggard," and attempted to win the princes to his cause. He told them that they were called upon to annihilate the foes of the true faith, the faith of the Chosen who are guided by God. "Dearest and beloved rulers, know your destiny from the mouth of God, and do not let the boastful priests cheat you by imaginary patience and kindness. For the stone that has been cast down from the mountain not by hands has grown big. Poor peasants and laymen see it far better than you. . . ." The day of the last reckoning approaches, and "Oh, how gloriously will the Lord smash the old pots with an iron rod." (28: p. 158) In this terrible hour one can learn the true way and foresee the future by one means only: through dreams and revelation. "This is in the true spirit of the Apostles, the Patriarchs, and the Prophets—to wait for visions and to trust in them." (28: p. 156) Müntzer cites example after example from the Bible. The chief difficulty, however, is to distinguish whether a vision is from God or from the Devil. For this, the princes ought to have faith in the new Daniel, the Chosen man. "Therefore, a new Daniel must rise and set forth revelation and must march at the head." (28: p. 159)

Müntzer urges relentless extermination of the enemies of the new teaching. "For the godless have no right to live except when the Chosen give their permission. . . . If you want to be true rulers, drive out the enemy of Christ, for you are the instrument to achieve this end. . . . Let the wicked who divert us from God live no longer." (28: p. 160) "It was not in vain that God commanded through Moses: 'You are the holy people and must not pity the godless. Smash their altars, smash to pieces their idols and burn them, lest I be wrathful with you." (28: p. 161)

At this point, Müntzer's sermon begins to shade into threats. Just as food and drink provide the means of living, he asserts, so, too, "is the sword needed for extermination of the godless. But for this to be done true, it must be done by our dear fathers, the princes, who profess Christ with us. But if they will not do it, their sword shall be taken away from them." (28: p. 161) "If they fail to believe in God's words, they ought to be removed, as Paul saith: 'Expel the depraved from amongst you.' And if they behave in contrary fashion, kill them without mercy. . . . Not only godless rulers, but priests and monks must be killed who call our Holy Gospel a heresy and claim to be the best Christians themselves." (28: p. 162)

It is a perplexing episode. How could an insignificant preacher undertake to lecture and threaten the most important princes of the empire? Some consider this proof of Müntzer's short-sightedness; for others it testifies to the princes' forbearance. Could there not be a more substantial explanation? Müntzer was a force to be reckoned with at the time. We learn this from other sources—from his letters and from the testimony presented before his execution. At the time of the sermon to the princes, he had organized a union "for the protection of the Gospel" and "as a warning to the godless" in Allstedt. He had some experience at such activities. While still a young man, Müntzer had founded a secret union directed against the Primate of Germany, Archbishop Ernst. But his new union was far larger in scope. At one gathering three hundred new members were inducted; at another, five hundred. Furthermore, Müntzer advised the citizens of neighboring towns to establish similar unions; reports were received that this plan was meeting with success. His contacts were very extensive, reaching even into Switzerland. Luther accused Müntzer of "sending to all countries messengers who fear light." In his letters, Müntzer emphasized the purely defensive nature of the union "against the oppressors of the Gospel." But after being captured, he testified that he caused the disturbances with the aim that "all Christians should become equal and the princes and lords reluctant to serve the Gospel be driven out or put to death." (28: p. 82) The motto of the Allstedt union was: *Omnia sunt communia* (Everything is common). Everyone was to share with others "as much as he could." And if a prince or a count refused to do so, "he was to be beheaded or hanged." (28: p. 82) Müntzer's union can be seen as the realization of his doctrine of the supremacy of the Chosen, as he calls the members of his union.

The situation in Allstedt grew ever more explosive. The neighboring knight von Witzleben forbade his subjects to attend Müntzer's sermons and dispersed a crowd of them, who nevertheless set out for Allstedt. Some of them fled to Allstedt and an order was sent for the fugitives to be returned to their lord. In a vehement sermon, Müntzer called Witzleben an "archbrigand" and referred to his enemies as "arch-Judases," saying that the princes were "acting not only against the faith but against natural law," and that they "must be killed like dogs." Crowds of local citizens and new arrivals filled the streets of Allstedt. The authorities lost all control over the town and could only appeal to Duke Johann of Saxony, who summoned Müntzer to Weimar for questioning.

The interrogation took place in the presence of the duke and his counselors. Müntzer denied having assailed the authorities and described his union as legal and purely defensive. Numerous witnesses, however, spoke against him. As a result, he was ordered to close his print shop, and the citizens of Allstedt were forbidden to form unions. A contemporary source describes how Müntzer, pale and trembling after the inquest, came out and, in reply to a question by Zeiss, answered: "It seems that I'll have to look for another state."

But upon returning to Allstedt, Müntzer took heart, refused to close the print shop and started writing protests. Kurfürst Frederick of Saxony intervened at this point and summoned Müntzer to Weimar for the second time. At first Müntzer surrounded himself with armed guards, apparently thinking to put up resistance, but in the night he climbed over the town wall and slipped away, leaving behind a letter in which he said that he was going to a village but would be back soon. After his flight, Müntzer wrote his compatriots another letter, calling for them to stand firm and be brave; he promised that he would be together with them soon "to wash hands in the blood of tyrants."

Müntzer went next to Mühlhausen, a town in central Germany. The choice was not accidental. For a year this place had been in a state of paralysis, without authority and on the verge of rebellion. A contemporary account of what was called the "Mühlhausen Disturbances" is extant. (28: pp. 85–115) It describes the events prior to Müntzer's arrival and his activities there. The disorders began with assaults on monasteries and churches. All the monasteries were robbed and religious objects in the churches smashed. The movement was headed by a fugitive monk, Heinrich Pfeiffer, who urged in his sermons rejection of the authority of the municipal council. On July 3, 1523, the alarm was sounded. A crowd surrounded the town hall and shots were fired. The council was compelled to make concessions, which were set forth in fifty-three points. In particular, complete freedom of preaching was announced. The insurgents were headed by a "council of eight," which retained its power on a par with the municipal council even after the agreement. Dual authority ruled in the town—people jailed by the municipal council were not infrequently released by the eight. The signing of the fifty-three points did not, however, pacify the town; in fact, it further aggravated the situation. Many priests' houses were robbed; leaflets were circulated telling that if the priests did not get out of town their houses would be burned. Priests who ventured into the streets were killed.

Such was the situation in Mühlhausen when Müntzer appeared there on August 24, 1524. He joined with Pfeiffer and their activity together soon began to bear fruit. Within a month, the town was in an uproar. This time the insurgents' demands mirrored Müntzer's ideas—no authority to be obeyed, all taxes and levies to be abolished, priests to be exiled. The burgomaster and some councillors fled the town and appealed for support from the peasants of the neighboring villages. At this time fires swept the villages, in all likelihood set by supporters of Müntzer and Pfeiffer. But the peasants stood firm on the side of the council. Promises of support also came in from towns round about. The insurgents were forced to yield. The authority of the council was restored and Pfeiffer and Müntzer were banished from Mühlhausen.

Müntzer set off for Nuremberg, where he printed two of his works. One of these, "An Interpretation of the First Chapter of St. Luke," had been written toward the end of his stay in Allstedt and revised in Mühlhausen. The other, "Discourse for Defense," was written in reply to Luther. Shortly before, Luther had written his "Letter to the Princes of Saxony Against a Rebellious Spirit," in which he drew their attention to the dangerously aggressive character of Müntzer's teaching. "It begins to seem to me that they wish to destroy all authority so as to become the lords of the world. . . . They say that they are led by the Spirit . . . but this is an ill spirit, one which is manifested in the destruction of churches and monasteries." (28: p. 204) "Christ and his Apostles never destroyed a single temple nor smashed a single holy image." Let them preach, argues Luther, "but those are not good Christians who pass from words to fists." (28: p. 209)

In his reply, Müntzer brought down a veritable cascade of abuse on Luther. He called him a basilisk, a dragon, a viper, an archpagan, an archdevil, a bashful Whore of Babylon and finally, in a fit of cannibalistic frenzy, he predicted that the devil would boil Luther in his own juice and devour him. "I would like to smell your frying carcass." (28: p. 200)

But Müntzer's Nuremberg works are especially interesting in that they demonstrate his social ideas in their most mature form. His "Discourse for Defense" begins with a dedication "To the Serenest, First-born Prince, the Mighty Lord Jesus Christ, the Gracious King of Kings, the Mighty Duke of All the Faithful." (28: p. 187) Here Müntzer expresses one of his basic conceptions—that power on this earth can belong only to God. The message ends with the following words: "The people will be free, and God will be the sole Lord over them." (28: p. 201) Princes had usurped power belonging to God. "Why do you call them serene princes? This title belongs not to them but to Christ." And: "Why do you call them highborn? I thought you were a Christian, but you are a Pagan!" (28: p. 197) Müntzer had forgotten that only a few months before, he had looked to the princes for aid. Now he says: "Princes are not lords, but servants of the sword. They must not do what they deem well but rather implement the truth." (28: p. 192) The role assigned to the princes was no more than that of executioner. It was not for nothing that Paul said that princes were not for the good but for the wicked. However, in Müntzer's view, they fail to fulfill even this function. "Those who ought to set an example for Christians, to which end they bear the name of princes, prove to the highest degree by all their deeds their unfaith." (28: p. 183) "Their hearts are vain and, therefore, all these mighty and arrogant godless ones must be thrown down from their throne. . . . God gave the princes and lords to men in His wrath and in His bitterness He will destroy them." (28: p. 171)

Müntzer also does not recall that shortly before, he saw in poverty and suffering a cross sent from above. Now the call to oppose the oppressors becomes one of the chief themes in his teaching: "The very stuff of usury, theft and robbery are our lords made of. Fish in the water, birds in the air, the fruits of the earth—they want to take everything. And beyond that they order that God's word be preached to the poor thus: 'God has commanded you not to steal' . . . and if a poor man takes the smallest thing, then he is hanged and Doctor Liar says, 'Amen.' The lords are themselves guilty of making the poor their foe. They do not wish to remove the cause of the indignation. How can the matter be set right? Since I speak so, perhaps I, too, rebel—well, so be it." (28: p. 192) By all their misdeeds the princes have deprived themselves of the right to the sword. "At the solicitation of the Chosen, God will no longer tolerate suffering." (28: p. 171) In actuality, the power of God on earth is pictured as the power of the Chosen, who are conceived of as a narrow, closed union. "It would be a wondrous Church in which the Chosen would be separated from the godless." (28: p. 182) The Chosen receive God's behests directly, by which means they execute his will on earth. (In various periods of his life, Müntzer asserted that he himself communicated directly with God.)

From Nuremberg, Müntzer set off for Switzerland and the border lands of Germany, where the Peasant War was already raging. While his role of agitator seems to have met with success, he did not stay long in the area. Seidman, the author of one of the most complete biographies of Müntzer, suggests that since disturbances had already broken out, Müntzer feared that he would be unable to gain an important enough place for himself. In February 1525, Müntzer returned to Mühlhausen.

By this time, the peasant rebellion was already spreading from the south into central Germany, toward the town of Mühlhausen. Authority had begun to slip from the hands of the municipal council. The "eight" demanded the keys to the city gates and the council had to comply. Anyone who disagreed with Müntzer and Pfeiffer's party was under constant threats of being banished. Monasteries and churches were robbed, sacred objects destroyed and monks and nuns assaulted. Finally, all Catholic clergy were driven from the town.

The sermons of Müntzer and Pfeiffer revolved around the ideas outlined earlier: princes and lords have no right to their power, authority must pass to the society of the Chosen, men have been created equal by nature and so must be equal in life, all who do not comply must be put to the sword. They preached that the rich cannot attain salvation; whoever loves beautiful chambers, rich ornaments and, above all, money cannot receive the Holy Spirit.

Finally, after the council refused to admit Müntzer and Pfeiffer into their number, it was decided at a huge gathering that the council be dismissed. A new, "eternal" council was elected.

The "History of Thomas Müntzer," a contemporary account long attributed to Melanchthon, describes the situation as follows:

This was the beginning of the new Kingdom of Christ. First of all, they drove out all monks, took over the monasteries and all their property. There was a monastery of Johannites with large holdings: it was taken over by Thomas.

And in order to take part in all proceedings, he came to the council and announced that all resolutions must be taken in accordance with God's revelation and on the basis of the Bible. And so whatever he liked was deemed just and a special commandment of God.

He also taught that all property must be common, as it is written in the Acts of the Apostles. . . . With this he so affected the folk that no one wanted to work, but when anyone needed food or clothing he went to a rich man and demanded it of him in Christ's name, for Christ had commanded that all should share with the needy. And what was not given freely was taken by force. Many acted thus, including those who lived with Thomas in the Johannite monastery. Thomas instigated this brigandage and multiplied it every day and threatened all the princes. (28: p. 42)

According to the same document, Müntzer's teaching included the destruction of authority and the communality of property: "According to the requirements of Christian love, no one ought to be superior to another, all must be free and there must be communality of all property." (28: p. 38)

Luther wrote that Müntzer had become a king and sovereign ruling in Mühlhausen.

Arms were produced in the town, the citizens given military training, and mercenaries (lansquenets) were hired. By this time, the peasant rebellion had enveloped all the neighboring areas. Large groups of Mühlhausen citizens and inhabitants of nearby villages assaulted castles round about. These they robbed, burned or destroyed. Müntzer ordered that "all castles and houses of nobility be destroyed and razed to the ground." (20: p. 519) Special arson units were organized. Booty was carried off to the town by the cartload.

Müntzer sent out messengers and issued detailed instructions on the torture of "villains" apprehended and the destruction of monasteries and castles. He called on other towns to join the uprising.

Here is what he wrote to the citizens of Allstedt:

Dear Brethren, will you sleep even now? The time is ripe. All German, French and Italian lands have risen. . . . Be there only three of you, but if you put your hope in the name of God—fear not a hundred thousand. . . . Forward, forward, forward! It is high time. Let not kind words of these Esaus arouse you to mercy. Look not upon the sufferings of the godless! They will entreat you touchingly, begging you like children. Let not mercy seize your soul, as God commanded to Moses; He has revealed to us the same. . . . Forward, forward, while the iron is hot. Let your swords be ever warm with blood! (28: pp. 74–75)

Though not "all German, French and Italian lands" had risen, the whole of central Germany—Thuringia, Saxony and Hessen—was in rebellion.

Toward the beginning of May 1525, the princes began to gather in force. A major part here was played by Luther's communication "On Disorderly and Murderous Peasant Gangs." By mid-May, two armies began to assemble in the environs of Frankenhausen. They were of approximately equal size—about eight thousand men each.

Müntzer rode out at the head of his army, surrounded by three hundred bodyguards and holding aloft a naked sword, which symbolized the goal of the rebels—annihilation of the godless. Some nobles had joined his camp. Müntzer wrote to others, threatening them and urging them to ally themselves with him. He wrote to Count Ernst Mansfeld: "So that you know that we have the power to command, I speak: The eternal, living God hath commanded that you be thrown off the throne and hath given to us the might to accomplish this. It is about you and those like you that God saith, 'Your nest must be torn down and trodden underfoot.'" The letter ends with the words: "I am marching after. Müntzer with Gideon's sword." (28: p. 78)

Nevertheless, panic began to spread through Müntzer's army. There were attempts at negotiating with the enemy, and executions of those suspected of treason took place. Müntzer sought to encourage his followers: "Sooner will the nature of the earth or of heaven be changed than God desert us." (28: p. 45) He promised that he would catch bullets in his sleeves. But when the first shots were fired, the rebel army broke and ran. Thousands of them were slaughtered on the field of battle.

In his hour of defeat, "Müntzer with Gideon's sword" lost all presence of mind. (For details, see 22: p. 225. He is the first of a long list of revolutionary leaders to act in this fashion.) Müntzer ran for the city, found an empty house and got into bed, feigning illness. A looting soldier came upon a packet of letters addressed to Müntzer that the latter had dropped in his haste, and Müntzer was seized. At the inquest, when asked about a certain execution of four men, Müntzer replied: "It was not I who executed them, my dear brothers, but God's truth."

Müntzer was subjected to torture, and when he cried out, the interrogator told him that those who had perished because of him had suffered worse. Müntzer burst out laughing and replied: "They wished for no different themselves."

He was sent to the castle of the very Count Mansfeld to whom he had written: "I am marching after." Müntzer confessed everything and betrayed the names of his comrades in the secret union. Before his execution, he wrote a letter to the citizens of Mühlhausen, appealing to them not to rebel against authority, according to Christ's commandment. "I wish to say in my farewell address, so as to unburden my soul, that you should avoid riot, lest innocent blood be shed in vain. . . . Help my wife if you can, and especially avoid bloodshed, of which I warn you sincerely." (28: pp. 83–84)

Müntzer took communion and died as a son of the Catholic Church. His head was put on a stake for show.

Contemporaries considered Müntzer to be the central figure in the Peasant War. Luther and Melanchthon believed him to be its most dangerous leader. Sebastian Franck referred to the war as the "Müntzer Uprising," and Duke Georg of Saxony wrote that with Müntzer's execution the war could be considered finished. (20: p. 257) This appreciation of Müntzer's role, however, could hardly have been meant to describe his activities as organizer; rather, the commentators most likely had in mind his function as the originator of an ideology of hatred and destruction. Luther must have been thinking along these lines when he wrote to Hans Rügel: "Whoever has seen Müntzer can say that he has seen the devil in the flesh, at his most ferocious." (28: p. 222)

*Johann of Leyden and the "New Jerusalem" in Münster.* In 1534–1535, the persecuted Anabaptists in Switzerland and southern and central Germany fled north, to northern Germany, Holland, Sweden and Denmark. The center of their activity became the town of Münster, where they established themselves at the time of the struggle between the Catholics and the Lutherans. They gained a strong position in the town by allying themselves with the Lutherans.

But when the Lutherans won, they found they had to reckon with the "Prophets," as the leaders of the Anabaptists described themselves. The latter had even succeeded in winning over the head of the Lutheran party.

At this time, a new and striking figure appeared among the Anabaptists— Jan Matthijs, a Dutch baker from Haarlem. In his preaching, the chiliastic and militant tendencies in Anabaptism were resurrected with their previous force. Matthijs called for armed rebellion and the universal extermination of the godless. "Apostles" sent by him went in pairs to all lands and provinces. They told about the miracles wrought by this new prophet and predicted the annihilation of all tyrants and godless people in the world. In Germany and in Holland, people underwent the second baptism and founded new communities. In Münster, fourteen hundred persons were baptized in eight days. In keeping with the growing success of the Anabaptists there, adherents from other countries, especially from Holland, streamed into Münster. The Dutch arrivals were headed by the Münster citizen Knipperdolling.

One of Matthijs's Apostles to arrive in Münster was Jan Bokelson (Beukels), who, under the name Johann of Leyden, was to become a central figure in later developments. Beginning as a tailor's apprentice, Bokelson married a rich widow but soon lost her fortune. He had traveled much, having been to England, Flanders and Portugal, had read fairly extensively and knew the Holy Scriptures as well as Müntzer's writings. In Münster he took up with Knipperdolling and soon married his daughter, thereby bringing the Anabaptist community under the influence of Matthijs. By this time, leadership of the Anabaptist movement in Münster had passed over from the local citizens entirely into the hands of the Dutch Prophets, preacher-conspirators who had been uprooted from their homeland.

Clashes between Anabaptists and Lutherans occurred in Münster, and Anabaptists raided monasteries and churches. Matthijs's Apostles proclaimed that the thousand-year kingdom was at hand for those who had accepted the second baptism: a happy life with community of property, without authority, laws or marital bonds. As for those who opposed the new kingdom, they could expect annihilation and death at the hand of the Chosen. The Chosen were prohibited to greet the faithless or to have anything whatever to do with them.

The municipal council banished some Anabaptist preachers from the town and arrested one who had violated the ban imposed on their sermons. This was early in 1534. Crowds of Anabaptists ran through the city, shouting: "Repent or God will punish you! Father, Father, annihilate the godless." On the ninth of February, armed mobs appeared in the town; they blocked off streets and occupied part of the city. The Lutherans also took up arms, occupied another part of town and began to push the Anabaptists back. Their forces proved to be greater and they surrounded the Anabaptists and brought up cannon. Victory was in the hands of the Lutherans, but the burgomaster Tilbeck, who sympathized with the Anabaptists, negotiated an agreement on religious peace: "So that everyone be free in his faith and every man come back to his own house and live in peace." (23: p. 701) This was the beginning of Anabaptist rule in the town. Anabaptists flocked to Münster from all sides. In an account that originated in Anabaptist circles, we read: "The faces of Christians again blossomed forth. Everyone in the marketplace, even seven-year-old children, began prophesying. The women made extraordinary jumps. But the godless said that they were demented, that they were drunk on sweet wine." (23: pp. 707–708)

On February 21, a new election was held for the municipal council, in which the Anabaptists won a majority. They took over the municipal administration and appointed their adherents Knipperdolling and Kibbenbrock as burgomasters.

The Anabaptists made a display of their power almost immediately in a terrible outburst of violence that took place on February 24, three days after the election. Monasteries and churches were destroyed, religious objects smashed and saints' relics thrown into the streets. Not only religion but everything connected with the old culture evoked their ire. Statues in the market square were smashed to pieces. A precious collection of old Italian manuscripts which had been collected by Rudolf von Langen was solemnly burned in the square. Paintings of the Westphalian school, famous at the time, were destroyed so thoroughly that at present this school of painting is known only by reputation. Even musical instruments were smashed.

Three days later, on February 27, the Anabaptists proceeded to one of the major points of their program—the expulsion of the godless, that is, of those citizens who refused to accept the teachings of the "prophets." Matthijs insisted that all the godless be put to death. The more wary Knipperdolling objected: "All peoples will then unite against us to revenge the blood of those killed." Finally, a decision was taken to drive out of town anyone who refused to accept second baptism. A meeting of armed Anabaptists was called. The Prophet sat in a trance while prayers were being said. At last, Matthijs rose and called for the expulsion of the faithless: "Down with Esau's offspring! The inheritance belongs to the children of Jacob." A shout of "Down with the godless!" rolled through the streets. Armed Anabaptists broke into houses and drove out everyone who was unwilling to accept second baptism. Winter was drawing to a close; it was a stormy day and wet snow was falling. An eyewitness account describes crowds of expelled citizens walking through the knee-deep snow. They had not been allowed even to take warm clothing with them, women carrying children in their arms, old men leaning on staffs. At the city gate they were robbed once more.

The next action was the socialization of all property. A chronicle of the time reads: "They decided unanimously that all property must be held in common and that everyone must hand in his silver, gold and money. In the end all did so." (29: p. 201) It is known that this measure was accomplished with some difficulty and only in the course of two months. Matthijs appointed seven deacons to watch over the socialized property.

To suppress discontent aroused by these measures, the Anabaptists began to resort to terror on an ever wider scale. One day Matthijs gathered all the men in the town square and ordered everyone who had taken baptism on the last day (mass baptism had gone on for three days) to step forward. There were three hundred; they were ordered to put down their arms. Matthijs spoke: "The Lord is wrathful and calls for sacrifice." The accused men prostrated themselves before the Prophet, in the manner of the Anabaptists, and begged for mercy. But they were locked in a deserted church, from which their appeals for mercy could be heard for hours. Finally, Jan Bokelson appeared and announced: "My dear brethren, the Lord has taken pity upon you!" And all were released.

But things did not always end so benignly. For example, a report was received that the blacksmith Hubert Ruscher had spoken against the actions of the Anabaptists. He was brought to a meeting; Matthijs demanded his death. Some of those present interceded for the man and asked that he be pardoned. But Bokelson shouted: "To me the power of the Lord is given so that by my hand everyone who opposes the commands of the Lord be struck down." And he struck Ruscher with a halberd. The wounded man was led away to jail. Disputation as to his fate continued. Finally, the man was again brought to the town square, where Matthijs killed him with a shot in the back.

Streams of incendiary Anabaptist literature flowed from Münster, calling the brethren to come together in the "New Jerusalem." For: "Bed and shelter are ready for all Christians. If there will be too many people, we shall use the houses and the property of the faithless. . . . Here you will have everything in abundance. The poorest among us, who earlier were scorned as paupers, now wear rich clothing like the highest and the noblest. The poor have become, by God's grace, as rich as burgomasters." (29: p. 147) It was reported that at Easter the world would be struck by a terrible plague and that, outside Münster, only every tenth person would be spared. "Let no one think either of husband or of wife or of child, if they are faithless. Do not take them with you; they are useless to God's community. . . . If anyone remains behind, I am innocent of his blood." Thus ends a leaflet signed "Emmanuel." (29: p. 148) The book *Restitution or Revival of the True Christian Teaching* was sent far and wide. It asserts that truth had been only partly open to Erasmus, Zwingli and Luther, but that it shone forth in Matthijs and Johann of Leyden. Much importance is attached to the Old Testament. The Kingdom of Christ on earth is conceived of in a purely physical fashion. It includes communality of property and polygamy. The book ends with the words: "In our time, Christians are allowed to turn the sword against godless authorities." The *Booklet Concerning Vengeance* was another popular work. It is nothing less than a call to murder and revenge. Only after vengeance had been carried out would the new earth and the new heaven appear to God's people. "Remember what they have done unto us; all this must be visited upon them in a like manner. Heed this and do not consider a sin what is no sin." (29: p. 149)

Apostles were sent from Münster to propagandize insurrection and to drum up support for the new Jerusalem. They were particularly successful in Holland. Erasmus Schet wrote to Erasmus of Rotterdam: "Hardly is there a town or a city where the ashes of rebellion are not smoldering. The communism that they preach attracts masses from all sides." (29: p. 153) In many towns the rebaptized were counted in the hundreds, among them many influential people. In Cologne it was reported that seven hundred had been newly baptized and in Essen, two hundred. Turbulence grew apace. One day five naked men, with swords in hand, ran through Amsterdam foretelling the imminent end of the world. Large crowds of armed Anabaptists were moving toward Münster. Sixteen hundred gathered in Vollenhove. Thirty ships with armed Anabaptists aboard left Amsterdam and landed near Genemuiden. This was followed by twenty-one more ships with three thousand men, women and children. The Dutch authorities were able to disperse these crowds only with great difficulty. In the town of Warenburg, an Anabaptist community began accumulating weapons, and the burgomaster became so frightened that he would appear only accompanied by a hundred guards. In Münster the Prophet Johann Dusentschur compiled a list of towns which were soon to be controlled by the "Children of God." First on the list was Soest. A delegation of Prophets set out for this city. They entered the town openly and solemnly, preaching insurrection. The authorities managed to oust them with great difficulty.

It is not surprising that this movement alarmed Bishop Franz von

THE SOCIALISM OF THE HERESIES / 63

Waldeck, in whose domain Münster was situated, as well as the rulers of the neighboring areas. Slowly an army was raised and Münster besieged. The town was well fortified and had large stores of provisions. The siege was a hard one, lasting fourteen months.

One of the first victims of the war turned out to be the Anabaptist leader Matthijs. During a common meal, he exclaimed: "Let Thy will be done and not mine!" Then he bade the others farewell, kissing them. It appears that he had had a vision that he was to challenge the unfaithful to a fight in the manner of Samson. The next day he actually went outside the city wall with a small group of volunteers and was hacked to pieces by the lansquenets.

His comrade in arms Bokelson (Johann of Leyden) thereupon delivered a sermon: "God will give you another Prophet who will be more powerful. God desired the death of Matthijs, lest you should believe in him more than in God." Within several days, Bokelson became that new Prophet, the heir to Matthijs. (29: p. 207) Once the Lord closed Johann's lips for three days. Upon recovering his speech, he proclaimed that he had had a revelation about a new order for the town. The power of the council was to be abolished, and twelve elders were to govern under the leadership of the Prophet. The names of the elders were announced; they turned out to be the most influential Dutch Prophets, and they were installed without any election.

Next came what was perhaps the most radical innovation—establishment of polygamy. Ideas of this sort are encountered earlier in Anabaptist preachings. They were supported by reference to the customs of the patriarchs of the Old Testament. The new law was facilitated by the fact that after banishment of the godless, there were two or three times as many women in Münster as men. The introduction of polygamy was accompanied by a regulation in accordance with which all women whose age did not prevent it were obligated to have a husband. The sharing out of women began. Eyewitnesses tell of violence and suicides. The atmosphere in which the law was implemented is intimated by another law, which forbade men to break into houses in groups to choose wives. One can only imagine what life was like in the new families. The authorities also interfered by staging frequent public punishment of recalcitrant wives.

The socialization of property and polygamy evoked considerable opposition in the town. The disaffected seized the chief Prophets and demanded abolition of these regulations. But they were surrounded by Anabaptists still loyal to Bokelson—mostly Dutchmen and Frisians—and compelled to surrender. They were tied to trees and shot. "Whoever fires the first shot does a service to God," Bokelson cried.

The defeat of the opposition within coincided with a major military victory—a large force assaulting the town had been beaten back. The army of the attackers was badly organized, and apparently there were Anabaptists in its ranks, for the time set for the assault had become known in Münster. The losses of the besieging army were such that a daring sally could have destroyed it entirely.

These events strengthened Johann's position considerably. The Prophet Dusentschur reported that he had had a vision that Johann would become king of the world and take the throne and the scepter of his father David until the coming of the Lord Himself. Bokelson confirmed that he had had the same vision. The election of the king culminated in the singing of psalms.

Bokelson surrounded himself with a splendid court, created court posts of various kinds and a detachment of bodyguards. He took new wives constantly, among whom the first was "the most lovely of all women," Divara—Matthijs's widow. Two crowns encrusted with precious stones—one royal, the other imperial—were made for Bokelson. His emblem was the globe with two swords crossed, a symbol of his power over the world.

The king appeared with a fanfare and accompanied by a mounted guard. A *Hofmeister* marched in front, carrying a white staff; splendidly dressed pages followed, one bearing a sword, the other the Old Testament. Next came the court, dressed in silk. Everyone they met had to kneel. At the same time, Johann had a vision from which he learned that no one should possess more than one coat, two pairs of stockings, three shirts and so on. Everyone outside the royal court was bound by this revelation.

One day 4,200 citizens were called to a royal banquet. The king and queen played host, and everyone sang the hymn "Glory to God in the Highest." Suddenly Johann noticed among the guests someone who seemed alien to him: "He was not in nuptial dress." Deciding that this must be Judas, the king cut off his head on the spot. Thereupon the banquet resumed.

Theatrical performances were staged for the townspeople; some of these parodied the holy service, others took a social turn—for instance, the dialogue of the rich man with Lazarus.

Streets and all important buildings in the town were renamed. Babies were given newly invented names.

Meanwhile executions took place almost daily: for example, on the third of June, 1535, fifty-two persons were executed; on the fifth of June, three; eighteen persons on both the sixth and the seventh, etc. Obstinate wives were executed, as well as a woman who had spoken against the new order. One woman who refused to become the king's wife, in spite of his several proposals, had her head chopped off in the town square by the king's own hand, while his assembled wives sang "Glory to God in the Highest."

The entire episode has the appearance of mass pathology, a madness to which the Prophets themselves eventually fell victim, when with blind fanaticism they joined their destinies to a doomed cause. But was it really? The Münster episode demonstrates a multitude of traits typical of all revolutions but where, confined to a single town and compressed into a single year, tragedy turns into a grotesque farce. The Swiftian device of attributing the vices of the world to tiny Lilliputians was here employed by history. In actual fact, the most eccentric of actions prove to have been entirely consistent with the inner logic of the movement. Extreme fanaticism stirred the Anabaptist mob and spread to larger and larger masses of people. Behind the absurd posturings of Jan Bokelson we can often discern a sly and calculating mind, examples of which we shall encounter later. Apparently, both he and the other Prophets had a very concrete goal in mind—"universal" rebellion and the establishment of themselves in power, if not over the "entire world," then at least over a large part of Europe. Although these hopes were not realized, they should not be dismissed as having been entirely groundless. Unrest was rampant in the whole of northwestern Germany and in Holland. It was widely thought at the time that if Johann would succeed in breaking through the siege, he would foster a change in the course of history comparable to the great migration of peoples. Anabaptist emissaries were active as far away as Zürich and Bern; in Münster they enticed lansquenets to their side with large salaries. The besieging force was once seized by panic over the rumor that the Anabaptists had taken Lübeck. This turned out to be untrue, but it is symptomatic of the prevailing sentiment.

There was, apparently, a plan to raise rebellion in four places simultaneously; it was partially implemented. In Frisia, Anabaptists seized and fortified a monastery, where they held out against a prolonged siege. Victory cost the imperial army nine hundred men killed. A squadron of Anabaptist ships approached Deventer intent on taking the town, but it was intercepted by the Duke of Heldern's fleet. Outside Groningen, an Anabaptist force of some one thousand men gathered, intending to break through to Münster. It, too, was scattered by the duke's men.

But the Anabaptists were strongest in Holland, the homeland of Matthijs and Jan Bokelson. In 1535, several large detachments of Anabaptists assembled there. They even succeeded in seizing the Amsterdam town hall for a time, although the authorities soon had the situation in hand. One of the reasons for the movement's failure was that its plans became known to the enemy. One of Johann's Apostles fell into the hands of the bishop and promised to disclose the Anabaptists' battle plans in exchange for his life. He returned to Münster, pretending to have escaped, then set out again on an Apostolic mission and informed the bishop of everything.

We can conclude that Bokelson's aspirations were far from illusory. He had amassed an army and was ready to break the siege, should the Dutch come to his aid. He was constructing a mobile barricade made of carriages. At night he ran around the town barefoot, wearing nothing but a shirt and shouting: "Rejoice, Israel, salvation is at hand." At one point he summoned the entire army to the square in order to move out of the town. He then appeared, wearing his crown and royal garments, and declared that the day had not yet come and that he had simply wanted to check the readiness of his forces. A feast was prepared for the populace— there were some two thousand men and eight thousand women altogether. After the meal Johann suddenly announced that he was stepping down. But the Prophet Dusentschur proclaimed that God called upon his brother Johann of Leyden to remain king and to punish the iniquitous. Bokelson was reelected.

There were apparently real frictions behind this masquerade. On another occasion, for instance, Knipperdolling started to leap and dance about strangely; he even stood on his head. But in the midst of these antics he suddenly cried out: "Johann is king of the flesh, but I shall be king of the spirit." Bokelson ordered him locked in the tower, as a result of which Knipperdolling soon thought better of things and the two were reconciled. Another political move in a similarly fantastic guise was the "election" of dukes. A secret vote was taken in the twelve districts into which the town had been divided. The names of candidates were put into a hat and drawn out by specially appointed young boys. The dukes elected in this manner all turned out to be Prophets close to Bokelson. Each received a dukedom of the empire, that is, one of the town districts, together with control of the town gate located in the corresponding district. This last point was the real meaning of the whole enterprise, for the lansquenets, whom Johann could no longer trust, were thereby removed from strategic positions in defense of the town.

These political maneuvers were supplemented by the sight of the royal guards engaging in daily military exercises on the main square.

In the end, however, the large stockpile of provisions ran out and famine set in. The horses were eaten, and this destroyed any hope of breaking the siege. The deacons confiscated all stores, and under threat of death it was forbidden to bake bread at home. All houses were searched and no one had the right to lock his door. The citizens began to eat grass and roots. The king pronounced that this was "no worse than bread." At this moment, he called together the dukes, the court and all his wives to a luxurious feast in the palace. An eyewitness who later escaped from the town reported: "They behaved as though they were planning to rule for the rest of their lives." (29: p. 237)

Fanaticism served as a lightning rod. The king commanded that "all that is high shall be destroyed." And the citizens began to destroy belfries and the tops of towers. Repression was practiced ever more widely. New conspiracies were revealed constantly. One of those accused was hacked into twelve parts, and a Dutchman ate his heart and liver.

The town was doomed. More and more of the defenders fled, despite the fact that trial, torture and possible execution awaited them in the besiegers' camp. Finally, on July 25, 1535, Münster was taken. The reign of the Anabaptists, who had come to power February 21, 1534, had lasted for a year and a half. Many of them were massacred by the lansquenets during the final assault; others were tried and many executed. Münster was no longer an evangelic city; it had returned to the realm of the Catholic bishop.

Jan Bokelson hid in the most impregnable tower but later gave himself up. Under torture, he renounced his faith and acknowledged that he "deserved death ten times over." He promised that if his life was spared he would bring all Anabaptists to obedience. But to no avail. In the square where once he had sat on a throne, he was tortured with hot irons, and then his heart was pierced with a red-hot dagger.

### 2. Chiliastic Socialism and the Ideology of the Heretical Movements

Above we have tried not to yield to the temptation to select from the sources on the history of the heretical movements of the Middle Ages and Reformation only those passages in which socialist ideas are expounded—the communality of property, the destruction of the family, etc. On the contrary, we tried to give a full review, though a necessarily schematic one, of the major aspects of the heretical doctrines. It will now be our task to determine the link between these two phenomena—i.e., to ascertain the role that the ideas of chiliastic socialism played in the overall ideology of the heretical movements.

To do this, it is first necessary to determine whether it is possible to speak of a single, unified world view in these movements, whether there are sufficient features common to the chaotic mass of heresies which appeared over the course of some seven centuries. In other words, we are dealing with the question of the interrelationship among different heretical doctrines. Beginning with the second half of the last century, this question became the object of much research which not only showed the existence of close ties between various heretical groups but also greatly extended the history of heresies into the past. It became clear that there is a direct continuity between the teachings of the medieval sects and the heresies of the first centuries of Christianity.

In most general terms, it is possible to divide the heresies of the Middle Ages into three groups: (1) "Manichean" heresies—the Cathars, Albigenses, Petrobrusians (from the eleventh to the fourteenth centuries). (2) "Pantheistic" heresies: Amalricians, Ortliebarians, Brethren and Sisters of the Free Spirit, Adamites, the Apostolic Brethren and the related groups of Beghards and Beguines (from the thirteenth to the fifteenth centuries). (3) Heresies which, long before the Reformation, developed ideas that were close to Protestantism—Waldensians, Anabaptists, Moravian Brethren (from the twelfth to the seventeenth centuries).

The majority of these doctrines have the same source—the gnostic and Manichean heresies which, as early as the second century A.D., spread through the Roman Empire and even beyond its borders, for example, into Persia.

The heresies of the "Manichean" group entered Western Europe primarily from the East. Very similar doctrines (dualism, belief in the connection of the Old Testament with the evil God, the division into narrow esoteric and broad exoteric circles) can be found in the gnostic sects of the second century, for example among the Marcionites, but these views achieved their full expression in Manicheanism.

The Paulicians, who appeared in the Eastern Roman Empire in the fourth and fifth centuries, served as a link between the early gnostic heresies and the medieval sects. They professed pure dualism, considering original sin to be a heroic deed: a refusal to obey the evil God. This led to a rejection of moral law and the denial of the difference between good and evil. This in turn was manifested in the various excesses of the sectarians, as described by their contemporaries. (One of the Paulician leaders was called Baan the Dirty, for instance, and there are accounts of brigandage.) In the ninth century, Paulicians occupied an area of Asia Minor, from which they carried out raids on neighboring towns, looting and selling captives into slavery to the Saracens. In 867, Ephesus was captured and sacked; the temple of St. John was turned into a stable. Defeated in the tenth century by the armies of the Byzantine emperor, the Paulicians were resettled wholesale in Bulgaria. Here they came into contact with the Bogomils, who derived from the Messalian sect (mentioned as early as the fourth century). Bogomil teaching was close to the views of the monarchic Cathars; it held that the physical world was created by God's apostate eldest son, Satanael. Paulicians and Bogomils alike rejected the baptism of children, hated and destroyed churches, sacred images and crosses.

From the Eastern Roman Empire, the Paulician and Bogomil doctrines penetrated into Western Europe. (See 10 and 12 for a more detailed account.)

The doctrines of the "pantheistic" trend can also be traced to the gnostic heresies. Epiphanes, a Christian writer of the fourth century, describes sects which are strikingly similar to the medieval Adamites. (He himself belonged at one time to such a group.) One hundred years later, Hyppolitus reports an analogous teaching among the sect of Simonians. In both cases, black masses were practiced, accompanied by an ostentatious disregard for moral norms, all of which was meant to reveal the superhuman character of "the possessor of gnosis." (16: p. 77)

There is ample evidence of numerous links among the doctrines of the different sects. We have already mentioned, for example, that the notion of the "divinity" of the Free Spirits was a development of the exclusive position of the *perfecti* among the Cathars. Some historians believe that the Free Spirits actually originated among the Cathars. In this connection we also note J. Van Mierlo's argument that the terms *beginus* and *begine* derive from "Albigensis." (15: p. 24. The Beghards and Beguines were the main source from which followers of the "Free Spirits" were drawn.)

It has furthermore been established that the Free Spirits influenced the Waldenses, specifically in the organization of the latter into a narrow circle of leaders or Apostles (who, according to the doctrine of the sect, received their authority from the angels, regularly visited paradise and contemplated God). The closeness of the two sects is illustrated by the example of Nicholas of Basel, who is variously assigned, by scholars thoroughly versed in the material, to either the Free Spirits or the Waldenses.

The Petrobrusian sect is another link between the Cathars and the Waldenses. Döllinger and Runciman consider them to be part of the Cathar movement, while other historians refer to them as predecessors of the Waldenses. Finally, there are numerous indications that Waldenses and Anabaptists are two names given at different periods to people in the same movement. Ludwig Keller devoted a number of works to elucidating the connections between the Waldenses and the Anabaptists. He brings forward numerous arguments to prove that they are in fact the same. (See 24 and 26.)

The impression of diversity created by the great variety of names cannot be taken as proof of the sects' distinctness. Their names were, for the most part, coined by their enemies after an influential preacher at a given time (Petrobrusians from Peter of Bruys; Heinrichians from Heinrich of Toulouse; Waldensians from Valdes; Ortliebarians from Ortlieb, etc., just as the term Lutheran later derived from Luther). The members of the sects called one another "Brethren," "God's people," "friends of God." The last term was used, for instance, by Waldenses and Anabaptists in Germany as late as the sixteenth century—*Gottesfreunde,* which also happens to be an exact translation of the word "Bogomil."

A striking feature that characterizes almost all the groups in the heretical movement is the rejection of baptism of the young and the related introduction of a second baptism for adults. The Justinian Code (sixth century) already contains clauses against heretics who preach a second baptism. Second baptism is mentioned repeatedly in the proceedings of the Inquisition and in the writings denouncing the Cathars and the Waldenses. The practice gives the Anabaptists their name and survives today among the Baptists.

The sectarians themselves insisted on the continuity of the heretical movement. In the first place, they asserted their ancient origins—from the disciples of the Apostles or from the Christians who refused obedience to Pope Sylvester and did not accept the bequest of Emperor Constantine. In the annals of the Toulouse Inquisition for 1311, there is the testimony of a Waldensian weaver who presented such a version of the sect's origin, quite traditional already at that time. (24: pp. 18–19) According to the Waldensian tradition, Valdes was not the founder of their church. For example, they called Peter of Bruys, who lived in the first half of the twelfth century, "one of ours." (Valdes preached in the second half of the century.) This point of view is typical not only for the Waldenses; for instance, the Anabaptist list of martyrs (which was also accepted by the Mennonites as early as the seventeenth century) begins with descriptions of the persecution of Waldenses which took place centuries before the Reformation. (24: p. 364)

Finally, the heretics' enemies, those who assailed their doctrines, as well as the representatives of the Inquisitors, all emphasized the unity of the heretical movement. St. Bernard of Clairvaux (twelfth century), who was well versed in the contemporary heresies, declared that the teaching of the Cathars contained nothing new but merely repeated ancient errors. In the work of a Roman Inquisitor known as the "pseudo-Raynier" (1250), we read the following: "Among the sects there is none more dangerous to the Church than the Leonites. And for three reasons: First, it is the most ancient of sects. Some say that it goes back to the time of Pope Sylvester, others to the Apostles. Further, there is no country where they are not met with." (24: p. 5) Bullinger, who wrote about the Anabaptists in 1560, says: "Many basic and grave errors of theirs they share with the ancient sects of Novatians, Cathars, with Auxentius and Pelagius." (25: p. 270) Cardinal Hosius (1504–1570), who fought the heretics of his day, wrote: "Still more harmful is the sect of Anabaptists, of which kind were the Waldensian Brethren also, who still recently practiced the second baptism. It is not yesterday nor the day before yesterday that this heresy grew up; it has existed since Augustine's time." (25: p. 267) In the *Substantial and Concise History of the Münster Rebellion* (1589), the Anabaptists are referred to by several names, including Cathars and Apostolic Brethren. (25: p. 247) In his *Chronicle* (1531), Sebastian Franck speaks of the connection among the Bohemian Brethren, the Waldenses and the Anabaptists: "Picards, who originate with Valdes, form a special Christian folk or sect in Bohemia. . . . They are divided into two or three groups—the largest, a smaller one and the smallest. These resemble Anabaptists in everything. . . . They number about eighty thousand." (26: p. 57) Similar evidence could be cited at length.

The notion of a unity among organized heretical movements is also tempting in that it makes more comprehensible the miracle of the Reformation, when within a few years organizations, leaders and writers crop up all across Europe. Links between the leaders of the Reformation (in its early phase) and the heretical movements are quite probable. This was asserted by opponents of the Reformation. For instance, during a disputation at the Reichstag in Worms, the papal nuncio reproached Luther: "Most of your doctrines are the already discarded heresies of the Beghards, Waldensians, Lyons Paupers, Wyclifites and Hussites." (25: pp. 122–123) Neither did the leaders of the Reformation deny these ties. For example, in the epistle "To the Christian Nobility of the German Nation" (1520) Luther writes: "It is high time for us to take up seriously and frankly the cause of the Bohemians so that we can unite with them and they with us." (25: p. 126) And Zwingli writes to Luther in 1527: "Many people, even earlier, understood the essence of evangelic religion as clearly as you do. But of all Israel no one dared to enter the battle, for they feared this mighty Goliath." (26: p. 9) It is thought likely that Zwingli belonged to the community of Brethren in Zürich, breaking with them around 1524. Luther apparently also had contacts in these circles. The first impetus to his subsequent rupture with the Catholic Church was given him when he was still an unknown young monk. Johann Staupitz, the general vicar of the Augustinian Order, took notice of him in one of his tours of inspection. Staupitz was highly esteemed among the Brethren. In a work of the day, for example, it is even said that he might be destined "to lead the New Israel out of Egyptian captivity," i.e., to save the societies of the Brethren from persecution. Staupitz's influence on Luther was exceptional at the time. Luther later said that it was he who "first lit the light of the Gospel" in his heart and raised his "dander against the Pope." Luther wrote to Staupitz: "You leave me too often. Because of you, I was like a deserted child pining for its mother. I beseech you, bless the Lord's creation in me also, a sinful man." (25: p. 133) It was only beginning with 1522 that certain differences between the two came to light, culminating, in 1524–1525, in a final break.

A striking picture emerges of a movement that lasted for fifteen centuries despite persecution by the dominant Church and by secular authorities.* A precisely fixed set of religious ideas affecting the general attitude toward life was preserved virtually unchanged, often down to the smallest detail. Throughout this period, the tradition of secret ordination of bishops was unbroken; general questions of import to the movement were decided at "synods," and wandering Apostles took the decrees to distant societies. On admittance to the sect, the initiates were given new names known only to their closed group. Secret signs were used (for instance, when shaking hands) so the brethren could recognize one another. Houses were also marked by secret signs so that traveling members could find accommodations with their kind. Among the sectarians it was said that you could travel from England to Rome, staying only at houses of fellow sectarians along the way. There were close ties among the national branches of the movement. Synods were attended by representatives from all over Western and Central Europe; literature was sent from country to country. There was mutual financial assistance during times of calamity; people would stream in from other countries to help their brethren.

Thus there are grounds for attempting to establish a common ideological underpinning for the entire movement in order to determine the place of the ideas of chiliastic socialism in these doctrines.

One of the fundamental traits observed throughout the history of the sects was their hostility toward secular authority—the "world"— and especially toward the Catholic Church. This could be active or passive, and could find expression in calls to "exterminate the godless," to kill the Pope or annihilate the Whore of Babylon (the Church), or in prohibitions of any kind of intercourse with the outside world.

This was the issue that led to the break between the leaders of the Reformation, Luther and Zwingli, and the "Brethren." The Ana-

---

* Our aim is to determine the fundamental principles that relate the doctrines of the various sects. We must, therefore, leave to one side the interesting question of precisely how the resemblance came into being: where it was a matter of direct succession, where of literary influence and in what cases it was engendered by similarity of historical circumstance.

baptist "Chronicles" for 1525 read: "The Church, long suppressed, has begun to raise its head. . . . As though they had used thunderbolts, Luther, Zwingli and their followers have destroyed everything, but they did not create anything better. . . . They let in a little light, but they did not go on to the end but joined the secular powers. . . . And therefore, although there had been a good beginning by God's will, the light of the truth was again extinguished in them." (29: p. 364)

The heretical movement, thoroughly hostile to the surrounding world, flares up from time to time with an all-consuming blaze of hatred. Such outbreaks are separated by intervals of a little more than a century: the movement fostered by Dolcino around 1300, the Hussite movement that started after Hus was burned at the stake in 1415, the aggressive form that Anabaptism assumed in the 1520s, and the English revolution of 1640–1660. In these periods we also observe socialist ideas in their starkest forms. At other times these tendencies are muffled, and we encounter sects that reject violence and teachings that contain no socialist ambitions whatsoever. (The Waldensian doctrine is an extreme example.) It is interesting, however, that the two extremes of the heretical movement were closely interwoven; they cannot be clearly distinguished. At times, in fact, a sect switched from one extreme to the other overnight. Thus we learn that the Cathars, whose doctrine forbade any violence, in 1174 attempted a coup in Florence. Merely touching a weapon, even for self-defense, was considered a sin, yet at the same time there were groups among the Cathars who permitted plunder and expropriation of churches. Historians explain events foreshadowing the Albigensian wars in terms of this sort of abrupt reversal, as more peaceful groups come under the influence of more aggressive ones: the Cathars, who had been forbidden even to kill an animal, suddenly erupted in a militant spirit that swept them into a war lasting more than thirty years. At certain periods, the Waldenses, considered the most peaceful group, burned the houses of priests who preached against their doctrine. They also killed individuals who left the ranks, or they placed prices on their heads. A similar abrupt shift can be seen in the Apostolic Brethren. Among the teachings ascribed to them is a prohibition against violence; killing a man was considered a mortal sin. This principle was soon transformed so that persecution of the sect was the capital sin, while any kind of action against the foes of the true faith was permitted. And a call for the destruction of the godless was raised as well. (9: II: p. 397) The same abrupt shift occurred with the Anabaptists in Switzerland and in southern Germany at the beginning of the Reformation. Apparently it was possible for a sect to exist in two states, "militant" and "peaceful," and the transition from one state to the other could happen suddenly, and for all practical purposes instantaneously.

The heretical world view, in its hatred for the Church and the way of life it engendered, can be understood ultimately as an antithesis to the ideology of medieval Catholicism. The Middle Ages represent a stupendous effort on the part of Western European humanity to build its life on the basis of lofty spiritual values, to comprehend life as a way toward achieving the ideals of Christianity. It was a question of reforming human society and the world, with the aim of their trans- figuration into a higher state. The religious principle that underlay this world view was the doctrine of the incarnation of Christ, an event that illuminated the physical world by means of a union of the divine and the material. In this way, the course of human action was indicated. Actual direction was in the hands of the Catholic Church and rested upon the doctrine of the Church as a mystical union of the faithful, embracing the living and the dead. Prayers for the dead were based on this teaching, as were appeals for the intercession of the saints, since all this was seen as various forms of communication between members of one Church.

The goals Western man had set for himself were not achieved. Undoubtedly, in this case as with any phenomenon of such scope, the *basic* cause of failure was *internal,* a result of free choice, of that which in relation to the Catholic Church may be called its sin. Much has been said on this subject, and we shall only mention the frequently encountered point of view according to which the fateful decision for the Church had been in choosing the *means* for achieving the goal. The forces of the world became such means—power, wealth, coercive authority. But it must not be forgotten that this choice was made in an atmosphere of unceasing struggle against forces hostile to Catholicism. Furthermore, these forces were *external,* and served as a substantial though not a main cause of the failure that had over- taken the Catholic Church. Among such forces, not the least were the heretical movements. Their activities belong to that border area where it is so difficult to distinguish between the free seeking after spiritual truth and a conspiracy having as its aim the forcible diversion of mankind from its chosen path. We have seen instances of the way that abstract mystical teachings could be interpreted, even a single generation later, as a basis for the destruction of churches and cruci-fixes, as a license for the killing of monks and priests. The common people, in turn, responded to heretical teaching with outbreaks of violence against the heretics. These were at first condemned by the Church, but gradually mutual bitterness, fear of the heretics' growing influence and, above all, the temptation of worldly power led to cam-paigns against the heretics and the institution of the Inquisition. The course that medieval society had set for itself became more and more twisted and the ideals it held became ever more blurred.

There is no doubt that the Middle Ages provided no less reason than other periods of history for dissatisfaction with life and for protest against its darker aspects. But even though criticism of society and of the Church played a great role in the heretics' message, it seems impossible to regard the heresies as mere reactions to injustice and the imperfection of life. In any case, the heresies that we have discussed did not call for the reform of the Church or an improvement in worldly life. The Anabaptists, for example, did not ally themselves either with the Protestant Reformation or the Catholic Counter-Reformation (the latter was quite effective). Instead, the doctrine of these sects called for the complete destruction of the Catholic Church, for the destruction of society as it was known, and, until this end could be accomplished, for withdrawal from the world.

It was against the *fundamental* ideas of the Middle Ages, which we have outlined above, that all the heresies were cast. Their teachings amounted to a downright denial of the propositions enumerated above, occasionally presented in mystical form. The Cathar doctrine of the creation of the material world by a wicked God or a fallen spirit was designed to destroy the belief that the incarnation of Christ had blessed the flesh and the world. The effect was to create a gap between material and spiritual life and to tear the members of the sect away from partici-pation in life as it was guided by the Church. In a more symbolic form, this juxtaposition of God and world was expressed in hatred for material representations of Christ and God the Father. It is interest-ing that one of the most ancient of the known heresies of Western Europe is connected with this. Claudius, Bishop of Turin (814–839), ordered crucifixes and sacred images to be removed from churches. (9: II: p. 50) Agobard, the Bishop of Lyons, who died in A.D. 842, also called for the destruction of sacred objects. (9: II: pp. 43–46) Undoubtedly, the iconoclast movement which spread throughout the Byzantine Empire in the eighth century was of the same origin. We mention only in passing that a leading role in this movement was played by Paulicians, the immediate predecessors of the Cathars. The same tendency to sever the ties between God and the world, between spirit and matter, led to the denial of resurrection of the flesh typical of the Cathars. The Waldensian hostility to graveyards and their tradition of burying their dead in wastelands or courtyards are also relevant.

The Cathar doctrine that good acts do not lead to salvation and, as a source of pride, are positively harmful was directed against individual participation in life. The prohibitions against carrying arms, taking oaths and going to court, which were common among Cathars and Waldenses, had a similar function. Cathars of some groups were forbidden all contact with laymen, except for attempts to convert them.

The ideas of the Free Spirits and the Adamites were even more radical—denial of property, family, state and all moral norms. The "divine" leaders of the sect clearly pretended to a much higher position in life than did the Catholic clergy. At the same time, their ideology denied all hierarchy, not only on earth, but in heaven as well. The polemical declarations that they were equal to God in all things, that they could perform miracles and that Christ had achieved a state of "godliness" only on the cross are to be taken in precisely this sense.

The denial of baptism for young children, common to almost all the sects, was based on their rejection in principle of the Church as a mystic union. In its place they set their own sect, admission into which was accompanied by baptism permitted solely to adults who consciously accepted its principles. Thus, in contrast to the Catholic Church, the sect was a conscious union of like-minded people.

All these individual theses can be reduced to one aim: overcoming the conjunction of God and the world, God and Man, which had been accomplished through Christ's incarnation (the fundamental principle of Christianity, at least in its traditional interpretation). There were two ways to achieve this: denial of the world or denial of God. The first path was taken by the Manicheans and the gnostic sects, whose teachings conceded the world to the domain of an evil God and recognized as the sole goal of life the liberation from matter (for those capable of it). The pantheistic sects, on the contrary, not only did not renounce the world, but proclaimed the ideal of the dominion over it (again, for a chosen few, while others, the "rude" folk, were included in the category of the world). In their teachings it is possible to find the prototype of the idea of "subjugating nature" which became so popular in subsequent periods. The dominion over the world was considered possible not through the carrying out of God's will—but by denying God and by transformation of the "Free Spirits" themselves into gods. The social manifestation of this ideology can be seen in the extreme trends of the Taborite movement. Finally, the Anabaptists apparently tried to find a synthesis of these tendencies. In their "militant" phase, they preached the dominion of the elect over the world; moreover, the ideas of dominion completely overshadowed the Christian features of their world view (for example, Müntzer wrote that his teachings were equally comprehensible to Christians, Jews, Turks and heathens). In their "peaceful" phase, as can be seen in the example of the Moravian Brethren, withdrawal from the world was predominant: a condemnation of the world and a breaking of all ties with it.

The ideas of chiliastic socialism constituted an organic part of this outlook. The demands to abolish private property, family, state and all hierarchies in the society of the time aimed to exclude the participants of the movement from the surrounding life. This had the effect of placing them in a hostile, antagonistic relationship with the "world." In spite of the fact that these demands did not occupy a quantitatively large place in the overall ideology of the heretical sects, they were so characteristic of it that they could serve to a great extent as an inherent distinguishing feature of the whole movement. Thus Döllinger, whom we have already cited, characterizes the attitude of the sects toward life as follows: "Each heretical doctrine that appeared in the Middle Ages bore, in open or concealed form, a revolutionary character; in other words, had it come to power, it would have been obliged to destroy the existing state structure and implement a political and social revolution. The gnostic sects, Cathars and Albigenses, who provoked the severe and implacable medieval laws against heresies by their activities, and with whom a bloody struggle was carried on, were socialist and communist. They attacked marriage, the family and property. Had they been victorious, the result would have been a traumatic social dislocation and a relapse into barbarism. It is obvious to anyone familiar with the period that the Waldenses with their doctrinal denial of oaths and criminal law could also not have found a place for themselves in the European society of the day." (41: pp. 50–51)

In the period when socialist ideas were developing within the framework of the ideology of the heretical movements, they acquired a series of new features which cannot be found in antiquity. In this epoch, socialism turned from a theoretical, scholastic doctrine into a rallying point and a motivating force behind broad popular movements. Antiquity knew harsh national catastrophes that culminated in the ruination of states. The most impoverished groups of the population did on occasion seize power, kill the rich or oust them from towns; property was taken and divided: in Kerkira in 427 B.C., in Samos in 412 and in Syracuse in 317. In Sparta, King Nabis, in 206 B.C., divided among his followers not only the property but also the wives of the rich. However, the popular movements of antiquity did not know the slogans of *communality* of property, *communality* of wives, and they were not directed against religion. All these traits emerge in the Middle Ages.

Socialist doctrines themselves change, acquiring an intolerant, embittered and destructive character.

The idea of dividing mankind into the "doomed" and the "elect" makes its appearance, followed by calls to destroy the "godless" or the "enemies of Christ," i.e., the opponents of the movement.

Socialist ideology is imbued with the notion of a coming fundamental break, of the end and destruction of the old world and the beginning of a new order. This concept is interwoven with the idea of "imprisonment" and "liberation," which, beginning with the Cathars, is understood as imprisonment of the soul in matter and as liberation in the other world. Later, the Amalricians and the Free Spirits saw the idea as spiritual liberation through the achievement of "godliness" in this world. And finally, the Taborites and the Anabaptists conceived of it as material liberation from the power of the "evil ones" and as the establishment of the dominion of the "elect."

Furthermore, socialist ideas in this epoch merge with the concept of universal history derived principally from Joachim of Flore. The realization of the socialist ideal is connected not with the decision of a wise ruler, as in Plato's conception, but is understood as the result of a predetermined process encompassing all history and independent of the will of individuals.

A new organizational structure is evolved as well; socialist ideas develop within it and attempts are made to implement them. This is a sect with the standard "concentric" structure—a narrow circle of leaders who are initiated into all aspects of the doctrine and a wide circle of sympathizers who are acquainted only with some of its aspects. The latter group tends to be linked with the sect by ties of an emotional character which are difficult to describe precisely.

The leading role in the development of socialism passes to a new type of individual. The hermetic thinker and philosopher is replaced by the fervent and tireless publicist and organizer, an expert in the theory and practice of destruction. This strange and contradictory figure will reappear in subsequent historical epochs. He is a man of seemingly inexhaustible energy when successful, but a pitiful and terrified nonentity the moment his luck turns against him.

In closing this chapter, we turn our attention to an interesting and apparently essential matter—something the reader has undoubtedly noted: the profound dependence of socialist ideology (in the forms it attained in the Middle Ages) on Christianity. In almost all socialist movements, the idea of equality was founded on the equality of all people before God. It was standard practice to refer to the community of Apostles in Jerusalem as a model founded on the principles of communality. It is to Christianity that socialism owes its concept of a historic goal, the idea of the sinfulness of the world, its coming end and the Last Judgment. Such a close link can hardly be explained by the desire to be in accord with accepted authority or (as Engels has argued) by the fact that the language of religion was the only available idiom in which to express general historical conceptions. The fact that socialism borrowed some of its fundamental ideas from Christianity shows that this was a matter not of mere transference but of a deeper interaction. The existence of certain related elements in Christianity and socialism is indicated, for example, by the phenomenon of the monastery, which seems to realize socialist principles within Christianity (e.g., the abolition of private property and of marriage). It would be extremely important to discern the aspects shared by Christianity and socialism, to trace how the Christian concepts are redirected within socialism and ultimately turn into a denial of the fundamental principles of Christianity (for example, when God's judgment over the world is reinterpreted as the judgment of the "elect" over their enemies, or when the resurrection of the dead is translated into "deification" in the sect of Free Spirits). Such an analysis would undoubtedly explain a great deal about socialist ideology.

# III   The Socialism
of the Philosophers

## 1. The Great Utopias

The English revolution of the seventeenth century was the last occasion when the heretical movement appeared as one of the major forces shaping the course of history.

In later years, the chiliastic sects that had shaken Europe became transformed into such peaceable movements as those of the Mennonites, the Baptists and the Quakers. The socialist ideas of the medieval sects live on, albeit in peaceful form, in their successors. The most graphic manifestation of these ideas are the numerous communist settlements founded by these sects in America during the eighteenth and nineteenth centuries. Here we encounter attempts to implement familiar socialist ideals: communality of property, the ban on marriage and family (expressed either as celibacy or as communality of wives and communal upbringing of children). But the socialist ideas themselves acquire a new coloration; they lose their aggressiveness. A lesser role is assigned to propagandizing the doctrine, and the center of gravity is transferred to the life of the isolated community. Thanks to this, the influence of the socialist doctrine does not in these cases extend beyond the limits of the communities that profess them. In this form, socialist ideas lose their incendiary force and cease to inspire massive popular movements.

The development of socialist ideas did not cease, of course. On the contrary, in the seventeenth and eighteenth centuries, socialist writings literally flooded Europe. But these ideas were produced by different circumstances and by men of a different mentality. The preacher and the wandering Apostle gave way to a publicist and philosopher. Religious exaltation and references to revelation were replaced by appeals to reason. The literature of socialism acquired a purely secular and rationalistic character; new means of popularization were devised: works on this theme now frequently appear under the guise of voyages to unknown lands, interlarded with frivolous episodes. By the same token, the audience to whom the message is addressed is also different. It is no longer pitched to peasants or craftsmen but to the well-read and educated public. Thus socialism renounces for a time a direct influence on the broad masses. It is as if after failing in its direct assault on Christian civilization, the movement launches an evasive maneuver which lasts for several centuries. It is only at the very end of the eighteenth century that socialism once again comes out into the street, and we meet with a fresh attempt to create a popular movement based on its ideology.*

This break in the development of socialist ideas had begun to take shape far earlier than the English revolution of the seventeenth century. In the beginning of the sixteenth century, at the time of the first tentative steps of the Reformation, a work appeared that exhibited numerous features of the new socialist literature—Thomas More's *Utopia*. In this work we first meet the literary devices that are later to become standard—e.g., a description of travel to a far-off land and the discovery of a previously unknown, exotic place where the ideals of socialism have been realized. Not surprisingly, the title of this work has become one of the terms denoting the teaching as a whole—"utopian socialism."

---

* It would be interesting to investigate the relation between these two periods in the development of socialist ideas—within the heretical movement and within the framework of Enlightenment literature. What is the influence of the former period on the latter? Through what channels was the tradition transmitted? The author is aware of only one historian who has studied this question—Ludwig Keller, who devoted a series of works to it. Keller points out two avenues by which this occurred; the first being the guilds and workshops, which were closely tied to the heretical movements throughout the Middle Ages and provided a refuge for persecuted heretics. This channel of influence leads to the Masonic movement and through it to the writers and philosophers of the Enlightenment. The second involves the academies of "poets" and "philosophers" of the Renaissance and Humanism. Of particular interest are the causes of such a sharp and sudden break in the character of chiliastic socialism and the decline of heretical movements in general. As one obvious explanation, we can point to the victory of the Reformation, which had achieved much of that which the sects had demanded (in particular, it satisfied those sects that had not set themselves the goal of destroying the entire social structure) and thereby decreased the destructive force of the sectarian movement.

*Utopia* by Thomas More. This book was first published (in Latin) in 1516, and its complete title is: "A Truly Golden Handbook, No Less Beneficial than Entertaining, About the Best State of the Commonwealth and the New Island of Utopia." At the time, its author was an influential English statesman with a brilliant career. In 1529, More became Lord Chancellor of England, the first office below the king. But in 1534 he emerged as a strong opponent of the Church reform that was being carried out by Henry VIII. He refused to swear allegiance to the king as head of the newly created Anglican Church, was accused of high treason and beheaded in 1535. Four centuries later, in 1935, he was canonized by the Catholic Church.

*Utopia* is written in the form of a conversation among the author, his friend Peter Giles, and the traveler Raphael Hythloday (Hythlodaeus). Hythloday had seen the world and was a keen observer of life. Taking part in the voyage of Amerigo Vespucci, he was left, at his own request, with a few companions "near the limits of the last voyage." After wandering over seas and wastelands, Hythloday came upon the island of Utopia, where he found a state organized according to the just laws established long ago by the wise legislator Utopus. In order to appraise correctly the impression made by *Utopia* on contemporaries, we ought to bear in mind that it was written in the very beginning of the age of discovery, before Defoe's and Swift's great novels.

The whole of *Utopia* relates one way or another to two subjects: criticism of contemporary European society and a description of the ideal state on the island of Utopia. This corresponds roughly to the division of the work into two parts. The central thesis of the first section is that contemporary European states are tools of the mercenary interests of the rich:

"When I weigh in my mind all the other states which flourish today, so help me God, I can discover nothing but a conspiracy of the rich, who pursue their own aggrandizement under the name and title of the Commonwealth." (42: p. 138)*

The true source of this situation is private property and money:

"But, Master More, to speak plainly what is in my mind, as long as there is private property and while money is the standard of all things, I do not think that a nation can be governed either justly or

---

* Quotations from More are based primarily on the English translation of H. V. S. Ogden. Page references are to the Russian edition.

happily." (42: p. 73) "As long as private property remains, the largest and by far the best part of mankind will be oppressed with an inescapable load of cares and anxieties." (42: p. 74)

By way of an example, criminal behavior is discussed; it is attributed entirely to flaws in the social system. "What else is this, I ask, but first making them thieves and then punishing them for it?" (42: p. 57) The laws of the day which punished thieves with death are considered to be not only unjust but ineffective as well. Instead, Hythloday offers the customs he had observed among people living in the mountains of Persia, the Polylerites. "I can find no better system in any country." (42: p. 59) The custom calls for a thief to be turned into a state slave. As a sign of his status, a thief's ear lobes are notched. The lazy "are sooner prompted with blows than punishment with fetters." (42: p. 60) Finally, as a measure against the escape of slaves, informing is encouraged—and rewarded by liberty (for slaves) or money (for a free man). A runaway slave who is caught is executed and any free man who helped him is turned into a slave. "You can easily see how humane and advantageous these laws are," concludes the narrator. (42: p. 61)

The gloomy depiction of contemporary Europe is contrasted with the ideal state on the island of Utopia. More's *Utopia* is no dry treatise on political systems, but a vivid picture of life. The clothing worn by the inhabitants is described, as are their occupations and amusements, the appearance of their towns, houses and temples. This enables us to discern those traits the author wishes to single out as essential.

Utopia is a republic governed by elected officials who are called "Fathers" by their subjects. All of life is regulated by the state. There is no private property and no money. The economy is based on universal labor conscription. In the first place, everyone (or almost so) is obliged to work for a certain period of time in agriculture: "For all men and women there is one common occupation—agriculture, from which no one is exempted." (42: p. 83) Upon reaching a certain age, citizens are sent to work in the countryside, where they labor for two years before being transferred back to the city. Apart from this, everyone learns some craft, which he practices when he is not at his assigned work. Work is done under the supervision of officials called "syphogrants." "The main and sole occupation of the syphogrants is care and observation lest anyone sit idle." (42: p. 84) The state also regulates the distribution of the population by means of mass resettlements. "Each community consists of households for the most part made up of kinsfolk. . . . In order that their cities may not have too many or too few inhabitants, they allow no city to have over six thousand households. . . . If the population of any of their cities happens to decline so much that it cannot be made good from other parts of the island . . . the population is built up with citizens from the colonies. This has happened only twice in all their history, both times the result of a devastating plague." (42: p. 88)

The narrator notes enthusiastically the uniformity and standardization of dress and way of life. "People wear the same sort of clothes throughout the island, except for the distinctions which mark the difference between the married and the unmarried. The fashion of the clothing never changes." (42: p. 83) "The color of the cloak is the same throughout the island. Furthermore, it is the natural color of wool." (42: p. 87) There is uniformity in other things as well. "There are fifty-four cities on the island, all large and well built, and with the same language, customs, institutions, and laws. All of them are built on the same plan, as far as the location permits." (42: p. 77) "Whoever knows one of the cities, will know them all, since they are exactly alike insofar as the terrain permits." (42: p. 80)

All products for consumption are distributed at public storehouses; moreover, everyone may take as much as he needs. Meals are taken in centralized facilities. "It is not forbidden to eat at home, though it is not thought proper. Besides no one would be so foolish as to prepare a poor meal at home when there is a sumptuous one ready for him so near at hand." (42: p. 90) The description of these common meals recalls food rationing more than simple distribution. "The best of each kind of food is first served to the elders, whose places are distinguished by some mark. Then the rest are served alike. The elders divide the choice bits, of which there is not enough to go around, as they wish. Thus due respect is paid them, yet all the rest fare as well as they." (42: p. 91)

Common meals are typical of the general tendency of the whole of life for the Utopians. "So you see no loafing is tolerated, and there are no pretexts for laziness, or opportunities. There are no taverns or ale houses, no brothels, no chances for corruption, no hiding places, no secret meetings. Because they live in full view of all, they must do their accustomed labor and spend their leisure honorably." (42: p. 92)

Every home has folding doors which, "easily opened by hand and then closing of themselves, give admission to anyone. As a result, nothing is private property anywhere. Every ten years they actually exchange their very home by lot." (42: p. 81)

In order to take a walk outside the town, it is necessary to get permission from one's father; a wife must ask her husband and a husband his wife. To leave for another town, permission must be obtained from the proper officials. "Several travel together, taking a letter from the prince, which certifies that permission to travel has been granted and states the day of return. . . . If any man goes outside his district without leave and is caught without a passport from the prince, he is treated scornfully, brought back as a fugitive and severely punished. If he does it again, he is made a slave." (42: p. 93) (We shall give more details on slavery in Utopia somewhat later.)

In Utopia marriage is monogamous, but there is nothing to indicate whether it is contracted at the will of the bride and groom or is decided by parents or officials. The state does supervise strictly the observance of chastity prior to marriage and the faithfulness of the spouses after. Anyone guilty of infraction of these rules is sold into slavery. Utopians compare the contracting of marriage to the selling of a horse, and for this reason, prior to entering into wedlock, the bride is shown to the bridegroom naked—and he to her—for, it is argued, is not the blanket taken off a horse before it is sold?

Utopians are not burdened with heavy work; they spend only six hours a day on the job, in fact, devoting the rest of the time to the sciences, the arts and "decent entertainment." In spite of this, they experience no material need. This is explained by the fact that in Europe the labor of the poor creates riches which go to support the idle, while in Utopia everyone works. (The enumeration of European idle folk is curious: "almost all the women" are first on the list, next come priests and monks, followed by landlords and their servants.)

Utopians seem to be equal in everything—universal obligatory labor, the color and cut of dress, housing. But this equality is by no means absolute. Officials are exempted from obligatory work, as well as those who have been officially "exempted for profound study of the sciences." (42: p. 86) From this exempted class the scholars, ambassadors, priests and high officials ("tranibors") are selected. Yet elsewhere it is stated that "for the most part everyone grows up learning his father's craft." (42: p. 83) It seems to follow that a closed class, almost a caste, controls the government. As for the rest of the citizens, the narrator has this to say of them (speaking of the necessity of making laws that are simple and require no complicated interpretation): "The common folk with their slow wits are unable to arrive at such conclusions, and their whole life would not suffice for it, as they spend it earning their living." (42: p. 116)

And the picture of equality is utterly destroyed when we learn that life in Utopia is largely based on slavery. Slaves do all the dirty work. But slavery seems to have more than just an economic function. Slaves are obtained from two sources: "Their slaves are either their own citizens who have been sentenced to bondage for some crime, or men of other nations who have been condemned to death. The Utopians buy these men at a low price, or more often obtain them free of charge and bring them home." (42: p. 110) "All kinds of slaves are kept constantly at work and are always chained. The Utopians treat their native slaves more harshly than the others, thinking them baser and deserving of greater punishment." (42: p. 111) It is thought that the labor of such people brings more use than their death would. At the same time, their example deters others. "If even after this treatment they still rebel and put up resistance, they are slaughtered like wild beasts." (42: p. 114)

The account of the Utopians includes a description of the prevailing philosophical views of the citizens, based as they are on the notion that pleasure is the supreme goal of life. But pleasure can be renounced: "Finally, they believe what religion easily persuades a well-disposed mind to believe, that God repays the loss of a short and transitory pleasure with great and endless joy." (42: p. 107)

Perfect freedom of conscience prevails in Utopia, with only this one reservation instituted by Utopus: "He made a solemn and severe law against any who sink so far below the dignity of human nature as to think that the soul dies with the body, or that the universe is carried along by chance without an over-ruling providence. The Utopians believe that after this life there are punishments for wickedness and rewards for virtue." (42: p. 128) Some Utopians consider the sun to be a god, others the moon, and still others, certain ancient heroes. But they all recognize some "universal deity, unknown, eternal, unfathomable, inexplicable, exceeding human intelligence, penetrating all this world not by its bulk but by its force. Him they call The Father." (42: p. 126)

The holy services of the Utopians are in keeping with this kind of abstract theism. The temples have no images of deities. The service consists of the faithful joining the priests in singing praise to God, to musical accompaniment. Women and married men may become priests, and priests may marry.

Of late, the narrator informs us, Christianity has become known in Utopia and has found many adherents there. It is true, however, that a preacher who had called other religions pagan and threatened their adherents with eternal fire was arrested and convicted. Of particular interest is the narrator's opinion that the rapid spread of Christianity in Utopia is explained by the resemblance between the communist structure of the Utopian state and the practices of the ancient Apostolic community which "are retained even now in the purest of Christian communities." (42: p. 127)

The reference to the communist character of the community described in the Acts of the Apostles was a favorite argument of the heretical sects. It is difficult to imagine what the author could have had in mind when he spoke of the "purest of Christian communities," except one or another of the heretical sects.

If we look upon More as a martyr who gave his life for the ideals of the Catholic Church, it is striking how remote his Utopia is from any such ideals. In addition to the sympathetic description of a hedonistic world view and of a colorless theistic religion, it is possible to find direct, if discreet, attacks on Christianity and the Pope. Apparently no one has yet succeeded in explaining away this disparity.

But if *Utopia* is considered as a work of chiliastic socialist literature, it seems surprisingly moderate. There is no mention of any abolition of the family or of communality of wives; there is no public upbringing of children. It seems that the new and secular movement in socialism did not at first base itself on the extreme beliefs that had been formulated within the heretical movement.

*City of the Sun* by Tommaso Campanella. Almost a century passed after the first "Utopia" before Utopian socialism was able to absorb and assimilate the more radical principles developed in antiquity and the heretical movements. Campanella's celebrated work illustrates the new synthesis.

Campanella lived at the end of the sixteenth and the beginning of the seventeenth centuries. Up to the age of thirty-four, he was a

Dominican monk; he was then arrested and spent the next twenty-seven years in prison. The remaining years of his life he spent in France.

Campanella was a philosopher, a religious thinker and a poet. He proclaimed (earlier than Bacon) the empirical nature of science, advocated the independence of science from Church authority and defended Galileo (while he himself was imprisoned by the Inquisition). In the theory of knowledge he was interested in the question of the means by which human consciousness, basing itself solely on subjective sensations, arrives at objective truth. His views on this subject are close to those later elaborated by Kant. His religious views, affirming that all things are with God, were pantheistic in character.

In Calabria in 1597, Campanella organized a conspiracy against the Spaniards, to whom the country belonged at that time. The conspiracy failed, and in 1599 Campanella was arrested and put to torture; in 1602 he was condemned to life imprisonment. In 1602, while in prison, he wrote his book *City of the Sun.*

The very title of the work—*Civitas Soli*—recalls St. Augustine's *Civitas Dei*—City of God. It is written in a sparse style, without any embellishments like exotic adventures in strange lands. The book takes the form of a dialogue between two speakers whose names are not even given: the Chief Host (apparently a reference to the Grandmaster of the Knights Hospitalers) and the Seafarer (of whom it is only said that he is a citizen of Genoa). The dialogue begins without any explanation with the words of the Host: "Please tell me of all your adventures during your last voyage." In reply, the Seafarer recounts that on an island in the Indian Ocean he visited the City of the Sun, the life of which he thereupon begins to describe.

The political system of the City of the Sun externally resembles a theocracy. "Their supreme ruler is a priest who is called Hoh, meaning 'Sun' in their language, but in our tongue we would call him the 'Metaphysic.'" (43: p. 146) This curious translation—Metaphysic for Sun—is not accidental. The role of the Sun priest could profitably be compared to the head of a technocratic hierarchy. The post is occupied by the most erudite inhabitant of the city. He knows "the history of all nations, their customs, religious rites and laws" and is well versed in all crafts, physical, mathematical and astrological sciences, and is especially knowledgeable in metaphysics and theology. He holds his office until "another man is found wiser than his predecessor and better capable to govern." (43: p. 153)

The Metaphysic has three co-rulers—Pon, Sin and Mor, meaning Might, Wisdom and Love. Each presides over the corresponding aspects of life. In some of its unexpected details, this division is reminiscent of Orwell. For instance, the area of Love's responsibility includes not only the supervision of the relations between men and women (of which, later) but also "agriculture, stock breeding and, in general, everything which pertains to food, clothing and sexual relations." (43: p. 149) The Metaphysic confers with his three co-rulers, but in major questions his decision is final. Numerous other officials are also mentioned; they are appointed by the four chief rulers or other members of the administration. There is also a Council, to which all citizens over twenty years of age belong, but it seems to possess only an advisory function. Candidates for office are nominated by the Council and confirmed at a conference of officials and finally by the four rulers. In this connection, one of Campanella's sentences remains unclear: "Officials are replaced according to the will of the people." (43 p. 175)

The social organization of the city is based on communal life, the implementation of which is directed by the administration.

"All things are common with them. The distribution of everything is in the hands of the officials, but since knowledge, honor and pleasure are common to all, no one can take anything for himself. They assert that among us property derives from and is maintained by our each having an individual dwelling and a wife and children of his own. From this self-love arises." (43: p. 149)

In the author's opinion, the communal principle is at odds with many other relations between men: "I am persuaded that the friars and monks and clergy of our country, if they were not seduced by love for their kin and friends, would be . . . more imbued with the spirit of charity." In the City of the Sun, citizens "get everything they need from the community, and the officials take care to see that no one should get more than he deserves and that no one be refused a necessity." (43: p. 150)

"Houses, dormitories, beds and all necessities they have in common. But every six months the superiors decide who is to sleep in what circle, and who in the first dormitory, who in the second . . ." (43: p. 154)

The Solarians (citizens of the City of the Sun) take their meals together, as in "monastery refectories," but the officials get "larger and better portions." (43: p. 155) The latter reward the children who excel in studies with part of the most desirable rations.

Production is based on universal obligatory labor. "There are no slaves among them," we read in one place. In another passage, however, there is the additional comment that "slaves taken at war are either sold away or used for digging ditches or other heavy work outside the city." (43: p. 169) Everyone has the duty of working four hours per day. (Like More, the author believes that with universal obligatory labor, this amount of work would suffice to provide the state with all the necessities.) However, only menial labor seems to be meant here, for later we read: "The remaining hours are spent in pleasant occupation with the sciences, in discourse and in reading." (43: p. 162) Thus scientific endeavors are not included in the four obligatory hours of "work."

That this labor is truly obligatory can be seen from the following description:

"But what is excellent and worthy of imitation with them is this: no bodily flaw compels them to idleness, excepting advanced age, when, however, they are still invited to consultations. The lame stand on guard since they have eyesight, the blind card wool and pluck fowl for cushions and featherbeds; those who are deprived of both eyes and hands serve the state with their ears, voice and so on. Finally, if someone possesses but a single limb, he makes use of it for work in the countryside, earning a good salary and serving as an informer to report to the state everything that he hears." (43: p. 163)

The Solarians work in detachments headed by a commander. "The commanders of both men's and women's detachments, that is, the heads of ten, fifty or a hundred persons," constitute the administrative body of the city immediately below the four supreme rulers. (43: p. 175) In the chapter on judicial procedures, we read that since the Solarians "always walk and work in detachments, there must be five witnesses to convict a criminal." (43: p. 177) It seems to follow that division into detachments continues even after work. At any rate, there is no question that Solarian life is regulated after work as well. For instance, during hours set aside for rest, even sedentary games are prohibited.

The uniformity of life is carried even further. Men and women wear almost identical attire; only the length of the cloak differs slightly. The form and color of clothing is prescribed, whether for wear inside or out of the city. Even the frequency with which clothes are to be changed is fixed. Violation of such prescriptions is a grave crime: "And they would certainly put to death a woman who in order to appear beautiful started to rouge her face or in order to appear tall began to wear shoes with high heels, or took to wearing long dresses in order to hide her unattractive legs." (43: p. 160)

The prescriptions concerning celebration of feasts are equally detailed, as are those covering the arts. At celebrations, "poets hymn the glorious commanders and their victories, but if one of them adds something of his own—even if adding to the glory of the hero—he is liable to penalty. Unworthy of the name of poet is he who engages in false fabrications." (43: p. 180)

The relations of the sexes are kept under a still stricter control. "The production of offspring bears directly on the interests of the state, and involves the interests of private persons only to the extent to which they are part of the state. And since individuals for the most part bear offspring wrongly and bring them up badly, to the peril of the state, the sacred duty of supervising this matter, which is considered the fundamental principle of state welfare, is entrusted to state officials, for it is only the community that can vouchsafe this and not private persons." (43: p. 160)

The procreation of children is compared to the breeding of livestock: "And they mock us in that we zealously care for improved breeds of dogs and horses but, at the same time, neglect the human race. . . . Therefore, male and female breeders of the best natural qualities are chosen in accordance with the rules of philosophy." (43: p. 160)

A series of officials—the heads of labor brigades, an astrologer and a physician—decide which man should share the bed of which woman and how often. Copulation itself takes place under the supervision of a special official. In this connection a number of rules are set forth which we will refrain from quoting. Relations between the sexes are considered to have—apart from procreation—only one other function: satisfaction of a purely physiological need. Therefore, in cases of extreme need, men are permitted to copulate with sterile or pregnant women. This is, however, possible only with the permission of a special Chief of Childbearing and on application from lower officials of the same agency, who keep this aspect of life in the city under constant supervision. The rights of a woman are determined by similar considerations: "If a woman does not conceive from one man she is joined with another; if she turns out to be sterile in this case too, she passes into common use but no longer enjoys respect." (43: p. 157)

It goes without saying that the upbringing of children is also in the hands of the state. "The children, once weaned, are placed in the charge of the mistresses, if they are girls, or with the masters, if they are boys." (43: p. 159) Children being educated are also divided into detachments. After their seventh year they start natural sciences, then proceed to other disciplines at the discretion of the administration. Less capable children are sent to the countryside, but some who prove to be more capable are accepted back in the city. (43: p. 152) Finally, education ends and the young individuals are ready to perform their basic function—to become officials in the state: "Subsequently, they all receive positions in the area of those sciences or crafts for which they have the greatest aptitude, in each case as advised by the leader or supervisor." (43: p. 152)

In this society, naturally, there are no kinship relations. "All persons of the same age call one another brother; those who are twenty-two years older they call father, and those who are twenty-two years younger, son. And the officials attend to it carefully that no one offends another in this brotherhood." (43: p. 149)

The last sentence shows that in order to maintain communal life in the City of the Sun, the abolition of family, property, freedom of work and creativity are insufficient. Campanella realizes this clearly and gives a detailed description of the system of punishments which guarantee the stability of the social structure.

Considered as crimes are: "Ingratitude, malice, failure to give due respect to another, sloth, despondency, anger, buffoonery and falsehood, which they hate more than the plague. And the guilty are deprived of the common table, or relations with women, or other honors and advantages." (43: p. 151) Sodomy is punished by forced wearing of disgraceful clothing and, if repeated, by death. "Those guilty of violence are subject to execution or punishment according to the principle of an eye for an eye, a tooth for a tooth and so on." (43: p. 176)

The punishments for military crimes are severe: "The first man who takes flight can avoid death only if the entire army pleads for his life and certain soldiers take it upon themselves to suffer punishment for the guilty party. But this indulgence is given rarely and only when there are extenuating circumstances. A man who failed to bring help when needed to an ally or a companion is punished by the rod;

for failure to follow orders, the culprit is thrown into a pit, to be torn to pieces by wild beasts; he is given a truncheon and if he succeeds in killing the lions and bears that attack him, which is almost impossible, he is pardoned." (43: p. 167) Particularly noteworthy here is this early formulation of the idea that the accused should be granted a semblance of rights in order to give the appearance of justice to his sentence.

There is no separation between the judicial and executive branches: "Everyone is judged by the senior master of his or her craft. Thus all the senior masters are judges and can sentence a person to exile, flogging, reprimand, deprivation of the common table and exclusion from the company of women." (43: p. 176) There are no professional executioners, either. "They have no hangmen . . . so as not to defile their state. . . . The death penalty is carried out only by the hand of the people, who kill or stone the transgressor. . . . Some are allowed to take their own lives: such persons surround themselves with small bags of powder which they set on fire and burn, while those present encourage them to die with dignity. All citizens meanwhile lament and beseech God to appease His wrath, grieving that they have been brought to the necessity of cutting off a rotten limb of the state. However, they persuade and cajole the transgressor until he himself acquiesces to his punishment and wishes for his death; otherwise he may not be executed. But if the crime is committed either against the liberty of the state or against God or the supreme authorities, then the sentence is carried out without delay or mercy." (43: pp. 176–177)

Punishment is regarded as an element in the education of citizens. "The defendant makes peace with his accusers and the witnesses as though with physicians who had treated his disease, embracing and kissing them. . . . And the sentences are genuine and reliable remedies and are seen as something pleasant rather than as punishment." (43: pp. 176, 173)

A religion of the sun is practiced in Campanella's state: "And in the Sun they perceive and recognize God, calling the Sun an image, a likeness and a living effigy of God from whom proceeds light, warmth, vital power and all things good. Therefore, they have erected an altar in the form of the Sun and their priests worship God in the Sun and the stars, regarding these as His altars and the sky as His temple." (43: p. 182)

Two specific aspects of these religious beliefs can be noted. First of all, this is a state religion, and the governing of the state coincides with the priestly function. Therefore, the head of state is simultaneously the chief priest, and since he is called "Sun" he is apparently perceived as an incarnation of God. "Of the officials, only the senior ones are priests. Their duties include purging the consciences of the citizens; the whole City in secret confession (which is also practiced among us) reveals its offenses to the authorities, who thus simultaneously purify souls and come to know the sins to which the people are particularly given." (43: p. 178) Hence administrative and priestly functions are concentrated in the same hands which, as we have seen earlier, possess the authority to impose any kind of penalty.

At the same time, the religion of the sun can be seen as veneration of the universe, rationalistically perceived as an ideal mechanism. In other words, it is a synthesis of religion and natural science (with an astrological bias). This accords with what we noted earlier: the title of the chief priest, "Sun," is translated as "Metaphysic," and the right to this post is determined by vast scientific knowledge.

A similar impression is produced by the description of the Temple of the Sun, which occupies the central position in the city. It resembles a museum of natural history far more than a church. "At the altar only a large globe representing the sky and another representing the earth are seen. Furthermore, on the vault of the main dome all celestial stars from the first to the sixth magnitude are depicted, with their names and their power to influence terrestrial events inscribed below each in three lines of verse." (43: p. 145) "The smaller dome is crowned only by a kind of weathervane showing the directions of the wind, of which they distinguish up to thirty-six." (43: p. 146) The word "only" seems to emphasize that the weathervane occupies the place given to the cross in Christian churches. In general, one gets the impression that throughout his work Campanella scattered remarks indicating hostility to the Catholic Church or to Christianity; moreover, these seem close in spirit to the attitude of some heretical sects. These hints are tendered obliquely and cautiously—and necessarily so, since *City of the Sun* was written in the prison of the Inquisition where Campanella was being kept in a cagelike cell. A veiled taunt of this type seems to have been intended by the enumeration of strange fish depicted on the town walls: the list begins with the "bishop fish" and ends with the "male-member fish." The following passage probably serves a similar function: "Dead bodies are not buried, but to prevent pestilence are burned and turned into fire, a noble and living element that comes from the sun and returns to the sun. By this method no chance is given for idolatry." (43: p. 180) The last sentence is clearly directed against the veneration of relics. This is an early attempt to reinforce the ideological objections to Christian rites by purely utilitarian and hygienic arguments.

The following ironic sentence is also intended as a thrust at Christianity: "After all is said and done, they recognize that happy is the Christian satisfied with the belief that such great confusion [the appearance of evil in the world] happened because of Adam's fall." (43: p. 186) And a gnostic concept in concealed form seems to be presented in the following sentence: "They also considered it possible that the acts of the lower world are governed by some lower deity at the connivance of the primary deity but now suppose this opinion to be ridiculous." (43: p. 185)

It is undoubtedly no accident that Jesus Christ is depicted on a wall of the city, in a gallery together with "all the inventors of the sciences and of armament and the legislators." True, Christ occupies "a most honorable place" next to Moses, Osiris, Jupiter, Lycurgus, Solon and others.

Several years after *City of the Sun*, Campanella wrote another work, *On the Best State*, in which he analyzes certain objections to the social concept expressed in his first book. He justifies, in particular, the communality of property by reference to the Apostolic community, and cautiously defends the communality of wives by quoting various Fathers of the Church. Especially interesting is the passage where he asserts that the possibility of such a state is confirmed by experience: "And this, moreover, has been demonstrated by monks and lately by the Anabaptists who live in communes; if they possessed the true dogma of the faith, they would have succeeded in this even more. Oh, were they not heretics and should they do justice as we preach it, then they would serve as an exemplar of this truth."

"The Law of Freedom" by Gerrard Winstanley. In the previous chapter, we spoke about the socialist movement of the Diggers of the time of the English revolution. We also quoted from pamphlets by the most important theoretician of this movement, Gerrard Winstanley. "The Law of Freedom" is the most systematic and complete exposition of his ideas. This work belongs to utopian literature and contains a detailed plan of the new society that is based, to a significant degree, on socialist principles.

"The Law of Freedom" was published in 1652. It begins with a salutation to "His Excellency Oliver Cromwell, General of the Commonwealth's Army in England, Scotland and Ireland." Winstanley points out to Cromwell that despite the victory of the revolution and the execution of the king, the position of the common folk has not improved. They continue to be burdened with taxes and to suffer under the sway of the rich, the lawyers and the priests. The promise that "all popery and episcopacy and tyranny should be rooted out" has not been kept; the soldiers now ask what they were fighting for. And Winstanley appeals to Cromwell to give true liberty to the oppressed common people.

The main part of the work begins with an attempt "to find out where true freedom lies." Winstanley believes that it resides in the free use of the fruits of the earth. "A man had better to have had no body than to have no food for it." (35: pp. 295) More specifically, true freedom consists of the free use of land. For the sake of land, kings declare wars, ministers preach, and the rich oppress the poor. And this "outer bondage" engenders "inner bondage": "the inward bondages of the mind, as covetousness, pride, hypocrisy, envy, sorrow, fears, desperation and madness, are all occasioned by the outward bondage that one sort of people lay upon another." (35: p. 295)

Proceeding from this materialist view of society, Winstanley develops a plan for a new social structure in which private land use is abolished and where "external" and "internal" bondage disappear as a result. Subordination of private interests to common interests is put forward as the basic principle of social organization. "There is but bondage and freedom, particular interest or common interest; and he who pleads to bring in particular interest into a free commonwealth will presently be seen and cast out, as one bringing in kingly slavery again." (35: p. 342)

More specifically, according to Winstanley's scheme, private land ownership, trade and money are done away with. Land is tilled by individual large families under the supervision and control of state officials. Implements are kept in each family but not as private possessions: the head of the family is responsible for their care, under penalty of law. Horses are allotted by the state. After the harvest, all produce is brought to a state warehouse.

Craftsmen are in the same position; they get raw materials from state storehouses and deliver their products there. They work either in families or in communal workshops. Citizens are transferred by the administration from one family to another, depending on the demand for manpower or their skills for a specific job.

Besides free citizens, those who have been deprived of their freedom by the courts also work. Sometimes Winstanley refers to them as bondsmen. They work at the same jobs as the free men but generally do the more menial tasks. They are supervised by officials called taskmasters.

"If they do their tasks, [the task-master] is to allow them sufficient victuals and clothing to preserve the health of their bodies. But if they prove desperate, wanton or idle, and will not quietly submit to the law, the task-master is to feed them with short diet, and to whip them, *for a rod is prepared for the fool's back,* till such time as their proud hearts do bend to the law. . . .

"And if any of these offenders run away, there shall be hue and cry sent after him, and he shall die by the sentence of the judge when taken again." (35: p. 335)

The status of slave does not automatically extend to relatives, if they have done no wrong. The purpose of slavery is to reeducate citizens who have strayed in order to "kill their pride and unreasonableness, that they may become useful men in the commonwealth." (35: p. 386)

All necessities are obtained from state shops free of charge. Here, a difficulty clearly arises, for "covetous, proud and beastly-minded men desire more, either to lie by them to look upon, or else to waste and spoil it upon their lusts; while other brethren live in straits for want of the use thereof. But the laws and faithful officers of a free commonwealth do regulate the unrational practice of such men." (35: p. 369) Indeed, according to the law, the head of a family that consumes more than it needs is punished first by public reprimand and then by being made a bondsman for a fixed term. The same solution is proposed for another difficulty—how to provide motivation for everyone to work the necessary time and with the necessary productivity in the absence of a material incentive. A citizen who refuses to carry out assigned work or a youth avoiding apprenticeship in a craft is first punished by public reprimand. If this does not help, he is then whipped, and should he repeat his offense once more, he is made a bondsman.

The basic economic and administrative unit of the state is the family. It is headed by a "father" or "master." The list of the officials of the free commonwealth begins thus: "In a private family, a father or master is an officer." (35: p. 324) Regarding his relationship to other family members, he is "to command them their work and see they do it, and not suffer them to live idle; he is either to reprove by words or whip those who offend, for the rod is prepared to bring the unreasonable ones to experience and moderation." (35: p. 325)

Apparently, blood relationships do not play a substantial role. The "father" can get dismissed for some offense and be replaced by another person; family members can be transferred to another family if necessary.

Beginning with the family, the state is built up of bigger and bigger units that are administered by the officials listed by Winstanley. Those who govern the unit immediately superior to the family are: "a peace-maker, a four-fold office of overseers, a soldier, a task-master, an executioner." The peace-maker is obliged to appeal to the conscience of offenders or to dispatch them to a province or county at the discretion of a judge. The task-masters supervise production and consumption within the families. As for soldiers, the author states that in fact, "all officials are soldiers." (35: p. 333) The function of soldiers (in the direct sense of the word) is to offer assistance to officials and to provide defense for them during times of disorder. The task-master is in charge of those sentenced to forced labor. The executioner is obliged to "cut off the head, hang or shoot to death, or whip the offender according to the sentence of law." (35: p. 335)

All posts, from the lowest to the highest, are filled by election on a yearly basis. The country is governed by a parliament, also reelected annually. All citizens may vote from the age of twenty and are eligible for election at forty. Many citizens, however, are deprived of active participation in governing; some are even disenfranchised. "All uncivil livers, as drunkards, quarrellers, fearful ignorant men, who dare not speak truth lest they anger other men; likewise all who are wholly given to pleasure and sports, of men who are full of talk; all these are empty of substance, and cannot be experienced men, therefore not fit to be chosen officers in a commonwealth; yet they may have a voice in the choosing.

"Secondly, all those who are interested in the monarchical power and government ought neither to choose nor be chosen officers to manage the commonwealth's affairs, for these cannot be friends to common freedom." (35: p. 321) Others deprived of rights include: "All those who have been so hasty to buy and sell the commonwealth's land, and so to entangle it upon a new account. . . . These are covetous men, not fearing God, and their portion is to be cast without the city of peace amongst the dogs." (35: pp. 322, 323)

Earlier, during the first period of the Digger movement, Winstanley had been an opponent of all coercion and state power. He believed that law was necessary for those living under the curse of property but that it becomes unnecessary for those who live under principles of justice and community. In the pamphlet "Letter to Lord Fairfax," he asserts that no one who obeyed just law would dare to arrest or enslave a neighbor.

Following the logic of all such movements, however, Winstanley, in his "Law of Freedom" (published just three years later), readily grants that in the state he is planning it will be possible to arrest and (literally) enslave one's neighbor. His work contains a detailed account of the punishments to be invoked: "He who strikes his neighbour shall be struck himself by the executioner, blow for blow, and shall lose eye for eye, tooth for tooth, limb for limb, life for life; and the reason is that men may be tender of one another's bodies, doing as they would be done by." (35: pp. 375–380) Striking an official is punishable by a year of forced labor. "He who endeavours to stir up contention among neighbours, by tale-bearing or false report," is at first reproved, then whipped; third offenders become servants for three months, and if the offense is reported once again, "he shall be a servant forever." (35: p. 380) Forced labor is the penalty for failing to render assistance to the task-master or for attempting to engage in buying and selling. An actual sale or purchase of land is punishable by death. A man who calls land his own is to be "set upon a stool" and held up to ridicule, and if he becomes abusive, he can be executed.

The army is fundamental to the state. It is divided into the officers corps, made up of all officials, and the soldiers, made up of the general population.

"The use or work of a fighting army in a commonwealth is to beat down all that arise to endeavor to destroy the liberties of the commonwealth." It must defend the state against those who "seek their own interest and not common freedom, and through treachery do endeavor to destroy the laws of common freedom, and to enslave both the land

and people of the commonwealth to their particular wills and lusts."
(35: p. 357) The army also opposes foreign enemies; it has one more
function—the establishment of the "Law of Freedom" in other lands.
"If a land be conquered and so enslaved as England was under the
kings and conquering laws, then an army is to be raised with as much
secrecy as may be, to restore the land again and set it free, that the
earth may become a common treasury to all her children." (35: p.
358)

In many respects, Winstanley's socialist concepts, as we have seen,
are much more moderate than those of his predecessors More and,
especially, Campanella. Only private ownership of land, labor products
and, partly, that which later came to be called the "means of production" are abolished. There is no mention of communal wives or
the communal upbringing of children. In fact, Winstanley frequently
objects to more extreme views, obviously attacking other more radical
trends. In the section "A short declaration to take off prejudice," he
writes: "Some, hearing of this common freedom, think there must
be a community of all the fruits of the earth whether they work or
no, therefore strive to live idle upon other men's labor. Others, through
the same unreasonable beastly ignorance, think there must be a community of all men and women for copulation, and so strive to live a
bestial life." (35: p. 302) The author asserts that, on the contrary, families will live separately and own their own furnishings in peace. (35:
p. 288) Laws must insulate citizens from those who hold such "false
opinions" and punish such "ignorant and insane behavior."

In one area, however, Winstanley went much further than More
and Campanella—in his attitude toward religion. The lukewarm attitude toward religion and the Church of the earlier two writers goes
hand in hand with their slant toward pantheism and their tendency
to deify the "mechanism of the Universe." In Winstanley, on the other
hand, we meet with an open hostility to the Church and a complete
replacement of religion by ethics and rational science. He sees the
chief goal of the religion of his day as assisting the rich in exploiting
the poor. "This divining doctrine, which you call spiritual and heavenly
things, is the thief and the robber." (35: p. 351) "This doctrine is made
a cloak of policy by the subtle elder brother, to cheat his simple younger
brother of the freedoms of the earth." Winstanley asserts: "They who
preach this divining doctrine are murderers of many a poor heart
who is bashful and simple." (35: p. 352) "So that this divining spiritual
doctrine is a cheat; for while men are gazing up to heaven, imagining

after a happiness or fearing a hell after they are dead, their eyes are put out, that they see not what is their birthright, and what is to be done by them here on earth while they are living." (35: p. 353) But the end of this deception is near, according to the author:

"And all the priests and clergy and preachers of these spiritual and heavenly things, as they call them, shall take up the lamentation, which is their portion, 'Alas, alas, that great city Babylon, that mighty city divinity, which hath filled the whole earth with her sorcery and deceived all people, so that the whole world wondered after this Beast; how is it fallen, and how is her judgment come upon her in one hour?' And further, as you may read, Rev. 18:10." (35: p. 354)

In Winstanley's future society, ministers of religion will be elected for one year, just as all the officials are. The duties of the commonwealth's clergy consist of carrying out functions that, from the usual point of view, have nothing whatever to do with religion. The minister is obliged to give sermons on "the affairs of the whole land, as it is brought in by the postmaster" and on "the law of the commonwealth," and to comment on "the acts and passages of former ages and governments, setting forth the benefits of freedom by well-ordered governments," as well as on "all arts and sciences . . . physic, chirurgery, astrology, astronomy, navigation, husbandry and such like." Finally, speeches "may be made sometimes of the nature of mankind, of his darkness and of his light, of his weakness and of his strength, of his love and of his envy." (35: pp. 345–346) Moreover, any experienced person may deliver a sermon, not only a minister.

Thus, under the name of clergy, Winstanley intends a class of people engaged in propagandizing the official world view and fulfilling, to an extent, the role of educators. To the objections of a hypothetical "zealous but ignorant professor," Winstanley replies: "To know the secrets of nature is to know the works of God; and to know the works of God within the creation is to know God himself, for God dwells in every visible work or body." (35: p. 348)

## 2. The Socialist Novel

In the sixteenth century and the first half of the seventeenth century, we encounter several works of socialist thought separated by lengthy intervals of several decades or even longer. Toward the end of the seventeenth century and in the eighteenth, the situation changes; a steady stream of socialist literature comes into being. Socialist ideology comes into fashion and acquires an influence; in one form or another, a majority of the thinkers of the time are affected by it.

We can distinguish two trends in the general course of things: entertaining socialist novels intended for a broad audience and the drier socialist literature of a philosophical and sociological character. The sources of both types of writing are in More and Campanella, but by the late seventeenth century the differences become substantial and the two currents each attain a distinct character.

*History of the Sevarites (L'Histoire des Sévarambes)* by Denis Vairasse may be considered the first of the typical socialist novels. Volume I, particularly interesting as a specimen of this new literature, was published in 1675. Adventures at sea are recounted, a shipwreck, landing on an unknown continent and the story of the travelers' life on shore. Finally, the travelers meet the inhabitants of the continent and become acquainted with their strange life. Instead of the dry descriptions of More and Campanella we are given vivid travel impressions rendered by the narrator, Captain Siden. Almost the entire book is devoted to the account of his travels across the land of the Sevarites and what he saw there. Only the last ten pages contain a description of the state and economic structure of the place.

The state was founded by a Persian named Sevarias, who discovered the continent and encountered the savage tribes living there in conditions of primitive communism—with communality of property and wives. By a series of ruses, he convinces them that he has arrived from the sun to tell them the laws and the will of the God of the Sun. These laws were accepted by the people and have shaped the structure of their state.

The religion of the Sun is accepted and the Sun itself is proclaimed king of the land. The Sun appoints a viceroy from among the inhabitants. In practice, the post of viceroy is filled by lot from among four candidates proposed by the council of high officials. The viceroy has absolute power, limited only by the right of the council to declare him mentally incapacitated. Beneath the viceroy there is a complex hierarchy of officials, partly elected by the people and partly appointed from above. These officials enjoy numerous privileges: they have more wives than other citizens, personal slaves, better houses, food and clothing.

The great mass of the population (all handsome and well-built people) live a carefree and happy life in well-organized cities and magnificent communal abodes. A third part of the day they work under the supervision of officials and spend the rest of the time sleeping or enjoying themselves.

Beneath them on the social ladder are the state and private slaves, who are obtained as tribute from conquered nations. They do the heavy work and their women serve as concubines to citizens and foreign guests.

The economy is based on complete state ownership: Sevarias "abolished the right of property, deprived private persons of it and willed it so that all land and wealth should belong exclusively to the state to dispose of it in such a way that subjects could receive only what was granted them by officials." (44: p. 422) The entire population lives and works in communes of a thousand persons; these are located in large square houses. The communes turn in the products of their work to the state warehouses, where they also receive all their necessities. In particular, they are all issued standard clothing; it varies only in color, depending on the age group of the owner.

"The state takes care of all this, demanding neither taxes nor tolls, and the whole people under the government of the monarch lives in happy affluence and with well-secured rest." All citizens are obliged to work to maintain the state warehouses and "for fear lest they grow restive in plenty and entertainment or be softened by idleness." (44: p. 423)

All the citizens of the land are beautiful and of fine bearing. Cripples are exiled to remote towns, as are sterile women.

The government painstakingly sees to the complete isolation of the country from the external world, but the Sevarites are aware of the latest developments in engineering and the sciences in Europe and Asia. This is possible because people are sent regularly to foreign lands in order to learn languages and all other useful knowledge. When abroad, citizens are forbidden to tell anything at all about their country. To guarantee that they return home, they are not permitted to leave their native land until they are able to put up at least three children as a pledge.

*History of the Sevarites* gives us a notion of the socialist novels that followed it. We shall therefore only briefly note a few other examples that illustrate various aspects of this genre.

*The Southern Land (La Terre australe connue)*, ascribed by Bayle to Gabriel de Foigny, a monk from Lorraine, appeared in 1676. It is the story of a voyage to the still unknown fifth part of the globe, in the Southern Hemisphere. The land discovered by the travelers is inhabited by an androgynous people—the "Australians." Their life is founded on complete freedom. Everyone acts as his reason dictates. There is only a single law according to which all must give birth to at least one child.

The inhabitants exist in complete innocence, knowing neither clothing nor government nor the words "thine" and "mine." Everyone receives an identical upbringing, which from early infancy instills in the inhabitant the idea that all are equal. (45)

*The Adventures of Telemachus (Les Aventures de Télémaque)* by Fénelon appeared in 1699. The interest of this book lies in the fact that it surveys not only the ideal socialist society but intermediate forms as well. The "first" and "second" phases of socialism are discussed. In quest of Odysseus, Telemachus visits two different communities: Boetica and Salentum. Land tenure in Boetica is communal. All property—land, fruit of the earth and trees, cows' and goats' milk—is held in common. Most of the inhabitants are tillers or herdsmen. The arts are considered harmful and there are almost no craftsmen. The citizens see their happiness in simplicity, thanks to which no one feels any deprivation. They live in families in conditions of perfect equality.

Salentum had been brought to economic ruin by the extravagant and proud King Idomeneus. Mentor, the wise old man who accompanies Telemachus, and who is in reality the goddess Minerva in disguise, establishes a new regime which is an intermediate stage on the path to complete communality. The population is divided into seven classes, each with its own prescribed type of dwelling, clothing, food, furniture and parcel of land. Private ownership is preserved, but in a limited form; no one possesses more land than is necessary for his subsistence. Trade is also permitted. (46)

*The Republic of Philosophers or the History of the Ajaoiens*, attributed to Fontenelle, appeared in 1768. A storm tosses some travelers onto an unknown shore, the island of Ajao. The island had many years before been conquered by the Ajaoiens, who annihilated a large part of the indigenous population and made slaves of the rest. Production is based on slave labor. The slaves live in barracks, where they are locked in at night. The number of slaves is strictly controlled; excess children were once killed, but at present they are taken to the shore of China and abandoned there.

The free population of the island—the Ajaoiens—live in complete communality. The words "mine" and "thine" are unknown to them. The entire land belongs to the state, which regulates its cultivation and distributes its products. Everyone is obliged to work in agriculture for a certain length of time. Crafts are organized in the same way.

It is the duty of all citizens to enter into marriage; moreover, every man has two wives. Children are brought up not by their parents but in state schools. The Ajaoiens have no cults, no priests or sacred books. They worship nature as their good mother. They recognize no supreme being but believe that everything living has intelligence. They believe that the soul is material and mortal. (47)

*The Southern Discovery by a Flying Man or the French Daedalus: Very Philosophical Novel* by Restif de la Bretonne appeared in 1781. The complicated plot (a love story, the invention of a means of flying with artificial wings, the founding of a new state in the Southern Hemisphere) leads to the discovery of Megapatagonia—the antipode of France. The basic law of this country is communality: "Without perfect equality there is neither virtue nor happiness. . . . Let everything be held in common among equals. . . . Let every one work for the common good." (48: p. 133) Twelve hours daily are given over to work in common and the other twelve to relaxation and sleep. Meals are taken in common. All social distinctions are determined solely by age: power is in the hands of the old men.

Marriage is temporary, contracted for one year. Emotions are not much taken into account; only services to the state entitles one to beautiful girls. The right of first choice therefore belongs to old men of 150 years or more.

When the wife becomes pregnant, the marriage is dissolved. The woman nurses her child at first, then hands it over to official tutors. The relations between fathers and children are "essentially the same as between persons who hardly know one another. All children are children of the people." (48: p. 138)

Dramatic works and painting are forbidden. The Megapatagonians assert that they "wish only real things and only have time to enjoy the genuine pleasures, never thinking of imaginary ones." However, there is music among them, and they sing songs glorifying great men, pleasure and love. All other subjects are banned from poetic expression.

The ethics of this society is based on obtaining the greatest possible pleasure: "Get rid of all unpleasant sensations; use everything that legitimately supplies pleasure, but without weakening or overstraining the organs." (48: p. 149) "What especially strengthens sound morals among us is the fact that moral questions are not left to the whim of private persons. Thanks to our equality and our communality, the accepted morality is uniform and public." (48: p. 151)

Megapatagonians describe the content of their religious doctrine thus: "To use one's organs in accordance with the intention of nature, abusing nothing and neglecting nothing." (48: p. 140) In answer to the question of temples, they point to the sky and to the earth. They esteem the sun as the universal father and the earth as the universal mother.

### 3. The Age of Enlightenment

We now turn to sociological and philosophical socialist literature, once again touching on but a few works which exerted the greatest influence on the development of chiliastic socialism.

Jean Meslier's *Testament* stands out among writings of this type by many aspects of its composition, by its unusual fate, as well as by the astonishing figure of its author. Throughout his adult life, Jean Meslier (1664–1729) was a priest in Champagne. His *Testament* became known in copies and excerpts only in 1733, after his death. Voltaire and other representatives of the Enlightenment found the book of great interest, but so dangerous that they never dared to publish its complete text. The first full edition appeared only in 1864, in Amsterdam.

The main distinguishing feature of the *Testament* is that its socialist conception is merely an outgrowth of the central idea of the work: the struggle with religion. Meslier saw nothing in religion other than a social role, which consists, in his opinion, of the furtherance of violence and social inequality by means of deceit and propagation of superstitions:

"In short, all that your theologists and priests preach to you with such eloquence and fervor . . . all this is in reality nothing but illusion, error, falsehood, fabrication and deception: these things were first in-

vented by sly and cunning politicians, repeated by impostors and char-
latans, then given credence by ignorant and benighted men from the
common folk, and finally supported by the power of monarchs and
the mighty who connived at the deceit and error, superstitions and
fraudulence, and perpetuated them by their laws so as to bridle the
masses in this way and make them dance to their tune." (49: I: pp.
67–69)

These two passions—hatred for God and for any kind of inequality
or hierarchy—are the driving forces of the *Testament*. Meslier considers
religion to be responsible for the majority of human misfortunes. In
particular, it sows dissent and promotes religious wars. But at the same
time, he himself calls with sincere conviction for an uprising, the killing
of kings, and the annihilation of all who could be considered more
fortunate and prosperous.

"In this connection, I am reminded of the wish of one man who
expressed the desire that 'all the mighty of this world and the noble
lords be hanged and strangled with loops made of priests' bowels.'
This judgment is certainly somewhat coarse and harsh, but there is
some naïve frankness about it. It is brief but eloquent and in a few
words expresses what people of this kind really deserve." (49: I: p.
71)

To Meslier religion was an absurd superstition that cannot survive
the slightest brush with reason. Of all the religions, the most absurd
is the religion of the Christians, whom he calls Christ-worshipers. But
it would be wrong to seek the reason for this attitude in an overly
rationalistic turn of mind of the author. Refuting Christianity, Meslier
is at the same time ready to believe the wildest superstitions and to
repeat the most absurd rumors. For instance, it seems nonsensical to
him that God could have had but a single Son, while much lesser
creatures are much better endowed. Many animals bear ten or twelve
offspring at once.

"They say that a Polish countess named Margaret has given birth
to thirty-six babies at once. And a Dutch countess, also Margaret, who
had laughed at a poor woman burdened with children, gave birth to
as many children as there are days in the year, that is, 365, and all
of them later got married. (See the Annals of Holland and Poland.)"
(49: II: p. 19)

It is clear that Meslier's point of departure is a hatred for God
and that his arguments are merely an attempt to justify this sentiment.

The person of Christ is especially hateful to him, and here he literally runs out of terms of abuse. "And what of our God—and Christ—worshipers? To whom do they ascribe divinity? To the paltry man who had neither talent, nor intelligence, nor knowledge, nor skill, and was utterly scorned in the world. Whom do they ascribe it to? Shall I say? Indeed I shall: they ascribe it to the lunatic, demented, wretched bigot and ill-starred gallows-bird." (49: II: p. 25) The champion of the rights of the poor perceives irrefutable proof of Christ's teaching in the fact that "he was always poor, and was merely the son of a carpenter." (49: II: p. 26)

Religion is the source of most social evils and, in particular, of inequality, which is maintained solely by its authority. Meslier recognizes the need for "some dependence and subordination" in every society. But at present, power is based on violence, murder and crime. In his *Testament* there is nothing said about concrete measures for improving the position of the poor nor about the rich doing something to help. The book merely fans the hatred of the former for the latter.

"You are told, dear friends, about devils; they frighten you with the devil's name alone; you are forced to believe that devils are the most evil and repulsive of creatures, that they are the worst enemies of humankind, that they strive only to ruin people and render them unhappy in hell forever. . . . But know, dear friends, that for you the most evil and true devils, those you ought to fear, are those people of whom I speak—you have no worse and no more evil enemies than the noble and the rich." (49: II: p. 166)

The essence and true cause of inequality is private property, which also is justified by religion.

"For this reason some drink and stuff themselves, wallowing in luxury, while others die from starvation. For this reason some are almost always happy and gay, while others are eternally sad and grieving." (49: II: p. 201)

Meslier's entire social program comes down to a few lines:

"What a great happiness it would be for people if they used all life's blessings together." (49: II: p. 209)

In a just society, Meslier feels, production and consumption must be organized according to principles of communality.

"People ought to possess all wealth and riches of the earth together and on equal terms and also use them together and equitably." (49: II: p. 198)

Food, clothing, education for children, ought not to differ greatly in different families. Everyone ought to work under the guidance of wise elders (in another passage, Meslier speaks about elected officials).

These measures would lead to miraculous results. No one would be in need; everyone would love his neighbor. Heavy work, deceit, vanity, would all disappear. Then, Meslier says, "no unhappy people would be seen on earth, whereas at present we come across them on every hand." (49: II: p. 217)

Family relations would also change, for a great evil introduced by the church would fall away—the indissolubility of marriage. "It is necessary to provide the identical freedom to men and to women to come together without hindrance, following their own inclination, and the freedom also to separate and leave one another when life together becomes intolerable or when a new attraction moves them to contracting a new union." (49: II: p. 214)

Meslier's *Testament* leaves the impression of a profoundly personal work revealing intimate aspects of its author's personality. Therefore, the passages that bear directly on this personality are especially interesting.

The book opens with Meslier addressing his parishioners:

"Dear friends, during my lifetime I was unable to say openly what I have thought about the order and method of governing men, of their religion and their rights, for this would have been fraught with highly dangerous and lamentable consequences. Therefore, I decided to tell you this after my death." (49: I: p. 55) Meslier says of himself: "I never was so foolish as to attach any significance to the sacraments and absurdities of religion; I have never felt bent to take part in them or even to speak of them with respect and approval." (49: II: p. 73) "With all my heart I detested the absurd duties of my profession and especially the idolatrous and superstitious masses and nonsensical and ridiculous holy communion that I was obliged to perform." (49: I: p. 77)

The book ends with these words:

"After all I have said, let people think about me, let them judge me and say of me and do whatever they please. I do not care. Let people adapt themselves and govern themselves as they please, let them be wise or mad, let them be kind or evil, let them speak of me as they please after my death. I will have nothing to do with it at all. I have given up almost any participation in the things of the world. The dead with whom I will travel the same road are troubled by nothing, they care for nothing. And with this *nothing* I shall end here. I myself am not more than nothing and soon will be, in the full sense of the word, nothing." (49: II: p. 377)

These were not idle words: Meslier committed suicide at the age of sixty-five.

The history of the *Testament* is curious. Its full text (or perhaps a series of extracts) came into the hands of Voltaire, who was greatly impressed. He wrote of the work: "This is a composition of absolute necessity for demons, an excellent catechism of Baal-zebub. Know that it is a rare book, a perfection." (49: III: p. 405)

To those he called "brethren," Voltaire wrote repeatedly, urging them to circulate extracts from the *Testament.*

"Know that God's blessing is on our nascent church: In one of the provinces, three hundred copies of Meslier have been distributed, which has produced many new converts." (49: III: p. 417)

The work was thought to be dangerous. In arguing for its publication, Voltaire wrote:

"Is it impossible, without compromising anyone, to turn to that good old soul Merlin? I would not wish for any of our brethren to take the slightest risk." (49: III: p. 416)

"Let us thank the good people who distribute it gratis and pray to the Lord to bless this useful reading." (49: III: p. 419)

"You have clever friends who would be not unwilling to have this book in a safe place; moreover, it is suitable for the edification of youth." (49: III: p. 408)

"Jean Meslier must convince the whole world. Why is his Gospel so little circulated? You are too retiring in Paris! You are hiding your lamp." (49: III: p. 410)

"In a Christian fashion, I wish for the *Testament* of the priest to be multiplied like the five loaves to nourish four or five thousand souls." (49: III: p. 411)

Later, in 1793, when the Convention was carrying out a program of de-Christianization and introducing the cult of Reason, Anacharsis Cloots proposed putting up in the temple of Reason a statue of the first priest to reject religious error—"the brave, magnanimous and great Jean Meslier."

*The Code of Nature or the True Spirit of the Law* by Morelly appeared in 1755. Almost nothing is known about the author; arguments are still going on as to whether he ever existed or whether "Morelly" is simply a pseudonym.

At the root of Morelly's system is a notion about the natural state or the "code of nature" to which mankind should adhere in order to live a moral and happy life. The breaking away from the natural state was caused by private property, the cause of all human misery. Only by abolishing it will mankind return to its natural and happy state.

Part four of the work contains a system of laws which, according to Morelly, ought to serve as the foundation of an ideal society.

A central place is occupied by three "fundamental and inviolable laws." The first abolishes private property. An exception is made only for things which a person uses "for his needs, his pleasures, or his daily work." The second law proclaims all the citizens to be public persons whom the state provides with work and maintenance. The third law proclaims universal obligatory service "in conformity with the Distributive Laws."

All citizens from the age of twenty to twenty-five are obliged to be engaged in agriculture; they are then either retained in their place or made artisans. At the age of forty, everyone has the right of free choice of profession.

Everything produced is distributed through communal storehouses. Trade and barter are forbidden by the "inviolable law."

The population lives in towns broken up into equal blocks. All buildings are of the same shape. Everyone wears clothing of the same fabric.

On reaching a certain age, everyone is to marry. Children are brought up in the family until the age of five, then they are placed in institutions designated for their further upbringing. The training (as well as the food and clothing) of all children is absolutely the same. At the age of ten, children move to workshops to continue their training.

The number of persons who devote themselves to science and the arts is strictly limited "for each type of occupation and for each town as well."

"Moral philosophy" is limited once and for all to the propositions worked out in Morelly's treatise:

"Nothing will be added beyond the limits prescribed by law." (50: p. 202)

On the other hand, unrestricted freedom of investigation is granted in the area of natural science.

The laws set forth by Morelly are to be engraved on columns or pyramids erected in the main square of each town.

Anyone attempting to change the sacred laws is to be declared mad and immured in a cave for life:

"His children and all his family will renounce his name." (50: p. 238)

We have already come across all these propositions in More and Campanella. But Morelly's system is of interest in that it contains the idea of the development of society from a primitive state to socialism.

Mankind once lived in a natural state, the Golden Age, the memory of which is preserved among all peoples. But this state was lost due to the mistaken introduction of private property by legislators. A return to a condition where no private property exists will take place thanks to progress, which Morelly considers to be the basic driving force of history.

"The phenomena that I observe demonstrate everywhere, even in a gnat's wing, the presence of a consistent development. I experience, I feel the progress of reason. I am justified, therefore, to say that by some miraculous analogy there also exist favorable transformations in the moral field, and that despite their power and pleasantness, the laws of nature do only gradually gain complete power over mankind." (50: p. 159)

Only after having experienced various forms of rule will the people understand what is truly good. The society described by Morelly will arise ultimately, as an inevitable triumph of reason, and mankind will come to the end of its journey from the unconscious Golden Age to the conscious one.

The spread of socialist ideas in the Age of Enlightenment may be judged by the open sympathy with which they are referred to in the most influential work of the day—the famous *Encyclopédie*. In an article on "The Legislator" (IX, 1765), the author of which is apparently Diderot, the fundamental goal of every legislator is described as the replacement of the "spirit of property" by the "spirit of community."

If the spirit of community is dominant in a state, its citizens do not regret that they have rejected their own will for the sake of the common will; love for their homeland becomes their only passion. These somewhat vague pronouncements are rendered more concrete by references to the laws of Peru as models of laws based on the spirit of community.*

"The laws of Peru strove to unite the citizens by bonds of humanity; while the legislation of other countries forbid doing harm to another, in Peru the laws prescribe tirelessly doing good. Laws establishing (to the extent possible in the limitations of a natural state) the communality of property weakened the spirit of property—the source of all evil. The most festive days in Peru were those days when the common field was being tilled, the field of an old man or an orphan. He who was punished by not being permitted to work in the common field considered himself a most unhappy man. Each citizen worked for all the citizens and brought the fruits of his labor to state granaries and received the fruit of other citizens' labor as reward." (Quoted in 51: p. 127)

Later, in 1772, Diderot returned to thoughts on the socialist form of state organization. In his work *Supplément au voyage de Bougainville*, he describes the life of the people of Tahiti, whose island the traveler is supposed to have visited.

The savages have everything in common. They work their fields together. Marriage does not exist and children are brought up by the community. Addressing the traveler, an old Tahitian says:

"Here, everything belongs to all, while you have preached a difference between 'mine' and 'thine.' " (52: p. 43) "Leave us our morals. They are wiser and more virtuous than yours. We do not want to exchange what you call ignorance for your useless knowledge. We have everything that we need and whatever is useful to us. Do we deserve contempt merely because we did not invent superfluous necessities? Don't inspire in us either your false necessities or your chimerical virtues." (52: p. 44)

"Our girls and women belong to all. . . . A young Tahitian girl giving herself up to the delights of a young Tahitian boy's embrace would wait impatiently for her mother to undress her and bare her

---

* In the first chapter of the next section of this book, the reader will find information on the social and economic structure of the Inca empire, which is what is meant here by Peru.

breasts. . . . Without shame or fear she accepts in our presence, surrounded by innocent Tahitians, to the sound of flutes and the dance, the caresses of him who was chosen by her youthful heart and the secret voice of her feelings. Are you capable of replacing with a more worthy and greater feeling the feeling that we instilled in them and which inspires them?" (52: pp. 43–45)

Diderot's attitude toward socialist theories may also be judged by the fact that when Morelly's *Code of Nature* was included in various collections of his works, he did not protest. This testifies not only to Diderot's moral principles but to his sympathy for socialist ideas as well.

**Deschamps's *Truth or the True System*.** In conclusion, we will take note of one of the theoreticians of socialism in the eighteenth century, the Benedictine monk Deschamps. During his lifetime, he published *Letters on the Spirit of the Times* (1769) and *The Voice of Reason Against the Voice of Nature* (1770), both anonymously. But his most original ideas are contained in his *Truth or the True System*, which remained in manuscript and was published only in our century (and in complete form only in the last few years; see 53).

Deschamps is the author of one of the most striking and internally consistent socialist systems. He is also a philosopher of the highest order, and is sometimes referred to as a precursor of Hegel. That is unquestionably correct, but while following a path similar to the one Hegel would take later, Deschamps also developed many concepts which were to be enunciated by Hegel's disciples of the left—Feuerbach, Engels, and Marx. And in his conception of Nothingness he anticipates in many respects the contemporary existentialists.

Deschamps's outlook is very close to materialism, although it does not coincide with materialism entirely. He sees only matter in the world, but his understanding of it is unusual.

"The world has existed always and will exist eternally." (53: p. 317) In it there is an unending process going on of the appearance of certain parts out of others and their destruction. "All beings emerge one out of the other, enter one into the other, and all the various species are essentially only aspects of a universal type. . . . All beings have life in them no matter how dead they seem, for death is merely a lesser manifestation of life and not its negation." (53: p. 127)

Life for Deschamps is equated to various forms of motion. He says of nature: "Everything in it possesses a capacity for feeling, life, thought, reason, i.e., motion. For what do all these words mean if not the action or motion of the particles we consist of?" (53: p. 135)

This determines man's place in the universe and, in particular, his freedom of action: "If we believe that we possess a will and freedom, that results, first, from the absurdity that forces us to believe in a God and consequently to believe that we have a soul which has its merits and faults before God, and, secondly, because we cannot see the inner springs of our mechanism." (53: pp. 136–137)

Deschamps considers God to be an idea created by mankind, a product of definite social relations based on private property. Religion did not exist before these relations took shape, and it will no longer exist when they are destroyed. Religion itself is not only the result of the oppression of people but also a means facilitating this oppression. It is one of the basic obstacles to the transition of mankind to a happier social condition.

Deschamps says: "The word 'God' must be eliminated from our languages." (53: p. 133) Nevertheless, he was a passionate opponent of atheism. Of his system he has the following to say: "At first glance, it might be possible to think that it is a concise formulation of atheism, for all religion is destroyed in it. But upon consideration, it is impossible not to be convinced that it is not a formulation of atheism at all, for in place of a rational and moral God (whom I do subject to destruction, for he merely resembles a man more powerful than other men) I set being in the metaphysical sense, which is the basis of morality that is far from arbitrary." (53: p. 154)

Deschamps has in mind his understanding of the universe, to which he ascribed three specific aspects. The first is *totality* [*le tout*], that is, the universe as a unity of all its parts. This totality is the "basis whose manifestations are all visible beings," but which has another, nonphysical nature which is unlike its parts. Therefore, it cannot be seen but can be comprehended by reason. The second aspect is *everything* [*tout*], that is, the universe as a single concept.

"*Totality* presupposes the presence of the parts. *Everything* does not presuppose this. . . . I understand *everything* as existence in itself, existence by itself . . . in other words . . . existence through nothing but itself." (53: pp. 87–88) "*Everything*, not consisting of parts, exists; it is inseparable from *totality*, which consists of parts and of which *everything* is simultaneously a confirmation and a negation." (53: p. 124)

But perhaps the most striking of Deschamps's three aspects of the universe is the third; it stresses the negative character of definitions of *everything*. "*Everything* is no longer a mass of entities but a mass without parts . . . not a single entity existing in many entities . . . but a singular entity which denies any existence apart from itself . . . about which it is possible only to deny that which is asserted in the other—for it is not sentient and not the result of sentient entities but, rather, *nothing* [*rien*], nonbeing itself, which alone cannot be anything but the negation of what is sentient." (53: pp. 125–126) "*Everything is nothing.*" (53: p. 129) "No doubt no one before me has ever written that *everything* and *nothing* are one and the same." (53: p. 130) For Deschamps, this principle is basic to his doctrine on existence: "What is the cause of existence? Answer: Its cause resides in the fact that *nothing* is something, in that it is existence, in that it is *everything.*" (53: p. 321) Here he finds a place for God as well: "God is *nothing*, nonexistence itself." (53: p. 318) Apparently, these principles, along with the deductions resulting from them, are what Deschamps opposes to atheism, which he declares a purely negative, destructive doctrine. He calls it the "atheism of cattle," i.e., of beings who have not *overcome* religion, and who have not even developed to the level of religion.

Deschamps's arrogant and scornful attitude toward contemporary philosophers of the Enlightenment is connected with this view. He accuses them of creating unscientific schemes based on fantasy.

"Let our destroyer-philosophers realize how futile and worthless were their efforts directed against God and religion. The philosophers were powerless to carry out their task, until they touched upon the existence of the civil condition, which alone is the cause of the appearance of the idea of a moral and universal being and of all religions." (53: p. 107) "The condition of universal equality does not derive logically from the doctrine of atheism. It always seemed, to our atheists as well as to the majority of people, to be a product of fantasy." (54: p. 41)

And fantasies of this sort are by no means harmless. There are only two ways out: the path proposed by religion and Deschamps's system. To undermine religion before the ground is prepared for the author's system is to hasten the coming of a destructive revolution. In *The Voice of Reason*, Deschamps says:

"This revolution will obviously have its source in the contemporary philosophical trends, although the majority does not suspect this. It will have much more lamentable consequences and bring much more destruction than any revolution caused by heresy. But is this revolution not already beginning? Has destruction not already befallen the foundations of religion, are they not ready to collapse, and all the rest as well?" (Quoted in 54: p. 6)

To the negative character of the *philosophes'* atheism Deschamps opposes what he sees as the positive character of his own system:

"The system I am proposing deprives us of the joys of paradise and the terrors of hell—just like atheism—but, in contrast to atheism, it leaves no doubt as to the rightness of the destruction of hell and paradise. Beyond that, it gives us the supremely important conviction, which atheism does not and can never give, that for us paradise can exist only in one place, namely, in this world." (53: p. 154)

Deschamps's social and historical doctrine is based on metaphysics. It is derived from a conception of the evolution of mankind in the direction of the greatest manifestation of the idea of oneness, of *totality:*

"The idea of *totality* is equivalent to the idea of order, harmony, unity, equality, perfection. The condition of unity or the social condition derives from the idea of *totality,* which is itself unity and union; for purposes of their own well-being, people must live in a social condition." (53: p. 335)

The mechanism of this evolution is the development of the social institutions which determine all other aspects of human life—language, religion, morality. . . . For example:

"It would be absurd to suppose that man came from the hands of God already mature, moral and possessing the ability to speak: speech developed along with society as it became what it is today." (53: p. 102)

Deschamps considers various manifestations of evil to be the result of social conditions; he includes even homosexuality, for example.

The social institutions themselves take shape under the influence of material factors such as the necessity of hunting in groups and the guarding of herds, as well as the advantages of man's physical structure; in particular, that of his hand.

Deschamps divides the entire historical process into three stages or states through which mankind must pass:

"For man there exist only three states: the savage state or the state of the animals in the forest; the state of law,* and the state of morals. The first is a state of disunity without unity, without society; the second

* Elsewhere Deschamps calls this the civil state.

state—ours—one of extreme disunity within unity, and the third is the state of unity without disunity. This last is without doubt the only state capable of providing people, insofar as this is possible, with strength and happiness." (53: p. 275)

In the savage state people are much happier than in the state of law, in which contemporary civilized mankind lives:

"The state of law for us . . . is undoubtedly far worse than the savage state." (53: p. 184) This is true with respect to contemporary primitive peoples: "We treat them with disdain, yet there is no doubt that their condition is far less irrational than ours." (53: p. 185) But it is impossible for us to return to the savage state, which had to collapse and give birth to the state of law by force of objective causes—first and foremost, by the appearance of inequality, authority and private property.

Private property is the basic cause of all the vices inherent in the state of law: "The notions of *thine* and *mine* in relation to earthly blessings and women exist only under cover of our morals, giving birth to all the evil that sanctions these morals." (53: p. 178)

The state of law, in Deschamps's opinion, is the state of the greatest misfortune for the greatest number of people. Evil itself is considered an outgrowth of this state: "Evil in man is present only due to the existing civil state, which endlessly contradicts man's nature. There was no such evil in man when he was in a savage state." (53: p. 166)

But those very aspects of the state of law that make it especially unbearable prepare the transition to the state of morals which seems to be that paradise on earth about which Deschamps spoke in a passage quoted earlier. His description, replete with vivid detail, contains one of the most unique and consistent of socialist utopias.

All of life in the state of morals will be completely subordinated to one goal—the maximum implementation of the idea of equality and communality. People will live without *mine* and *thine*, all specialization will disappear, as will the division of labor.

"Women would be the common property of men, as men would be the common possession of women. . . . Children would not belong to any particular man or woman." (53: p. 206) "Women capable of giving suck and who were not pregnant would nurse all children without distinction. . . . But how is it, you will object, that a woman is not to have her own children? No, indeed! What would she need that property for?" (53: p. 212) The author is not alarmed by the fact that such a way of life would lead to incest. "They say that incest goes against nature. But in fact it is merely against the nature of our morals." All people "would know only society and would belong only to it, the sole proprietor." (53: pp. 211–212)

For transition into this state, much that is now considered of value would have to be destroyed, including "everything that we call beautiful works of art. This sacrifice would undoubtedly be a great one, but it would be necessary to make." (53: p. 202) It is not only the arts—poetry, painting, architecture—that would have to disappear, but science and technology as well. People would no longer build ships or study the globe. "And why should they need the learning of a Copernicus, a Newton and a Cassini?" (53: p. 224)

Language will be simplified and much less rich, and people will begin to speak one stable and unchanging language. Writing will disappear, together with the tedious chore of learning to read and write. Children will not study at all and, instead, will learn everything they need to know by imitating their elders.

The necessity of thinking will also fall away: "In the savage state no one thought or reasoned, because no one needed to. In the state of law, one thinks and reasons because one needs to; in the state of morals, one will neither think nor reason because no one will have any need to do this any longer." (53: p. 296) One of the most vivid illustrations of this change of consciousness will be the disappearance of all books. They will find a use in the only thing that they are in reality good for—lighting stoves. All books ever written had as their goal the preparation for the book which would prove their uselessness—Deschamps's study. It will outlive the rest, but finally it, too, will be burned.

People's lives will be simplified and made easier. They will scarcely use any metals; instead, almost everything will be made of wood. No large houses will be built and people will live in wooden huts. "Their furniture would consist only of benches, shelves and tables." (53: p. 217) "Fresh straw, which would later be used as cattle litter, would serve them as a good bed on which they would all rest together, men and women, after having put to bed the aged and the children, who would sleep separately." (53: p. 221) Food would be primarily vegetarian and, thus, easy to prepare. "In their modest existence they would need to know very few things, and these would be just the things that are easy to learn." (53: p. 225) This change of life style is connected to fundamental psychic changes, which would tend to make "the inclination of each at the same time the common inclination." (53: p. 210) Individual ties between people and intense individual feelings would disappear. "There would be none of the vivid but fleeting sensations of the happy lover, the victorious hero, the ambitious man who had achieved his goal, or the laureled artist." (53: p. 205) "All days would be alike." (53: p. 211) And people would even come to resemble one another. "In the state of morals, no one would weep or laugh. All faces would be almost identical and would express satisfaction. In the eyes of men, all women would resemble all other women; and all men would be like all other men in the eyes of women!" (53: p. 205) People's heads "will be as harmonious as they now are dissimilar." (53: p. 214) "Much more than in our case, they would adhere to a similar mode of action in everything, and they would not conclude that this demonstrates a lack of reason or understanding, as we think about animals." (53: p. 219)

This new society will give rise to a new world view. "And they would not doubt—and this would not frighten them in the least— that people, too, exist only as a result of the vicissitudes of life and someday are destined to perish as a consequence of the same vicissitudes and, perhaps, to be eventually reproduced once more by means of a transformation from one aspect to another." (53: p. 225) "Because they, like us, would not take into account that they were dead earlier, that is, that their constituent parts did not exist in the past in human form; they would also, being more consistent than we, not place any significance on the termination of this existence in this form in the future." (53: p. 228) "Their burials would not be distinguishable from those of cattle." (53: p. 229) For: "their dead fellows would not mean more to them than dead cattle. . . . They would not be attached to any particular person sufficiently so that they would feel his death as a personal loss and mourn it." (53: p. 230) "They would die a quiet death, a death that would resemble their lives." (53: p. 228)

## 4. The First Steps

We have seen how socialism was nurtured by the philosophy of the Enlightenment. The new infant came into the world at the time of the Great Revolution and was suckled by Mother Guillotine. But it took its first steps down life's path after the heroic epoch of the Terror had already passed. It is touching to see traits of the future shaker of kingdoms and shatterer of thrones emerge from the charming infantile awkwardness.

In 1796, after Robespierre's fall and during the rule of the Directoire, a secret society was founded in Paris. It planned a political coup and worked out a program for a future socialist organization of the nation. The society was headed by the Secret Directory of Public Salvation, which relied on a network of agents. Among its leading members were Philippe Buonarroti and François Émile (who later called himself Caius Gracchus) Babeuf. A military committee was created to prepare for the uprising. The conspirators hoped for the support of the army. According to their calculations, seventeen thousand men would come to their active aid. After an informer's tip, the leaders of the conspiracy were arrested; two of them, including Babeuf, were exiled.

When he returned from exile, Buonarroti continued to propagandize his views. The majority of the socialist revolutionaries of the day were under his influence. In particular, he founded a circle in Geneva which was to exert a great influence on Weitling (whose role in the formation of Marx's views is well known).

Numerous documents in which the society set forth its views were published by the government immediately after the conspiracy was uncovered. A detailed description of the conspiracy and its plans was later given by Buonarroti in his book *Conspiracy of Equals.*

The central principle of this society's program was the need for equality at any cost. This was reflected in the very title of the work. The principle of equality was laid down in their "Manifesto" with invulnerable Gallic logic:

"All men are equal, are they not? This principle is irrefutable, for only a man who has lost his reason can in full earnestness call night day." (55: II: p. 134)

Having established this unshakable foundation, the "Manifesto" proceeds to draw conclusions from this axiom:

"We truly want equality—or death. This is what we want." (55: II: p. 134) "For its sake, we are ready for anything; we are willing to sweep everything away. Let all the arts vanish, if necessary, as long as genuine equality remains for us." (55: II: p. 135) "Let there be an end, at last, to the outrageous differences between the rich and the poor, the high and the low, the lords and the servants, the governors and the governed." (55: II: p. 136)

This led directly to the communality of property:

"The agrarian law, that is, the division of arable land, was a temporary requirement of unprincipled soldiers, of certain tribes, who were prompted more by instinct than by reason. We aspire to something more lofty and just—the community of property." (55: II: p. 135)

The right of individual property was to be abolished. The country was to be turned into a single economic unit built exclusively on bureaucratic principles. Trade, except for the smallest transactions, was to be stopped and money withdrawn from circulation.

"It is necessary that everything produced on the land or in industry be kept in general storehouses for equitable distribution among citizens under the supervision of the appropriate officials." (55: II: p. 309)

Simultaneously, universal obligatory labor is introduced.

"Individuals who do nothing for the fatherland cannot enjoy political rights of any kind; they are as foreigners afforded the hospitality of the Republic." (55: II: p. 206)

"To do nothing for the fatherland means not to serve it by useful labor. . . . The law treats as useful labor the following endeavors: agriculture, stock raising, fishing, navigation, mechanical and artisan crafts, petty trade, transportation of men and goods, military arts, education and scientific activities. . . . Persons engaged in teaching or science must submit certificates of loyalty. Only in this case is their labor considered useful. . . . Officials supervise work and see to it that jobs are equitably distributed. . . . Foreigners are forbidden to take part in public gatherings. They are under the direct supervision of the supreme administration, which can deport them to a place of corrective labor." (55: II: pp. 296–297) Under pain of death they are forbidden to possess weapons.

The creators of this plan were aware that carrying it out would entail an unprecedented growth in the number of officials. They pose this question in broad terms:

"Indeed, never before has a nation possessed them in such great numbers. Apart from the fact that in certain circumstances every citizen would be an official supervising himself and others, it is beyond doubt that public offices would be very numerous and the number of officials very great." (55: I: p. 372)

Here is how the interrelationship of individuals with the bureaucracy is conceived:

"In the public structure devised by the Committee, the fatherland takes control of an individual from his birth till his death."

The authorities begin by educating the child:

"Protect him from dangerous false tenderness and by the hand of his mother lead him to a state institution where he will acquire the virtues and knowledge necessary for the true citizen." (55: I: p. 380)

Youths are transferred from state schools to military camps; only later, under the guidance of officials, do they undertake "useful labor."

"The municipal administration is to be kept constantly aware of the position of the working people of every class and of the assignments they are fulfilling. It is to inform the supreme administration in this regard." (55: II: p. 304) "The supreme administration will sentence to forced labor . . . persons of either sex who set society a bad example by absence of civic-mindedness, by idleness, a luxurious way of life, licentiousness." (55: II: p. 305)

This punishment is described lovingly and in great detail:

"The islands of Marguerite and Honoré, the Hyères, Oléron and Ré are to be turned into places of corrective labor, where foreigners who are suspicious and persons arrested for addressing proclamations to the French people will be sent. There will be no access to these islands. They will be administered by an organization directly subordinate to the government." (55: II: p. 299)

After these dark pictures, the section called "Freedom of the Press" is a positive joy.

"It will be necessary to devise means by which all the assistance that can be expected of the press can be extracted from it, without the risk of once again endangering the justice of equality and the rights of the people or of abandoning the Republic to interminable and fatal discussions." (55: I: p. 390)

The "means" turn out to very simple:

"No one will be allowed to utter views that are in direct contradiction to the sacred principles of equality and the sovereignty of the people. . . . The publication of any work having a psuedo-critical character is forbidden. . . . All works are to be printed and disseminated only if the guardians of the will of the nation consider that its publication may benefit the Republic." (55: I: p. 391)

One cannot but admire how the creators of this system managed to concern themselves with the slightest need of the citizen of the future Republic.

"In every commune, public meals will be taken, with compulsory attendance for all community members. . . . A member of the national community will be able to obtain his daily ration only in the district of his residence, except when he is traveling with the permission of the administration." (55: II: pp. 306–307)

"Entertainment that is not available to everyone is to be strictly forbidden." (55: I: p. 299) This is explained in another passage: ". . . for fear lest imagination, released from the supervision of a strict judge, should engender abominable vices so contrary to the commonweal." (55: I: p. 348)

The "Equals" inform us that they are friends of all nations. But *temporarily*, after their victory, France is to be stringently isolated.

"Until other nations would adhere to the political principles of France, no close contacts with them can be maintained. Until then, France will only see a menace for herself in their customs, institutions and, especially, their governments." (55: I: p. 357)

It appears that there was disagreement among Equals over one question. Buonarroti felt that a divine principle and immortality of the soul should be recognized, since for a society "it is essential that citizens recognize an infallible judge of their secret thoughts and acts, which cannot be persecuted by law, and that they should believe that a natural result of faithfulness to humanity and the fatherland will be eternal bliss." (55: I: p. 348) "All so-called revelation ought to be banished by law, together with maladies the germs of which ought to be gradually eradicated. Until that occurs, all were to be free to give vent to whims, so long as the social structure, universal brother-hood and the force of the law would not be disrupted." (55: I: pp. 348–349) Buonarroti believed that "the teaching of Jesus, if depicted as flowing out of the natural religion from which it does not differ, could become a support of a reform based on reason." (55: I: p. 168) But Babeuf held a more narrow view: "I attack relentlessly the main idol, until now venerated and feared by our philosophers, who dared to attack only his retinue and surroundings. . . . Christ was neither a *sans-culotte* nor an honest Jacobin nor a wise man nor a moralist nor a philosopher nor a legislator." (55: II: p. 398)

Academician V. P. Volgin, an eminent specialist on the literature of utopian socialism, notes the important innovation introduced by Babeuf and the Equals in comparison with other socialist thinkers. While predecessors like More, Campanella and Morelly focused on a picture of a fully formed socialist community, Babeuf pondered the problems of the transitional period as well, suggesting methods for establishing and strengthening the newly born socialist system. Indeed, the records of the Equals yield much that is fascinating and instructive in this connection.

It goes without saying that in an already established socialist society, legislative power is to be entirely in the hands of the people. In all districts, "assemblies of popular sovereignty" are created; each is made up of all the citizens of a given district. Delegates appointed directly by the people constitute the "Central Assembly of Legislators." (The procedure for "appointment" is not further specified.) The legislative power of these assemblies is restricted, however, by certain basic principles which "the people themselves are not empowered to violate or to alter." In addition to legislative assemblies, and parallel to them, senates consisting of old men are to be instituted. Supreme power was to be given over to a corporation of "Guardians of the National Will." This was conceived as a kind of "tribunal responsible for overseeing the legislators, so that those who abuse the right of issuing decrees would not encroach upon legislative power." (55: I: p. 359)

In the period immediately following the revolution, however, a different structure of government was envisaged. *"What kind of authority would this be?* Such was the delicate question that the Secret Directory has subjected to thorough scrutiny." (55: I: p. 216) The answer to this "delicate question" could be summed up as follows: power would be concentrated in the hands of the conspirators or partly shared with individuals appointed by them.

"It will be proposed to the people of Paris to institute a National Assembly vested with supreme power and consisting of democrats, one from every department; meanwhile the Secret Directory will investigate thoroughly as to which of the democrats ought to be put forward after the revolution is completed. The Directory will not cease to act but will carry on supervision of the new Assembly." (55: I: p. 293) After prolonged hesitation, the conspirators almost made up their minds to "ask the people for a decree which would entrust the legislative initiative and the implementation of laws" to them alone. (55: I: p. 290)

In the section entitled "In the Initial Stage of Reform the Agencies Must Be Entrusted Only to Revolutionaries," we read:

"A true Republic should be founded only by those selfless friends of humanity and the fatherland whose wisdom and courage exceed the wisdom and courage of their contemporaries." (55: I: p. 375)

Therefore, a committee composed of these "selfless friends of humanity" would see to it that "public institutions consisting solely of the best revolutionaries" should have only a very gradual change of personnel. (55: I: p. 375)

In more concrete terms, sixty-eight deputies chosen from among those serving in the Convention of the day were designated by the Committee to be left in place. To these were to be added another one hundred deputies "selected by us jointly with the people."

Beginning with the first day of the revolution, economic reforms were to be undertaken, as set forth in their "economic decree." How good to learn that implementation was to be on a purely voluntary basis. All those who would renounce their property voluntarily would make up a large national community. But everyone would retain the right not to join this community. Those who did not would acquire the status of "foreigners" with all the attendant rights and duties sketched in above. The economic position of "foreigners" is defined in the "Decree on Taxation," which contains, among other points, such things as:

"1. The sole taxpayers are the individuals who do not join the community. . . .

"4. The sum of tax payments in each current year is twice the amount of the preceding year. . . .

"6. Persons not party to the national community may be required, in case of necessity and against payment of future taxes, to supply produce and manufactured goods to the storehouses of the national community." (55: II: pp. 312–313)

The decree "On Debts," article three, states that debts owed by "any Frenchman who has become a member of the national community to any other Frenchman are annulled." (55: II: p. 313)

Other measures designed to strengthen the newly established regime and to promote its reforms were elaborated. For instance, "distribution of the possessions of emigrants, conspirators and enemies of the people to defenders of the fatherland and to the poor." (55: II: p. 253)

It is tempting to think that it was profound knowledge of life, based on personal tragic experience, that prompted the "selfless friends of humanity" to plan instituting the following highly important reforms, on the very first day of the revolution:

"Objects belonging to the people [!] and in hock will be immediately returned without charge. . . . On completion of the uprising, indigent citizens now residing in poor lodgings will not return to their habitual abodes; they will be immediately installed in the houses of the conspirators." (55: II: p. 281) (The reader should note that the participants in the "Conspiracy of Equals" used the term "conspirator" not to refer to themselves but rather to the government and to representatives of hostile classes.)

Unfortunately, the disciples of the Age of Reason did not leave a more detailed account of this operation. Had the economy of the time attained so high a level that the number of indigent citizens no longer surpassed that of the "conspirators"? Or, if the lodgings of the "conspirators" would not suffice to accommodate all the indigent, in what way would the lucky new owners of apartments be chosen? The documents of the "Conspiracy of Equals" are of little help on these points,* but we learn some other interesting details.

"The furniture of the above-mentioned rich will be confiscated as necessary for the adequate furnishing of the dwellings of the *sans-culottes.*" (55: II: p. 282)

Finally, terror was envisaged as one of the measures of strengthening the regime. The tribunals which had acted during the Jacobin terror until the ninth of Thermidor, 1794, were to be restored. And: "On pain of being held outside the law, return to prison all persons who were held there until the ninth of Thermidor of year II, if they have not complied with the call to limit themselves to the necessities for the benefit of the people." (55: I: p. 404) "Any resistance must be immediately suppressed by force; the persons involved are to be exterminated. Also liable to capital punishment are persons sounding an alarm themselves or causing others to do so; and foreigners, no matter what their nationality, who are apprehended on the street." (55: II: p. 232) Members of the existing government—members of the two Councils and of the Executive Directorate—were to be executed. "The crime was evident and the punishment had to be death—a great example was essential." (55: I: p. 283)

"In the Insurgent Committee, views were current to the effect that the condemned were to be buried under the rubble of their palaces, whose ruins would serve to remind future generations of the just punishment meted out on the enemies of the people." (55: I: p. 284)

In elaborating their system of reforms and practical measures, the

---

* Although there is the following remark: "It would be an error to confuse the systematic distribution of lodgings and clothes with pillage." (55: I: p. 282)

activists of the "Conspiracy of Equals" did not close their eyes to objections which they might encounter: "Disorganizers, rebels, they say to us, all you want is massacre and plunder." Such charges are swept aside, however: "Never has so broad a plan been conceived and brought into existence." (55: II: p. 136) "Let them show us," they would exclaim, "another political system with which such great results could be obtained with more easily implemented means." (55: I: p. 339)

We note with sorrow how such a perfectly conceived system was constantly hampered in practice by a host of petty and squalid difficulties. First of all, the conspirators did not avoid what Rabelais called "the incomparable grief," that is, lack of money. In the section entitled "The Participants in the Conspiracy Despised Money," Buonarotti says:

"Certain steps were undertaken to obtain means, but the greatest sum that the Secret Directory ever had at its disposal was 240 francs in cash, contributed by the ambassador of an allied [?] republic." (55: I: 251)

We cannot help but sympathize when Buonarotti laments: "How difficult it is to do good armed only with means acknowledged by reason." (55: I: p. 251)

And a second misfortune befell our heroes—internal discord over dividing power not yet seized. The Committee was at first joined by a small group that called itself the Montagnards. But soon, "the Committee was informed that they had secretly undertaken maneuvers to get around the conditions which had been agreed upon so as to guarantee that supreme power in the Republic would be in the Montagnards' hands. The Committee was so thoroughly convinced they could do no good that it considered the slightest movement which gave them any power to be an unforgivable crime." (55: I: p. 286)

And finally, a third misfortune: The Committee turned out to be under the influence of an *agent provocateur*. Grisel, a member of the military committee, "hurried his trusting colleagues along, overcame obstacles, suggested new measures and never forgot to encourage those around him with exaggerated pictures of the loyalty of the Grenelle democratic camp." (55: I: p. 265) And it was this Grisel who was denouncing the Committee to the authorities!

The Insurgent Committee was already working out the details of the uprising. One of its members was writing a proclamation called: *"The Insurgent Committee of Public Salvation . . .* The people have triumphed, tyranny is no more. . . ." (55: I: p. 400)

"At this point, the writer was interrupted and seized," says Buonarotti, who seems not to have lost his French wit. The army and the people had not supported the conspirators: "The standing army, with weapons in hand, helped the campaign against democracy, while the population of Paris, persuaded that those arrested were thieves, remained a passive witness." (55: I: p. 417)

The circumstances of this astonishing episode prompted us to resort to a form of presentation that perhaps seems out of place in our narrative. But this dissonance reflects a curious objective property of the phenomenon under study. At the moment of their inception, socialist movements often strike one by their helplessness, their isolation from reality, their naïvely adventuristic character and their comic, "Gogolian" features (as Berdyaev put it). One gets the impression that these hopeless failures haven't a chance of success, and that in fact they do everything in their power to compromise the ideas they are proclaiming. However, they are merely biding their time. At some point, almost unexpectedly, these ideas find a broad popular reception, and become the forces that determine the course of history, while the leaders of these movements come to rule the destiny of nations. (In this way a frightened Müntzer climbed over the Allstedt city wall, having deceived his supporters, only to become, soon thereafter, one of the leading figures in the Peasant War which shook Germany.) It would seem that there was no contradiction when Dostoyevsky peopled his novel *The Possessed* with "three and a half" nihilists incapable of making a serious disturbance in a provincial town, while at the same time predicting an imminent revolution that would carry away one hundred million lives.

## Summary

We shall attempt to sum up those new features of socialist ideology that we have encountered in utopian socialism and in works of the Enlightenment.

1. If in the Middle Ages and during the Reformation socialist ideas developed within movements that were religious, at least formally, utopian socialism tends to break with religious form and gradually acquire a character hostile to religion. In More and Campanella we were able to point out an alienated and at times ironic attitude toward Christianity. Winstanley is openly hostile to contemporary religions.

Deschamps rejects all religion, declaring the idea of God to be a human invention, the result of mankind's oppressed state and an instrument of oppression. In its stead, he puts forward the enigmatic conception of God who is Nothing. Finally, Meslier bases his world outlook on a hatred of religion and Christianity—and of Christ in particular. Thus one can speak of a gradual merging of socialist ideology and atheism.

2. The Socialism of this epoch borrows the idea derived from medieval mysticism (Joachim of Flore's, for instance) that history is an immanent and orderly evolutionary process. However, the goal and the driving force invested in this process by the mystics—knowledge of God and merging with Him—is eliminated. Instead, *progress* is recognized as the motivating force of history, and human reason is seen as its supreme product.

3. Socialist doctrines preserve the notion of the medieval mystics about the *three stages* in the historical process, as well as the scheme of the *fall* of mankind and its return to the original state in a more perfect form. The socialist doctrines contain the following components:

a. The *myth* of a primordial "natural state" or "golden age," which was destroyed by that bearer of evil called private property.

b. A *castigation* of the way things are. Contemporary society is pronounced incurably depraved, unjust and meaningless, ready only to be scrapped. Only on its ruins can a new social structure be built, a structure that would guarantee people every happiness of which they are capable.

c. The *prophecy* of a new society built on socialist principles, a society in which all present shortcomings would disappear. This is the only path for mankind to return to the "natural state," as Morelly put it: from the unconscious Golden Age to the conscious one.

4. The idea of "liberation," which was understood by the medieval heresies to be liberation of the spirit from the power of matter, is transformed into an appeal for liberation from the morality of contemporary society, from its social institutions and, most of all, from private property.

At first, reason is recognized to be the driving force of this liberation, but gradually its place is taken over by the people, the poor. In the world view of the participants in the "Conspiracy of Equals," we can see this conception in finished form. As a result, new concrete features appear in the plan for the establishment of the "society of the future": terror, occupation of the apartments of the rich by the poor, confiscation of furniture, abolition of debts, etc.

# PART TWO

# STATE SOCIALISM

# IV   South America

## 1. The Inca Empire

In the first part of this study, we have seen how the stable set of social ideas that we have called chiliastic socialism was expressed in various periods of human history, over the course of at least two and a half millennia. We shall now try to trace the attempts to implement these ideas in particular social structures. Our primary goal is to show that here, just as in the case of chiliastic socialism, we are dealing with a universal phenomenon, one by no means limited to our century. We shall review several examples of states whose life was built, in great part, on socialist principles.

We encounter here a far more difficult task than the one that occupied us in Part I of this study. After all, an author of a work in which socialist principles are propounded must proceed from the notion that these ideas are novel and unusual to his reader. He is therefore compelled to explain them. But in the scant economic and political documentation that has been preserved from remote epochs (and sometimes cultures without written languages are involved), the meanings of the terms used are not elucidated for the reader of the future. Such documents were intended for people to whom the terminology would have been understandable. To reconstruct from scattered hints the way of life, to comprehend the legal and economic relations of the members of a society far removed in time, is therefore a task of extreme difficulty, much more difficult than to reconstruct the appearance and behavior of a prehistoric creature from the fossil remains. In most cases, we see the historians offering a series of opinions rather than any definitive formulation.

If the present epoch is excluded, it was only once that Europeans were able to observe at first hand a state of this type. Many intelligent and observant travelers left accounts of this state, and certain of its natives acquired European culture and left narratives about the way of life of their fathers. This phenomenon, which is far more important for the historian of socialism than descriptions of the appearance and behavior of a dinosaur would be for a paleontologist, is Tawantinsuyu—the Inca empire conquered by Spanish invaders in the sixteenth century.

The Spaniards discovered the Inca state in 1531. At that time, it had existed for some two hundred years and had achieved its peak, encompassing the territory of contemporary Ecuador, Bolivia, Peru, the northern half of Chile and the northwestern part of Argentina. According to several sources, its population was twelve million.

The empire, as the Spaniards found it, was as well organized as it was huge. According to their accounts, the capital, Cuzco, rivaled the biggest European cities of that time. It had a population of about 200,000. The Spaniards were struck by the magnificent palaces and temples, with façades as much as two hundred meters long, the aqueducts and the paved streets. The houses were built of large stones so finely polished and fitted together that they seemed to be of one piece. Outside Cuzco, there was a fortress that was built of stones weighing twelve tons each; it so amazed the Spaniards that they refused to believe it could have been made by men, without the help of demons. (56: p. 114, 57: pp. 72–82)

The capital city was joined to the outlying parts of the empire by excellent roadways, in no way inferior to Roman roads and far better than the ones in Spain at the time. The roads ran along dikes in swampy terrain, cut through rock and crossed gorges by means of suspension bridges. (56: pp. 106, 113, 57: pp. 93–96) An efficiently organized service of foot messengers guaranteed communications between the capital and the rest of the country. Around the capital and other towns, as well as along the roads, there were state storehouses full of produce, clothing, utensils and military equipment. (56: pp. 61–67, 57: pp. 100–101, 58: pp. 61–67)

In stark contrast to the superb organization of the Inca state, its level of technical knowledge was astonishingly primitive. Most tools and weapons were made of wood and stone. Iron was unknown, as was the plow, and land was tilled with a wooden hoe. The only domestic animal was the llama, from which meat and wool were obtained but which was not used for farming or transportation. All farm work was performed manually, and travel was either by foot or by palanquin. Finally, the Incas had no writing system, although they could transmit great amounts of information by means of quipu, a complex system of knotted strings.*

Hence the low level of technology had to be compensated for by perfect organization of huge masses of the population. As a natural result, private interests were to a considerable extent subordinated to those of the state. And so, as we might expect, we encounter certain socialist features in Inca society.

What follows is a brief sketch of its structure. Fortunately, much information is available. The conquistadors proved to be more than mindless military men; they grasped much of what they saw and some of their accounts have survived. In their wake came Catholic priests, who also left detailed descriptions. Finally, the conquistadors married girls from the Inca ruling circles, and the children of these unions, who belonged to the Spanish aristocracy, at the same time retained close ties with the local population. To them belong the most valuable descriptions of life in the Inca state prior to the Spanish conquest.

The population of the Inca state was divided into three strata:

1. Incas—the ruling class, descendants of a tribe that in the past had conquered an ancient state near Lake Titicaca. Various authors refer to them as aristocracy, the elite, the bureaucracy. From this class came the administrators, the army officer corps, priests and scholars— and of course, the absolute ruler of the country, the Inca. This class was hereditary, but chiefs of conquered tribes and even soldiers distinguished in war might occasionally enter it.

2. The bulk of the population—peasants, herdsmen, artisans. They had two types of obligation to the state: military and labor. Both of these will be described below. Sometimes they were utilized in other ways by the state, for instance to settle a newly conquered territory, or to provide material (women) for human sacrifices.

3. The state slaves—yanacuna. According to legend, they descended from a tribe that had once rebelled against the state, had

* Cf. 58: p. 358. According to legend, writing had been prohibited by the founder of the Inca empire.

been crushed, and had been sentenced to extermination. But in response to a plea by his wife, the Inca changed the sentence to perpetual slavery. Thereafter the members of this group occupied the lowest position in the country. They worked the state lands, herded the llamas belonging to the state and served as servants in the houses of the Incas. (57: pp. 124–125)

The basic form of property in the Inca empire was land. Theoretically, all land belonged to the Inca and was distributed by him to the Incas and peasants for their use. The lands received by the Incas were hereditary, but they were apparently managed by administrators, while the Incas themselves merely made use of the produce. These lands were worked by peasants in a manner described below. Peasants also received land for use from the state. The basic unit was the *tupu*— a plot large enough to sustain one person. Every Indian received one tupu at marriage, another for each son and half a tupu for each daughter. After the death of a tenant, the land reverted to the state. (56: pp. 68–69, 57: pp. 126–127, 58: p. 274) Land not divided into tupu was treated as belonging to the Sun God and served to support the temples and the priests. The remaining land belonged to the Inca class or directly to the state. All these lands were worked by peasants according to a detailed schedule. Control over all farm work was exercised by clerks. For example, they gave the daily signal for the peasants to begin work by sounding a conch from a specially constructed tower. (56: pp. 70–71, 58: p. 247)

The peasants were liable to military service and to obligatory labor—tilling the land of the temples and the Incas, building new temples and palaces for the Inca or the Incas, mending roads, building bridges, working in the gold and silver mines owned by the state, and so on. Some of these duties required moving the peasants to distant areas of the empire, in which case the state undertook to feed them. (56: p. 88–89)

The raw materials for crafts were provided by the state; finished products were delivered to it. For example, llamas were shorn by state slaves, the wool distributed by officials to peasants for spinning and the finished material subsequently collected by other officials.

The law divided the life of a male peasant into ten periods and prescribed the obligations of each age group. Thus, from age nine to sixteen, the peasant was to be a herdsman, from sixteen to twenty, a messenger or a servant in the house of an Inca, etc. Even duties of the last age group (over sixty) were specified: spinning rope, feeding ducks, and so on. Cripples formed a special group, but they too, as Guamán Poma de Ayala reports, were designated for certain work. Similar prescriptions existed for women. The law required constant activity from the peasants. A woman on her way to another house was to take wool with her and to spin on the way. (56: p. 80, 57: pp. 129–131) According to the chronicle of Cieza de León, peasants were sometimes made to perform completely useless work simply so as not to be idle—for example, they were forced to move a hill of dirt from one place to another. (56: p. 81, 57: p. 132) Garcilaso de la Vega informs us that work was found for cripples. (58: p. 300) He also cites a law against idlers—a man who tilled his field badly was hit several times with a stone in the shoulders or flogged with a rod. (56: p. 276) The completely incapacitated and the aged were maintained by the state or the rural community.

For work, the peasants were joined into groups of ten families, five such groups into a larger group, etc., up to ten thousand families. There was an official head for each group. The lower members of this hierarchy were appointed from the peasantry; higher posts were occupied by Incas. (57: pp. 96–97, 59: p. 77)

Not only work but the whole life of the citizenry was controlled by officials. Special inspectors continuously traveled about the country observing the inhabitants. To facilitate supervision, peasants, for instance, were obliged to keep their doors open during meals (the law prescribed the time of meals and restricted the menu). (56: p. 96, 57: p. 132) Other aspects of life were also strictly regimented. Officials issued every Indian two cloaks from the state stores—one for work and the other for festivals. Within each individual province, the cloaks were indistinguishable in style and color and differed only according to the sex of their bearers. The cloak was to be used until it was worn out. Changes in cut and color were forbidden. There were laws against other extravagances: it was forbidden to have chairs in the house (only benches were allowed), to build houses of a larger size than authorized, etc. Each province had a special obligatory hair style. (55: p. 91, 57: p. 132) Such prescriptions extended to other classes, for instance, the quantity and size of gold and silver vessels that an official of lower rank could possess were strictly limited according to his station. (56: pp. 91–92)

The inhabitants of newly conquered areas were under especially severe control. Residents from central provinces were dispatched to new regions, where they were entitled to enter the houses of the subjugated people at any time of day or night and were obliged to report on any sign of discontent.

Peasants were not allowed to leave their villages without special permission. Control was made easier by the differences in the color of clothing and the varied hair styles. Special officials supervised traffic on bridges and at gates. The state itself, however, carried on compulsory resettlement on a large scale. Resettlement sometimes was occasioned by economic factors—people were moved to a province devastated by an epidemic or transferred to a more fertile area. Occasionally, the reason was political, as with the resettlement of inhabitants from the original provinces of the empire to newly conquered lands or, on the contrary, the dispersion of a newly conquered tribe throughout the more loyal population of the empire. (56: pp. 99–100, 59: p. 58)

Family life was also under the control of the state. All men were obliged to enter into marriage upon reaching a certain age. Once each year, every village was visited by a special official who conducted a public marriage ceremony, in which everyone who had come of age the previous year took part. Spaniards who described the customs of the Inca state often asserted that the preference of the person being married was not asked for. And Santillán, writing at the end of the sixteenth century, reports that objections were punishable by death. On the other hand, Father Morúa reports that a man could indicate that he had already promised to marry another girl, and the official would then review the matter. It is clear, however, that the opinion of the bride was never solicited. (57: pp. 158, 160)

Members of the top social group—the Incas—had the right to several wives, or more precisely, concubines, since the first wife had a special position while the others were relegated to the role of servants. Marriage with the first wife was indissoluble; concubines could be driven out and would thereafter not be allowed to marry again. (57: p. 156) The number of concubines permitted by law depended on the social status of the man; it could be twenty, thirty, fifty, etc. (57: p. 134) For the Inca and his immediate family, there was no limitation whatever. The multitude of wives and the consequently large number of offspring resulted in an ever increasing proportion of Incas in the general population.

There was a special category of women—the so-called elect. Each year, officials were sent to all sections of the country to select girls eight or nine years old. These were called the "elect." They were brought up in special houses (called "convents" in some Spanish accounts). Every year during a special celebration, those who had reached thirteen years of age were sent to the capital, where the Inca himself divided them into three categories. Some, called Solar Maidens, were returned to the "convent," where they were to engage in activities associated with the worship of the gods of sun, moon and stars. They had to observe chastity, although the Inca could give them to his circle as concubines or take them for himself. Girls from the second group were distributed by the Inca as wives or concubines. A gift of this kind from the Inca was regarded as a high distinction. Finally, a third group was intended for the human sacrifices that took place regularly, but on a particularly large scale at the coronation of a new Inca. The law provided for the punishment of parents who showed their grief when their daughters were chosen for the "elect." (57: pp. 161–162)

Apart from the "elect," all unmarried women were also at the disposal of the Incas, but not as private property; rather, they were allotted to them by government officials for use as concubines and servants. The oppressed status of women in the Inca state is particularly notable against the background of the neighboring Indian tribes, where women enjoyed much independence and authority. (57: p. 159)

It is clear that such total regulation of life and the omnipresent state control would have been impossible without a multifaceted bureaucratic apparatus. The bureaucracy was built on a purely hierarchical principle. Every official had contact only with his superior and his subordinates; officials of the same rank could communicate only through their common chief. (56: p. 96) The main function of this bureaucracy was the keeping of accounts by means of the sophisticated and as yet undeciphered system of knotted strings.

The idea of the quipu was a curiously accurate reflection of the hierarchical structure of the state machinery. A hierarchy was introduced into the material area as well; for instance, all types of arms were arranged by "seniority." The lance was considered to be senior to other weapons; next came the arrow, then the bow, and so on. According to the seniority of these objects, they were denoted by knots tied higher or lower on a string. Learning the art of quipu began with learning the principles of "seniority" by rote.

Information encoded in this way was passed up the bureaucratic ladder to the capital, where it was examined and preserved by types: military, population, provisions, etc. In the Spanish chronicles it is asserted that even the number of stones for slings, the number of animals killed in hunting and other such data were kept. Guamán Poma de Ayala writes: "They keep an account of everything that occurs in their state, and in every village there are secretaries and treasurers for that. . . . The state is governed with the help of quipu." (56: pp. 94–95)

There are accounts of truly remarkable administrative achievements, such as the creation of armies of workers numbering 20,000 men or an operation in which 100,000 bushels of maize are distributed among a population of a large region according to strictly fixed norms. (56: p. 102)

The workers in the bureaucracy were trained in schools that only children of the Incas were permitted to attend. (The law forbade education for the lower levels of the population.) Teaching was performed by the *amautas* or "scholars." Their duties included the writing of history in two versions: one, objective records in the form of quipu, which were preserved in the capital and intended only for special authorized officials, and the other in the form of hymns to be narrated to the people at festivals. If a dignitary was deemed unworthy, his name was removed from the "festival" history. (56: pp. 75–76, 78)

The laws regulating life in the Inca state relied on a sophisticated system of punishment. Penalties were severe—almost always death or torture. This is to be expected: when all life is regulated by the state, any infringement of the law is a crime against the state and, in turn, affects the very foundation of the social system. Thus a man guilty of cutting down a tree or stealing fruit in a state plantation was subject to the death penalty. Abortion was punished by death for the woman and for anyone who may have assisted her. (59: p. 173)

The system provided for an extraordinary variety of capital punishments: the victim could be hanged by the feet or stoned or thrown into a gorge or hanged by the hair over a cliff or thrown into a pit with jaguars and poisonous snakes. (57: p. 42) For the most serious offenses, there were provisions for the execution of all relatives of the accused. Guamán Poma de Ayala's manuscript contains a drawing of the slaughter of a whole family whose chief member had been determined to be a sorcerer. Burying the bodies of executed criminals could be prohibited as a further punishment. Burial of the bodies of mutineers was forbidden, for example. Their flesh was thrown to wild beasts, and drums were made of their skin, bowls of the skulls and flutes of the arm and leg bones. Finally, a victim could be put to torture before execution. "He who kills another to rob him will be punished by death. Before the execution he will be tortured in jail so that the penalty should be harder. Then he will be executed." (57: p. 143)

Many forms of punishment differed little from execution. For instance, Cieza de León, Cobo, Morúa and Guamán Poma de Ayala describe jails in underground caves in which jaguars, bears, venomous snakes and scorpions were kept. Incarceration in this type of prison was used as a test of guilt. Generally, this form of trial was used in the case of people suspected of plotting rebellion. Persons sentenced to life imprisonment were kept in other underground jails. (57: p. 142) A penalty of five hundred lashes (provided by law as a punishment for theft) probably was the equivalent of a death sentence. There was a punishment called the "stone execution," where a huge stone was tossed onto the victim's shoulders. According to Guamán Poma de Ayala, this killed many and crippled others for life.

Other punishments consisted of forced labor in state gold and silver mines or on coca plantations in difficult tropical climates. Forced labor could be either for life or for a fixed term. Finally, minor offenders were subject to various corporal punishments. (57: p. 144)

It goes without saying that equality before the law did not exist. For one and the same crime a peasant might be executed, while an Inca would get off with a public reprimand. As Cobo reports: "The premise here was that for an Inca of royal blood (all Incas were theoretically related), a public reprimand was a heavier penalty than death for a pleebeian." (56: p. 79, 57: p. 143)

Seduction of another's wife was accorded corporal punishment. But if a peasant seduced an Inca woman, both were executed; as Guamán Poma de Ayala recounts, both were hanged naked by the hair over a cliff until they died. (57: p. 146)

A crime against property was also punished differently depending on whether the interests of the state or a private party were involved. Someone guilty of picking fruit on a private estate could avoid punishment, if he could prove that he had done so out of hunger. But if the owner was an Inca, the guilty party was subject to death. (57: p. 145)

The complete subjugation of life to the prescriptions of the law and to officialdom led to extraordinary standardization: identical clothing, identical houses, identical roads. Repetition of the same descriptive details is characteristic of the old Spanish accounts. The capital city, built of identical houses made of identical block stone and divided into identical blocks, undoubtedly created the impression of a prison town. (56: p. 117)

As a result of this spirit of standardization, anything the least bit different was looked upon as dangerous and hostile, whether it was the birth of twins or the discovery of a strangely shaped rock. Such things were believed to be a manifestation of evil forces hostile to society. Events were to show that the fear of unplanned phenomena was quite justified: the huge empire proved powerless against less than two hundred Spaniards. Neither their firearms nor their horses (animals unknown to the Indians) can explain this extraordinary turn of events. The same difference in armaments was after all involved in the subjugation of the Zulus, but they were able to mount a long and successful resistance to large detachments of English forces. The reason for the collapse of the Inca empire must apparently be sought elsewhere— in the complete atrophy of individual initiative, in the ingrained habit of acting only at the direction of officials, in the spirit of stagnation and apathy.

Ondegardo, a Spanish judge who served in Peru in the sixteenth century, noted a similar phenomenon. In his books, he constantly laments the complete regimentation of life and the removal of all personal stimuli which led to a weakening of and, sometimes, the complete destruction of family relationships. Grown children, for instance, often refused to take care of their parents. (56: p. 127) Baudin, a French student of Latin American history, sees in many traits of the contemporary Indians the aftermath of Inca rule—indifference to the fate of the state, lack of initiative, apathy. (56: pp. 124–125)

To what extent is it possible to call the Inca state socialist? Without any doubt, it is much more entitled to this designation than any of the contemporary states that regard themselves as belonging to this category. Socialist principles were clearly expressed in the structure of the Inca state: the almost complete absence of private property, in particular of private land; absence of money and trade; the complete elimination of private initiative from all economic activities; detailed regulation of private life; marriage by official decree; state distribution of wives and concubines. On the other hand, we do not encounter either communal wives or communal upbringing of children. A wife, though given by the state to the peasant, was his alone, and children grew up in the family (if the special class of girls chosen to be "elect" is excluded). Nevertheless, the Inca state seems to have been one of the fullest incarnations of socialist ideals in human history.

This is indicated by the striking similarity between the Inca way of life and numerous socialist utopias, sometimes down to the smallest detail. In his work *The Incas of Peru*, Baudin tells that during a report on the Inca state at the Paris Academy of Sciences, a member asked whether it would not be possible to show an influence of the Incas on Thomas More's *Utopia*. (56: p. 165) This would have been quite impossible, of course: More's *Utopia* was written in 1516, while Peru was discovered by the Spaniards in 1531. The similarities are, therefore, all the more striking and show how socialist principles inevitably led to the same conclusions in the centuries-long practice of the Inca administrators and in the mind of the English philosopher.

But later socialist writers undoubtedly were under the strong influence of what they had heard of the "Peruvian Empire." In one of his works, Morelly describes a society that lives in "natural conditions" and without distinction between "thine" and "mine," and says that the "Peruvians" had laws of this kind. We have already quoted (in Part I) a similar passage from the article "The Legislator" in the *Encyclopédie,* and we invite the reader to compare Diderot's description (pp. 112–114 above) with the historical facts. It is quite possible that the Inca model provided numerous details in the depiction of the future society by the writers of the seventeenth and eighteenth centuries. It is easy enough to imagine how readily they absorbed the stories then current in Europe of a real society so close in spirit to their ideals. This leads to a general problem of great interest—that of the influence exerted on the socialist literature, beginning with Plato, by the "socialist experiment," that is, by the practical implementation of socialist ideals in Egypt, Mesopotamia and Peru.

## 2. The Jesuit State in Paraguay

Although one would have thought that the Spanish conquistadors had written an end to socialism in South America, it had a continuation nevertheless. Some one hundred to one hundred fifty years later, in an area not far from the former Inca state, a political system in the

Inca tradition was established in Paraguay by the Jesuits.

The history of Spanish penetration into Paraguay begins in 1516, when Don Juan Díaz de Solís discovered the mouth of the Paraná river and conquered the surrounding territories. In 1537, Juan de Salazar de Espinoza founded Asunción, the capital of the new province of Paraguay.

The native inhabitants of Paraguay were Indians of the Guaraní tribe. Missionary work among them was first undertaken by the Dominican monk Las Casas. The Jesuits took part in this effort later. With the realistic approach so typical of their order, they decided to make acceptance of Christianity practically advantageous and so attempted to protect their converts from the Indians' main enemy, the slave traders called paulistas (from the state of São Paulo, the center of the slave trade at the time). Suppression of the slave trade had been beyond the Spanish crown's capabilities for years. Yet the Jesuits succeeded in providing security against raids for Indians in large areas of Paraguay. To achieve this, they accustomed the Indians to a sedentary life, placing them in large settlements called reductions. The first reduction was set up in 1609. It seems that a plan existed at first for the creation of a great state with access to the Atlantic Ocean, but paulista raids made this impossible. Beginning in 1640, the Jesuits armed the Indians and fought through to an area where they settled their flock. It was almost inaccessible, bordered on one side by the Andes and on the other by the rapids of the rivers Paraná, La Plata and Uruguay. The entire territory was covered with a network of reductions. As early as 1654, the Jesuits Macheta and Cataladino obtained from the Spanish crown an exemption of the realm of the Society of Jesus from subordination to the Spanish colonial forces and from paying tithes to the local bishop. The authorization to arm the Indians was a further exception to the absolute ban introduced by the Spanish government in all parts of South America. The Jesuits soon had a strong fighting force at their disposal.

In their dealings with the Spanish government, the Jesuits steadfastly denied that they had created an independent state in Paraguay. It is true that certain accusations were exaggerated, as for example the book about the "Emperor of Paraguay," which included his portrait, as well as coins allegedly minted at court, both being nothing but a contrivance of the Jesuits' enemies. But it is also a fact that the area controlled by the Jesuits was so isolated from the external world that it could in fact be considered an independent state or a dominion of Spain. Jesuits were the only Europeans in the region. They prevailed on the government to pass a law that allowed no European to enter the territory of the reductions without the Jesuits' permission. In any case, no visitor was allowed to stay longer than three days. The Indians were not able to leave their reductions except in the company of the Fathers. In spite of numerous government demands, the Jesuits refused to teach the Indians the Spanish language; they devised a writing system for the local Guaraní language. The Jesuits who lived in the area were not Spaniards for the most part, but included Germans, Italians and Scots. The territory had an army of its own and engaged in independent foreign trade. All this does tend to justify the term "Jesuit state," which is used by most scholars who have written on the subject.

The population of the Jesuit state at the height of its development was 150,000 to 200,000 inhabitants. Most of these were Indians; in addition, there were some twelve thousand black slaves and between one hundred fifty and three hundred Jesuits. The state came to an end in 1767–1768, when the Jesuits were driven out of Paraguay as part of the general campaign of the Spanish government against the movement. In 1773, the Society of Jesus was abolished altogether by Pope Clement XIV.

The main organizational principles of the reductions were worked out by Father Diego de Torres. It is significant that he began his missionary work in Peru, where the Inca state had not yet been entirely forgotten. The Spanish authorities were exploiting the rich silver mines in the area, and they were concerned about keeping the Indians in one place. To this end, it was proposed that the social structure of the Inca period be maintained in its essentials. As he called for the setting up of reductions in Paraguay, Diego de Torres wrote that "the locality must be governed by the same system as in Peru." (61: p. 117) Many observers have come to the conclusion that the Jesuits consciously copied the structure of the Inca empire.

As already mentioned, the entire population of Jesuit Paraguay was concentrated in the reductions. These usually numbered some two thousand to three thousand Indians, with the smallest ones containing about five hundred inhabitants and the biggest mission (St. Javier) numbering thirty thousand. Each reduction was run by two Jesuit Fathers, one being as a rule much older than the other. There were generally no other Europeans in the settlement. The senior Father, or "confessor," devoted himself primarily to religious functions, while the younger acted as his assistant and directed economic matters. Together the two possessed absolute power in the reduction. As the Jesuit Juan de Escadón states, in a letter written in 1760: "Secular power belongs totally to the Fathers, as much as or even more than spiritual power." (61: p. 146)

The priests normally appeared before the Indians only at divine services. At other times, they communicated with them through intermediaries drawn from the local population. These local officials, called corregidors and alcaldes, were selected annually from a list compiled by the Fathers. Election was by a show of hands. The corregidors and alcaldes were completely subordinate to the Fathers, who could abolish or change any of the formers' orders. De Escadón writes that the corregidors and alcaldes reported to one of the Fathers every morning to get their decisions approved and to receive instructions as to the work order of the day. "This was accomplished as in a good family, where the father tells everyone what he must do for the day." (61: p. 148) "The limited intelligence of the Indians compelled the missionaries to take care of all affairs and to guide them in secular as well as in spiritual matters," as the Jesuit Charlevoix (in *History of Paraguay*) quotes his contemporary Antonio de Ulloa.

There were no laws—only the decisions made by the Fathers. They heard confession, which was obligatory for the Indians, and assigned penalties for all offenses. Penalties included: face-to-face reprimand, public reprimand, flogging, imprisonment, and banishment from the reduction. Many authors assert that there was no capital punishment, although Charlevoix writes about a certain unsubmissive local official who was burned up in a fire sent by God. (62: p. 13) An offender was first made to repent in church, was dressed as a heretic, and was then subjected to the punishment. De Ulloa writes: "They had such great confidence in their pastors that they regarded even an unprovoked penalty as deserved." (60: p. 140, 62: p. 31)

The entire life of the reduction was based on the principle that the Indians were to possess practically nothing of their own—neither land nor houses nor raw materials nor handicraft tools. The Indians did not even belong to themselves. Thus, de Escadón writes: "These plots, as with the other lands of the mission, belong to the community and no inhabitant has more than the right to use them. Therefore, they never sell anything to one another. The same is true of the houses in which they live. . . . The community takes care of all the houses, makes repairs and builds new ones as needed." (61: p. 148)

The reduction was divided into two parts: tupambé (God's land) and abambé (private land). The difference was not in the form of tenure, since both types belonged to the mission, but simply that tupambé was tilled collectively, while abambé was divided into plots and distributed among individual families.

Muratori writes that abambé was *lent* to the Indians for working. (60: p. 145) A plot of land was granted to an Indian when he married. It was not hereditary, and if the man died, his widow and children did not retain the plot. The land reverted to a common fund and the dependents became wards of the mission. Charlevoix says that work on individual plots was regulated by the administration in the same way as on common land. (60: p. 145) In the monthly *Catholic Missions*, it was reported that seeds and tools for working the individual plots were lent by the community. In the majority of missions, families lived on crops harvested from their individual plots. However, in certain reductions they were required to deliver a part of their harvest to the mission, with rations later dispensed in return. In any case, work on the individual plots and the crops produced on them were under strict control everywhere. Charlevoix writes: "It was known how much a plot of land yielded and the crops from it were under the supervision of those who were particularly concerned with looking after it. And if there had been no strict hand over the Indians, they would soon have found themselves with no means of subsistence." (62: p. 37)

Work on the communal land was obligatory for all Indians, including administrators and artisans. Before work, one of the Fathers delivered a sermon. The Indians then set out for the fields in columns, to the sound of drum and flute. They returned from work singing uplifting songs. Work was supervised at all times by inspectors and spies who apprehended idlers. "Culprits were severely punished," writes Muratori. (60: p. 159)

All crops essential to the mission's economy were grown on communal land. Eyewitnesses are unanimous in pointing out differences in the cultivation of individual and communal lands: while communal lands were carefully tilled, the individual plots looked neglected. The Jesuits constantly complained of the indifference of the Indians to working their own fields; they preferred to be punished for a badly cultivated plot and to live on the communal stores. The Indians were capable of eating the seed grain distributed to them and coming back for more—and a sound flogging—several times over. The Jesuits saw the reason for this not in the peculiarities of the social system they had established but in the "childish" nature of the Indians. Father J. Cardiel wrote in 1758: "For 140 years we have been fighting this, but there has hardly been any improvement. And so long as they have but a child's intelligence, things will not get better."

The communities possessed huge herds of horses and oxen that were pastured in the pampas. Communal oxen were given to the Indians to work their plots. "Sometimes the Indian kills one or both oxen to eat meat at his pleasure. He later reports that they have become lost and pays for the loss with his back." (Escadón, 61: p. 149)

The meat of communal oxen was distributed among the residents two or three times a week. On the appointed day, the inhabitants came to the storehouse, where the storekeeper called everyone's name and dispensed a standard portion of meat. Indians also received a ration of local tea.

Various crafts were encouraged in the reductions, and a high level of workmanship was achieved. Wool was dispensed to the women to be spun at home, the finished cloth being collected on the following day. All tools and raw materials belonged to the reduction and not to the individual craftsman. Moreover, a large part of the craftsmen worked in communal workshops. José Cardiel writes: "All craft work is done not in the home, since that would be very ineffective; it is performed in the courtyards of the collegium." (61: p. 164) The missions had stonemasons, brickmakers, arms makers, millers, clockmakers, artists, jewelers and potters. Construction included brick factories, kilns for producing quicklime, mills powered by horses and by men. Organs were made, bells cast, books printed in foreign languages (for export). By the beginning of the eighteenth century, every reduction had a sundial or a mechanical clock of local manufacture, according to which the workday was regulated.

All products were delivered to the storehouses, where Indians who could write and keep accounts were employed. Part of the production was distributed to the population. Fabrics were divided into equal pieces and distributed by name, one day to girls, the next to boys, then to men and finally to women. Each man was given 5.5 meters of canvas for clothing a year and each woman, 4.5 meters. Each received a knife and an ax once a year.

The major portion of the articles produced in the reduction was for export. Given the large herds, vast amounts of tanned skins were produced; there were tanning and shoemaking shops in the missions, with the entire production being exported—Indians were not allowed to wear shoes.

The artisan skills of the Indians amazed many observers. Charlevoix writes that the Guaraní succeeded "as though instinctively in any craft they undertook. . . . For instance, it was enough to show them a crucifix, a candlestick, an amulet and to give them the necessary material for them to make an identical copy. Their work could be distinguished from the original model only with difficulty." (60: pp. 115–116) Other observers also stress the imitative character of the Indian craftsmanship.

Trade did not exist either within reductions or between them. There was no money. Each Indian held a coin in his hands only once in his lifetime—during the wedding ceremony, when he handed it as a gift to his bride, the coin being returned immediately thereafter to the priest.

On the other hand, foreign trade was conducted on a large scale. Reductions exported, for instance, more local tea than all the rest of Paraguay. The Jesuit state was also compelled to import some items—above all, salt and metals (especially iron).

All reductions were built according to one plan. In the center there was a square plaza on which a church was situated. The square was bordered by the jail, the workshops, storehouses, the armory, a weaving shop in which widows and female offenders worked, a hospital and a guesthouse. The rest of the territory was broken up into equal square blocks of houses.

Clay-plastered cane cabins served as dwellings for the Indians. A hearth was located in the middle of the structure; smoke was allowed to go out through the door. People slept without beds, either on the floor or in a hammock. The Austrian Jesuit Sepp, who came to Paraguay in 1691, describes these houses as follows: "The dwellings of the natives are simple one-room cabins made of earth and brick. They have little to recommend them. Inside, father, mother, sisters and brothers crowd together with the dog, cats, mice, rats, etc. There are cockroaches everywhere. The stench is unbearable to someone unaccustomed to it." Funes writes in *The Civil History of Paraguay* that "the houses had neither windows nor any means of ventilation; there was also no furniture—all residents of the missions sat on the ground and ate on the ground." (63: p. 26) It was only shortly before they were driven out of Paraguay that the Jesuits began to build more suitable quarters for the Indians. The dwellings were not considered private property, and an Indian was not permitted to give his house away.

In contrast to the Indian dwellings, the churches were impressive in their splendor. They were built of stone and richly decorated. The church in the mission of St. Javier accommodated between four thousand and five thousand persons; its walls were overlaid with shiny plates of mica, the altars were covered with gold.

At dawn a bell was rung to wake up the Indians and to call them to prayers (obligatory for all). They then went to work to another peal of the bells. They retired to bed on signal also, and after dark the settlement was patrolled by detachments of the most reliable Indians. Special permission was required to be outside at night. (61: p. 176, 62: p. 29)

The reduction was surrounded by a wall and a moat. Gates were guarded carefully; entry and exit was forbidden without a pass. Contact among Indians from different reductions was not permitted. None of the Indians, except for soldiers and herdsmen, had the right to ride horseback. All means of conveyance—boats, canoes, carriages—belonged to the community. (63: p. 44)

All Indians wore identical clothing made from material obtained from the communal stores. Only officials and officers dressed differently, but only when on duty. At other times, their uniforms and their arms were kept in a storehouse.

Marriages were contracted twice a year at solemn ceremonies. The choice of a wife or husband was under control of the priests. If a youth took a liking to a girl or vice versa, this was taken into account and the party concerned was informed. But the Fathers, apparently, also functioned independently and decided on marriages themselves, regardless of the young people's preferences. In at least one recorded instance, a large group of young men and women took flight in protest over these practices. After prolonged negotiations, they returned to the reduction, but the Fathers were forced to sanction the marriages they demanded. (63: p. 43)

Children began working at an early age. Charlevoix writes that "as soon as a child reached the age at which he could work, he was brought to a workshop and assigned to a craft." (60: p. 116) The Jesuits were concerned that the population of the reductions grew very little, despite unusually good conditions from the Indian point of view, such as medical aid and safeguards against famine. To stimulate the birth rate, they did not allow Indian males to wear long hair (a sign of adulthood) until the birth of a child. The same purpose was sought by ringing a bell at night summoning them to perform their "marital duties." (64: p. 31)

The Jesuits justified their control over all aspects of the Indians' lives by reference to the latter's low development. The following judgment by Funes is typical: "Never acting according to reason, they ought to have several centuries of social childhood before reaching that maturity which is the preliminary condition of the full enjoyment of liberty." (62: p. 371) In the letter quoted earlier, the Jesuit Escadón writes: "In truth and without the slightest exaggeration, none of them has greater faculty, intelligence and capacity of common sense than as we observe in Europe in children who can read, write and learn, but who are nevertheless in no condition to decide for themselves." (61: p. 146) Meanwhile the Jesuits themselves were doing everything possible to stifle the Indians' initiative and interest in the results of their labor. In the Reglamento of 1689, we find the following advice: "It is permissible to give them something to make them feel satisfied, but this needs to be done in such a way that they do not develop a sense of interest." Only toward the end of their rule did the Jesuits try (no doubt for economic reasons) to promote private initiative, for instance, by turning over cattle to individuals. But these experiments failed to bring any results. One exception, recorded by Cardiel, was a case in which a small herd was built up, though its owner was a mulatto. (60: p. 146)

The Jesuits' enemies, the anti-clerical writer Asara in particular, reproached them for having starved the Indians and burdened them with work. But the impression gained from Jesuit sources seems more convincing and logical: hunger-free existence, rest every Sunday, guaranteed dwelling and a cloak. . . . Yet this almost successful attempt at reducing hundreds of thousands of people to a life as lived in an ant hill seems far more terrible a picture than that of a hard-labor camp.

The Jesuits in Paraguay (and elsewhere in the world) fell victim to their own success. They became too dangerous: in the reductions, they had created a well-equipped army of up to twelve thousand men, which was apparently the predominant military force in the region. They interfered in internal conflicts and took the capital of Asunción by assault on more than one occasion. They defeated Portuguese troops and delivered Buenos Aires from a British siege. During a mutiny, the viceroy of Paraguay, Don José de Antequera, was defeated by them. Several thousand Guariní participated in the battles, equipped with firearms and including some cavalry units. The Jesuit army began to inspire more and more apprehension in the Spanish government.

The fall of the Jesuits was greatly hastened by the widespread rumors of the enormous riches they were supposed to be accumulating. There was talk of gold and silver mines and of fabulous revenue from foreign trade. The latter rumor seemed particularly plausible in view of cheap Indian labor and the unusual fertility of the land.

After driving the Jesuits out, government officials rushed in to look for hidden treasure—and discovered nothing. The storehouses in the reductions proved bitterly disappointing and contained none of the riches that they were supposed to yield: the economy had not been profitable!

After the collapse of the Jesuit state, most of the Indians drifted away from the reductions and returned to their former religion and their nomadic way of life.

It is interesting to note the appraisal given to Jesuit activity in Paraguay by the spokesmen of the Enlightenment. Although the Jesuits were considered their greatest enemies, the *philosophes* could not find lofty enough terms to characterize the Paraguayan state. In *The Spirit of the Laws* (Book 4, Chapter 6), Montesquieu writes: "The Society of Jesus had the honor . . . of proclaiming for the first time ever the idea of religion in combination with the idea of humanity. . . . The Society attracted tribes scattered in villages, provided them with secure livelihood and clothed them. It will always be admirable to govern people so as to make them happy."

And Voltaire, in this case speaking about *"l'infâme,"* expressed even greater respect in his *Essay on Rights:* "The spread of Christianity in Paraguay by the efforts of the Jesuits alone was, in a certain sense, a triumph of humanity."

# v    The Ancient Orient

The Inca empire (as well as the other states of pre-Columbian America, the Aztecs and the Mayans) developed in complete isolation from the Old World and exerted no appreciable influence on our civilization. Therefore, it is much more important for us to study the manifestation of socialist tendencies in those ancient civilizations which are directly linked to our cultural tradition. In this chapter, we present certain facts that bear on ancient Mesopotamia and Egypt.

## 1. Mesopotamia

The state structure in Mesopotamia developed out of the holdings of individual temples that were able to gather together great numbers of farmers and artisans thanks to the widespread use of irrigation. This social pattern took shape in ancient Sumer toward the end of the fourth and the beginning of the third millennia B.C. Extant inscriptions (most of them were pictographs predating cuneiform writing) provide little information about this society. It was headed by a priest—sangu—while the main work force consisted of peasants who were tenants on the land around the temple, which provided them with draft animals and seed grain.

Toward the middle of the third millennium B.C., a new type of social organization emerged—small regions coalesced into separate "kingdoms" headed by a king called ensi or patesi. The economic system of this period is usually called royal or ensial. Inside each kingdom, the temples remained the basic economic units. A classic example of an economic center of this kind is the estate of the temple of the goddess Bau in Lagash (twenty-fifth and twenty-fourth centuries B.C.). Detailed accounts and records have been preserved in the form of a huge number of cuneiform tablets. The data permits a reconstruction of many features of life in Sumer during this epoch.

There were two means of providing for the people employed in the domain of the goddess Bau: allowances in kind and the granting of land plots for "sustenance." The lesser part of the temple's land was given over to the latter function; the bulk of the land was tilled by parties of workers under the supervision of the temple. These workers were looked upon as part of the estate and were called "people of the estate of the Bau goddess." (65: p. 142) They received a monthly allowance in kind from the temple stores. In the temple's records numerous lists of these workers have been preserved; some lists were reproduced year after year. Here we meet such groups as "porters" and "men-who-do-not-raise-their-eyes" (interpreted as unskilled laborers), "slave women and their children," "men who receive their allowances according to separate tablets." All received approximately the same allowance. In the lists, workers figure in parties headed by a foreman—"the chief farmer." Men did not receive subsistence for their families, but appeared only as individuals. Women and children are mentioned separately; orphans formed a special category. (65: p. 166) The workers seem to have had no private holdings; they could not store provisions for themselves, but neither were they obliged to buy what they needed elsewhere. The temple storehouses provided them with all the necessities. Tablets record the names of the party chief, the recipient and the dispensing official. Evidently, workers (usually every month) came to the storehouses in parties to get their rations, which consisted primarily of grain. (65: p. 151)

Another group consisted of "men getting sustenance." They received allowances less frequently (three or four times a year), but as a rule the amount was proportionally larger. In addition, they received plots of land, which in most cases were tiny. These plots were redistributed frequently. (65: p. 174) The most numerous category in this group consisted of "shub-lugal," who also worked on the temple estate under "chief farmers." They carried out irrigation work and performed military duties. They received plows and grain for working the allotted plots from the temple storehouses. Their position changed from time to time. Thus, for example, the "reformer-king" Urukagina granted them the right to have their own houses and cattle. The group of "men getting sustenance" also included clerks and officials who supervised the agricultural work in the fields. Their plots were frequently many times larger (65: pp. 154–155)

A certain amount of land was rented. However most of it was tilled by the work force of the temple estate. (65: p. 175) The management of agricultural work was in the hands of the ensial administration. Workers did not till separate plots individually, but worked in parties under the supervision of a chief farmer. The plots allotted to individuals were also worked in this manner. (65: pp. 170–171) We note that the same system was employed in the Inca state. Workers delivered all produce to the administration. All implements of production, including draft animals, were issued to the foremen of the working parties from the storehouses on a daily basis. Plows, hoes, flails, packs, collars and yokes for oxen were all kept in the stores. Skins of animals that had died were delivered by the "chief farmers" to the storehouse. The central store provided fodder for the oxen and donkeys. All these transactions were recorded in great detail. (65: pp. 176–177)

The harvested grain was delivered by the individual chief to the administration of the estate, and after milling, it was brought to the storehouse for distribution. Accounts were kept of everything, including the size of the fields from which the grain had been received.

Date plantations and vineyards were cultivated in the same manner. It seems that fixed norms existed. One document lists an amount of dates received in excess of the norm as "arrears" from the previous year. (65: p. 179) The foresters, who got sustenance in kind, worked in detachments in wood lots, from which timber (highly valued in a lightly forested country) was brought to the storehouses. Livestock was raised in the same way, herdsmen of temple cattle receiving food rations for themselves and fodder for the animals according to fixed norms. (Fishermen also worked in parties and had norms to fill and the obligation of delivering their entire catch to the storehouses.) (65: p. 184)

Artisans worked in the same fashion. Animal skins, metal (copper and bronze), and wool were received from the stores; manufactured articles were in turn delivered there. They, too, received food supplies from the estate. (65: p. 187)

All workers employed by the temple of the goddess Bau were guaranteed clothing or material for clothing. (65: p. 192)

In the documentation on the temple estates, prisoner-of-war slaves are rarely mentioned. Inscriptions speaking of victories in battle tell of enemies killed but not of prisoners taken. And the names of the farm workers are of purely Sumerian origin. Slaves are seldom treated as a separate group, and when they are, women are generally meant.

Apart from workers permanently employed on the temple estate, there was another group of inhabitants who were recruited for irrigation and farm work or military service only occasionally. It is possible that these were semi-independent farm workers. Since the character of their work outside the temple estate is not recorded, we know nothing about it. The number of these workers is estimated differently by various historians. A. Deimel, who has translated and commented upon a great number of cuneiform inscriptions from this period, believes that the temple economy was typical of the "entire economic life of that time. . . . Almost all property was in the possession of the temple. . . . Almost the entire little kingdom of Urukagina* was, in all likelihood, divided among temples." (67: p. 78) Many historians today do not share this view. (66, 68, 69) I. M. Diakonov cites a number of calculations estimating the amount of temple land in the entire state. (66: Chapter 1) He believes that "in the time of Urukagina, the temple economy comprised perhaps half the total territory of the state." (66: p. 251) The size of the populations of this epoch can also not be determined exactly. The work force of the Bau estate is estimated at 1,200 persons. (67: p. 78) But this was only a single small temple estate in the kingdom of Lagash. The king of Lagash, Urukagina, was himself the head of a far larger temple estate belonging to the god Mingirsu. Using deliveries as a measurement, it may be assumed that this temple alone had dozens of times more workers than the temple of the goddess Bau.

The epoch of small states and royal households in Mesopotamia (the twenty-fifth and twenty-fourth centuries B.C.) was followed by a period of fierce warfare which ended in the conquest of Mesopotamia by the Akkadian king Sargon, who subjugated the ensi of the other cities. It was about this time, apparently, that the idea of a "world empire" first arose, something which later inspired Cyrus, Alexander and Caesar. Sargon's state was truly huge in comparison with the small city-states of the preceding epoch. It extended from the Persian Gulf

* The temple of the goddess Bau was part of this kingdom.

to the Mediterranean. A high price had to be paid for the creation
of this empire; famine spread in the land and there were numerous
rebellions which did not cease even under Sargon's successors. The
state ultimately disintegrated under the impact of the mountain tribe
of Gutiyas, who seized part of Mesopotamia.

In the twenty-second century, Mesopotamia was again united under
Utuchegal, the ruler of the city of Uruk, who took the title "King of
the Four Lands of the World." After his death, a new dynasty was
established by King Ur-Nammu; this is referred to as the third dynasty
of Ur. Mesopotamia, Elam and Assyria came under its rule in the
twenty-second and twenty-first centuries. It was a centralized state
with a single economy managed by an imperial bureaucracy.

The king headed the state as an absolute sovereign. He was surrounded by a bureaucracy of "king's men" or "slaves to the king,"
among whom the highest post belonged to the "great emissary." (66:
pp. 256, 259, 262) In this epoch, we no longer encounter a nobility
aware of its genealogy and tracing its roots to a deity. The top element
in the state consisted of bureaucrats, administrators, royal war chiefs,
priests, all living on government allowances. The governing body itself
did not reflect the former city-states. The ensi, although retaining their
title, were merged with the royal officials; they were appointed by
the king, sometimes only for a limited period, and were shunted about
from one town to another. Their primary duty was to manage the
royal estates and perform administrative, judicial and religious functions. Temples began to lose their economic independence and came
under the protection of the king. (65: pp. 247, 250)

Production was centralized to the same degree as the administration
of the country. Former ensial estates entered into the state economy
as subordinate units. Parties of workers, in cases of necessity, were
shifted from one town to another. Numerous records have been preserved concerning the distribution of allowances to such newly arrived
parties (from Lagash to Ur, from Ur to Uruk, etc.) (65: pp. 248, 264)
All lines of authority came together in the capital, Ur. Control was
accomplished by means of envoys, inspectors and messengers of various
ranks. These obtained supplies in the towns through which they passed.
A small tablet, for instance, records a routine transaction in which a
messenger was supplied with provisions. Local records were kept by
scribes, who affixed their signature to almost all archival documents:
"Scribe at the Storehouse," "Scribe at the Granary," etc. (65: p. 251)

The system of accounting developed to the point of virtuosity. The chiefs of large (former ensial) estates submitted annual reports to the capital, while certain artisan workshops had to present reports several times per month. Descriptions of all fields and households were kept, together with maps characterizing individual plots: stony, fertile, clayey, etc. Date plantations were registered, with indications of the yield of each tree. There were inventories of the goods in the storehouses—grain, raw materials, finished articles. (65: p. 249, pp. 253–254, 255) An equally detailed record of manpower was kept: there were separate lists of workers of full strength, of two-thirds strength, of one-sixth strength. Norms for their allowances were adjusted accordingly. Lists of the sick, the deceased and those absent from work (including the cause of absence) were submitted regularly. (65: pp. 256–257)

State agriculture was based almost exclusively on cultivation of land by parties of workers receiving permanent allowances from the state. Rental of plots is met with only as an exception. (65: pp. 339, 312–313) The fact that certain fields are identified with a particular person or group indicates only that crops harvested from the fields in question supported these persons—not that they were the owners of them. Thus there were fields for supplying high priests, scribes, foremen of workers, diviners (a lower order of priests), craftsmen, herdsmen, etc. All these lands, as well as land intended for sustaining farm workers, were under the direction of supervisors. (65: pp. 301, 316–317, 398, 411)

Groups of ten to twenty men worked in the fields all year round. The workers were sometimes transferred from one supervisor to another or even from one city to another or sent to the workshops. With the work quotas, the notion of a "man day" of work was introduced (it was determined by dividing the work done by the norms). These figures were reported in accounts. The ration allowance depended on the amount of work performed. Foremen received seed, draft animals, plows, hoes and other tools from the central stores. (65: pp. 271, 273, 274, 275, 299–300, 302)

The same system existed in cattle breeding. Dairy products, cattle and hides delivered by herdsmen to the storehouses were recorded. A basket of tablets has been preserved that contains the records on a certain estate's animals that had died or had been slaughtered over a period of thirteen years. Feed for livestock also was dispensed at the storehouses.

In the crafts, a new form of large state workshop appeared. In

Ur, eight big workshops were united under the supervision of a single person. This manager inscribed all accounts (submitted several times a month). The products of the workshops went to the state stores, from which the manager received, in turn, raw materials and half-finished goods, as well as the craftsmen's provisions. (65: p. 286, 343) For instance, wool and linen fabrics from the weavers went to sewers for borders and hems, then to fullers and finally to the storehouses. Plain clothing was made for the workers and a better sort of dress for administrators. Reports from the workshops contain data on the output, expenditure on linen, expenditure on grain for the sustenance of the craftsmen and figures on numbers absent and deceased. (65: pp. 349, 350)

For dispensing metals and receipt of metal articles there were special officials who weighed the goods and inscribed the records.

Craftsmen were divided into parties headed by foremen. Workers could be transferred from one foreman to another. The allowance a craftsman received depended on his production (relative to the norm) and his skill. Chiefs of workshops could obtain manpower from outside in case of necessity. By the same token, craftsmen from the state workshops could be sent to work on the land, in river transportation, etc. The same term (gurushi) was often used to denote craftsmen and farm workers. (65: pp. 267, 299–300, 346)

The construction of ships was organized on the same principles as the crafts.

Like the crafts, trade was a monopoly of the state. (66: p. 262) In both state and temple records, slaves are mentioned—but slave women appear much more frequently. At first these were mostly weavers, but later they came to be employed in other work as well. Male slaves are mentioned almost exclusively in reference to the capital. Evidently, the children of slave women were absorbed into the general mass of unskilled labor. (65: pp. 279–280)

As earlier (for example, in the estate of the Bau temple), there existed workers who were not fully tied to the state but were recruited only for the height of the working season and paid in grain. Their proportion in the overall population is unclear.

A. I. Tiumenev cites data according to which hired workers constituted from 5 to 20 percent of the work force. (65: p. 362) I. M. Diakonov believes that the "percentage of the land seized for the king's household (including the temple household) was enormous." For the third dynasty of Ur, he argues, we must take 60 percent as a minimum figure. (66: p. 151) Diakonov does not, however, substantiate this calculation.

A series of extant documents testifies to the fact that private property played a certain role in economic life: for example, certain bills of sale for children sold into slavery. But in the main sphere of economic life, agriculture, the significance of private property could not have been great. Among the huge number of surviving records of business transactions of that epoch, there is not a single one extant that deals with land sales. (66: p. 250) Specialized handicraft existed only within the king's household; I. M. Diakonov asserts that there existed no trade workshops other than those of the state. (66: p. 262)

During the third dynasty of Ur, material inequality reached extraordinary proportions. The allowances for administrators exceeded those of the workers by a factor of ten or twenty. (65: p. 405) The difficult existence led by the lower segments of the population is reflected in the great number of records dealing with escapes. We have reports (with an indication of the names of the relatives of the escapee) on the flight of a gardener, a fisherman's son, a herdsman's son, a barber, a priest's son, a priest, etc. (65: pp. 367–368)

Another index of the conditions is the striking mortality figures preserved in the archives. In connection with the apportioning of grain, it is recorded that, in one party, 10 percent of all workers died in one year's time; in another party, 14 percent; in a third, 28 percent. One tablet states that two women out of seventeen died during a certain month, and in a year's time, eighteen of 134. In one list the death of more than 100 women out of 150 is reported. Still higher was the mortality rate for children, who (together with women) were employed in heavy work, such as barge hauling. In general, the notation "deceased" is encountered with extraordinary frequency. The general mortality rate is estimated at 20 to 25 percent, and in field work it is thought to have been even higher—up to 35 percent. (65: pp. 365–367)

This system of exploitation undermined the foundations of the state, which abruptly began to disintegrate under the onslaught of the Amorite tribes. The fall of Ur is dated 2007 B.C. A hymn describing this event was later incorporated into a liturgy; it tells of corpses rotting in the streets, of gutted storehouses, of towns turned to ruins, and of women abducted to foreign cities. The destruction of temples in Nip-

pur, Kish, Uruk, Isin, Eridu, Lagash and Umma is also mentioned.
The catastrophe was all-inclusive. The state crumbled into small
principalities, and there followed a period of internecine conflict
which came to an end only in 1760 B.C. with the accession to the
throne of Hammurabi in Babylon. (65: pp. 269–271)

The question of the social structure in ancient Sumer and of the
social position of its rural population has long interested historians.
The view of Soviet scholars that Sumer belonged to a slave-owning
type of system is not generally accepted elsewhere, nor is the usual
Soviet designation of Sumer as a kind of *patriarchal* slave state with
two economic sectors (a state sector, where slaves belonged to the
state, and an independent sector based on family membership). (See,
for example, 69.) The most widely accepted point of view assigns the
main part of the work force to the status of the half-free gurushi.
According to I. J. Gelb, these were native inhabitants who were "undoubtedly free at first but gradually lost their means of sustenance
for some reason or other and as a result of direct or indirect force
were compelled to work continually or periodically in other households." (69: p. 84) They were not slaves and could not be sold; they
had families of their own. But they had no right to move freely from
place to place and were obliged to work on state lands, for temples
or for the aristocracy (in the latter's capacity as state officials). Along
with these, there was another category of workers (mentioned in the
"gemé-duma" texts), who apparently had no families and were permanently employed in temple households. The great majority of war prisoners could not have been effectively utilized in the economy. The
gap between the large figures reported for prisoners taken and the
small number of such persons in the household records leads Gelb
to the conclusion that most captured enemy soldiers were killed. On
the basis of a certain text, I. J. Gelb even argues that war prisoners
were driven to special "death camps" and killed later. (70: p. 74) Those
who managed to survive were turned into state slaves, but their status
gradually changed from that of slaves to that of the semi-free workers.
(70: pp. 95–96) McAdams also believes that the economy of ancient
Sumer was a kind of amalgam of several kinds of dependence—from
an obligation to work on state fields permanently to a dependence
based on allowances of water, grain and tools—with only a small contin-
gent of actual slaves.

There were few slaves in the service of the elite, and their condition did not differ substantially from the numerous other forms of dependence. (68: p. 117) The bulk of the work force, at least in the larger estates, consisted of the semi-free gurushi. Even the small plots of land not belonging to the temple or to the state were nevertheless subject to controls. Purchases had to be sanctioned by the administration; cultivation depended on obtaining grain and plows from the central storehouses. (68: pp. 105–106) The majority of records dealing with land transactions consists of notations of transfer of small plots of land to the large estates belonging to representatives of ruling families. (68: p. 106)

## 2. Ancient Egypt

The period of history to which the preceding section is devoted was not an anomaly or a paradox discontinuous with the basic development of history. On the contrary, we have seen an example, perhaps the most striking one, of a style of life *typical* of the third and second millennia B.C. in the region that takes in Crete, Greece, Egypt and Asia Minor. These were the most developed countries of the ancient world. To a great extent, the same tendencies were apparent in the states of the Indus basin.

This epoch marks the rise of a *new social structure* which was destined to play a decisive role in the future history of mankind: the *state.* The basic social unit of the earlier period was a settlement around a temple or a village closely tied to territory familiar to the fathers and grandfathers of the inhabitants. All this was now replaced by the state, which frequently united heterogeneous ethnic groups and controlled vast territories, which it constantly strove to increase still further. "World empires" appeared, pretending to hegemony over the "whole" world and actually succeeding in gaining control over a considerable part of the civilized world of the time.

The first such empire was that of Sargon. Instead of comparatively small groups in which most members knew each other personally, a society appeared for the first time in history that united hundreds of thousands or millions of individuals who were ruled from a single center.

This upheaval in the course of history cannot be explained by technological or cultural progress, despite such achievements as the invention of writing, the widespread use of irrigation, the construction of cities, the use of the plow and the potter's wheel, and the systematic use of metals. In spite of these advances, the new epoch was based chiefly on the mass application of the achievements of the neolithic and bronze ages. The force that provoked the changes must be sought elsewhere: it resulted from the uniting of human masses on an unprecedented scale and the subjugation of these masses to the will of a central power. The "technology of power" and not the "technology of production" was the foundation upon which the new type of society was based. (68: p. 12) The state, by means of its bureaucracy of scribes and clerks, took control of the fundamental aspects of economic and spiritual life, justifying this by the idea of the king's absolute power over his subjects and over all sources of income.

To illustrate the general tendencies of this epoch, we shall cite some data on two periods in the history of ancient Egypt.

*The Ancient Kingdom (First–Sixth Dynasties).** All land was considered to be the pharaoh's. Part was transferred to temporary individual use, but most of it made up the king's domain—i.e., it was used directly by the state. The peasants were looked upon for the most part as fruit of the earth and were transferred together with land. Acts of transfer typically contain formulations like "the land with men is given," or "land with men and cattle." Peasants worked under the supervision of officials. The officials determined the norms for delivery (calculated anew each year, depending on the harvest and the annual flood). Moreover, the peasants were subjected to obligatory labor ("the hours") for building and other state work, most notably for construction of the pyramids. According to Herodotus (later confirmed by F. Petri's research), the scale of building was such that to construct the Cheops pyramid, 100,000 men worked for twenty years. The peasants did mandatory work for the king's relatives as well, and for the nobility. All these "hours" and norms were regulated and recorded in each region by four departments, which were in turn subordinated to the central storehouses and central offices.

It seems that the category of agricultural worker, denoted by the word *mrt*, was especially common. Pharaoh Pepi II decreed the removal of these workers to other regions to provide for the fulfillment

---

* A survey of the period can be found in 71, which is the source of most of our information.

of their state duties. According to some sources, these laborers lived in special workers' houses.

The crafts were concentrated, for the most part, in state and temple workshops, where the workers were supplied with tools and raw material, while the finished products were turned over to storehouses. Shipbuilders, carpenters, joiners, masons, potters, metal workers, glass and ceramics workers, either worked in palace and temple shops or depended on them for raw materials and orders. Highly skilled artisans with the status of hired free workers were in the minority. A number of important branches of craft production were monopolized by royal and temple workshops. For example, the temples manufactured papyrus for writing material as well as for mats, ropes, footwear and shipbuilding.

While Meyer (72) considers it possible that the Ancient Kingdom had a number of independent artisans and traders, Kees (73: p. 164) thinks there was no such category.

Trade was exclusively in the form of barter. Gold, copper and grain were used sometimes as a measure of value, but the entire process of exchange was based on real value. Exchange of this sort is depicted in numerous tomb frescoes. And among the objects donated to the cult for the repose of the dead, none seems to have a monetary character. The famous "Palermo Stone" enumerates the pharaoh's donations to the temples. These include a most diverse list of valuables, including land, people, rations of beer and bread, cattle and fowl.

Officials also were paid in produce. At court "they live from the king's table"; in the provinces, on the deliveries due to them, in keeping with their rank.

Certain persons of high standing received grants of land. But such lands did not form single holdings (with the exception of instances near the end of the period); they were scattered in various parts of the country. The persons to whom lands were assigned had no political rights within these territories.

The social structure was built around the bureaucracy. Beginning with the Second Dynasty, an inventory of all property in the state took place every two years. (It was called the "inventory of gold and fields" or the "inventory of large and small livestock.") To accomplish this task, the king's scribes were sent from house to house, accompanied by a detachment of soldiers. Norms for deliveries and taxes were established on the basis of the inventory. The representatives of central authority in the villages were the "village judge" and the "village scribe."

The multitude of titles for the officials is an indication of the degree of bureaucratic control over life: village scribe, village judge, chief of canals, lake scribe, chief of sea construction (the fleet), builder of palaces, overseer of grains and granaries, etc. Beginning with the Fourth Dynasty, the economic life of the country was regulated by two departments: one for fields, the other for personnel.

The officials who governed separate regions were not its rulers in the feudal sense. Although they usually came from the "aristocracy" by birth, and their official title was not infrequently passed from father to son, nevertheless the position of an official was determined not by his birthright but by the king's grace—in other words, by the given official's position in the bureaucratic hierarchy. No one possessed the automatic right to rule by birth. Service began usually in the lower ranks, and a successful official moved from one province to another frequently, without acquiring stable connections anywhere. On official seals, the name of an official was never indicated—only his position and the pharaoh's name. Inscriptions found in tombs make no reference to the social origin of the deceased or even to his father's name (except in the case of princes of the blood). An official's career and material welfare depended entirely on the state as personified by the pharaoh, who could even grant immortality (by allowing construction of a tomb near his own burial place). As Meyer says: "Egypt by the time of Mena [creator of a united state comprising Upper and Lower Egypt] was not an aristocratic state but a bureaucratic state." (72: p. 156) Furthermore: "The Ancient Kingdom is an extreme example of a centralized absolute monarchy ruled by a bureaucracy that depended only on the royal court and was educated in state schools for the training of officials." (72: p. 193)

*The Eighteenth Dynasty (Sixteenth–Fourteenth Centuries* B.C.)* More than a millennium later, we observe a system of economic relations based on almost identical principles. The state, in the person of the pharaoh, owned all sources of income, and anyone making use of them was under his permanent control. Periodic censuses were used to keep track of land, property, occupations, positions. All activity was to be sanctioned by the state; any change of occupation could take place

* Based on the survey presented in 74.

only with official authorization. With the exception of the priests and the military nobility, the population—both urban and rural—was united into communities or guilds controlled by state officials.

Land relations during this epoch were shaped by the recent war for the liberation of the country from the Hyksos invaders. The military nobility, which arose during this struggle, possessed a small portion of the land. Their holdings were passed down, as a rule, by right of primogeniture from father to son, but ultimate control of even these lands belonged to the pharaoh. Thus heirs assumed possession of land only after this was confirmed by the central authorities.

With the exception of these lands and the temple lands, other land belonged to the state in the person of the pharaoh and was tilled by peasants under state control. In the tomb of Vizier Rekhmara, for example, the agricultural workers are shown along with their wives and children getting sacks of grain and returning empty ones in exchange, under the supervision of an official.

The norms for delivery of agricultural goods were determined in advance on the basis of the Nile floods.

Cattle breeding was also subordinated to a broad governmental administration headed by the "overseer of horned cattle, hoofed and feathered livestock."

With the rare exception of individuals in some crafts that required special skill, all artisans were united in guilds and controlled by officials. The heads of agricultural communities and craft workshops were responsible for the timely fulfillment of the plan for state deliveries. If the plan was not carried out, those responsible were punished by being sent to agricultural and construction work.

Merchants sent abroad acted as the state's agents. All imports were also controlled by the administration; often foreign merchants were obliged to deal only with state officials. The administration controlled internal trade as well; all markets were under its supervision.

Despite the fact that almost the entire population was to a great extent directly dependent on the state, the society of the time cannot be called either a slave system, as in classical antiquity, or a feudal system. Written records contain numerous terms indicating dependence on the state—i.e., people sent to compulsory work or war prisoners used in building and other state works. However, not one of these terms can be interpreted as slave under the personal control of another individual and employed in economic activity.

**Appendix**
**Religion in Ancient Egypt and Mesopotamia**

While there is some documentation that throws light on the economic structure of the ancient states of Egypt and Mesopotamia, it is much more difficult to form an idea of the intellectual life and general outlook of these societies. The only sources of information at our disposal bear on religion.

Characteristic of the religions of the ancient East is the special role that the king played both in a given cult itself and in all religious notions of the time. Not only was he an earthly incarnation of a god, but godhood was the king's second, heavenly nature, his soul. Hence, religion was to a large extent transformed into worship of a deified king.*

Hocart (75) has amassed a great amount of material on the cult of king worship. However, his observations refer to more primitive societies when the deified king played an almost exclusively cult role. It was characteristic of Mesopotamia and Egypt to merge this function with the role of an absolute ruler of the country.

A great number of facts supporting this point of view are available in J. Engnell's study (76), from which we shall quote several examples.

*Egypt.* The king is held to be divine from birth and even before birth; he is conceived by god who became incarnated in his earthly father. The gods form the child in the mother's womb. He has no earthly parents. As one hymn reads: "Among the people thou hast no father that conceived thee, among the people thou hast no mother that conceived thee." (76: p. 4)

The main function of the king is to be the high priest; all other priests are only his surrogates. The main goal of the cult is the identification of the king with god. The king is identified with Ra—the Sun. This identification is reflected in the so-called royal name—Horus. That which is characteristic of the supreme god is relevant to the king—by the might of his words he creates the world, he is the support of worldly order, he is all-seeing and all-hearing. "Thou art like father Ra arising in the firmament. Thy rays of light penetrate to caves, and there is no place on earth not lit by thy beauty." (76: p. 6) To the pharaoh is attributed the dual nature of the supreme god, both good and wrathful.

The king is also identified with Horus, the son of Osiris, hence with Osiris as well. Horus is the living king; Osiris is the dead king. Osiris is the personification of the function of fecundity in the supreme god and in that capacity was incarnate in the pharaoh. The death of Osiris was depicted in ritual festivities—his passage through the underworld and his resurrection, his incarnation in Horus, the earthly king. This was simultaneously the festivity of the pharaoh's coronation.

---

* At least this is true of the official religion. Touching inscriptions uncovered in barracks occupied by the builders of the pyramids show that there also existed a popular religion based on deep feelings of personal merging with the deity.

The identification of the pharaoh and Osiris has even given rise to speculation (Sothe, Blackman) that Osiris is the deified image of a real king whose archetypal activities and death serve as the basis of the cult of Osiris. (76: p. 8)

The pharaoh's function as defender of the state against its enemies is identified with a mythical struggle between Ra and a dragon. The pharaoh's victories are described in vivid metaphors: he attacks like a storm, like a devouring flame, dismembering his enemies' bodies; their blood flows like water during the flood, their bodies are heaped higher than the pyramids, etc. The pharaoh's enemies are called children of destruction, the condemned, wolves, dogs. They are identified with the dragon Apopi.

In his state activities the pharaoh is likened to a good shepherd, shelter, a rock, a fortress. The very same epithets are applied to the supreme god.

Hymns addressed to the pharaoh include such sentiments as:

"He hath come to us, he hath made the people of Egypt to live, he hath opened the throats of the people."

"Rejoice, thou entire land: the goodly time hath come, the Lord hath appeared in the Two Lands." (76: p. 13)

"The water standeth, and faileth not, the Nile is running high.

"The days are long, the nights have hours, the months come aright.

"The gods are content and happy of heart, and life is spent in laughter and wonder." (76: pp. 13–14)

*Mesopotamia.* The king was considered to be born of a goddess; his father was Anu, Enlil or some other god who was called the "father conceiver." In his mother's womb, the king's body and soul are endowed with divine qualities. (76: p. 16)

During the ritual celebration of the coronation, the king dies symbolically and is reborn as a god.

It is interesting that the more ancient texts are the more definite about the divinity of the king. In visual representations, the king often cannot be distinguished from a god; he might have the same hair style, for instance. The king's name has a divine character and is used as an oath. (76: p. 18) In the god-king identity there are two aspects. The king is the supreme sun god and, at the same time, the god of fertility.

Thus the king Pursin of Ur is called the "true god," the sun over his land. Hammurabi says: "I am the sun god of Babylon, who causes light to rise over the land of Sumer and Akkad." (76: p. 23) During ritual ceremonies the king acted as the god of the sun—Marduk. This identification was proclaimed as dogma in relation to the role of the king in the cult, but in an earlier period it evidently was seen in literal terms.

On the other hand, the notion of the king as an embodiment of the god of fertility Tammuz seems so fundamental that scholars like Feigin consider Tammuz a historical king whose deification initiated the cult. (76: p. 24)

In the religion of Mesopotamia, the image of a tree of life that grants the water of life plays a great role. The king is often identified with it. Thus it is said of King Shulgi: "Shepherd Shulgi, thou who hast the water, shed water . . . God Shulgi is the seed of life . . . the aromatic plant of life." The lives of people are from the king: "The King gives life to men . . . life is with the King." (76: p. 28)

In a certain hymn the king speaks: "I am the king, my reign is endless. . . . I am he who rules over all things, the master of the stars." (76: p. 29)

Identical epithets are usually applied to king and to god: master, ruler, shepherd, lawful shepherd, ruler of lands, ruler of the universe.

We quote several more fragments from the hymns:

"He that overfloweth the face of the land with the flood . . ." (76: p. 39)

"He whom the great gods look upon with bright regard . . ." (76: p. 42)

"Who brings back life to those who have been sick for many days . . ." (76: p. 44)

And in connection with nature:

"The corn grew five ells high in its ears."

## 3. Ancient China

The history of China is an extraordinarily interesting example of how the tendencies of state socialism find expression in a multitude of forms over a tremendous span of time. Below we shall cite some data bearing on the period between the thirteenth and the third centuries B.C. This epoch is divided into two parts: the ancient (the Yin and the early Chou of classical Chinese historiography) and the late Chun-Chiu and Ch'in. The boundary between them lies in the fifth century B.C.

The Yin era comprises the earliest nonmythic period in Chinese history. Songs and chronicles supply some information on it, in addition to archaeological evidence. Some of the most important knowledge about the Yin comes from inscriptions on bones and tortoise shells used for divining. These inscriptions are assigned by Maspero (77) to the twelfth to eleventh centuries B.C. and by Kuo Mo-Jo (78) to the fourteenth to thirteenth centuries. The sources point to a society based on hunting and agriculture. Cultivation was by and large confined to riverbanks; artificial irrigation was little used. The manufacture of bronze utensils and spinning and weaving achieved a high level of technical proficiency. A writing system had been developed and the calendar was in use.

Power belonged to the king or wang. In a later chronicle a legendary king, Pan-Keng, in ordering his people to populate new areas, says: "You are all my cattle and people." (78: p. 22) He warns that in case of disobedience they will have their noses cut off and all their descendants will be destroyed "so that bad seed should not get into the city." (78: p. 22) The commentary to an ancient chronicle (sixth-fifth centuries B.C.) states that "Chou [the wang of Yin] had hundreds of thousands, millions of people." (78: p. 22) That the wang occupied a central place in Yin society is indicated by the huge number of human sacrifices that accompanied his burial. The grave of a wang was surrounded by up to one thousand corpses. On the other hand, such mass slaughter, apparently of war prisoners, made the spread of slavery rather improbable.

In agriculture no trace of individual land allotment has been found. Control over work on the land was in the hands of agricultural officials. The bureaucratic nature of agriculture is suggested by inscriptions on dice used in fortune-telling. For example, the augury directs the wang "to order the common folk to go to the fields for the harvest." Or: "The common folk are to be ordered to sow millet." (79: p. 125)

The conquest of the Yin empire by the nomadic Chou tribe transformed the latter into a privileged class of society, but little changed in the general structure of life. As before, work on the land was controlled by officials subordinate to the king. Numerous songs describe agriculture based on the use of large groups of peasants directed by officials who indicate where, when and what to sow. For example, land officials were instructed as follows: "our ruler summons us all . . . orders you to lead the plowmen to sow grain . . . quickly take your instruments and begin to plow. . . . Let ten thousand pairs go out . . . this will be enough." (79: p. 125) Elsewhere a similar scene is pictured: "A thousand pairs of people on the plain and on the mountain slope weed and plow the field." (79: p. 129) Of the harvest it is said: "There are large granaries everywhere. . . . In them, millions of *tan* of grain . . . A thousand granaries must be prepared. . . . Ten thousand grain baskets must be prepared." Finally, the wang gives his approval—the ultimate goal of labor: "All the fields are completely sown. . . . The grain is truly good. . . . The wang was not angry; he said, 'You peasants have labored gloriously.' " (79: pp. 128, 134)

The historical book *Han-Shu*, written in the first century A.D., describes the organization of agricultural work thus: "Before the population went out to work, the village head took up his place on the right of the exit, the agricultural officials on the left; they left their places after everyone had departed for the fields. In the evening, the same thing was repeated." (78: p. 31)

A line in a song runs: "Rain falls on our common land and on our own fields." (79: p. 135) Thus, apart from the fields in which thousands toiled under the supervision of officials, there were individual plots analogous to those that existed in Peru and in the Jesuit state.

Historical sources point to the state distribution of land. "At definite times the population was counted and the land distributed." (80: p. 149) And: "The individual at the age of twenty received a field, at the age of sixty returned it, at an age over seventy lived in state dependency, up to ten years of age was brought up by elders, on reaching age eleven was forced to work by the elders." (78: p. 31)

All land and all people were considered to be the wang's property: "Under-the-heavens, there is no land that does not belong to the wang, in the whole world from one end to the other there are no people who are not the wang's underlings." (78: p. 29)

Land and folk were granted by the wang to the aristocracy for temporary use, without the right of sale or transfer even by inheritance. Many cases are recorded of land being confiscated and even of aristocrats being reduced to the rank of the common people. Officials, scholars and artisans got their sustenance from specific plots of land tilled by the peasants who lived on them.

Besides their immediate obligations, peasants had a number of other duties. In case of war, they were to "put on armor and take poleaxes in hand." (78: p. 32) They were obliged to work on construction projects. In one song, it is said: "Tillers! . . . This year the harvest is already in. . . . It is time to build a palace. . . . By day make ready reeds. . . . In the evening weave rope. . . . Hurry and finish the building." (79: p. 147)

The crafts were partly the peasants' obligation as well. In the *Han-Shu* it is said: "In winter, when the population returned to the village, the women gathered together in the evenings and were engaged in spinning. In one month they fulfilled the norm set for forty-five days." (78: p. 31)

There were, however, professional artisans also. They belonged to a special organization in which the artisans of similar specialties formed closed corporations directed by overseers. Artisans and overseers, as well as merchants, received allowances from the state.

All the essential aspects of life were under the control of the king's administration. There were three basic areas of supervision: agriculture, war and public works. The heads of these three departments were called the three elders and were regarded as the highest-ranking officials of the empire. All agricultural production was subordinated to the department of agriculture or "plenty."* Its officials scheduled the rotation of crops, the time of sowing and of harvesting. They assigned the duties to groups or to individual peasants and supervised the private exchange of agricultural products at the markets. The life of the peasant was also under their control: marriage, village holidays and litigation.

The primary task of the military department was the suppression of uprisings. Also among its functions were recruiting and training and all questions of the conduct of and preparation for war—the arsenal, food stores, horses. This department also organized the huge hunting expeditions that took place four times each year. The department of public works had authority over the land (while the people who worked the land were managed by the department of "plenty"). It established "boundary lines," that is, undertook the periodic redistribution of land; it directed irrigation work, the building of roads, the cultivation of virgin lands. Artisans, architects, sculptors and armorers were at its disposal. (77: pp. 73–75)

Although there were objects (shells, copper bars) that were used as convenient means of exchange, all deliveries to the state consisted of produce: grain, canvas, etc. Private transactions, in most cases, also had the character of exchange in kind.

In many respects, marriage had nontraditional forms. Among the inscriptions from the Yin period, we find listings of wives belonging to two husbands. (81: p. 12) In the Chou epoch, marriage among the peasants was to a large extent regulated by the state. For example, in one source we read: "Men are ordered to marry by age thirty, girls, by age twenty. This means that the deadline for marriage both for men and for women cannot be extended." (80: p. 147) At a specific time in spring, the emperor announced the day for weddings. A special official called a mediator informed the peasants that the time for "the joining of youths and girls" had come. The French Sinologist Maspero believes that marriage in the true sense existed only for the aristocracy, for which it had the effect of sustaining the religious cult. Common

* This translation was suggested by Maspero (77) in 1927, long before Orwell's *1984*.

folk did not establish clans and the family did not have a religious character. Marriage was denoted by different terms for the aristocracy and the peasantry; Maspero translates the former term as "marriage" and the latter as "union." (77: p. 117)

Legal functions were divided between the civil administration and the legal department. Civil authorities assigned penalties for minor crimes—a specific number of blows with a stick. In cases of repeated offense, the guilty party was handed over to the law department. Five kinds of punishment were provided for by law for serious offenses: capital punishment, castration (or, for women, incarceration), cutting off of the heel, cutting off of the nose, branding. A codex attributed to King Mu of the beginning of the Chou period contains a list of three thousand offenses, of which two hundred were punishable by death, three hundred by castration, five hundred by cutting off the heel, one thousand by cutting off the nose and one thousand by branding. The codex from the end of this epoch lists 2,500 offenses, five hundred in each of the five categories of punishment. (77: p. 77)

In many respects, the society of the Chou period resembles that of the Inca empire at the time of the Spanish invasion. But in China, history made possible a further elaboration of the social structure. The Chou state did not fall victim to a foreign invader, but rather developed under the influence of internal factors. And quite unexpected features appeared. By the fifth century B.C., the empire, officially under the dominion of the Chou king, broke up into what were in reality small independent states that engaged in permanent warfare. (This age is, in fact, called the "epoch of the fighting kingdoms.") But the collapse of the monolithic state mechanism was compensated for by the development of individual factors. The teachings of Confucius proclaimed man's primary goal to be the moral and ethical perfection of his personality and the integration of culture with such spiritual qualities as justice, love of mankind, loyalty, nobility. A multitude of philosophical schools came into being; vagrant scholars began to play a great role in the life of society.

This is a period of rapid cultural and economic growth. The language and writing systems of the different kingdoms was codified. The number of cities and towns increased rapidly, and they began to play a greater role in the life of the country. The chronicles tell of cities in which carriages collided in the streets and the crowds were such that clothing put on in the morning got worn out by evening. Large irrigation systems were constructed. A network of canals was built, connecting all the kingdoms of China. Implements made of iron came into wide use. Almost all agricultural instruments, such as hoes, spades, axes, sickles, were made of iron. Throughout China large iron deposits were being worked; there were huge smelting furnaces run by crews of hundreds of slaves. Cities and whole regions specialized in producing different articles: silk, arms, salt. Under the influence of increasing trade links, almost all kingdoms began to mint identical coins. (83: pp. 24–32)

Somewhat later, however, a new tendency appeared: the desire to make use of the higher technical and intellectual level in order to create a strictly centralized society in which the individual, to a far greater degree than before, would be under control of the state. It seems that this is not the only time in history that developments have taken such a turn. For example, H. Frankfort (83) believes that the first states in Mesopotamia and Egypt arose in an analogous fashion, i.e., as a result of subjecting the economic and intellectual achievements of the temple economies to the goals of a central government.

A unique place in the thought and activity of the China of the "fighting kingdoms" period is occupied by Kung-sun Yang, better known as Shang Yang. He was the ruler of Shang province in the middle of the fourth century B.C. and his theoretical views are set forth in *The Book of the Ruler of Shang*. (84) This work is believed to have been written in part by Shang, in part by his disciples.

According to Shang's teaching, two forces determine the life of society. One of them Shang calls the ruler or the state, evidently regarding them as different terms for essentially the same thing. Shang identifies himself with this force. The aim of the whole treatise is to point out the best paths and means for achieving the goals of this force in the most perfect fashion. The goal consists essentially of increasing to the maximum degree possible the ruler's influence and power both inside the country and beyond its borders through expansion. The ideal is full dominion under-the-heavens. The other force is the people. The author describes the interrelations between the ruler and the people as analogous to those between the artisan and his raw material. The people are likened to ore in the hands of a metal worker or to clay in the hands of a potter. And even more—the aspirations of the two forces are diametrically opposed; they are enemies, the one getting stronger only at the expense of the other. "Only he who has conquered his own people first can conquer a strong enemy." (84: p. 210) "When the people are weak the state is strong; when the state is weak the

people are strong. Hence the state that follows a true course strives
to weaken the people." (84: p. 219) The section in Shang's book from
which the last quotation is taken is in fact entitled: "How to Weaken
the People."

In order to transform his people into clay in his hands, the ruler
is advised to renounce love of man, of justice and of the people—
qualities that the author categorizes collectively as virtue. These qualities should not be assumed among the people either; they must be
ruled like a collection of potential criminals with an appeal made only
to fear and selfish advantage. "If the state is governed by virtuous
methods, large numbers of criminals are sure to appear." (84: p. 156)
"In a state where the depraved are treated as if they were virtuous,
sedition is inevitable. In a state where the virtuous are treated as if
they were depraved, order shall reign and the state surely shall be
powerful." (84: p. 163) "When the people derive profit from the ways
in which they are used, they can be made to do anything the ruler
wishes. . . . However, should the ruler turn away from the law and
begin to rely upon his love for the people, there will be an outbreak
of crime in the land." (84: p. 220)

The law is at the basis of life; it rules over the people through
fear and, to a lesser extent, through the profit motive: "The law is
the basis for the people. . . . A situation is considered just when digni-
taries are loyal, when sons are respectful to their parents, when juniors
are observant of their seniors, when the distinction between man and
woman is established. But all this is achieved not through justice but
by means of immutable laws. And then, even a starving man will not
strain to reach for food, just as a condemned man will not cling to
life. He who is perfectly wise does not value justice, but he values
laws. If the laws are absolutely clear and decrees are absolutely obeyed,
nothing more is needed." (84: pp. 215–216)

Of the two key factors, punishment and reward, with the help of
which the law governs the people, considerable preference is given
to the first: "In a state striving for dominion under-the-heavens, there
are nine punishments to one reward, and in states doomed to disintegrate, there are nine rewards to one punishment." (84: p. 165) It is
only punishment that breeds morality: "Virtue originated with punishment." (84: p. 165) Speaking of how to apply punishment, the author
sees only the following alternatives: mass punishment applied across
the board or the less frequently used but particularly harsh punishment.
He definitely recommends the second course: "People can be made

worthy without mass punishment, if the punishment is severe." (84: p. 212) In this he even discerns a mark of the ruler's love for his people: "Should punishments be severe and rewards few, the ruler loves his people and the people are ready to give up their lives for the ruler. Should rewards be considerable and punishments mild, the ruler does not love his people, and the people will not give up their lives for his sake." (84: pp. 158–159)

The primary goal of punishment is to sever the ties that bind people together; therefore, a whole system of informers must supplement punishment. "If the people are ruled as virtuous, they will love those closest to them; if they are ruled as depraved, they will become fond of this system. Unity among people and their mutual support spring from the fact that they are ruled as virtuous; estrangement among the people and mutual surveillance spring from their being ruled as depraved." (84: pp. 162–163) The ruler "should issue a law on mutual surveillance; he should issue a decree that the people ought to correct each other." (84: p. 214) "Regardless of whether the informer is of the nobility or of low origin, he inherits fully the nobility, the fields and the salary of the senior official whose misconduct he reports to the ruler." (84: p. 207) Denunciation is tied to a system of extended mutual liability. "A father sending his son to war, the elder sending his younger brother, or the wife seeing off her husband, shall all say: 'Don't come back without victory!' And they will add 'Should you break the law or disobey an order, we shall perish together with you.' " (84: p. 211) "In a well-regulated country, husband, wife and their friends will not be able to conceal a crime one from the other without courting disaster for the relatives of the culprit; the rest will not be able to cover each other either." (84: p. 231)

The author pictures this entire system as a more profound and significant form of humanity, a path toward the dying away of punishment, execution and denunciation, almost a withering away of the state—through its maximum increase in strength. "If punishment be made severe and a system of mutual responsibility for crime is established, people will not dare to expose themselves to the force of law. And when people begin to fear the results, the very necessity of punishment will disappear." (84: p. 207) "Therefore, if by war, war can be abolished, then even war is permissible; if by murder, murder can be abolished, then even murder is permissible; if by punishment, punishment can be abolished, then even harsh punishment is permissible." (84: p. 210) "Such is my method of returning to virtue, by the path of capital punishment and reconciliation of justice and violence." (84: p. 179)

What is the social structure that Shang Yang proposes to achieve by these means? He singles out two concerns for the sake of which other human interests should be suppressed and to which everything should be subordinated: agriculture and war. He ascribes such exclusive importance to these entities that he introduces a special term to define them, translated as "concentration on the One Thing" or "unification."· The whole future of the country depends upon this factor: "The country that achieves unification, be it for one year, will be powerful for ten years; the state that achieves unification for ten years will be powerful for a hundred years; the state that achieves unification for a hundred years will be powerful for a thousand years and will achieve dominion under-the-heavens." (84: p. 154) Only the following activities must be encouraged by the state: "He who wants the flowering of the state should inspire in the people the knowledge that official posts and ranks of nobility can be obtained only by engaging in the One Thing." (84: p. 148)

All economic activity was to have a single goal—agriculture. Two explanations are given for this: in the first place, "when all thoughts are turned to agriculture, people are simple and easily governed." (84: p. 153) Secondly, agriculture helps feed the army during prolonged wars. Colonization and cultivation of virgin lands is proposed; peasants are to be attracted from other lands to this end by promises of release from labor and military duties for three generations. It seems that the peasants who settled on virgin lands were usually under greater control and belonged to a "royal domain." Thus the proposal to be free for three generations must have sounded especially attractive. Over and over, proposing this or that official measure, Shang Yang concludes the passage with the words: "And then the virgin lands are certain to be cultivated."

For the nobility, the only way to riches and a career must be through military service: "All privileges and salaries, official posts and ranks of nobility, must be given only for service in the army; there must be no other way. For only by this path is it possible to take a clever man and a fool, nobles and common folk, brave men and cowards, worthy men and those good for nothing, and extract all that is in their heads and their backs and force them to risk their lives for the sake of the ruler." (84: p. 204)

In military activity there is no place for moral considerations. On the contrary: "If the army commits actions that the enemy would not dare to commit, then this means that the country is strong. If in war the country commits actions the enemy would be ashamed of committing, then it will have gained an advantage." (84: p. 156)

The ruler, too, is released from moral obligations toward his soldiers. He rules over them, as over all people by means of rewards and punishments. Three enemy heads cut off results in a promotion to the rank of nobility. "If after three days a commander has not conferred this title upon anyone, he is sentenced to two years hard labor. . . . A warrior displaying cowardice is torn to pieces by carriages, a warrior daring to disapprove of an order is branded, his nose is cut off and he is thrown down at the city wall." (84: pp. 218–219) As with the general population, the warrior is bound by extended responsibility. Soldiers are divided into fives and for an offense by one all are executed.

Thus: "It is necessary to drive people into such a state that they should suffer if not engaged in agriculture, that they should live in fear if they are not engaged in war." (84: p. 234) Therefore, all "external" occupations (that is, not part of the One Thing) are systematically suppressed. As a result, activities outside direct state control, those in which personal initiative and individuality were displayed, were the first to be cut off. Hence the abolition of private trade in grain is proposed. Then merchants will be compelled to turn to working the land, and "wastelands are certain to be cultivated." Taxes were to be raised sharply so as to make trade unprofitable. And in general the role of gold was to be diminished so that it should play the least possible role. "When gold appears, grain disappears—and when grain appears, gold disappears." (84: p. 161) Merchants and their people should be drawn into performing state labor duties. The crafts are also not to be encouraged: "Common people are engaged in trade and are masters of various crafts so as to avoid agriculture and war. If such things take place, the state is in danger." (84: p. 148) Hired labor should be abolished so that private persons would not be able to undertake construction work. Mining and water transportation should become state monopolies: "If the right of ownership to mountains and reservoirs is concentrated in the same hand, then lands lying fallow will certainly be cultivated." And inhabitants should be attached to the land. "If the people are deprived of the right of free migration, then lands lying fallow will certainly be cultivated." (84: pp. 144–145) All these measures can be summed up in one general principle: "Under-the-heavens there hardly was ever a case where a state did not perish when infested with worms or when a crack appeared. That is why a wise ruler makes laws eliminating private interests, thereby delivering the state from worms and cracks." (84: p. 198)

The implementation of these principles, however, is prevented by a force which the book deals with at length. To denote this force Shang Yang uses a term that is translated as "parasites" or (literally) "lice." Sometimes six parasites are enumerated, sometimes eight, in still other instances ten. These are the *Shih Ching* and the *Shu Ching* (*The Book of Songs* and *The Book of History*, the sources of artistic and historical education), music, virtue, veneration of old customs, love of mankind, selflessness, eloquence, wit, etc. Elsewhere, knowledge, talent and learning are added. What seems to be meant is culture in its broadest understanding and involving a certain level of ethical and moral demands. The existence of such "parasites" is incompatible with the One Thing that the author elaborates, as well as with his whole program. "If there are ten parasites in a state . . . the ruler will not be able to find a single man whom he might use for defense or to wage war." (84: p. 151) "Wherever there exist these eight parasites simultaneously, the authorities are weaker than their people." (84: p. 162) In this case, the state will be torn apart. "If knowledge is encouraged and not nipped in the bud, it will increase, and when it will have increased, it will become impossible to rule the land." (84: p. 182) "If the eloquent and the intelligent are valued, if vagrant scholars are brought into the service of the state, if a man becomes well known thanks to his learning and personal glory, then ways are open in the land to the unrighteous. If these three kinds of persons are not checked in their path, it will be impossible to engage the people in war." (84: p. 224) And Shang Yang warns darkly: "The people in the whole country have changed, they have taken to eloquence and find pleasure in study; they have started to engage in various crafts and trade; they have begun to neglect agriculture and war. If this trend continues, the hour of death is near for the land." (84: p. 152) In olden times, he says, things were not this way: "The gifted were of no use and the ungifted could do no harm. Therefore, the art of ruling well consists precisely in the ability of removing the clever and the gifted." (84: p. 231) Finally, this idea is expressed in its most naked form: "If the people are stupid, they can be easily governed." (84: p. 237)

Shang Yang's teaching is reminiscent of a social utopia, a description of an "ideal state," in which "private interests are eliminated," love for kindred beings is replaced by love for state order, all aspirations are concentrated on the One Thing and the entire structure is maintained by a system of informers, guilt by association and harsh punishments. But in one respect Shang Yang occupies a special place among authors of such treatises. Many of them made attempts to implement their ideals. Plato, for instance, sought a ruler who would organize a state in the spirit of his teaching. Plato's attempts ended when the Syracuse tyrant Dionysius, upon whom he had set his hopes, sold him into slavery. Shang Yang, however, found his ruler and had the opportunity to realize his ideals. The prince of the state of Ch'in made him first minister and Shang Yang succeeded in carrying out a number of reforms. Here is what is known of Shang Yang's legislation:

1. Farmers ("those engaged in the essential thing") were freed from obligatory service.

2. Those discovered engaging in "nonessential" activities were turned into slaves.

3. Ranks of nobility were obtainable only through military service. High positions in the government could be given only to those who had already earned the rank of nobility. Those without rank were forbidden to display luxuries. (In this way, the ruling class was transformed from a hereditary aristocracy into officials dependent on the favor of their superiors and the monarch.)

4. The state was divided into provinces ruled by state officials.

5. Large families were split up, and grown sons were forbidden to live with their fathers. (This measure is seen as an attempt to destroy the village community.)

6. Fields were marked off with boundary lines. A number of historians see in this the destruction of community and the subordination of the peasantry directly to officials; others view it as indicative of the freedom to buy and sell land. (The spirit of Shang Yang's book would seem to render the latter interpretation quite unlikely.)

7. Capital punishment was introduced for the theft of a horse or an ox.

8. Every five households were united into a unit of shared responsibility and linked to another five. If one member of the group of ten households committed a crime, the others were to report him—otherwise they were to be cut in half. The informer was to be rewarded in the same manner as one who had killed an enemy.

These laws met with great resistance, but Shang Yang managed to cope with the opposition. Individuals expressing their discontent were removed to the frontier regions. Danger struck from quite a different quarter. His patron died and the heir to the kingdom, who hated Shang Yang, executed him along with his entire family. But Shang Yang's reforms were left in effect and led, as he had asserted, to the achievement of hegemony under-the-heavens by the Ch'in kingdom. In the third century B.C., China was united in the highly centralized Ch'in empire in which the ideas of Shang Yang were implemented even more consistently and on a greater scale.

At the head of the state stood the ruler, who took the title Huang-ti, a term which existed right up until 1912. It is translated as "emperor," although it has more elevated connotations, something like "Divine Sovereign of the Earth." The first emperor proclaimed that he should be called Shih Huang-ti; his heirs were to be called the Second shih, the Third shih, and so on up to ten thousand generations. (In fact, the dynasty was overthrown in the reign of his son.) The emperor was proclaimed the sole high priest of the state. Inscribed on a stele erected by the emperor are the words: "Within the limits of the six points [the four directions, plus up and down] everywhere is the land of the Emperor. Wherever man's foot has trodden there are no people who do not submit to the Emperor." (82: p. 162)

A historical concept current at the time held that the history of under-the-heavens consisted of a succession of five epochs, corresponding to the five elements: earth, wood, metal, fire and water. Black was designated the state color, corresponding to water, and the word "people" was replaced by the term "the black-headed." The number six, which indicated water, was declared to be sacred, and counting was to be based on this number. The "responsible unit," which had contained five people, now included six.

The historically produced division of the country was abolished. Instead, the empire was divided up into thirty-six regions, and those in their turn into districts. The country was run by a centralized bureaucracy. Inspectors, who were directly responsible to the emperor, supervised the work of all officials and reported on it to the capital. During critical periods such inspectors were also appointed to the army. District authorities were in charge of the rural elders, of the keepers of public morals, of the keepers of barns and granaries, of watchmen and postmasters. Cults and rituals were unified and local observances suppressed; temples directly subordinated to the state were built. Officials of special departments were charged with keeping track of these activities. Other special officials were in charge of military and economic affairs, or of service to the person of the emperor. The overwhelming majority of officials received regular allowances in grain. Only high officials and the emperor's sons utilized the income of certain regions, in which, however, they did not enjoy any political rights.

In accordance with Shang Yang's teaching, agriculture was proclaimed to be the "essential thing." On the emperor's stele it said: "The emperor's merit consists in his having forced the population to engage in the essential thing. He encouraged agriculture and eradicated the secondary." (82: p. 161)

The emperor was considered to be the owner of all land. It seems that when the Emperor Wang Mang proclaimed all land to belong to the crown (first century A.D.), he was only calling to mind an already established tradition. This arrangement was reflected in obligatory deliveries and a series of military and labor duties the peasants performed. Nevertheless, there exists information concerning the buying and selling of land by private persons. Still, agriculture was apparently based on the commune, which was used as a means of subordinating the peasantry to the state. Commune officials were obliged to see that the peasants went to the fields on time and were not to allow back into the village a peasant who had not fulfilled his norm. One treatise of the day relates that during an illness of one of the Ch'in kings, communes that sacrificed oxen for his recovery were punished. Evidently, the central authorities did not consider that communes had the right to dispose of livestock in any way. A historical record of later times tells about an inscription someone cut on a stone: "When Emperor Ch'in Shih Huang dies, the land will be divided." The guilty party was not found, but the stone was ground to powder and all inhabitants of the vicinity were executed. (82: p. 180) This incident suggests that in Ch'in Shih Huang's reign certain measures taken to socialize the land provoked discontent among the populace.

An important means by which subordination of agriculture to state control was implemented was the emperor's monopoly on water. A special department oversaw sluices, dikes and irrigation canals. (It should be kept in mind that in the Ch'in epoch, irrigation began to play an extremely important role in agriculture.) Another measure that served the purpose of extending the authority of the state was the resettlement of great masses of peasants to newly conquered territories, where they were evidently under more direct control.

Little information about private crafts in the Ch'in empire has survived. There are references to owners of iron-smelting workshops who became extremely rich. On the other hand, there are descriptions of large state arms-manufacturing works, whose entire production went to state storehouses. It is known that the state confiscated iron arms from the populace, and it is therefore likely that all production of arms was concentrated in the hands of the state. An imperial stele reads: "All implements and arms were made after one pattern." (82: p. 161) The state had a monopoly on the mining of salt and ore. Whole armies of workers labored in state workshops and on state construction sites. It is known that some of them were state slaves; the status of others is unclear. The state carried out construction projects on an unprecedented scale. Immensely long roads, the so-called imperial highways, were built, crisscrossing the country from one end to the other. The width of these roads reached fifty paces, and there was a raised section in the middle some seven meters wide. This latter was intended for use by the emperor and his court. The fortifications erected earlier by the various states were demolished and the celebrated Great Wall of China constructed to defend the northern frontier. The region of the Wall was connected with the capital by a road that went directly from north to south without attempting to bypass the natural obstacles. ("Mountains were dug through; valleys filled in, and a straight road was built.") (82: p. 171) Tremendous resources were expended on the building of palaces (in the vicinity of the capital, 270 were erected) and on constructing the emperor's mausoleum.

These activities of the state, as well as the wars that were being constantly waged on the southern and northern frontiers, required the employment of colossal masses of people. The state resorted to a policy of resettlement on a wide scale; unreliable segments of the population were moved to the former Ch'in kingdom and more reliable groups sent to the newly conquered regions. The resettlement of 120,000 families is recorded in one place; 50,000 in another case, 30,000 elsewhere.

The entire population, except officialdom, was subject to innumerable military and labor duties. Military service included an obligatory month of training for all men at age twenty-three, one year of service in the regular army, and border patrol apart from mobilization. The number of men employed in military service was immense: armies of 500,000 and 300,000 are mentioned. Even more people were involved in labor duties. In the building of a single palace, 700,000 were employed. The basic labor obligations included the building of canals, palaces, the Great Wall, etc.; the transportation of goods for the state (mainly military supplies), transportation work on canals and rivers. Military and labor duties were not always distinguished one from the other. In the south, the army built canals for transport of supplies; in the north, a 300,000-man army, alongside mobilized inhabitants and state slaves, were engaged in the building of the Great Wall. One source gives the following picture: "Men who had come of age were being driven to work. . . . Along the roads there lay so many corpses that they could have filled the ditches." (79: p. 395)

Such measures evoked mass flight of the population to forests, mountains and marshy regions. Others joined the northern nomads, or migrated to the Korean state. A new term appears in the sources—the category of "people in hiding." It was not only the poor who fled. The emperor who came to power after the overthrow of the Ch'in Dynasty decreed that those who returned to their districts would get back their fields and ranks.

The Ch'in penal code was consistent with the ideas of Shang Yang. It is based on the principle of guilt by association. Six relatives answered for each person. The criminal was executed; the others made into state slaves. Officials were bound by another form of mutual liability: the official who had appointed a guilty party and any others who knew of the crime but did not report it were subjected to the same punishment as the culprit. In other cases, execution of "relatives of the three branches" could be carried out—i.e., relatives on the father's side, the mother's and the wife's. This edict reads: "First, brand all the criminal's relatives of the three branches of relationship, cut off their left and right heels and beat them to death with sticks. Their heads are then to be cut off and their flesh and bones thrown on the city square. If the criminal was a slanderer or a conjurer, his tongue is first cut out. This is known as execution through the five punishments." (79: p. 379) A milder form of punishment was the extermination of the criminal's immediate relatives only.

There existed an extraordinary variety of execution: quartering, cutting into halves, cutting into pieces, decapitation with exhibition of the head on the square, slow strangulation, burying alive, boiling in a cauldron, breaking of ribs, smashing of the crown of the head.

Other kinds of punishment included the cutting off of the kneecap or of the nose, castration, branding and beating with sticks. Conviction to hard labor for from several months to several years was widely used, as was enslavement. One chronicle recounts: "All the roads were crowded with the condemned in scarlet shirts. And the jails were filled to overflowing like markets crowded with people." (85: p. 58)

Perhaps the most notorious event in the reign of Ch'in Shih Huang is the so-called book burning. The idea was to suppress any thought independent of the state and to obliterate historical sources that differed from official ones. The emperor's chief counselor proposed the form of the decree. In his letter he wrote: "At present, Your Majesty has performed great deeds whose glory will spread through ten thousand generations. This, of course, cannot be understood by foolish scholars. . . . At present, when You the Emperor have united the country, separated black from white and established unity, they honor their science and associate with people who disapprove of laws and directives. When they learn of an edict they discuss it in accordance with their scholarly principles. When they enter the palace they disapprove in their souls; when they come out again they engage in open discussion. . . . And if this is not forbidden, then the condition of the ruler at the top will become worse, and at the bottom the parties will gain strength. It would be useful to forbid it." (81: pp. 150–152)

There follow suggestions for concrete measures that were, in fact, acted upon by the emperor. The edict in question reads: "All books which are not concerned with the official history of the Ch'in state, except books which are under the keeping of high officials, are to be burned. . . . All who still dare under-the-heavens to conceal [books deemed seditious] are to be brought to the chiefs and the guards and burned together with their books. All who discuss these works are to be publicly executed. All who use the examples of the past to condemn the present are to be executed. . . . Officials seeing or knowing anything about the hiding of books who do not take measures are to be treated like those who conceal books. . . . Those who do not turn in books within thirty days after the proclamation of this edict are to be branded as criminals and exiled to the building of the Wall. . . . Books on medicine, divination and plant growing are not subject to destruction." (79: p. 381)

The point of these measures was to deprive the population of the means of independent study. Private persons had no right to possess any books except those devoted to very narrow utilitarian problems.

Many books were preserved in state depositories to which only special officials had access. But historical works on kingdoms other than the Ch'in empire were completely destroyed.

Books were not the only victims of persecution. At the order of the emperor, 460 Confucian scholars were buried alive, and a far greater number were exiled to frontier regions.

Subsequently, when Confucianism became the official ideology of the Chinese empire, Ch'in Shih Huang's persecutions came to be seen as an epitome of barbarism. But hostility toward Confucian teachings on the part of rulers manifested itself in the later periods as well. It is said of the founder of a dynasty that succeeded the Ch'in that he "does not like Confucian scholars. When a man in the headdress of a 'guest' or a Confucian enters, he quickly tears the headdress off and urinates into it on the spot." (79: p. 389)

In our day, the Communist Party of China has called the people to a struggle against the "followers of Confucius and Lin Piao." And back in 1958, at the second plenary meeting of the Central Committee of the Chinese Communist Party (Eighth Congress), Mao Tse-tung said of Emperor Ch'in Shih Huang:

> He issued an order that read: "The kin of him who for the sake of antiquity rejects the present will be eradicated to the third generation." If you adhere to antiquity and do not recognize the new, all your family will be slaughtered. Ch'in Shih Huang buried only 460 Confucians alive. However, he has a long way to go to catch up with us. During the purge, we did away with several tens of thousands of people. We acted like ten Ch'in Shih Huangs. I assert that we are better than Ch'in Shih Huang. He buried alive 460 people, and we, 46,000—one hundred times more. Indeed, to kill, then to dig a grave and bury someone—this also means to bury alive. We are abused and called Ch'in Shih Huangs and usurpers. We accept this and consider that we have still done little in this respect— much more can be done.

**Appendix**
**Was There Such a Thing as an "Asiatic Social Formation"?**

> Everyone who has ever passed an examination on "historical materialism" is familiar with the basic outline of human history. History is seen as a sequence of social formations: primitive-communal, slave-owning, feudal, bourgeois and communist. This fundamental historical law, however, did not crystalize with perfect clarity at once and certain comrades still have confused ideas on the question.
> The problem is that the Founders of the Scientific Method of History occasionally referred to one other type of information—the "Asiatic,"

elsewhere referred to as the "Asiatic Mode of Production." (See the correspondence between Marx and Engels, Marx's essay "British Rule in India" and his preface to "Toward a Critique of Political Economy.") The distinguishing feature of this formation, the trait that constitutes the basis of the political and religious history of the East and the "key to the Eastern sky," was identified as the absence of private ownership of land.

There was lively discussion of this question in Soviet historical scholarship in the twenties and thirties, especially in connection with the history of the ancient Near East. The argument was won by academician V. V. Struve and his followers, who maintained the correct Marxist point of view, according to which the ancient kingdoms of the Near East were slave-owning societies. The question might have been considered completely closed with the publication of Stalin's famous Chapter 4 of the *Short Course on the History of the CPSU* (1938), wherein the now universally familiar "fivefold" scheme of historical development was enunciated: it did not include any "Asiatic formation."

This atmosphere of perfect clarity was clouded by the appearance in print, in 1939, of a manuscript by Marx that the author had not originally intended for publication: "The Forms Preceding Capitalist Production." (86) Marx here places "Asiatic, ancient, feudal and modern bourgeois modes of production" in a single line of development as the "progressive epochs of economic social formation." Soon after this publication, an article designed to prevent any misinterpretation appeared in *Vestnik drevnei istorii*. (87) It was by academician Struve, who wrote: "By this, once and for all, an end is put to the attempts of certain historians to ascribe to Marx the idea of a special 'Asiatic' socioeconomic formation." He warns sternly: "Asiatic society is a slave-owning society." What Marx says about slavery in the East in the work in question is of course very good, but he unfortunately uses the rather vague concept of "universal slavery," which is difficult to fit into a historical framework that is based on the idea of class.

Representatives of various other schools of thought were quick to respond. The Communist renegade and reactionary K. Wittfogel stooped to filthy insinuations about an alleged analogy between the "Asiatic" and "socialist" formations. He even attempted to use this analogy to explain why Marx and Engels, by the end of their lives, had stopped mentioning the "Asiatic mode of production."* Needless to say, the slanderous character

---

* Reference to Wittfogel's argument (in 89) that Marx borrowed the notion of a specific "Asiatic" type of state from the works of Adam Smith, James Mill, John Stuart Mill, Richard Jones (the concept itself goes back to Montesquieu and Bernier), and used it in his scheme of the development of society on the basis of production. From the 1860s on, however, Marx and Engels engaged in sharp polemics with Bakunin and his adherents. Bakunin asserted that Marx and Engels' ideal of state socialism would "engender despotism at one extreme and slavery at the other." In this context, the analogy to Asiatic despotism became too obvious for comfort. Here is the reason, Wittfogel believes, why Marx and Engels refrained from mentioning the "Asiatic mode of production" in their later works.

of Wittfogel's statements was thoroughly exposed by Marxist historians, although a number of them also started to show an interest in this question, which, one would have thought, had been fully settled. In foreign Marxist journals, dozens of authors took part in the discussion. The response came in the form of a collection of articles. (88) (In this collection see the survey entitled "Discussion of the Asiatic Mode of Production in the Foreign Marxist Press," which is the source of the information given below.)

One of the first contributions to this discussion was an article published in 1957 by B. Welskopf, a historian from the German Democratic Republic. She expresses the opinion that the ancient Orient cannot be adequately categorized by either the concept of "classical" slavery or the concept of "patriarchal" slavery. Those societies, the author believes, fit the rubric of "Asiatic mode of production" in the same way as ancient China, India and America. In 1958, F. Tökei, reviewing property relationships in the Chou epoch, came to the conclusion that there was no private ownership of land at the time. And in studies published in 1963, he characterizes this epoch as a period of "Asiatic mode of production." R. Pokora comes to the same conclusion regarding ancient China.

Studies in which the "Asiatic mode of production" is discovered in ever new countries and new historical periods have been multiplying rapidly. J. Suret-Canale, a "Marxist-Africanist" (and the author of the survey under review here) sees this formation in precolonial, tropical Africa. P. Boiteau discerns it on Madagascar; R. Gallissot, in precolonial Maghreb and Algiers (in the latter, however, in an imperfect form); M. Tchechkov, in precolonial Vietnam; K. Manivanna, in Laos of the fourteenth to the seventeenth centuries; M. Olmeda, in pre-Columbian Mexico; S. Santis, in Inca, Aztec and Mayan states; S. Divitcioglu, in the Ottoman empire of the fourteenth and fifteenth centuries. It turns out that traces of the "Asiatic mode of production" can be found in present states (but of course not in the sense proposed by the renegade Wittfogel). J. Chesneaux writes of the "Asiatic mode of production":

"It does not belong only to the past, however. No doubt it has left deep traces on subsequent history. The tradition of 'supreme unity' is an example. Has it not, in numerous Afro-Asian countries, prompted the establishment of a system controlled by an all-powerful head of state who also enjoys the confidence of the masses?" (88: p. 55)

These historians acribe the following new features to the "Asiatic mode of production":

1. A special concept of property. First of all, this is expressed in the absence of private ownership of land, as noted in Welskopf's first study. Tökei even asserts that no private land ownership ever existed in Asia. Gallissot speaks about "public property." And L. Sedov writes: "That which distinguishes all stages in the development of the Asiatic mode of production . . . is an almost complete absence of private property as a system of relations."

2. A minor role for trade. Chesneaux believes that commercial turnover

and commercial exchange played only secondary roles and were limited to "additional foodstuffs" in the consumption of the communities.

3. A special means of exploitation that was, as Chesneaux puts it, "fundamentally different from classical slavery or from serfdom—universal slavery." C. Perrin singles out the basic features of this means of exploitation:

a. Use of a large mass of essentially unpaid peasants temporarily cut off from their farms and families.

b. Extravagant use of the labor force not only on the building of canals, dikes, and so on, but on construction of the despot's palaces, pyramids, etc.

c. The masses forced into hard, unskilled physical labor.

d. Peasant communities compelled by the despot to provide labor for public works on a grand scale.

e. Such exploitation is implemented by means of collectives formed from the rural communities; this requires a despotic, centralized rule.

4. A special role for the state when it acts as "supreme unity" to exploit rural communities (Welskopf, Perrin) and "controls directly the basic means of production" (Gallissot).

The "Asiatic formation" presents extraordinary difficulties for scientific Marxist study. In particular, it has proved almost impossible to subject it to class analysis. Chesneaux, for instance, is compelled to come to the conclusion that class contradictions are present here "in an original way," viz., they exist without any clear appropriation by the ruling class of the ownership of the means of production. The ruling class turns out to be not a group of people (!) but "the state itself, in its essence."

Tökei writes: "Of all the related problems, the most frequently discussed is the question of how societies of the Asiatic mode of production were divided into classes." (88: p. 62) Tökei and Chesneaux come to a "functional class theory," according to which the division into antagonistic classes is based not on the exploiters' ownership of the means of production but rather on "socially useful functions" defined by the ruling class. Sedov shares this view and advocates a theory of a "state as a class." Finally, Tchechkov asserts that the term "class" is not applicable at all to the ruling social group in precolonial Vietnam. There was instead a hierarchy of "functionaries," with the emperor as "first among functionaries." This elite was constantly replenished through a system of examinations and tests. For this group of elite "scholar functionaries," ownership of the means of production did not determine their place in the hierarchy, but on the contrary, their rank in the hierarchy determined their economic position. The ruling "state as a class" exploited the peasant members of the community not by owning the means of production but by virtue of its functional role in governing society and the economy.

The tried and tested tool of scientific research—quotation from the Marxist classics—proved to be of no help in solving this extremely difficult problem:

"What was Marx's opinion on social stratification and the class structure under the 'Asiatic mode of production'? We search the works of Marx in vain for a formula or a simple and clear analysis bearing on this question. Due to the press of time, Marx did not even give a complete analysis of the class structure under capitalism. In Chapter 52, Volume III, of his *Capital,* Marx began to expound his ideas on the subject* but was able to write only the first lines of a preface." (88: p. 63) One cannot help sharing Tökei's sad thoughts on this score.

Why is the matter so complicated that it does not yield even to the refined tool of the Marxist scientific method?

Apparently this is to be explained by the fact that we are speaking about phenomena that are so remote in time and so alien to our way of thinking that the modern Marxist historian finds it exceptionally difficult to visualize all these unknown and strange social relations.

## Summary

We have brought forward a series of examples which allow us to draw some conclusions on the character of socialist tendencies in the economics (and to an extent, in the ideologies) of certain states of South America and the ancient East. All these states were of a very primitive type, more so than the ancient classical civilizations or the medieval and capitalist societies. (We did not touch on the socialist states of the twentieth century, assuming them to be familiar to the reader.) In the literature on the subject we find indications of analogous states elsewhere (for example, the ancient states of the Indus valley or of pre-Columbian Mexico). We now wish to summarize the basic features of this type of society, relying mainly on Heichelheim (90).

All economic relationships were based on the assumption that the state, in the person of the king, was the proprietor of all sources of income. Any use of these sources was to be redeemed by deliveries to the state or by performance of obligatory work. Labor conscription by the state was considered just as natural as universal military conscription is today. Laborers were organized into detachments and armies (often under the command of officers) and were set to work on tremendous construction projects. They worked state fields, repaired, dug and cleaned irrigation and navigation systems, built roads, bridges, city walls, palaces and temples, pyramids and other tombs. They were used in transporting the goods of the state. Sometimes such duties were imposed on conquered peoples, and, as Heichelheim believes,

* I.e., the class structure of capitalist society.

it was precisely this that gave rise to the whole system of duties—
i.e., the state began to take the exploitation of conquered peoples as
a model in the treatment of its own subjects. (90: p. 176)

Most land either belonged to the state or was controlled by it.
Temple lands were usually under the control of the state officials who
directed work on them. The peasants got tools, seeds and cattle from
the state and were often told exactly what to sow. They were obliged
to work the state and temple fields on a set schedule. The bulk of
the agricultural population depended to a large degree on the state,
but in most cases the peasants were neither slaves nor private chattel.
I. J. Gelb (69) applies the term "serfs" to them—i.e., "attached" and
"protected peasants." He writes: "The productive labor population
of Mesopotamia and the ancient East in general, in Mycenaean and
Homeric Greece, later in Sparta and on Crete, in Thessalia and in
other parts of Greece (with the exception of Athens), as well as in
India, China, etc., is the basic work force employed either all the time
or part of the time on the public lands of the state, of the temple or
of the large landowners, who as a rule acted simultaneously as state
officials. This work force was half independent." (69: p. 83)

Slaves in the majority of cases were house servants. In connection
with the classical East, Meyer says: "It is hardly possible that slavery
. . . played a basic role in the economy." (91: p. 190, quoted in 89)

Trade and handicrafts were controlled by the state in an analogous
way. To a great extent, the state supplied artisans with their tools
and raw materials, and merchants with money. Both artisans and merchants were organized into guilds headed by state officials. In Egypt,
for instance, all foreign trade was monopolized by the state, right up
to the time of the Middle Kingdom. Internal trade was strictly controlled by the state, including the pettiest dealings. Most goods were
distributed directly by the state.

Money did not play any significant role in trade. Even quite valuable
objects were frequently exchanged without money payment, although
a price was mentioned in the records. M. Weber calls this "exchange
with money valuation." From twelve to twenty forms of primitive
money were usually employed, their value strictly regulated by the
state. This was one more important lever in controlling the economy.

The king's household was the basic economic force in the country.
Weber describes this structure as the king's *oikos*, underlining the
fact that the entire state was ruled from one center as the estate of

a single master. In Egypt, the name Pharaoh ("big house") corresponds literally to the word *oikos*. Heichelheim asserts that the state controlled about 90 percent of the whole economy. He writes:

"The kings of the ancient Orient were economically the center points from which the greater part of the capital investment and the economic life of the empires radiated. From here only capital surplus which had been amassed by the people could be reinvested or distributed, for productive purposes, among individuals or to whole groups of people. Scholars have attempted, and not without some justification, to describe the system of government of the ancient Orient as a patriarchal socialism." (90: pp. 169–170)

Just as economic life was directed by the state, as embodied in the king, so too the dominant pattern in ideology was the concept of a deified king, seen as the benefactor and savior of mankind. In another passage Heichelheim characterizes this concept:

"He saved the human race by becoming a human being, an eschatological breakthrough for each generation which made the king completely different from even the most powerful high priest or noble. The king saved mankind by his overpowering mystical strength in peace and war, by his justice in upholding a fair and benevolent law, and by sharing and investing the enormous capital at his disposal to the benefit of his poorer subjects." (90: p. 166)

Naturally, such an ideological and economic centralization made the most drastic measures of suppression of the population both morally permissible and technically necessary. Thus in India, in the laws of Manu, it is said: "Order in the world is maintained through punishment. . . . Punishment is the king." (Quoted in 89: p. 138) In Egypt every official had the right to impose physical punishment on his subordinates. The awe inspired by the pharaoh is symbolized by the snake in his crown; he is sometimes depicted as killing, dismembering and boiling people in the nether world. (Cited in 89: p. 142) The ritual name of one of the first pharaohs was "The Scorpion."

Socialist tendencies in the ancient states were studied in detail by Wittfogel (89), from whom we have already borrowed a number of specific facts. The author's general approach involves uniting a series of states (in the ancient Orient, pre-Columbian America, East Africa and some regions of the Pacific, particularly the Hawaiian Islands) into a special historical formation that he calls "hydraulic society" or "hydraulic civilization." According to Wittfogel, artificial irrigation played a fundamental role in all these societies.* The author defines the concept of a "hydraulic society" very broadly, including in this category almost all noncapitalist countries, with the exception of Greece, Rome and the states of medieval Europe. But he singles out the Inca state, Sumer, ancient Egypt and the Hawaiian Islands as "primitive hydraulic societies"—in other words, almost the same group of states that interests us. Wittfogel points out numerous features these societies have in common with the socialist states of the twentieth century. Thus he notes the similar roles played by irrigation and heavy industry. Both are activities that do not directly produce any goods but constitute a necessary basis for production. (89: pp. 27–28) This key sector of the economy is the property of the state, which in this way achieves complete control over the economic and political life of the country.

Heichelheim points to similar parallels:

> For scholars who have studied this development in detail, it is no secret that the planned economy and the collectivism of our modern Age of Machines has returned subconsciously to ancient Oriental conditions wherever we try to abolish or to modify the individualistic and libertarian forms of society which have been characteristic for the Iron Age of the last three glorious millennia. Instead our turbulent twentieth century shows a tendency to link together our own traditional state organization, society, economic and spiritual life with the rudiments of ancient Oriental collectivist forms of organization as they have survived subconsciously in the life and customs of many modern nations. . . . The modern great powers are closer in analogy to the great empires of the cuprolithic and bronze ages than is generally realized, or to similar later forms of rule which developed from ancient Oriental foundations either directly or indirectly. Whenever our century shows some attempt to achieve not personal liberty but widespread control it has strong affinities to the planned city life of the kings of Mesopotamia and Asia Minor, the rule of the pharaohs in Egypt, the early Chinese emperors. . . . The spiritual ties which the nineteenth century had with . . . Israel, Greece and Rome are more often replaced, to a greater degree than we know, by a return to ancient Oriental foundations. (90: pp. 99–100)

---

* McAdams (68) cites the examples of ancient Mesopotamia and pre-Columbian Mexico to assert that irrigation, contrary to Wittfogel's opinion, did not play a determining role in the formation of such societies (pp. 67–68). It should be noted, however, that Wittfogel does allow that an "agrodespotic state" *could* come into existence without an economy based on irrigation. (89: p. 3)

# PART THREE

# ANALYSIS

# VI  The Contours
# of Socialism

In the preceding sections of this book we have gathered together certain data in order to indicate when and in what forms socialism has appeared in human history. The data presented do not, of course, constitute a systematic history of socialism. It is rather a dotted outline, a collection of disparate facts selected in a manner that makes possible a judgment about some general features of the entire phenomenon. Utilizing these facts, we can now approach the main subject of our investigation—socialism as a historical concept.

It is natural enough to begin with an attempt to formulate a *definition* of socialism, if not a formal definition then at least an explanation in general terms of the meaning that we attribute to this concept. It is of course not simply a matter of providing empirical data in the first part of the book, and then extracting common unifying features. After all, the material was selected on the basis of specific indicators, as we pointed out in the beginning. Nevertheless, there is nothing circular here.* We have drawn attention to similar features in a series of historical phenomena. Now we must try to determine whether these phenomena possess sufficient unity to make it possible to look on them as a manifestation of the same general concept. In this way, the problem of definition converges with the question of the *existence* of socialism as a historical category. Such an approach seems to be appropriate in the consideration of any general concept, as for example in the identification of a new biological species.

We begin, therefore, with an enumeration of the basic principles

* Although we did use the term "socialism" long before undertaking to define it.

manifested in the activities of socialist states and in the socialist ideologies described earlier.

## 1. The Abolition of Private Property

The fundamental nature of this principle is emphasized, for instance, by Marx and Engels: "The theory of Communism may be summed up in a single sentence: 'Abolition of private property,'" *(Communist Manifesto).*

This proposition, in its *negative* form, is inherent in all socialist doctrines without exception and is the basic feature of all socialist states. But in its *positive* form, as an assertion about the actual nature of property in a socialist society, it is less universal and appears in two distinct variants: the overwhelming majority of socialist doctrines proclaim the *communality of property* (implemented in more or less radical fashion), while socialist states (and some doctrines) are based on *state property.*

## 2. The Abolition of the Family

The majority of socialist doctrines proclaim the abolition of the family. In other doctrines, as well as in certain socialist states, this proposition is not proclaimed in such radical form, but the principle appears as a de-emphasis of the role of the family, the weakening of family ties, the abolition of certain functions of the family. Again, the negative form of the principle is more common. As a positive statement about specific relationships between the sexes or between parents and children, it appears in several variants as the total obliteration of the family, communality of wives and the destruction of all ties between parent and child to the point where they may not even know each other; as an impairment and a weakening of family ties; or as the transformation of the family into a unit of the bureaucratic state subjected to its goals and control.

## 3. The Abolition of Religion

It is especially easy for us to observe socialism's hostility to religion, for this is inherent, with few exceptions, in all *contemporary* socialist states and doctrines. Only rarely is the abolition of religion legislated, as it was in Albania. But the actions of other socialist states leave no doubt that they are all governed by this very principle and that only external difficulties have prevented its complete implementation. This same principle has been repeatedly proclaimed in socialist doctrines, beginning with the end of the seventeenth century. Sixteenth- and seventeenth-century doctrines are imbued with cold skeptical and ironic attitudes toward religion. If not consciously, then "objectively," they prepared humanity for the convergence of socialist ideology and militant atheism that took place at the end of the seventeenth century and during the course of the eighteenth. The heretical movements of the Middle Ages were religious in character, but those in which socialist tendencies were especially pronounced were the ones that were irrevocably opposed to the actual religion professed by the majority at the time. Calls to assassinate the Pope and to annihilate all monks and priests run like a red thread through the history of these movements. Their hatred for the basic symbols of Christianity—the cross and the church—is very striking. We encounter the burning of crosses and the profanation of churches from the first centuries of Christianity right up to the present day.

Finally, in Plato's socialist system, religion is conceived as an element in the state's ideology. Its role amounts to education, the shaping of citizens' opinions into the forms necessary to the state. To this end, new religious observances and myths were invented and the old ones abolished. It seems that in many of the states of the ancient Orient, official religion played an analogous role, its central function being the deification of the king, who was the personification of the all-powerful state.

## 4. Communality or Equality

This demand is encountered in almost all socialist doctrines. Its negative form is seen in the striving to destroy the hierarchy of the surrounding society and in calls "to humble the proud, the rich and the powerful," to abolish privilege. This tendency frequently gives rise to hostility toward culture as a factor contributing to spiritual and intellectual inequality and, as a result, leads to a call for the destruction of culture itself. The first formulation of this view can be found in Plato, the most recent in contemporary leftist movements in the West which consider culture "individualistic," "repressive," "suffocating," and call for "ideological guerrilla warfare against culture."

We see that a small number of clear-cut principles inspired the socialist doctrines and guided the life of the socialist societies in the course of several millennia. This unity and interrelatedness of various socialist doctrines was fully recognized by their representatives: Thomas Müntzer cites Plato as an authority; Johann of Leyden studies Müntzer, Campanella considers the Anabaptists as an example of the embodiment of his system. Morelly and the anonymous author of the article in the *Encyclopédie* point to the Inca state as a corroboration of their social views, and in another article from the *Encyclopédie* ("The Moravians," written by Faiguet), the Moravian Brethren are cited as an example of an ideal communal order. Among late socialists, Saint-Simon in his last work, *New Christianity,* declares: "The New Christianity will consist of separate tendencies which for the most part will correspond to the ideas of the heretical sects of Europe and America." Further examples of this sense of kinship among the socialist currents of different epochs could easily be produced. We shall only point here to the numerous works with titles such as *Forerunners of Scientific Socialism* produced by spokesmen of the socialist camp, where among "forerunners" one can find Plato, Dolcino, Müntzer, More and Campanella. . . .

It is of course true that in different periods the central core of socialist ideology was manifested in different forms: we have seen socialism in the form of mystical prophecy, of a rationalistic plan for a happy society or of a scientific doctrine. In each period, socialism absorbs certain of the ideas of its time and uses the language contemporary to it. Some of its elements are discarded; others, on the contrary, acquire especially great significance. This is not unusual: such a pattern applies to any other phenomenon of such historical scope.

In another work on socialism, I referred to religion as an example of the same kind of historical phenomenon which is transformed in the course of time just as socialism has been. Now, however, it seems to me that this juxtaposition rather underscores the unique character of socialist ideology—its unprecedented conservatism. Since the time when socialism's basic principles were formulated in Plato's system, the religious concepts of mankind have been completely transformed:

the idea of monotheism has acquired universal significance in the world; the concept of a single God in three essences, God-manhood, salvation by faith and a series of other fundamental ideas have arisen. At the same time, the basic principles of socialism have not changed to this day; it has only altered its form and motivation.

The unity and cohesiveness of the system of socialist conceptions becomes apparent, together with an astonishing conservatism, in the way that certain *details* recur again and again in socialist societies and doctrines that are little related one to the other and sometimes widely separated in time. The probability of accidental recurrence is negligible, unless we assume that the similarities are inexorably determined by their exceptional spiritual closeness. We shall cite only four examples from the large number of such coincidences:

a. The coincidence of many details in More's *Utopia* and the accounts of the Inca state, which lead to the question posed in the French Academy concerning the influence of these accounts on More (which would have been chronologically impossible).

b. The custom of mummification of the heads of state and burial in stepped tombs of pyramid-like design, which is met with in states with strong socialist tendencies (although the states in question may be separated by many thousands of years).

c. In Deschamps's *True System* we find this vivid detail: Describing the future socialist society, he says that "nearly all people will have almost the same appearance." Dostoyevsky expresses the same thought in the notebooks to *The Possessed*. The character who is called Pyotr Verkhovensky in the novel and Nechayev in the notebooks has this to say about the future society: "In my opinion even men and women with particularly attractive faces should be prohibited." (92: XI: 270) Dostoyevsky gathered material for his novel from the ideological pronouncements of the nihilists and the socialists, but neither he nor they could have known Deschamps's work, which was published only in our century.

d. In *The Republic*, Plato wrote that, among the guardians, "none have any habitation or storage area which is not open for all to enter at will." Aristophanes speaks about this in almost the same words in his *Ecclesiazusae:* "I'll knock out walls and remodel the city into one big happy household, where all can come and go as they choose."

This particular coincidence may be explained by the fact that the authors lived during the same epoch, but the motif is encountered again in More, who, in order to underscore the kind of communality in which the Utopians lived, describes the entrances to their dwellings: "The doors are made with two leaves that are never locked or bolted and are so easy to open that they will follow the slightest touch and shut again alone. Whoever wishes may go in, for there is nothing inside the house that is private or any man's own."

More, of course, had read Plato and could have borrowed the thought from him. But we meet with a law against the closing of doors in the Inca state as well. Still later, in *Crime and Punishment,* the character Lebeziatnikov expounds on the question of free entry into rooms in the future society: "It has been debated of late whether a member of the commune has the right to go into the room of another member, male or female, at any time . . . well, it was decided that he does." (92: VI: p. 284) This is not merely an artistic contrivance. Dostoyevsky understood the nature of socialism and anticipated its future role perhaps more astutely than any other thinker of the last century. Of the multitude of petty details that he knew about nihilist circles, he selected some of the most characteristic, among these the very same free entrance into dwellings mentioned almost two and a half thousand years earlier by Plato.

And finally, we encounter this motif in the first years after the revolution in Russia. The force of the explosion experienced then dislodged and threw to the surface deeply buried elements of socialist ideology that had earlier remained almost unnoticed and that were later again displaced from view. We will therefore be turning frequently to this period, which presents multiple facets of socialism in an entirely new light. In particular, there appeared at the time numerous ideas on how the new forms of life could overcome the old ways and make life more collective—for example, by replacing individual kitchens with huge factory-like kitchen facilities, or by housing the population in dormitories instead of apartments. One enthusiast published a book based, as he claims, on Trotsky's ideas (93): "It should be made clear that I do not consider the idea of rooms necessary; I believe that it will be possible to consider a room only as the living space of an individual person. After all, isolation in a room is quite unnecessary for collective man. . . . The isolation needed in certain hours of love can be had in special pleasure gardens where the man and his female companion will be able to find the necessary comforts."

It would seem that socialist ideology has the ability to stamp widely separated or even historically unlinked socialist currents with indelible and stereotyped markings.

It seems to us quite legitimate to conclude that socialism does exist as a unified historical phenomenon. Its basic principles have been indicated above. They are:

- Abolition of private property.
- Abolition of the family.
- Abolition of religion.
- Equality, abolition of hierarchies in society.

The manifold embodiments of these principles are linked organically by a common spirit, by an identity of specific details and, frequently, by a clearly discernible overall thrust.

Our perspective on socialism takes into account only one of the dimensions in which this phenomenon unfolds. Socialism is not only an abstract ideological system but also the embodiment of that system in time and space. Therefore, having sketched in its outlines as an ideology, we now ought to be able to explain in what periods and within what civilization socialism arises, whether in the form of doctrine, popular movement or state structure. But here the answer turns out to be far less clear. While the ideology of socialism is sharply defined, the occurrence of socialism can hardly be linked to any definite time or civilization. If we consider the period in the history of mankind which followed the rise of the state as an institution, we find the manifestations of socialism, practically speaking, in all epochs and in all civilizations. It is possible, however, to identify epochs when socialist ideology manifests itself with particular intensity. This is usually at a turning point in history, a crisis such as the period of the Reformation or our own age. We could simply note that socialist states arise only in definite historical situations, or we could attempt to explain why it was that the socialist ideology appeared in virtually finished and complete form in Plato's time. We shall return to these questions later. But in European history, we cannot point to a single period when socialist teachings were not extant in one form or another. It seems that socialism is a constant factor in human history, at least in the period following the rise of the state. Without attempting to evaluate it for the time being, we must recognize socialism as one of the most powerful and universal forces active in a field where history is played out.

In a general sense, such an approach is not new. Book titles alone testify to that: *The Socialist Empire of the Incas; The History of Communism and Socialism in Antiquity; State Socialism in the Fifteenth Century* B.C., and so on. Wittfogel (in the work quoted above, 89) gathers vast amounts of material about the states of the ancient Orient, pre-Columbian America, East Africa and certain areas of the Pacific, for example the Hawaiian Islands, characterizing the states he describes as "hydraulic societies" and tracing the multitude of parallels between them and the contemporary socialist states. The history of the socialist doctrines is no less thoroughly researched, as can be seen from the numerous "Histories of Socialist Ideas," which usually begin with Plato. Koigen has even remarked ironically: "Socialism is as old as human society itself—but not older." (94)

It would seem that this should be taken as the starting point of any attempt to understand the essence of socialism. Despite being quite general, such a point of view strictly limits the range of those arguments that are applicable: any explanations based on the peculiarities of a given historical period, race or civilization must be discarded. It is necessary to reject the interpretation of socialism as a definite phase in the development of human society which is said to appear when conditions are ripe. On the contrary, any approach to socialism ought to be based on principles broad enough to be applicable to the Inca empire, to Plato's philosophy and to the socialism of the twentieth century.

# VII Survey of Some Approaches to Socialism

Before we apply the conclusions formulated in the preceding section to further analysis of socialism, they can be tested in a simpler procedure of a purely critical character. We shall examine those points of view which are representative of the majority of conceptions of socialism that have been formulated in the past.

### 1. *The Marxist standpoint*

*Socialism as a state system is a specific phase in the historical development of mankind; it inevitably replaces capitalism when the latter reaches a definite level of development. Socialism as a doctrine constitutes the world view of the proletariat (itself engendered by capitalism), and at the same time it is the result of scientific analysis, a scientific proof of the historical inevitability of the socialist state system.*

This view is contradicted by the known facts. If a socialist state comes into being only under the conditions created by the development of capitalism, if, as Lenin wrote, "socialism originates in capitalism, develops historically from capitalism, and results from the action of a social force that is engendered by capitalism," then whence did it come and as a result of what social force did it develop in the Inca empire or the states of the ancient Orient? History only reinforces the doubts engendered by the contemporary situation: socialist states have arisen in China, North Korea and Cuba—that is, in the countries where the influence of capitalism can in no way be considered a determining factor.

It is just as difficult to see any connection between the ideology of socialist movements and the proletariat: for example, in the movement of Mazdak or the Taborites. Furthermore, the link between the proletariat and socialism was not at all strong in the nineteenth century either. Bakunin, for example, felt that socialism was most congenial to the peasantry; he considered peasants and brigands (at least in Russia) to be the main revolutionary force. "The brigand is the true and only revolutionary in Russia." (95: p. 353) "And when these two kinds of rebellion, the rebellion of the brigands and of the peasants, are joined together, a popular revolution takes place." (95: p. 354) In replying to Bakunin, the prominent Marxist historian M. N. Pokrovsky refers, strange as it may seem, not to the immanent laws of history with which he is familiar, but to far more concrete circumstances: "Of course, this was outdated for the sixties, the epoch of the railroads. . . . It was extremely difficult to commit robberies on the railroads." (96: p. 65) But when even the founders of Marxism, recognizing the proletariat as the main force of the future social upheaval, stressed that the proletariat had "nothing to lose but its chains," their differences with Bakunin were more technical than theoretical. And in fact, some time later the role of the proletariat was reconsidered—without any change of basic historical concepts. The neo-Marxists who make up the New Left believe that the working class has ceased to be a revolutionary force, that it has been "integrated into the system" and that the "new working class" is the "favorite child of the system and ideologically subjugated to it." (4: p. 57)

Hope for the future has been transferred to the peoples of the developing countries, to disaffected national minorities (for example, the blacks in the U.S.A.) and to students. On the other hand (or perhaps it comes to the same thing), the proletariat is apparently assigned a very modest role in Chairman Mao's concept of the confrontation of the "world city" with the "world village."

The third proposition in the Marxist view of socialism is that socialism (in the form of Marxism) is a scientific theory.

### 2. Socialist teachings as scientific theory

The evident weakness of such a point of view is that it is applicable only to a few socialist doctrines. Most of them never pretended to be a part of science and assumed instead the form of philosophical systems, divine revelation or theories on the most reasonable social structure. But the nineteenth century was so imbued with the cult of science that even an adventure novel could count on success only if, as in the Sherlock Holmes stories, the "scientific method" was used. Only in these circumstances did "scientific socialism" appear.

Hence we need only consider to what extent the socialist doctrines of the nineteenth century were a product of scientific activity. The assertions about the scientific character of its conclusions play an especially large role in Marxism, but other socialist teachings, as those of Fourier, for example, had similar pretensions. While Marx and Engels mock Fourier as a "utopian socialist" and apply the term "scientific socialism" only to their own doctrine, Fourier maintained that he had made an analysis of social phenomena that was as precise as Newton's physics and, in fact, constructed in its image. He wrote: "The theory of passionate attraction and repulsion is something stable to which geometric theorems are wholly applicable. . . . And thus, of the connection amongst the new sciences: I soon understood that the laws of passionate attraction correspond at all points to the laws of material gravitation discovered by Newton and Leibnitz, and that *there exists a unity in the movement of the material and the spiritual worlds."* (97: p. 43)

Juxtaposition of these two teachings—Fourier's and Marx's—may help us to understand what role the theme of science played in both.

Strictly speaking, the founders of Marxism did not always deny the significance of Fourier's scientific constructions. For example, comparing them with Saint-Simon's doctrine, Engels wrote:

"It is true that there is in [Fourier's theories] no shortage of mysticism as well. . . . Still, if we set that aside, something remains which cannot be found among the followers of Saint-Simon—scientific inquiry, sober, bold and systematic thinking, in a word: *social philosophy."* (3: II: p. 395)

It is very difficult today to understand such a point of view. Fourier's system is far removed from any contemporary notion of what constitutes a scientific theory. He held that planets and other celestial bodies are living beings, that they live, die and copulate. "A planet is a being, having two souls and two sexes. In the act of conception, just as with animals and plants, two productive substances are joined together. . . . A heavenly body may copulate: (1) With itself, the south pole with the north pole, as with plants. (2) With another heavenly body through the emission of fluids from the opposite poles. (3) With something intermediate." (97: p. 69)

SURVEY OF SOME APPROACHES TO SOCIALISM / 205

The life of the planet earth, also perceived as a single organism, is inherently linked with the life of mankind. There is a correspondence between the various epochs of their respective developments. There had been seven epochs up to then, and Fourier speaks of an eighth epoch which is on the verge of being born: "Meanwhile, the earth thirsts for creation; the frequent emission of northern light is witness to this, an indication that the planet is in heat, and a sign of a useless emission of its fertile fluid. It cannot copulate with the fluid of other planets until the human race accomplishes certain preliminary tasks. These tasks can be performed only by the eighth society, which must now be formed." (97: p. 71)

This eighth society of "combined structure" is to bring socialist ideas to life. In the description of this society, we encounter the famous "phalansteries" and numerous forms of free love, together with Fourier's criticism by contemporary civilization. On entering the "eighth society," mankind will accomplish the tasks that serve as the preconditions for a new act by copulation by the earth. This will bring about changes which, in their turn, will have a fructifying influence on mankind and will lighten the task of developing the "combined structure." The seas and oceans will acquire the taste of lemonade; instead of sharks and whales, there will appear anti-sharks and anti-whales, together with a multitude of amphibia that will promote transportation and fishing. And in the deserts, instead of lions and tigers, there will be anti-lions and anti-tigers, which will carry out people's wishes.

We have here the ancient and mythological notion according to which human activity is necessary for the functioning of the universe. It is precisely the same sort of notion that underlies the ceremony of the Australian aborigines which aims to assure the fertility of nature. Similarly, the Aztecs sacrificed thousands of people in order to preserve the life-giving power of the sun. It would seem that this ancient notion was the real foundation of Fourier's teaching, and not "the application of geometric theorems," which are completely absent in his speculations. His theory seems to have been "revealed" to him, and in this direct perception there is a sincerity that partly accounts for his success.* As for the imitation of scientific phraseology, which is quite clumsy in Fourier, this was only a gesture in the direction of nineteenth-

---

* When Fourier writes of "a ray containing five other [colors] invisible and unnoticed by us—pink, crimson, chestnut, green with a shade of dragoon, lilac (I am perfectly sure only of pink and crimson)," one can readily believe that he saw the pink and crimson with his own eyes. (See 97: p. 104)

century tastes, an attempt to make his system more attractive.

This conclusion, so obvious in the case of Fourier, forces us not to accept on faith Marxism's claims to being a scientific theory. And the very feature which the creators of Marxism proclaimed to be fundamental—the "criterion of practice"—seems to provide the clearest response to Marxism. According to this criterion, a scientific theory ought to be tested according to its concrete conclusions. But with almost perverse consistency, most of the projections of Marxism have proved to be incorrect. A better percentage of correct predictions could probably have been achieved by making random guesses. Examples have been cited repeatedly, and for this reason we limit ourselves to three in order to underscore the typical and in most cases *fundamental* nature of the errors: the truth proved to be not merely different but in fact the opposite to that which had been predicted.

a. The national question:

"National differences and antagonistic interests among various peoples are already vanishing more and more thanks to the development of the bourgeoisie, to freedom of commerce, to the world market, to uniformity in the mode of production and in the corresponding conditions of life. The supremacy of the proletariat will accelerate the disappearance of differences." (3: V: p. 500)

b. In particular, the Jewish question, which was to disappear as soon as financial operations and petty trade became impossible. "The chimerical nationality of the Jew is the nationality of a merchant, in general of a man who deals with money." (3: I: p. 382) "An organization of society which could remove the preconditions of petty trade, and therefore the possibility of petty trade, would make Jewry impossible." (3: I: p. 379)

c. The role of the state:

"The first act in which the state truly comes forward as a representative of the whole of society—the taking possession of the means of production in the name of society—is, at the same time, its last independent act as a state. Interference of the state in social relations becomes superfluous in one sphere after another, and then ceases of itself. The government of persons is replaced by the administration of things and the direction of the process of production. The state is not 'abolished'; it withers away." (98: p. 285)

"With the disappearance of classes the state inevitably disappears. A society which organizes its production in a new fashion based on the free and equal association of producers will send the machine of the state to the place where it will then belong: the museum of antiquity, next to the spinning wheel and the bronze ax." (3: XVI: p. 149)

The unquestionably immense *success* of Marxism in the nineteenth and the beginning of the twentieth centuries by no means proves its correctness as a scientific theory. Other movements, Islam, for instance, have enjoyed no less success without ever having laid claim to being "scientific."

The direct impression left by the works of the founders of Marxism leads to the same conclusion—they lack the climate characteristic of scientific inquiry. For the authors, the world of science is divided into two unequal parts. One part consists of a narrow circle of followers, the other of enemies, plotting against them and ready for any crime against the truth for the sake of attaining their goals. Thus German economists are said to have willfully ignored *Capital* for years, while stealing from it constantly, and English specialists on primitive society are said to have treated Morgan's book in the same way. But the founders of Marxism hardly stood on ceremony themselves and again and again attacked their colleagues for "liberal falsifications," "banality and commonplaceness of the worst kind," "virtuosity in pretentious idiotism," etc.

The basic works of Marxism are utterly alien to the most fundamental characteristic of scientific activity—the disinterested striving for truth for its own sake. And although the scientist's duty is sometimes proclaimed, the truth, in practice, always remains a "party truth"—i.e., it is subordinated to the interests of the political struggle. This attitude toward science is expressed, for instance, in the conclusion of the preface to Marx's *Critique of Political Economy:* "My views, no matter how they are judged and how little they agree with the egotistical prejudices of the ruling classes, are the result of many years of conscientious research." (3: XII: p. 9) In this way, Marx immediately suggests that any objections to his views are the product of "egotistical prejudices."

Thanks to this indifference toward truth in Marxism, we so often come across contradictions even a few of which would ruin any genuinely scientific theory. We have cited, for instance, Wittfogel's remarks on the appearance and sudden disappearance of the "Asiatic formation" in the works of Marx and Engels. Numerous examples of this kind could be brought forward. In the *Communist Manifesto* we read:

"The lower middle class, the small manufacturer, the shopkeeper, the artisan, the peasant . . . they are all not revolutionary but conservative. Nay, more, they are reactionary, for they try to roll back the wheel of history." (3: V: p. 493) Lassalle incorporated the same thought in his Gotha program: "In relation to the proletariat, all other groups constitute a single reactionary mass."

But it was precisely at this time that Marx was competing against Lassalle (and not very successfully) for influence on the German social democratic movement.

And he writes: "Lassalle knew the 'Manifesto' by heart, and if he distorted it so grossly, he did so only to justify his own betrayal of the working class."* (3: XV: p. 277)

Marx's *Capital* of course imit. tes the style of a scientific treatise far better than Fourier's *Theory of Four Movements.* Marx includes tables and a great number of quotations (even from Greek, as he was fond of noting). But in its essence, Marx's *Capital* is equally far from being a scientific work, for the basic statements in it are merely asserted and not deduced. It was Bulgakov who (in 100) drew attention to a footnote in Volume I of *Capital:* "Of course, it is much easier to find the earthly essence of religious notions by means of analysis than the other way round, i.e., from the given real relations to deduce their religious forms. The latter method is the only materialistic one and, therefore, the only scientific one."

But Marx only remarked on this matter in a note and nowhere attempted to apply his "only scientific" method. In the same way, neither Marx nor Engels tried to show in what manner "the hand mill yields a feudal society with a suzerain at its head." They simply could not have done so, of course, since the hand mill was known in ancient Sumer and in other societies as well. Examples such as these could be cited at length.

The attitude of the classics of Marxism toward science is vividly illustrated by what Engels wrote about mathematics. Indeed, it is in this connection that he says (in the preface to *Anti-Dühring*):

"Awareness of the fact that I have not sufficiently mastered mathematics has made me careful: no one will be able to find me trespassing against the facts." (98: p. 7)

---

* This example and most of the others in this section are taken from a study (99) in which the question of the scientific character of Marxism is analyzed more systematically.

Nevertheless, in that work we find the following statements:

"We have already mentioned that one of the main principles of higher mathematics involves a contradiction which consists of the fact that under certain conditions a straight line and a curve are one and the same thing. And higher mathematics provides another example of a contradiction: two lines that intersect before our eyes must nonetheless be considered parallel lines five or six centimeters from the point of intersection, i.e., lines that cannot intersect even if extended to infinity." (98: p. 120)

"The virgin state of absolute signification, the indisputable proof of everything mathematical, is gone forever; an era of discordant opinion is upon us, and we have gotten to the point that the majority perform differentiation and integration not because they understand what they are doing, but simply because they believe in something that up till now has always obtained correct results." (98: p. 85) (We must point out that when this was written, *half a century* had already passed since Cauchy proposed a rigorous foundation for differential and integral calculus and his ideas had long become textbook knowledge.)

"Mathematical axioms are an expression of an extremely limited intellectual content, which mathematics is obliged to borrow from logic. They may be reduced to the following two:

"1. The whole is larger than the part. . . .

"2. Two quantities separately equal to a third are equal to one another." (98: p. 34)

(It would seem that even a mediocre secondary school student ought to have remembered at least the axiom on parallels!)

As for political economy or history, Marx and Engels clearly did not believe that they had "not sufficiently mastered" these subjects; nothing prompted them to be "careful" as with mathematics. One may well imagine how resolutely they operated in these areas.

The correspondence between Marx and Engels provides further striking examples of views that are extremely difficult to reconcile with the usual understanding of the scientific method. For instance, Engels points out to Marx one passage in *Capital* that would obviously provoke objections and suggests this objection be taken into account. Marx replies: "Had I wished to foresee all objections of that kind I should have spoiled the dialectical method of exposition. On the contrary. This method has the advantage of setting traps for these gentlemen at every step and compelling them to reveal their impenetrable stupidity." (3: XXIII: p. 425)

Or in another letter to Engels: "Dear Fred! In my opinion you are unjustly afraid to treat the English philistine reader of the magazine to such simple formulae as M-G-M, etc. If you were compelled to read, as I am, the economic articles of Lalor, Herbert Spencer, Macleod and others in *The Westminster Review,* you would see that they all abound in economic banalities (all the while knowing that their reader is thoroughly bored with it all) and that they try to spice up their articles with pseudo-philosophic or pseudo-scientific jargon. Despite the imagined scientific character, the content (equal to nothing, of course) becomes in no sense clearer. On the contrary, the trick is to mystify the reader." This paragraph closes with the advice: "In fact, you are too shy. The new is required—the new in form and in content." (3: XXIV: pp. 60–61)

It is interesting to juxtapose the attitude of Marxism toward science with a closely related question—Marx's use of Hegel's dialectical method. Here we may again refer to S. Bulgakov. In a work already cited (100), he shows that *Capital,* especially the first chapter of Volume I, is written in a Hegelian fashion but that, at the same time, it demonstrates a very superficial grasp of Hegel's philosophy and of German classical philosophy in general, a quite primitive manipulation of subtle and profound categories. In fact, Marx at times seems to see dialectics in a quite unexpected light.

"I took the risk of prognosticating in this way, as I was compelled to substitute for you as correspondent at the *Tribune.* Nota bene— on the supposition that the dispatches we have gotten up till now are correct. It is possible that I may be discredited. But in that case it will still be possible to pull through with the help of a bit of dialectics. It goes without saying that I phrased my forecasts in such a way that I would prove to be right also in the opposite case." (3: XXII: p. 217)

Returning to the comparison of Fourier's "scientific method" with Marx's, it must be stated that in some instances they differ very little— e.g., in their use of mathematics. Take, for instance, the argument Fourier gives in support of his idea that society is ruled on the "basis of geometric principles":

"The properties of friendship duplicate the properties of the circle.

"The properties of love, those of the ellipse.

"The properties of fatherhood, of the parabola.

"The properties of ambition, of the hyperbola.

"The collective properties of these four passions duplicate the properties of the cycloid."

This is quite comparable with the passage in *Capital* in which Marx writes (in connection with one of his conclusions): "This law clearly runs counter to experience." But he extricates himself from the predicament as follows: "The solution of this seeming contradiction requires many more intermediary links, as in elementary algebra, where many intermediary links are required to comprehend that $\frac{0}{0}$ may represent a real quantity." (3: XVII: p. 337)* Karl Jaspers is closer to the truth, no doubt, when he sees Marxism not as science but as "mythmaking" based on certain notions borrowed from magic, as for instance the belief that the destruction of the existing world will lead to the birth of new man. (101)

The concept of "the scientific method" was of extraordinary importance for the development of nineteenth-century socialism. Hence it was steadily and persistently elaborated, first by Fourier and Saint-Simon (in a very naïve form), and later in a much more sophisticated manner by Marx and Engels. The scientific method provided the socialist doctrines with a "sanction" of the first order. Furthermore (and this is especially important), the theses of socialist doctrine thereby

---

* Marx employs this unusual argumentation in a passage that is by no means secondary in importance for his system. His theory of value, a cornerstone of his political-economic theory, proved to be in complete contradiction to well-known facts of economic life! Concerning Marx's promises to present further evidence (or "intermediary links") on the question, the Italian economist Loria wrote: "I have justly asserted that this second volume with which Marx constantly threatens his opponents, and which, however, will never appear, was most probably employed as a cunning subterfuge in those cases where Marx lacked scientific arguments." In the sixteen years that separate the publication of Volume I of *Capital* from his death, Marx did not offer a continuation of his study. In 1885, Engels published Marx's manuscripts as the second volume of *Capital*. In the preface, he mentions the contradiction cited above and remarks that "because of this contradiction the Ricardo school and 'vulgar economy' collapsed." Marx, so Engels claimed, resolved this contradiction in Volume III, which was to appear in several months. Volume III appeared in 1894—i.e., nine years later. In his preface, Engels again returns to the "contradiction" and quotes Loria in this connection. He points out that in the preface to Volume II, this question was "publicly proposed" by him and that, therefore, Loria might have taken this into account. . . . But Engels does not mention his own promise that the contradiction would be resolved in Volume III, nor does he indicate the place where it is resolved. In reference to Loria, however, he does use such expressions as: "falsification," "distortion," "mistakes unforgivable in a schoolboy," "careerist," "scientific charlatan," "shamelessness," "literary adventurer who in his heart of hearts spits on the whole of political economy," "a conscious sophist," "a braggart," "an irresistible rush to appropriate the works of others," "importunate charlatanism of self-aggrandizement," "success achieved with the help of clamorous friends," etc.

acquired the appearance of objectivity and a certain inevitability, being presented as a consequence of immanent laws independent of human will. In calling for the destruction of society, revolutionaries of the Babeuf and Bakunin type had to argue that it was loathsome and unjust. But in doing so, they made each person a judge and left open the opportunity for the counter-argument that the process of destruction itself was even more loathsome and unjust. But when, for example, Bukharin (102) proclaimed that execution by shooting constituted one of the forms for the "elaboration of communist humanity," he was invulnerable from the Marxist point of view. Indeed, Engels could think of only one function in history for the concept of justice—as a phrase useful for agitation. (98: p. 352) How, then, is one to verify an expert in Marxism like Bukharin? Perhaps his method of elaborating communist humanity does proceed from the "immanent laws" or the "dialectics of production?"

In the contemporary world, hypnotized as it is by the notion that science can solve any question and sanction any action, will many find the courage in such a situation to adhere to the unscientific ten commandments rather than to the scientifically proved "immanent law"?

It was natural enough, therefore, that socialist Marxists of the nineteenth century were highly attracted to science as the supreme sanctioning authority. In particular, Marx and Engels, with their prodigious energy and capacity for work, processed huge amounts of data from the fields of political economy and history. But what they were seeking in science was not the source but the confirmation and sanction of the age-old theses of socialist ideology. The logic of their endeavor is explicitly stated in the preface to *Anti-Dühring:*

"In 1831, in Lyons, the first uprising of workers took place; in the period between 1833 and 1842, the English Chartist movement, the first national working movement, reached its climax. . . . It was impossible not to take all these facts into consideration, as well as French and English Socialism, which constituted their theoretical, albeit extremely imperfect expression." (98: p. 21) "Although it criticized the capitalist mode of production and its consequences, the socialism of earlier periods could not cope with it. It could only pronounce it to be good for nothing. But the task is twofold: on the one hand, to explain the inevitability of the appearance of the capitalist mode of production in its historical context and thus to show why its death is inevitable;

on the other hand, to explain the hitherto unclear nature of that production. Previous criticism has been directed more toward the harmful consequences than against capitalist production itself." (98: p. 22)

Marxism here emerges not as a result of objective scientific research but as a response to a set task—to prove the inevitability of the collapse of capitalism and its replacement by socialism. This task became relevant for the creators of Marxism as the result of a series of labor disturbances in Europe.

3. *Socialism is the theory of preparing and implementing revolution: it is a series of rules which must be followed in order to seize power. At the same time, it is the technology of power, the philosophy of the absolute state to which all life is subjected—i.e., statism.*

In contrast to the views considered earlier, serious arguments may be brought forward in support of this point of view. It is difficult to deny that socialist doctrines constitute a powerful driving force capable of inspiring masses of people and serving as a means of seizing power. Furthermore, many socialist utopias describe a society in which all aspects of the citizen's life are controlled by the state, while socialist states carry out these ideals to a certain extent. In some cases (for example, in Shang Yang's teaching), it is impossible to draw a line between certain aspects of socialism and statism taken to an extreme—if all of life is controlled by the state, the degree to which private property is legally permitted ceases to be significant.

The first objection aroused by such a definition is not based on specific arguments but is primarily aesthetic. The characterization seems far too shallow in comparison with the phenomenon it seeks to explain; it recalls the view of religion as the "contrivance of priests." Furthermore, many actual features of socialism cannot be accounted for by this means.

In fact, viewing the socialist doctrines as a technique for seizing power leaves the basic principles of socialism unexplained. How is one to interpret the principle of *communality* of property from this point of view? In order to gain control over a poverty-ridden tattered mob, it is far more natural to promise a *redivision* of property—such was the character of social upheavals in antiquity. The slogan of communality could even turn out to be an obstacle to taking power, as was the case in the revolution of 1917, when the Bolshevik Party, which until April of that year had advocated nationalizing land, temporarily retreated from this position and accepted the S.R. principle of "equalized land use" in order to assure victory in October.

The call for communal wives is equally inexplicable from this perspective. In the *Communist Manifesto*, Marx and Engels say that the entire bourgeoisie accused the Communists of intending to introduce communality of wives. Why did they not reply to this accusation less ambiguously than they did? They wrote: "Bourgeois marriage is in reality a system of wives in common and thus at the most, what the Communists might possibly be reproached with is that they desire to introduce, in substitution for a hypocritically concealed, an openly legalized communality of women."

This obviously leaves the impression that the reproach is true. Indeed, this passage caused so much trouble later that numerous "elucidations" were required. (The sort of problem that arose is illustrated by the fact that in the second Russian edition of the works of Marx and Engels, published in 1955, this text was altered to read: ". . . what the Communists might possibly be reproached with is *the allegation* that . . .") Why were these accusations not simply declared bourgeois slander? And what is most remarkable of all, such an idea did in fact occur to Engels. He raises precisely this question in "Principles of Communism," his first draft of the Manifesto. But later, after he met with Marx, the text was changed.

There are many other particular features of socialist doctrine that remain completely incomprehensible, if one looks at socialism solely as a method of seizing power. One example is the notion of the "forerunners of scientific socialism," which plays an important role in Marxism. Why was it necessary for Marx, Engels, Kautsky, Bernstein and others to declare Plato, Dolcino, Müntzer and More their forerunners? What strange logic, for example, made Kautsky, speaking of proletarian movements that came to power "too early," exclaim: "They are all dear to us, from the Anabaptists to the Paris Communards." (103: p. 166) Nothing could be more obviously contrary to their view of socialism as a product of the contradiction between production forces and production relations under capitalism. It would seem that they should have denied any connection; any common features could have been declared to be a matter of coincidence.

It is impossible to suppose that such obvious theoretical difficulties went unnoticed by the founders of socialism. Evidently, the concept of forerunners contained something essential to the ideology—some elements that had to be preserved at any cost, even at the risk of doctrinal inconsistencies. And this indicates that certain strata of socialist ideology cannot be understood in terms of any coldly calculated plan for the seizure of power.

It is possible to come to power preaching religious ideas (as the example of Mohammed shows) or by taking advantage of national feelings, but we do not therefore think of either of these routes to power as mere means.

Furthermore, the view of socialism as the ideology of an absolute state makes incomprehensible one of the main properties of socialist doctrines—their infectiousness, their capacity to influence the masses. It would be absurd to suppose that people face torture and the gallows or go to the barricades for the sake of becoming a soulless cog in the all-powerful state machine. Moreover, the large proportion of socialist doctrines belongs to the *anarchical-nihilistic* tendency, which is quite hostile to the idea of state control. Such is the spirit that informs the medieval heresies, the movements of the Reformation period, Meslier, Deschamps, Fourier, Bakunin and numerous modern socialist movements.

4. The last objections apply fully to the view that *socialist states are a manifestation of a social structure based on compulsory labor.* This idea is expressed, for instance, by R. Vipper in his book *Kommunizm i kultura* [*Communism and Culture*], which was published shortly after the Revolution. (This book is presently inaccessible to me and I am obliged to cite from memory.) Vipper suggests that socialism should be regarded not as a prophecy about a happy *future* society but as a real social structure which has appeared *in the past* more than once. His examples: ancient Egypt, the Inca state, the Jesuit state in Paraguay . . . In his opinion, compulsory labor is the cornerstone of all these societies.

It is true that noneconomic compulsion, to a greater or lesser degree, plays a significant role in all socialist states. But one would like to discover not only the sort of trait that would serve as a distinguishing feature but some relevant property that would render their other essential features comprehensible. Yet the presence of compulsory labor in no way explains either the attraction of socialist ideology or such of its principles as the destruction of the family or of hierarchy.

5. *Socialism as such does not exist. That which is called socialism is one of the lines of development of capitalism—state capitalism.*

The evident defect of this point of view is that it applies only to the socialist states of the twentieth century, without any effort to ascertain the place of these states within the millennia-long tradition of socialism. But it would be interesting to determine to what degree this view is applicable even to this admittedly short period of history.

Wittfogel believes that the concept of state capitalism is not pertinent to contemporary socialist states. From the point of view of economics, he asserts, it is impossible to consider capitalist a society in which there are neither private means of production nor any open market for goods and manpower.

The inadequacy of this approach is even more apparent when one takes into consideration the basic point that socialism, unlike capitalism, is not merely an economic formation but is also, and perhaps first of all, an ideology. Indeed, we have never heard of "capitalist parties" or "capitalist doctrines." The ideological character of socialism is a basic factor in the activities of the socialist states. Their policy is far from being determined only by economic factors or by state interests. History provided a clear-cut experiment a few years ago, when the governments of two countries in the same socialist camp simultaneously permitted themselves to deviate from group policy. The deviation of one of these states was purely ideological, while the other state preserved a complete ideological conformity but demonstratively asserted the independence of its foreign policy. As a result, drastic measures were taken against the first state, while the other only benefited from its policy. Another example of political action motivated by ideological principles is the support given by the socialist states to revolutionary socialist movements and newly formed socialist states. And this in spite of considerable experience which shows that this is the way to create the most dangerous rivals, aggressive and armed with more radical ideology.

We shall point out only one more crucial peculiarity of socialist states, something that has no analogy in capitalist society: all socialist states are based on a "new type" of parity. We have here a phenomenon that is completely different, despite its name, from the political parties of bourgeois society. Members of liberal or radical parties are united by a desire to realize definite political or economic ends, without circumscribing their conduct or views in other areas. In this sense, they are guided by the same kind of principles as trade unions or animal protection societies. The "new type" of party, however, not only demands that its members subordinate *all* aspects of their lives to it, but also develops in them an outlook according to which life outside the party seems in general *unthinkable*. The spirit of the special relationship that exists between the individual and the party may be gleaned from the following three examples.

A German essayist, W. Schlamm, relates that in 1919, at the age of fifteen, he became a "fellow traveler" of the Communists but never managed to penetrate into the narrow circle of the party functionaries (104). Twenty years later, one of these functionaries, who had broken with the party, explained to Schlamm the reason why. When Schlamm was invited to join the party, he had said: "I'm ready to give the party everything but the two evenings of the week when I listen to Mozart." This answer proved fatal! A man who has interests he does not wish to subordinate to the party does not fit.

Another aspect of the relationship between party and individual is revealed by Trotsky's last speech at a Party Congress. He had already been defeated by his opponents. He said: "I know that it is impossible to be right against the party. It is possible to be right only with the party, for history has created no other road for the realization of what is right." (105: p. 167)

Finally, here is how Piatakov, already expelled from the party and in disgrace, described his view of the party to his former party comrade Valentinov. Piatakov reminded him of Lenin's statement that the "dictatorship of the proletariat is a regime implemented by the party, which relies on violence and is not bound by any law." (From the article "The Proletarian Revolution and the Renegade Kautsky.") Piatakov explained that the central idea here was not "violence" but the fact of being "unbound by any law." He says:

> Everything that bears the imprint of human will must not and cannot be considered inviolable or tied to any insuperable law. A law is a limit, a ban, a definition of one phenomenon admissible and another inadmissible, one action possible and the other impossible. When thought holds to violence in principle and is psychologically free, unbound by any laws, limits or obstacles, then the field of possible action expands to gigantic proportions and the field of the impossible contracts to the point of zero. . . . Bolshevism is a party whose idea is to bring into life that which is considered impossible, not realizable and inadmissible. . . . For the honor and happiness of being in its ranks we must sacrifice our pride and self-esteem and everything

else. Returning to the party, we put out of our heads all convictions condemned by it, even though we defended them while in opposition. . . . I agree that non-Bolsheviks and the category of ordinary people in general cannot make any instantaneous change, any reversal or amputation of their convictions. . . . We are a party of men who make the impossible possible. Steeped in the idea of violence, we direct it against ourselves, and if the party demands it and if it is necessary and important for the party, we can by an act of will put out of our heads in twenty-four hours ideas that we have cherished for years. In suppressing one's convictions or tossing them aside, it is necessary to reorient oneself in the shortest possible time in such a way as to agree, inwardly, with one's whole mind. . . . Is it easy to put out of mind things that only yesterday you considered to be right and which today you must consider to be false in order to be in full accord with the party? Of course not. Nevertheless, through violence directed against oneself, the necessary result is achieved. Giving up life, shooting oneself through the head, are mere trifles compared with this other manifestation of will. . . . This sort of violence against the self is acutely painful, but such violence with the aim of breaking oneself so as to be in full accord with the party constitutes the essence of a truly principled Bolshevik Communist. I am familiar with objections of the following kind. The party may be absolutely mistaken, it is said, it might call black something that is clearly and indisputably white. To all those who try to foist this example on me, I say: *Yes, I shall consider black something that I felt and considered to be white, since outside the party, outside accord with it, there is no life for me.* (106: p. 148)

Some entomologists (see, for example, 107: pp. 110–115) believe that the functioning of a beehive can only be understood in terms of a *superorganism* having its own metabolism and respiration and capable of reproduction and of the kind of action quite impossible for individual bees (for instance, holding the temperature within to the necessary narrow range around 34°C.). The existence of each bee has meaning only to the extent that it is involved with the life of the entire hive. We are no less justified in considering the parties of the socialist states to be similar *superorganisms* capable of performing actions impossible and unthinkable for its individual human cells. Their life has meaning only when they are carrying out the aims of the superorganism without which they cannot exist.

This enables us to understand the enigmatic psychology, described so precisely by Solzhenitsyn, of the "orthodox" true believer who even in a concentration camp continues to glorify Stalin and the party.

Any such world view is, of course, utterly alien to rational capitalism. It is not among the Tories and Whigs that the forerunners of the "new type" of party must be sought, but in the Society of Jesus or among the medieval sects, with whom they also have some common organizational traits.

The presence of such a party seems to be a necessary condition for the existence of all socialist states of the twentieth century, while in capitalist countries it serves as one of the main instruments of destruction. This points to cardinal differences between the two social structures.

### 6. Socialism is the expression of the quest for social justice.

It is an indisputable fact that almost all socialist doctrines and movements assign an extremely important role to protest against the injustices of the contemporary social order. Sympathy for the oppressed and the condemnation of oppressors are motifs that may be found in the works of Müntzer (especially in his "Discourse for Defense"), More (in Part One of *Utopia*), Winstanley, Meslier, Fourier, Bakunin, Marx and the Marxists.

Many who are not supporters of socialism (or who accept it only partially) also see its main driving force in its advocacy of justice. For example, the prime minister of India, responding to a correspondent who inquired what the word "socialism" meant to him, answered: "Justice. Yes, socialism means justice, the desire to work in a more equal society." To a certain extent this point of view is shared by Karl Jaspers: "Socialism today is seen as that quest, tendency or plan which has as its aim universal cooperation and coexistence in the spirit of justice and in the absence of privilege. In this sense, today, everyone is a socialist—socialism is the main tendency of our time." (108)

But Jaspers distinguishes socialism in the sense of gradual progress from communism, which preaches total planning and the achieving of happiness for humanity according to a scientific prognosis.

The view of socialism as an attempt to achieve social justice was widespread in Russian philosophy. For instance, Vladimir Soloviev wrote: "The attempt of socialism to achieve the equality of rights in material welfare, its efforts to transfer this material welfare from the hands of the minority into the hands of the popular majority, is absolutely natural and legitimate from the point of view of the principles proclaimed by the French revolution and which underlie all modern civilization." (109: III: pp. 7–8) While he rejects socialism's claim to being a supreme moral force, Soloviev does acknowledge that it "has the character of morality in its demand for social truth. . . . In any case, socialism is right to rise up against existing social untruth." (109: III: p. 9) It is here that he evidently sees that "truth of socialism" which must be recognized in order to vanquish the "lie of socialism."

Bulgakov, a former Marxist himself, developed this view of socialism in detail, especially in a pamphlet (110) that appeared in 1917, while the Revolution was at its height. Socialism, in his opinion, is a reaction to the misery, hunger and suffering of mankind. It is the thought that "first of all one must defeat hunger and break the chains of poverty." (110: p. 5) Man is the prisoner of natural forces and his spirit longs for liberation from that captivity. Socialism shows him the way. It promises "freedom from economic factors . . . through economic factors, by means of the so-called development of productive forces." (110: p. 9) But this is a false promise. "The economic captivity of man is not a root cause but a consequence; it is called forth by the shift in man's relation to nature—the result of the sinful corruption of the human essence. Death came into the world; life became mortal, whence appeared man's fateful dependence on food and the forces of nature, control over which will not save him from death." (110: p. 11)

The idea of socialism was foreshadowed in Christ's first temptation. By "turning stones into bread," Christ would have become an earthly Messiah, who instead of overcoming the sinful condition of the world would have submitted to that condition. This temptation, to which a considerable part of modern mankind has yielded, constitutes the spiritual essence of socialism. But every temptation contains within itself some truth. In this case, it is a protest against human bondage to matter and the suffering that ensues from it. The positive meaning of socialism, however, is extremely limited. Bulgakov writes: "Socialism cannot be seen as a radical reform of life; it is *philanthropy*, or one form of it, evoked by modern life—and nothing more. The triumph of socialism would introduce *nothing essential* to life." (110: p. 41)

Let us now move to a consideration of these views. First of all, it seems that socialism can by no means be *identified* simply with a striving for justice nor with a reaction to the suffering of mankind. This is already clear from the fact that we would not need to invent a new term for such a desire: "compassion," "sympathy," "active love," are all old-fashioned words quite suitable for the definition of this equally old aspiration. But let us assume for a moment that socialism is a definite way to achieve social justice. In that case we should be able to see numerous confirmations of this fact in the known socialist doctrines as well as in the experience of the socialist states. Since it is unquestionably true that appeals to justice and the condemnation of the defects of contemporary life occupy a central place in socialist ideology, this question must be formulated more precisely: *Is the aspiration for social justice the goal and the driving force of socialism or is the appeal to this aspiration only a means to achieve some other goals?*

To simplify our argumentation, we exclude from our discussion the practice of socialist states. After all, if it could be shown that dreams of socialist justice have not been realized in these states, that would not in itself contradict the possibility that these dreams did inspire the participants and the leaders of socialist movements: Life has a way of deceiving the best-laid plans. But in the socialist doctrines themselves, at least, we should uncover compassion for the sufferings of the victims of injustice and the impulse to lighten their burden. Yet this is precisely what is lacking! The alleviation of suffering is set aside until the victory of the socialist ideal, and all attempts to improve life at the present time are condemned as possibly postponing the coming victory. Particularly in the modern socialist doctrines proclaiming atheism, this point of view is in no way compatible with compassion for *today's* victims of oppression, who will have no share in the future just society. It will be objected that striving to achieve justice in life for *future* generations is the very thing that inspires the followers of socialism. This point of view seems hardly plausible from a psychological point of view. We are asked to believe that a man can be indifferent to the suffering of those around him and at the same time devote his life to the happiness of a future world he will never see.

We list below several examples illustrating the approach of socialist doctrine toward the injustice of their day.

The Cathars, whose doctrines included some elements of socialism, categorically forbade charity, in stark contrast to the theory and practice of the Catholic Church. In the Cathar sects the "faithful" were obliged to make numerous donations but only to the leadership, the "perfect." This doctrinal feature is extremely old and, consequently, is linked to the sect's fundamental precepts. We meet the same principle among the Manicheans, in the second century A.D.

The society of the Moravian Brethren is a vivid example of the strictest community of property and of all aspects of life. In the sect's voluminous writings, Christ's law of brotherly love is often mentioned, but it is never used to justify communality. On the contrary, the demand for communality is closely linked to the striving for suffering. Communality is perceived not as an expression of compassion, but as a "yoke," a voluntary cross. Communist life is a narrow path, leading through suffering to salvation.

Turning to the humanist literature, we might point to Thomas More, who gave a detailed commentary on the suffering of the poor; he condemned unjust life as a "conspiracy of the rich" and formulated a thesis, which later became popular, to the effect that criminality is in reality a crime of the unjust society. At the same time, he suggested what he thought was a more just approach: criminals should be made into slaves! Just how familiar More was with the life of the common folk is indicated by his list of idle parasites in society, in which women appear first.

The history of the socialist movement in Russia serves as another striking example. The appearance of revolutionary nihilist circles coincides exactly in time with the abolition of serfdom. The peasants were liberated in 1861. Chernyshevsky's "Appeal to the Peasants of Landowners" appeared in the same year and his "To Young Russia," where the style and spirit of the new movement were formulated, appeared in 1862. Chernyshevsky and others openly explained their antipathy to the reform of 1861 by asserting that a certain improvement in the peasants' lot might turn them from the revolutionary path. Somewhat later we have Nechayev proclaiming the following: "The government itself might at any moment come upon the idea of reducing taxes or instituting similar benefits. That would be a real misfortune, because even under the present terrible conditions the folk are slow to rise. But give them a little more pocket change, set things up even one cow better, and everything will be delayed another ten years. And all our work will be lost. On the contrary, you should use any opportunity to oppress the people, the way the contractors do, for example." (111: p. 137)

Apropos of the attempt to effect a socialist coup in France, Bakunin wrote: "Frenchmen themselves, even the workers, were not inspired by it; the doctrine seemed too frightening. It was, in fact, too weak. They should have suffered greater misery and disturbances. Circumstances are coming together in such a way that there will be no shortage of that. Perhaps then the Devil will awaken." (Letter to Ogarev, 1871, 95: p. 246)

This pronouncement coincides with the views contained in the writings of the Moravian Brothers: there should be no attempt to seek release from suffering since suffering is essential in achieving the supreme goal. There is of course an important difference—the Moravian Brethren saw the goal in Christ, while Bakunin uses different terminology.

Finally we come to Marxism. Despite the role that the exposure of the injustice, cruelty and inhumanity of capitalism plays in it, we can encounter quite similar views. Thus, in the article "Exposé of the Cologne Trial of Communists," Marx writes: "We say to workers: you must survive fifteen, twenty, fifty years of civil war and international strife not only to change existing relations but to change yourselves and become capable of political supremacy." (3: VIII: p. 506) If we recall the cruelty and hunger which were the consequence of three years of civil war in Russia, we may imagine vaguely what those fifty years of civil war would mean—the years that the workers *must* survive, according to Marx. In describing the terrible living conditions of the workers of the day, Marx and Engels showed no interest in any improvement. On the contrary, they actually tried to see features of the future society in these conditions. It was impossible for the worker to have an uninterrupted family life? Well, in the future society the bourgeois family will wither away. Proletarian children were compelled to work? In the future society children would "combine education with productive labor." At a time when "bourgeois philanthropists" such as Dickens and Carlyle were fighting against child labor, the Geneva Congress of the First International adopted a resolution composed by Marx: "The Congress regards the tendency of contemporary industry to draw on the labor of children and juveniles of both sexes in the great task of social production as a progressive, sound and lawful tendency, though under the rule of capitalism it turns into a terrible evil. In a rationally organized society, each child from the age of nine ought to be a productive worker." (Cited in 112)

In the correspondence between Marx and Engels there are numerous utterances in the following vein:

"Dear Engels! I have just received your letter which brings up the very pleasant prospect of a trade crisis." (Marx to Engels, 3: XXI:

p. 228) "It would be a good thing to have a bad harvest next year in addition, and then the real fun will begin." (Engels to Marx, 3: XII: p. 249) "It's the same with me. Since the beginning of the crash in New York, I could find no rest in Jersey and feel fine amidst the general breakdown. The crisis will be as useful for my organism as the sea baths." (Engels to Marx, 3: XXII: p. 255) "There is an improved mood in the market. May this be damned!" (Engels to Marx, 3: XXII: p. 295) "Here only two or three very bad years could help, but it seems that they won't be quick to come." (Engels to Marx, 3: XXII: p. 368) "Our fatherland presents an extremely pitiful sight. Without being battered from outside, nothing can be done with these dogs." (Marx to Engels, 3: XXIII: p. 162)

During World War I, Lenin wrote as follows about war: "If the war now evokes among reactionary Christian socialists and the whimpering petite bourgeoisie only horror and fright, only an aversion to any use of arms, to blood, death and so on, then we must answer that capitalist society has always been and remains *a horror without end*. And if now the most reactionary of all wars is preparing an *end with horror* to this society, we have no reason to fall into despair." (113: XXX: p. 136)

It is striking how socialist thinkers, in exposing injustice and exploitation of the people, refer so often to these very people with contempt and even malice. For instance, Meslier wrote on the cover of his *Testament:* "I came to know the errors and the misdeeds, the vanity and the stupidity of the people. I hated and despised them." Describing the peasants' suffering, he wrote: "It is justly said of them that there is nothing more corrupt, more crude and more deserving of contempt." (114: p. 56) Fourier calls the same French peasants "living automatons" and adds: "In their extreme crudity, they are nearer to animals than to the human race." (97: p. 93) In a letter to Marx, Engels calls the peasants Germanic bumpkins. (3: XXI: p. 39) And the French peasants are referred to as "a barbaric race," that is "by no means interested in the form of government, etc., striving first of all to destroy the tax collector's house . . . to rape his wife and to beat him to death if they should manage to catch him." (Letter to Marx, 3: XXI: p. 312) About the workers he writes: "The masses are frightfully stupid." (Letter to Marx, 3: XXIV: p. 160) Speaking of certain unjust contracts, Marx for his part calls them "contracts to which only the completely degenerate rabble could agree." (Letter to Engels, 3: XXIV: p. 30)

Another time he exclaims: "To hell with these popular movements, especially if they are pacifist into the bargain. The Chartist movement drove O'Connor mad (have you read his last speech at the trial?) made Garny weak in the head and caused Johnson to go bankrupt. *Voilà le dernier but de la vie dans tous les mouvements populaires.*" (Letter to Engels, 3: XXI: p. 328)

It is possible to suggest various logical explanations for such statements, but it is absolutely improbable psychologically to consider that they are engendered by compassion for the people or by sympathy for the victims of hunger and war. And we can see that the main achievements in social justice of the last century in the West—the reduction of the working day, social insurance, an extraordinary rise in the living standard of the workers—were accomplished with very little participation on the part of socialist movements. The main factors were the struggle of the trade unions (condemned by the socialists as "economism"), increased productivity of labor due to technological progress, and the moral influence of "bourgeois philanthropy."

How, then, is socialist ideology connected with the idea of struggle for social justice? It seems that we have here two quite different approaches toward life which, nevertheless, intersect in a certain area. Their point of contact is the condemnation of social injustice and the exposure of the suffering it brings. From this starting point, they develop in two entirely different directions, one being the path of correcting social injustice, the struggle against the concrete evils of the present. The other path regards social injustice as an absolute evil, an indication that the existing world is doomed and must be completely destroyed. Sympathy for the victims of injustice is more and more squeezed out of the picture by all-consuming hatred of the existing social structure.

### 7. Socialism as a special religion

Bulgakov, among others, formulated this thought in the following way: "For socialism nowadays emerges not only as a natural area of social policy but usually also as a religion, one based on atheism and the deification of man and man's labor and on recognition of the elemental forces of Nature and social life and as the only meaningful principle of history." (115: p. 36) More specifically, Bulgakov believes, socialism can be seen as a rebirth of Judaic Messianism. "Karl Marx, along with Lassalle, are the proclaimers of the apocalypse in fashionable dress, the announcers of the Messianic Kingdom." (110: p. 17; Bulgakov treats this idea in greater detail in his "Apocalyptics and Socialism," in the collection *Two Cities*, Volume II). Semyon Frank also calls revolutionary socialism "a religion of absolute realization of the people's happiness" and the "religion of service to material interests." Frank points to "a train of thought which unites nihilistic morality with the religion of socialism." (116: p. 192) An analogous point of view is developed by Berdiaev in the article "Marxism and Religion."

Such a view was expressed occasionally by the adherents of socialism themselves, for instance, by the social democrat participants in the "God-building" [*bogostroitel'stvo*] tendency at the beginning of this century. Bazarov, Gorky and Lunacharsky took part in this attempt to link Marxism and religion. A book by G. Le Bon (117) is based on the same view. Among more recent works, this approach is taken, for instance, in 118.

A forceful argument can be made for this definition. For example, the religious aspects of socialism may explain the extraordinary attraction of socialist doctrines and their capacity to inflame individuals and to inspire popular movements. It is precisely these aspects of socialism which cannot be explained when socialism is regarded as a political or economic category. Socialism's pretensions to be a universal world view comprising and explaining everything (from the transformation of a liquid into steam to the appearance of Christianity) also make it akin to religion. A characteristic of religion is socialism's view of history not as a chaotic phenomenon but as an entity that has a goal, a meaning and a justification. In other words, both socialism and religion view history teleologically. Bulgakov draws our attention to numerous and far-reaching analogies between socialism (especially Marxism) and Judaic apocalyptics and eschatology. Finally, socialism's hostility toward traditional religion hardly contradicts this judgment—it may simply be a matter of animosity between rival religions.

However, all these arguments indicate only that socialism and religion have some important features in common. They do not prove that the basic traits of socialism can be *reduced* to a religion. And in point of fact, there are a number of cardinal distinctions that set them apart.

In the first place, religion proceeds from concrete experience: the religious feelings of people who then describe these feelings as an encounter with God. Such experiences on the part of individuals gifted in this respect become fixed and are passed on to others in the form of a cult, of a tradition and of theological literature. It would be of great interest if it could be established that similar experiences lie at the root of socialist philosophy, but we hear nothing of the kind. And this in itself is a clear objective difference between the socialist world view and religion. For even if such experiences do occur within socialism, those to whom it is accessible categorically deny the fact. The most prominent representatives of socialist ideology either adhere to a rational outlook (in recent centuries) or profess some other, nonsocialist religion (earlier).

An even more radical contrast between socialism and religion emerges from their views of the essence of man and his role in their respective "anthropologies." All religions proceed from a recognition of some higher meaning in life, some goal deriving from a higher sphere. Presupposing the existence of God and the possibility of man's communication with Him, religion thereby admits a certain commensurability between God and man, which is indispensable if only to make possible some sort of contact. (An ant, for instance, cannot enter into contact with man.) Socialism, on the other hand, proceeds in almost all its manifestations from the assumption that the basic principles guiding the life of an individual and of mankind in general do not go beyond the satisfaction of material needs or primitive instincts. What is more, this view becomes more explicit, the more clearly formulated the given socialist ideology. Below, we shall cite several illustrations of this tendency.

With Plato, *justice* was still among the basic organizing principles in the ideal state. The ideology of medieval heresies included spiritual goals, although they generally set God and the world at such odds that the *earthly* activity of man came to be devoid of any higher meaning. But More recognized (or more precisely, he wrote that the Utopians recognized) satisfaction as the supreme goal in life. Still, More does believe that a reasonable man can refuse lesser satisfactions in order to receive greater ones from God. However, this line of reasoning soon brings us to Fourier's doctrine, according to which the satisfaction of instincts (or as he puts it, passions) is the only goal and even the basic force shaping human society.

According to Fourier, all instincts are equally fruitful and useful for society—it is only necessary to combine them and direct them in the proper way: "There is not a single useless or bad passion; all personalities are good as they are." (97: p. 292) "Passions, whatever they might be—even the most repulsive—both in man and in animals, lead to their various consequences according to geometrical principles observed by God." (97: p. 60) As a result, citizens who are most useful to the societal mechanism are those "who are most inclined to refined pleasures and who boldly give themselves up to the satisfaction of their passions." (97: p. 292) The future "combined" social structure is built along the same lines: "In the eighteen communities of the combined structure, the trait that is the most useful for the triumph of truth is love of wealth." (97: p. 95) "The whole arrangement of the combined structure will be the direct opposite of our habits and will compel the encouragement of everything we call vice, for instance, the passion for sweets and the pleasures of love." (97: p. 96)

The moral principles restricting freedom of expression of instincts are harmful. In particular, there is nothing so harmful as the sense of duty invented by philosophers. "All these philosophical whims called *duty* have nothing to do with truth; duty proceeds from people, while attraction proceeds from God. If you want to recognize God's intentions, study attraction, only nature, and do not accept duty." (97: p. 98) The functioning of society is to be ensured by placing people in situations in which what is advantageous for them will be for the benefit of all. At this point even the most dishonest man will become a useful member of society. "Show him that he can earn a thousand écus by lying and three thousand by the truth, and he will prefer the truth no matter what a cheat he is." (97: p. 96)

It is revealing, however, that Fourier *refuses* to recognize the existence of clearly instinctive attractions if they engender acts which do not fit an egoistic framework. For instance, he never speaks about love as such but only about the "delights of love" or about "amorousness." He considers the feelings of parent for child and child for parent to be mere invention. "Since he does not know the 'act' that is at the basis of his paternity, the child cannot experience filial feelings." Parents, for their part, love only "the recollection of past delights connected with conception." A child cannot feel "indebted to parents to whom he has given so much delight unshared by him, delight of which people want to deprive him at the best time of his life." (97: p. 100)

It is possible to consider Fourier as an immediate predecessor of Freud: in his striving to understand man and human society in the light of the most primitive instincts, in a pathological underdevelopment of the emotional sphere which prevents any appreciation for the higher aspects of the human psyche, in the hypertrophied role he ascribes to relations between the sexes. (According to Fourier, even economics ought to be based on attracting young people into labor armies by the prospect of love affairs; in this way huge industrial building projects could be carried out.) Of course, Fourier's mythological construct describing the cooperation of man and the cosmos finds no continuation in Freud's works. (As we shall see below, Freud had his own mythology.) But while Fourier, with the infantilism so characteristic of him, sees amid "the passions we call vices" nothing more terrible than "passion for sweets and the delights of love," Freud goes much further. Among the forces to which he attempts to reduce culture and the spiritual life of man, Freud does not bypass either malice or lust for domination, destruction or the death wish. He considers all culture to be based on the suppression of the instincts—the deepest part of the human psyche, which strives to act according to the "pleasure principle." Unhappiness, in Freud's view, is a necessary cost for civilization. Happiness does not fall within the range of cultural values. Moral norms, elaborated by that part of the psyche that is of later, cultural, origin, are factors which are destructive and mortally dangerous to the organism. Freud compares morals with products of decay which are manufactured by a cell and then become the cause of its death.

The next episode in the history of socialist doctrine after Fourier—Marxism—was based on analogous concepts of human personality. Dividing all human activity into "base" and "superstructure," Marxism assigned to the "base" that mode of production "from which, by force of inner dialectics and immanent laws, a social and state system is derived with all its legal, philosophical and religious views." In an even more striking formulation, Marxism proclaimed that this superstructure is "given" by the hand or steam mill. The mechanism by which the base creates a superstructure is held to be the struggle of material and economic *interests* (that is, egotism in the form of the class struggle). In its more general views of man, Marxism denies the freedom of will and any independent spiritual life or consciousness, the last being determined by one's "social existence." In the preface to the first volume of *Capital,* Marx wrote: "For me the ideal principle is a material one that has passed through the brain."

Still, the negation of the higher aspects of human existence in Marxism is not as radical as it is in the movement given shape by Fourier and later developed by Freud. Marxism sees the basic stimulus of human life and the explanation of the riddle of history in man's baser actions, but nevertheless in *human* activity and even in activity that unites people in a "social existence." Freud, however, reduces mankind to a still lower, purely biological level. While Marxism proclaims the division of *human society* into antagonistic classes (at least throughout recorded history), Freud strives to accomplish the same stratification in the *human personality*. He singles out the most ancient and the most extensive area—the id, the unconscious—which functions exclusively according to the pleasure principle, outside any notion of time or contradiction. There is no distinction here between good and evil, no morality or any other kind of value, save pleasure. Under the influence of the external world a derivative area—the ego—is formed, and from this, in turn, the superego takes shape under the influence of social factors. Here we can observe (under the name of suppression or repressive organization) the same exploitation and oppression in which Marxism sees the basic factor of social life. Freud compares the role of the areas of the psyche created under the influence of civilization to that part of the population which "seized power and exploits the rest of the population for its own profit. The fear of an uprising of the oppressed becomes the source of more severe measures." *(Civilization and Its Discontents)* In particular, sexuality, which has for the id the sole aim of deriving pleasure from different parts of the body, is forcibly subordinated to the function of childbearing and is transferred exclusively to the genitalia. Subconsciously the organism retains a recollection of the ideal condition of unlimited rule of the pleasure principle (cf. pre-class society) and attempts to break out of bondage. The ego and superego create in response the concept of morality and classify such attempts as "perversion" or "amoral actions." This results in a civilization where labor brings no satisfaction and instead becomes a source of unhappiness, a civilization which inevitably breeds suffering. One may add to this picture the conception of history as a traumatic reaction to an ancient crime—the murder of the father, the leader of a primitive band.

It might seem that Freud has distracted us from the main task of sketching the concept of human personality in socialist ideology. In fact it would have been a miracle if systems like those of Freud, so close to the views elaborated by socialist thinkers (Fourier and Marx), had not been incorporated into the socialist world view. No miracle occurred: the attempt to achieve a synthesis of Freudianism with socialist concepts (called "neo-Marxism" or "neo-Freudianism") became the biggest event in the development of socialist ideology in the post-World War II years; it had a very strong ideological impact on socialist trends that took shape during this time. In this regard Marcuse's book (119) stands out as the most consistent and vivid attempt to achieve such a synthesis.

Freud's system is skeptical and pessimistic; he considered suffering and mental diseases to be the inevitable cost of civilization, which in its turn is more and more undermined by elements of the psyche that have broken away from its control. Marcuse, in contrast, undertakes to alter this view so that its pessimistic evaluation is directed only against modern society. Furthermore, he adds the prediction of a future "liberation." To do this, he divides the suppression to which the instincts are subjected into two parts: the repression that inevitably comes from the objective claims of the external world on each organism and another type, which is caused by the striving of certain groups of individuals to attain privileged positions in society. The second form of repression he calls *surplus-repression,* and he considers the excessive burden that this factor imposes on the human psyche to be a peculiarity of modern civilization. Included in surplus-repression by Marcuse are the following: the necessity of work that does not bring direct satisfaction and whose reward appears in the form of ever more delayed pleasure; the repressive role of genital sexuality and the suppression of more primitive forms of libido, which permit the whole body to be the instrument of pleasure; the dominant role of reason, which subjects all life to itself; the transformation of science and religion into a means of the total mobilization of man; the control exercised by such categories as "conscience" and "morality" over man's inner world. Surplus-repression is directly connected to the fact that the demands of society are not satisfied collectively and in accordance with individual needs but are *organized* by the dominant part of society.

Marcuse is in agreement with Freud that repression is the necessary price for survival, but he asserts that surplus-repression with all its consequences may be overcome with the help of the latest achievements in technology. Without going into the details of this process (as a rule, one word is used: "automation"), Marcuse draws a picture of a future unrepressed society. It is based on the liberation of the instincts from the control of "repressive reason." This will lead to *regression*, in comparison to the level of civilization and reason that had been achieved: "It would reactivate early stages of the libido which were surpassed in the development of the reality ego, and it would dissolve the institutions of society in which the reality ego exists." (119: p. 198) "The regression involved in this spread of the libido would first manifest itself in a reactivation of all erotogenic zones and, consequently, in a resurgence of pregenital polymorphous sexuality and in a decline of genital supremacy." (119: p. 201) The body as a whole will become an instrument of satisfaction. "This change in the value and scope of libidinal relations would lead to a disintegration of the institutions in which the private interpersonal relations have been organized, particularly the monogamic and patriarchal family." (119: p. 201) Reason, which is the instrument of the ego, will to a large extent give way to fantasy connected with the id. And this will open up new ways to understand the future; it will reveal the reality of the possibilities formerly perceived only as elements of a utopia. The liberation of sexual instincts will lead to the development of "libidinal rationality," which will show the way to a higher form of free civilization.

The satisfaction of needs understood in an ever wider sense will become possible without heavy—i.e., alienating—work. Working relations will be simultaneously libidinal relations. "For example, if work were accompanied by a reactivation of pregenital polymorphous eroticism, it would tend to become gratifying in itself without losing its *work* content." (119: p. 215) On the other hand, work will become play, "a free play of human faculties." (119: p. 214) In a later work (4), Marcuse speaks about "play with automation." Here he considers it essential to correct Marx, who was not bold enough, and to adhere to Fourier.

Marcuse speaks here of the end of culture in the old sense of the word: "It would still be a reversal of the process of civilization, a subversion of culture—but *after* culture had done its work and created the mankind and the world that could be free." (119: p. 198) The essence of this upheaval Marcuse describes in poetic terms by juxtaposing Prometheus, the hero of repressive culture, with the heroes of his own New World—Orpheus and Narcissus. He ends as follows: "The classical tradition associates Orpheus with the introduction of homosexuality.

Like Narcissus, he rejects the normal Eros, not for an ascetic ideal, but for a fuller Eros. Like Narcissus he protests against the repressive order of procreative sexuality. The Orphic and Narcissistic Eros is to the end the negation of this order—the Great Refusal. In the world symbolized by the culture hero Prometheus, it is the negation of *all* order; but in this negation Orpheus and Narcissus reveal a new reality, with an order of its own, governed by different principles." (119: p. 171)

The most active socialist current of recent times, the New Left, proved to be extraordinarily receptive to Marcuse's teaching and was to a considerable extent influenced by it. Marcuse's basic propositions are closely paralleled in the slogans of this movement and serve as their theoretical foundation. For instance, the liberation of sexual instincts finds expression in the "sexual revolution," and the suppression of repressive reason is demonstrated in the "psychedelic revolution," that is, in the mass use of hallucinogens. Even ostentatious slovenliness can be theoretically justified, for according to the theory, ego and superego suppress the instincts connected with the sense of smell and enforce the perception of strong smells as "disgusting." (Furthermore, the dominant classes associate garbage with the lower classes, which are perceived negatively as "the dregs of society.") These views also serve as a theoretical basis for "left art," which fosters the idea of "anti-cultural" (or "cultural") revolution, of the destruction of "repressive" or "stifling" culture, up to and including a heightened interest (in both literature and art) in garbage and excrement as means of "exploding bourgeois culture."

We provided several examples to illustrate the "anthropology of socialism.".Had we considered other developed socialist theories in this connection (for instance, Deschamps's system), we would have been obliged to come to the same conclusion, namely, that *socialist ideology seeks to reduce human personality to its most primitive, lowest levels and, in each epoch, relies upon the most radical "criticism of man" available.* For that reason, the concepts of man in socialism and in religion are diametrically opposed.

So that if socialism is a religion, it must be recognized as a quite special religion, different in principle from all others and antithetical to them in many basic questions. (How else are we to understand Bulgakov's statement that socialism is "a religion based on atheism"?)

Otherwise it would be necessary to expand the definition of religion to the point where it would have no meaning at all.

8. *Socialism is the consequence of atheism, the conclusion to which atheism leads in the field of social relations.*

Dostoyevsky expressed this view with particular clarity, and his comments deserve special consideration. The majority of the thinkers of the nineteenth century completely overlooked the spiritual crisis of their time, which paved the way for the triumph of socialism in our day. Dostoyevsky was one of the few who saw clearly that mankind would not follow the path of liberalism, humanism and progress, and that terrible calamities awaited it in the not too distant future. He foresaw that socialism was destined to play the central role in the future tribulations of mankind, and most of his works touch upon various aspects of the problem. We shall here limit ourselves to what can be found on the subject in his essays appearing in *The Diary of a Writer.* Here are some of his views:

"French socialism, that is, the assuaging and the arrangement of human society without Christ and outside Christ . . ." (1877, January, Chapter 1) "For socialism sets itself the task of solving the fate of mankind, not according to Christ but outside God and outside Christ, and it was natural for it to arise in Europe, on the ruins of the Christian principle in proportion to the degree that this had become degenerate and lost in the Catholic Church itself." (1877, February, Chapter 3) "When Catholic humanity turned away from the monstrous image in which Christ was presented to them, then after many centuries of protests . . . there finally appeared, at the beginning of this century, attempts to arrange things outside God and outside Christ. Without the instincts of bees or ants that create their beehives and ant hills faultlessly and precisely, people undertook to create something like a faultless human ant hill. They rejected the formula for salvation which proceeds from God and was revealed as 'Love thy neighbor as thyself' and replaced it by practical conclusions such as *'chacun pour soi et Dieu pour tous'* or by scientific axioms such as 'the struggle for existence.' Lacking the instincts of animals . . . people placed great confidence in science, forgetting that for a task like the creation of society, science was still in its infancy. Dreams appeared. The future tower of Babel became the ideal and, on the other hand, the fear of all mankind. But the visionaries were soon followed by other doctrines, simple and to the point, such as 'rob the rich, drown the world in blood and then everything will somehow arrange itself.' " (1877, November, Chapter 3)

There are two essential points here. First, socialism is seen as the natural consequence of the decline of religion (Dostoyevsky has in mind socialism in Western Europe and the decline of Catholicism). Socialism is in this sense that which remains of the spiritual structure of mankind if the link with God is lost.

Second, socialism aims at organizing human society according to new principles which are compared to the instinctive actions of insect societies.

It appears to us that the second idea is in complete accordance with all the known facts about socialism, and later we shall try to specify the attitude of socialism toward the forces that shape human society.

As far as the first point is concerned, it is certainly true that socialism is hostile to religion. But is it possible to understand it as a *consequence* of atheism? Hardly, at least if we understand atheism as it is usually defined: as the loss of religious feeling. It is not clear just how such a negative concept can become the stimulus for an active attitude toward the world (its destruction or alteration) or how it can be the source of the infectiousness of socialist doctrines. Furthermore, socialism's attitude toward religion does not at all resemble the indifferent and skeptical position of someone who has lost interest in religion. The term "atheism" is inappropriate for the description of people in the grip of socialist doctrines. It would be more correct to speak here not of "atheists" but of "God-haters," not of "atheism" but of "theophobia." Such, certainly, is the passionately hostile attitude of socialism toward religion. Thus, while socialism is certainly connected with the loss of religious feeling, it can hardly be reduced to it. The place formerly occupied by religion does not remain vacant; a new lodger appeared. This is the only true source of the active principle of socialism, and the aspect which determines the historical role of this phenomenon.

We may draw the following conclusion from our critical survey: Socialism can apparently not be reduced to familiar social categories. The very abundance of such attempts points to the futility of such an exercise.

# VIII The Embodiment of the Socialist Ideal

In the light of the preceding section, two possibilities remain: either socialism is a fundamental historical force irreducible to other factors, or it is a manifestation of forces which up till now have not received sufficient attention. Our basic goal is a discussion of these alternatives. To prepare the ground for it, we shall try to look at the entire question from a new perspective. If earlier we attempted to specify what the various manifestations of socialism have in common, we shall now try to dissect this phenomenon into its elements in order to observe their interrelations and to evaluate the role of each element in the evolution of socialism.

The starting point for such an analysis is the observation with which we began the present study: Socialism manifests itself in life in two forms—as a doctrine (chiliastic socialism) and as a state system (state socialism). These forms differ so significantly that a question arises as to whether their content is in fact the same. Is it proper to categorize them as a single historical phenomenon? For example, the demand for destruction of the family, which in chiliastic socialism so often takes the more radical form of community of wives, has been realized in practice only in narrow circles: the gnostic sects described by Epiphanes, among the Brethren of the Free Spirit or in contemporary Berlin's "Commune No. 1." But we are not aware of any instance of this principle's implementation on the level of state policy. The same is true of another aspect of the abolition of the family—the break-up of ties between children and parents, with state upbringing of all children from the earliest age.

We shall begin with a discussion of this question. We shall argue that chiliastic and state socialism are two embodiments of one and the same ideal. Later, the role of these two forms in the historical evolution of socialism will be examined.

It would be natural to ascribe the difference between the doctrines of chiliastic socialism and the practice of state socialism to the fact that the former have as their aim the destruction of an existing social order and the establishment of a new one, while the latter aims to preserve an already existing social order. In this case, the specific features of chiliastic socialism which call for the destruction of the family could be considered tactical devices designed to disrupt the hostile system or to arouse fanaticism. It follows that after the establishment of a new order, these devices are no longer needed and can be discarded. They must therefore not be taken into consideration in a discussion of socialism's practical goals. Any argument about the fundamental difference between chiliastic and state socialism would probably follow such a pattern.

This point of view seems to us to be unconvincing a priori and devoid of inner logic. So gigantic a movement as socialism cannot *in principle* be based on a deception. For all their superficial demagoguery, these movements are honest at bottom—they proclaim their *fundamental* principles clearly for all to hear (except those who consciously try not to hear). And those propositions of socialist ideology which we formulated in chapter VI appear so consistently over such a vast period of time that they obviously are to be taken as fundamental principles. Moreover, they are often expressed in writing not by the leaders of popular movements but by abstract thinkers such as Plato and Campanella, whom it is hard to suspect of demagogic effects and who evidently produced the entire complex of basic socialist notions in response to the inner logic of this world view.

Below, we shall bring forward a number of specific arguments to support our contention. However, we must not forget that considerable differences in the spirit of socialist doctrines and the practice of socialist states are inevitable. We may speak only about the *coincidence in principle* of the ideals proclaimed in each case. The leader of a popular socialist movement and the representative of a socialist state have to deal with different practical tasks. The more radical and striking is the form in which the former expresses his ideal, the more accessible and effective his ideas will be. But the latter must contend with many real and complex difficulties, which limit the possibility of enacting his ideology in a consistent fashion and which may even threaten the very existence of his state.

One of the typical limitations imposed by reality is the necessity of contact with other, differently organized societies. Isolation is posited as a basic condition for the existence of a socialist state in the majority of the socialist utopian writings. More, Campanella, Vairasse and many others placed their utopias on remote islands. Vairasse, for example, makes the special reservation that only the most reliable Sevarites may go on "errands" to the outer world and they are permitted to do so only on the condition that their families remain behind as hostages. The organizers of the "Conspiracy of Equals" suggested that France should be surrounded by "spiked hedges" after the victory. The stability of the Jesuit state, to a marked degree, depended on its isolation. The unexpectedly high level of the crafts among the Guaraní, in the context of a generally primitive level of life, apparently was a result of an attempt to make the country independent of the outside world. On the other hand, the breakdown of isolation permitted a handful of Spanish adventurers to destroy the Inca empire. Is not this difficulty reflected in the vexed problem of "building socialism in one country"? Engels once answered this question most categorically: "Nineteenth question. Can the revolution take place in one country? Answer. No." (3: V: p. 476) Thanks to this factor alone, a socialist state that is not sufficiently isolated is forced to forgo the most radical elements of the ideal. And the contrary also holds: when the socialist movement is on the ascent, taking control in more and more areas and holding out the promise of the destruction of the old system in the entire world, the socialist states prove to be much more radical in their practical activity. From this point of view, the epoch of "War Communism" in postrevolutionary Russia is extremely interesting for an understanding of the peculiarities of socialist ideology; the impulses aroused then, in the hope of world revolution (or at least a European revolution), continued to be prominent until the middle of the twenties. We shall cite a necessarily limited number of examples to show how the realization of socialist principles was conceived at the time.

The term "War Communism" itself is misleading; it is not at all a description of the measures dictated by wartime needs (as was suggested, for example, in Stalin's *Questions of Leninism*). In fact, at the time this policy was being implemented (1918–1921), the term "War

Communism" was not used at all. It came into being later, together with the notion that this policy was conceived as temporary and was forced upon the Soviet regime by events. In a series of speeches in 1921–1922, Lenin characterized the policy of the preceding three years as something consciously undertaken that had perhaps gone too far. He compared it with the storming of a fortress: if this tactic would not bring victory, it should be replaced by a systematic siege. For example: "Regarding our preceding economic policy, although it cannot be said to have been planned (in such situations one calculates little), it nevertheless assumed that there would be an immediate transition from the old Russian economy to state production and to distribution based on Communist principles." In Lenin's opinion, it was a necessary experiment which forced the transition to a new policy of "state capitalism," which, albeit still in vague form, had been considered as early as 1918 as a possible line of retreat. (See Lenin's "NEP and the Tasks of Political Enlightenment," "The Report on NEP at the VIIth Moscow Regional Party Conference," and "Five Years of the Russian Revolution and the Prospects for World Revolution.")

There were many similar statements by numerous leaders of the state. In addition, the fact that the most radical measures in implementing the policies associated with War Communism were taken in the spring of 1920 and the winter of 1920–1921—when there was no military action going on—leads to the conclusion that the policy of the day was not necessitated by the Civil War but had been motivated by general theoretical considerations.

Let us take up a more detailed discussion of the policy in question.

## 1. Economy

All industry was nationalized, including the smallest operation. Everything was "supercentralized," subordinated to Central Boards (Glavki) in which separate plants were deprived of any economic independence. In agriculture, the proclaimed goal was the most radically conceived form of collectivization. The decree of the Central Executive Committee issued on March 1, 1919, reads as follows: "All aspects of individual land use should be regarded as transient and dying forms." ("On the Socialist Use of Land and on Measures for the Transition to Socialist Agriculture") The preferred form of organization of peasant labor was the *commune*. For example, in another section of the same decree, state farms and communes are listed first among the priorities in the regulation of land allotments. In a resolution "On the Collectivization of Agriculture" (adopted by the All-Russian Congress of Land Sections [Zemotdely]), it is stated that "the main task is large-scale organization of agricultural communes, of Soviet Communist farms and of the public cultivation of land, all of which will inevitably lead to a unified Communist organization of agriculture."

In the commune, as a rule, all means of production were socialized—buildings, instruments, livestock, land, etc., as well as consumption and services. What life was supposed to be like may be gleaned from stories about model communes published, during NEP, in *Izvestia*'s regular section called "Competition for the Best Collective Farm." For example: "No one has his own money; all money is kept in the general treasury." (September 11, 1923) Some members live in separate houses and take their meals separately, but when a new building is ready "everything individual will be done away with." (September 5, 1923) In another commune, there is a dormitory, a common dining hall and kitchen. "Work and meals are announced by bells." (September 8, 1923) People eat in public cafeterias and live in a dormitory, where each family has its own room. "Children still live with their parents, going out only by day to the kindergarten. It is only due to the absence of bedding that children cannot be interned separately." (September 11, 1923) "Children under school age live and eat separately."

Agricultural products were delivered to the state according to the "surplus appropriation system," at prices dozens of times lower than those paid on the black market. In other words, products were taken for practically nothing. The *Soviet Encyclopedia* puts it quite delicately: "The economic relations of the town and the country were essentially one-sided in character." In other areas, too, requisitions and confiscation were regulated. A decree of the Council of People's Commissars (SNK) from April 16, 1920, allows the Presidium of the VSNKh (Supreme Council of the People's Economy) and The People's Commissariat of Produce to carry out requisition and confiscation directly as well as through local organizations. Another of the SNK's decrees (December 4, 1920) sanctions free distribution of foodstuffs to the population (more accurately, to those groups of the population that were being supplied with foodstuffs). Frequently, the complete abolition of money was formulated as an immediate aim of economic policy. Yu. Larin, head of the department of financial policy of the VSNKh wrote: "And now, after a few years of effort on the part of the victorious proletariat, the thousand-year-old foundations of the commodity production system are collapsing like a house of cards. When our children grow up, money will be nothing but a memory, and our grandchildren will learn about it only from the colored pictures in history books." (*Pravda,* October 17, 1920, "The Transformation of Everyday Life") In an article by L. Obolensky in *The People's Economy* (published by VSNKh), we read: "At the present time in Soviet Russia, a system of moneyless accounts is the first step toward the abolition of money relations in general." (No. 1–2, 1920) "Naturalization of the economy" became a commonly used term, derived from the phrase *platit' naturoi*—"to pay in kind." *Pravda* states: "The tendency to the *general naturalization of our economy* must be consciously undertaken by us with all possible energy." (February 14, 1920)

## 2. The Organization of Labor

Let us recall that Marx and Engels themselves recommended the following measure, among others to be carried out immediately after the socialist revolution: "Identical duties regarding work. Establishment of industrial armies, especially in agriculture." (3: V: p. 502)

In a note called "Ten Theses on Soviet Power" which was presented to the Seventh Party Congress, Lenin formulated the task thus: "A quick beginning of the complete realization of general labor conscription, with a careful and gradual extension of it to the small peasants living on their own without hired labor." (113: XXXVI: p. 74) This idea was developed in great detail somewhat later.

At the Ninth Party Congress, Trotsky proposed a system of militarization under which workers and peasants would be in the position of mobilized soldiers. The plan set forth in Trotsky's report is worth considering in more detail.

He begins with an attack on Smirnov, whose position he formulates as follows:

"Insofar as we have begun a wider mobilization of the peasant masses in the name of tasks requiring extensive application of labor, militarization is becoming mandatory. We mobilize the peasantry and from this mobilized work force we form labor detachments that resemble military units. We supply commanders and instruction staff. We must include Communist cells so that these units are not soulless, but are inspired by the will to work. This amounts to a close approximation of military structure. The word 'militarization' is appropriate here, but Comrade Smirnov says that when we enter the field of industry, the field of skilled labor where there are professional and production organizations of the working class, there is no need to apply the military apparatus for the formation of units—militarization in this sense is out of the question. The trade unions will fulfill the task of organizing labor. Such an approach to the question reveals a complete lack of understanding of the essence of the economic changes that are taking place at the present." (120: p. 92)

Trotsky's point of view, as expressed in his report, comes to this: "In the military there is an appropriate mechanism which is set in motion to make soldiers fulfill their duty. This ought to be introduced in one form or another in the labor area. It is clear that if we wish to speak seriously of a planned economy that is directed from the center by a single design, where the work force is distributed in accordance with an economic plan at a given stage of development, this work force cannot be nomadic Russia. It must be capable of being moved quickly, of being given tasks and commanded just as soldiers are." (120: p. 93) "This sort of militarization is unthinkable without the militarization of the trade unions as such, without the establishment of a regime under which each worker feels he is a soldier of labor who cannot freely arrange his life. If there is an order for him to be transferred, he ought to obey it, and if he does not, he will be considered a deserter who must be punished." (120: p. 94) Trotsky even puts forward a theory in this regard: "Those arguments which were directed against the organization of a labor army are wholly directed against the socialist organization of the economy in our transitional period. If we take at face value the old bourgeois prejudice—or, to put it more precisely, an old bourgeois axiom which has become a prejudice, about forced labor being unproductive—then we must apply this not only to a labor army but to labor conscription as a whole, to the foundation of our economic plan and therefore to socialist organization in general." (120: p. 97) "If labor is organized according to an incorrect principle, according to the principle of compulsion, if compulsion is hostile to the productivity of labor, then we are doomed to economic decline no matter how much we dodge and shift. But this is a prejudice, comrades! The assertion that free labor, freely hired labor is more productive than forced labor was undoubtedly correct when applied to the feudal and bourgeois systems. . . . But the development of labor productivity prepared for the shift from a capitalist economy to a new Communist economy, and to apply to this colossal historic change that which was correctly applied to the old situation means to remain within the framework of bourgeois and philistine prejudices. We say: it is not true that compulsory labor is unproductive under any and all circumstances and conditions." (120: p. 98)

Trotsky developed the same thoughts in greater detail in his book directed against Kautsky. (121) Once again we encounter the idea of militarization, labor armies and the theory according to which forced labor under conditions created by the dictatorship of the proletariat will be more productive than free labor. Trotsky supports this conception by means of the following significant analogy: "Even serfdom was, under certain circumstances, progressive and led to an increase in the productivity of labor." (121: p. 119)

The question was posed on a more theoretical plane by Bukharin. (102) Noneconomic compulsion is presented here not as a measure necessitated by the war but as an organic feature of the transition from capitalism to socialism. In Chapter 10, entitled "Extra-Economic Compulsion in the Period of Transition," we read: "In regard to the non-kulak peasant mass, compulsion on the part of the proletariat is an instance of the class struggle, insofar as the peasant is a proprietor and a speculator." As it turns out, the question has a more elevated aspect: "From a broader point of view, proletarian compulsion in all its forms, from execution by shooting to labor conscription, is—no matter how paradoxical this sounds—a method for the elaboration of Communist humanity from the human material of the capitalist epoch." (102: p. 146)

These constructs were far from being pure theory. General labor conscription was actually announced. Instead of passports, which had been abolished, working papers were introduced for the entire work force. In Moscow and Petrograd, anyone venturing out on the street was obliged to have his working papers with him. By the time of the introduction of NEP (1921), eight labor armies had been organized.

## 3. Family

Practical actions as well as theoretical considerations in this field were based on Marxist theory, as set forth in its most complete form in Engels' book *The Origin of the Family, Private Property and the State.*

Engels had the following view of the contemporary family: "Monogamy arose from the concentration of great riches in a single hand—that of the man—and from the need to bequeath these riches to the children of that man and not of any other." (3: XVI: p. 56) About the future of the family he says: "With the transfer of the means of production into common ownership, the individual family ceases to be an economic unit of society. Private housekeeping is transformed into a social industry. The care and education of children become a public affair; society looks after all children equally, whether they are born in or out of wedlock." (3: XVI: p. 57)

It would seem that since the family is deprived of all social functions, it must inevitably disappear, at least from the point of view of historical materialism. The *Communist Manifesto* does in fact proclaim the abolition of the "bourgeois family." What, then, will replace it? The answers to that question in the classic writings of Marxism are strikingly ambiguous. We have already pointed out the passage in the *Manifesto* where the authors, in speaking about the accusation that Communists wish to introduce communality of wives, clearly avoid rejecting this explicitly. In another document used by Marx in writing the *Manifesto* ("Proceedings of the German Workers' Self-Education Society") we read: "Question 20: Will communality of wives be proclaimed together with the abolition of private property? Answer: Absolutely not. We shall interfere in the private relations between man and woman only to the degree that these relations disrupt the new social order. We know very well that family relations have been subjected to change in the course of history, depending on the phase of development of property, and because of this the very abolition of private property will have a most decisive influence." (Quoted in 112)

Here again, it is impossible to comprehend what it is that the author so decisively rejects—the fact that communality of wives will occur or merely the fact that it would be "proclaimed" and introduced through the interference of society.

In *The Origin of the Family, Private Property and the State*, a work written in the least radical period of his activities, Engels asserts of the future: "Far from disappearing, monogamy will then on the contrary be fully realized for the first time." (3: XVI: p. 57) But in what way, if its economic preconditions have disappeared? Answer: "Here a new factor comes into play . . . individual sex-love." (3: XVI: p. 57) But one waits in vain for a materialistic analysis of this "factor" from the founder of historical materialism. It is not a biological category because: "Before the Middle Ages individual sex-love was out of the question." (?!) (3: XVI: p. 58) Then perhaps we should expect an explanation in the spirit of the "base" and the "superstructure," so as to show how this "factor" is "given" by the hand mill! But instead, the author only points mysteriously to adultery as a source of sexual love—i.e., to a factor which could be ascribed to production relationships only with great difficulty. To add to the confusion, Engels speaks, in a note at the end of the book, with sympathy of Fourier's "brilliant critique of civilization": "I only note that already in Fourier's writings, monogamy and property in land are treated as the chief characteristics of civilization." (3: XVI: p. 153)

It is not surprising that these general principles were interpreted in a multitude of ways in the early postrevolutionary years. But there is one thing that unites most of the views current then—the attitude toward the family as an institution opposed to the party, the class or the state, and therefore dangerous. Here are some examples:

"The frequent conflicts between the interests of the family and that of the class, as for example during strikes, and the moral standard that is used by the proletariat in these cases characterize the basis of the new proletarian ideology with sufficient clarity. . . . To the detriment of individual happiness, to the detriment of the family, the morality of the working class will demand the participation of women in the life unfolding beyond the threshold of the house." (122: p. 59) "From the moment the family begins to oppose itself to society, enclosing itself in the narrow circle of purely domestic interests, it begins to play a conservative role in the whole social structure of life. This sort of family we are certainly obliged to destroy." (123: p. 156) "The spirit of solidarity, comradeship, readiness to give oneself up to the common cause is well developed wherever the exclusionary family does not exist. This has been carefully taken into account by the leaders of almost all large social movements. . . . Under the socialist system, when there will no longer be a domestic household and children will be brought up by society from the day of their birth, other forms of the union of the sexes rather than the family will undoubtedly come into being." (124: p. 12) "In future socialist society, where the obligation for the upbringing, education and maintenance of children will be shifted from the parents to society as a whole, it is clear that the family must wither away." (125: p. 121) "It makes little sense for us to strive

for an especially stable family and to regard marriage from that angle."
(126: p. 26)

The practical conclusions derived from this general tendency varied
sharply. Aleksandra Kollontai called for the spread of free love with
a frequent change of sexual partners: "For the working class, greater
'fluidity,' less rigidity in the union of the sexes completely coincides
with and even follows from the basic tasks of this class." (122: p. 59)
In the play *Love of the Worker Bees* and the article "Make Way for
Winged Eros!" she developed these propositions vividly. Lenin objected (see Klara Tsetkin's "On Lenin"), as did Solts, who writes: "A
disorderly sex life undoubtedly weakens anyone as a fighter." ("On
Party Ethics") On the other hand, M. N. Liadov (pseudonym of Man-
delshtam, a Bolshevik who had been one of the earliest members of
the Social Democratic Party) called for the abolition of the upbringing
of children within the family. "Is it possible to bring up collective
man in an individual family? To this we must give a categorical response: No, a collectively thinking child may be brought up only in
a social environment. . . . Every conscientious father and mother must
say: If we want our child to be liberated from that philistinism which
is present in each of us, he must be isolated from ourselves. . . . The
sooner the child is taken from his mother and given over to a public
nursery, the greater is the guarantee that he will be healthy." (127:
pp. 25–27)

Let us recall here the reference cited above on the "interning of
children" in communes.

Finally, extensive state interference in family relations was proposed and justified on historic grounds: "Wherever the state held control over all economic resources, as in ancient Peru, it attempted to
control the contracting of marriage as well as the family life of man
and wife." (124: p. 12) Radical eugenic measures also were proposed,
for example: "We have every reason to assume that under socialism
childbearing will be removed from the realm of nature." This dubious
consolation is offered: "But this, I repeat, is the only aspect of marriage
that, in our opinion, socialist society may control." (128: p. 450)

Preobrazhensky, who was extremely influential at the time, wrote:
"From the socialist point of view, it is quite senseless for a separate
member of society to look on his body as his own private property,
for an individual is only an isolated point in the transition of the race
from past to future. But it is ten times more senseless to view one's

'own' progeny that way." The author recognizes "a full and uncondi-tional right of society to introduce regulation, including interference in sexual life for the improvement of the race through natural selec-tion." ("About Moral and Class Norms," cited in 112)

And occasionally the problem was phrased even more radically than in any of the examples above. For instance, a unit of the Young Communist League at the Liudinov factory in Briansk adopted the following resolution concerning a report "On Sexual Intercourse": "We must not avoid sexual intercourse. If there is no sexual intercourse, there will be no human society." (123: p. 168)

Practice, of course, lagged behind ideology. But a number of meas-ures were taken, which, though less far-reaching than theoretical pro-nouncements, nevertheless pointed in the same direction. The legal formalities in contracting and breaking a marriage were greatly liberal-ized; registration was regarded merely as one of the means to confirm marriage. "Registration is a survival of old bourgeois relations, and it will ultimately cease to exist." (A speech by Larin, 126: p. 210)

Divorce was granted upon the request of either party. Paternity was ascertained on the basis of the mother's claim: "Our legal practice . . . placed responsibility on all the defendants [laughter], giving the woman the opportunity of recovering something from each. . . . The court, as a general rule, will be guided by the indications of the plaintiff: whoever is indicated by the plaintiff will be recognized by the court as the father [laughter]." (From a speech by People's Commissar of Justice Kursky, 126: pp. 232–233)

New dwellings were not divided into separate apartments but were built as dormitories.

"And one should by no means blame those working men and women who do not want to move into common quarters. It must always be kept in mind that the former life of the working class was deeply rooted in bourgeois society, built as it was on the isolation of separate families. This individual family of bourgeois origin is what stands in the way of the collectivization of our existence." (123: p. 12) Dormitory quarters did not as a rule have kitchens, since it was assumed that everyone would take his meals at common dining rooms and "factory kitchen" facilities. In his "Ten Theses on Soviet Power," Lenin suggests that "steadfast and systematic measures should be undertaken for re-placing the individual food preparation . . . by the common dining of large groups of families." (113: XXXVI: p. 75) Dormitories, common meals, the upbringing of children apart from parents—all these measures were tried in various communes. And they did in fact lead to a weakening of the family. In 123, which has already been cited, there is the following letter from a certain "highly placed member" of the Komsomol: "Today, marriage between Komsomol members hardly ever takes place." The author of the letter asserts that sexual relations outside marriage prevail, but he is taken to task for not understanding that this is indistinguishable from marriage. After all, "for a Marxist it would seem that the very fact of sexual intercourse should testify to matrimonial relations." (123: p. 164) Between 1924 and 1925 in the European area of Russia, the number of marriages per 100,000 of population declined from 1140 to 980, while the number of divorces rose from 130 to 150. In 1924, of those obtaining divorces, a considerable number had been married for less than a year. (In Minsk this was true of 260 per 1,000 divorces; in Kharkov, 197; in Leningrad, 159. Compare the same statistic for: Tokyo—80; New York—14; Berlin—11.) (129: pp. 412, 416)

The deplorable situation with regard to homeless children at the time is well known.

"The present number of homeless children may be attributed to a large degree to the disintegration of the family." (126: p. 255) The following words seem to come from the heart: "If we continue along this path, I fear we shall turn Russia into a country where each will be married to all." (126: p. 270)

## 4. Culture

In the postrevolutionary period there appeared numerous theories and plans for the destruction of culture, science and art. Certain of them originated in anarchist circles. For instance, in a work published in 1917 (129), the anarchist A. Borovoi asserts that only by overcoming culture could anarchist ideals be realized. The prolific Gordin brothers (anarchist writers who in their political activity were close to Bolshevism) proclaimed the slogan "Down with science!" They meant this as an appeal for freedom from the oppression of logic: "Down with spiritual oppression, coercion through science, deception, pseudo-convictions!" And: "Down with science—with the spiritual government, and its logical power and army, its logical coercion." (130: p. 144) The anarchist "proclaims terror against science." (130: p. 137) Their entire book is devoted to the comparison and condemnation of two superstitions—religion and science. The brothers Gordin consider the Party to be the church of science, the university its synagogue, the philosopher a holy fool of intellect. (130: pp. 142, 194, 202) "The history of culture is the history of our superstition. . . . The history of culture once fulfilled its honorable role as the gravedigger of religion, serving as its tomb at the same time. It must fulfill the same role in respect to science. After the collapse of science, after the disenchantment with it as the source of truth, after its extinction as 'civilization,' it must become 'culture' and retire to the museum of human superstitions." (130: pp. 226–227) Here is the ideal: "At present a true anarchist, a panarchist, outgrows his petty-negative anarchism and, rejecting science and social science, thereby rejects his own petty idols, his shallow and cheap ascetic ideals, replacing them with one great destructively negative truth which lies at the very base of his innaturism/aphysism, of the anti-scientific spirit." (130: p. 137)

In his *The Theory of the New Biology*, E. Enchmen, citing Marx as his authority, comes to even more extreme conclusions. His work, which is reminiscent of Fourier in spirit, contains a highly ambitious plan for the biological regeneration of mankind through a change in the structure of consciousness which will be brought about by a series of so-called organic cataclysms. "The Revolutionary Scientific Council of the World Commune will accomplish organic cataclysms both in the masses of rebels and, systematically and by means of force, in the conservative organisms of the recent oppressors and their minions." (131: p. 43) As a result of these cataclysms, almost all received ideas in the human consciousness will be erased. "All theories of logic, cognition, scientific methodology will disappear, as will all social and sociological theories which still label themselves 'humanitarian,' and all the old biological theories." All are to be replaced by fifteen concepts which the author calls "analyzers." He explains that "past mankind divided into thousands of groups of differently reacting people—groups of more or less 'educated' and 'cultured,' and completely 'uneducated' and 'uncultured.' All will unite under the Communist economic system and become absolutely equal through the penetration into all human organisms of a new, completely identical combination of fifteen analyzers . . . that the epoch of Communism will be regarded by Communist mankind not according to the modern artistic formula 'from each according to his abilities, to each according to his needs' but as an epoch of the complete equalization of all human organisms strenuously involved in 'continuous joy' . . . that the Communist economy will be based on a system of 'physiological passports' for all human organisms . . . that such a 'physiological passport' will serve for the organism, using modern language, as a 'ration card' both for work and consumption in the broad sense of these words." (131: p. 34)

Bukharin devoted an article to the criticism of "Enchmenism" in the collection *Attack*. Another author deals with Enchmen in this way: "Of course, it would not have been worth mentioning had not Enchmenism attracted a number of students." (132: p. 19)

Whereas in respect to general culture such statements were sporadic and unsystematic, in the areas of art and philosophy a coherent system evolved. Some of the most influential groups (LEF—the "Left Front of the Arts") proclaimed the transformation of art into a branch of material production. B. Arvatov, a prominent theoretician of this group, wrote: "The goal of LEF is to transform all art into a contribution to the material culture of society in close touch with engineering." (133: p. 90) "When artistic work is structured in this way, individual artists will become the collaborators of scientists, engineers, scholars, administrators in organizing the common product; they will be guided not by personal motives but by the objective needs of social production, fulfilling the tasks set by the class through organizational centers." (133: p. 104) Ultimately, the result will be as follows: "According to the preceding, it is possible to maintain that in an organized, integrated, socialist order, figurative art as a special profession will wither away." (133: p. 129)

This same attitude found expression in hostility toward the treatment of human personality in literature; this was branded "psychologism," and was generally considered representative of "bourgeois" values. Osip Brik expressed views typical of this approach in an article on Fadeyev's novel *The Rout*: "One must set literature the task of describing not people but their deeds, to evoke interest not in people but in deeds. We value a person not for his experiences, but for the role he plays in our common cause. Therefore, interest in the deed is basic for us, while interest in the person is derivative." (134: p. 79) B. Kushnir, in his article "Why We Are Falling Behind," writes: "In all its permutations, the slogan 'living man' always preserved its invariable class essence. . . . According to this theory, the author is supposed not only to work out the psychology and the interrelationship of his characters but also as it were to metamorphose himself into each of them. This is clearly a difficult, time-consuming and harmful thing. Transformation into one's characters can hardly sharpen the author's class vigilance and class perceptivity. After all, there are characters and characters. Among them there may even be some unambiguous class enemies." (134: p. 85) I. Nusinov opines: "The further to the right a writer is, the stronger his tendency to psychologize." (134: p. 88) I. Altman, in an article entitled "From the Biography of a Living Man," thinks it necessary to "expose utterly the opportunistic slogans of psychologism—'the living man'—which interfere with the decisive and triumphant advance of proletarian literature!" (134: p. 91)

A negative attitude toward *philosophy* was also supported by references to the classic writings of Marxism. Kautsky had written: "Marx did not proclaim any philosophy—but the end of all philosophy." (135: p. 452)

In Russia, the view of philosophy as a "product of the bourgeoisie," a "semi-religion," "intellectual atavism," was developed by S. Minin, particularly in the article "Philosophy Overboard" (136), and by P. P. Blonsky. (137)

## 5. Religion

The fate of religion in this period is replete with features that have no parallel in either Russian history or the history of the world. A study of this phenomenon would undoubtedly shed light on a number of aspects of War Communism that remain unclear. A great deal of systematic research is required.

This was the time when the most decisive attempt was undertaken to destroy the Russian Orthodox Church (in connection with the so-called campaign for the removal of church valuables). It was a time when tribunals were convened to try God and He was sentenced to death by unanimous vote. At Easter, there were demonstrations with blasphemous pictures and slogans. . . .

This extremely fragmentary survey of War Communism will nevertheless, we hope, convey a certain impression of that fascinating period. We see there a system of views and measures that is much more radical than what is to be found in any other socialist state known to us. If War Communism is the most striking example of the appearance of radical tendencies in a socialist state, it is nevertheless not unique.

Only continuing famine and devastation coupled with "capitalist encirclement" forced a retreat from this system. The New Economic Policy was such a retreat and we must believe the sincerity of the declarations of the day that it would be only a temporary withdrawal. NEP was indeed temporary. Stalin promulgated a law which foresaw imprisonment for laborers and office personnel who were absent from work or merely late: they were "militarized." In the last years of his life, Stalin "reassigned" more and more scientists and technicians to prison research institutes *(sharashki)*. The internal security agency ran innumerable factories and scientific institutions.

But Stalin had visions of even more radical changes ahead. In a work written in the last year of his life, *The Economic Problems of Socialism,* he expresses the thought that money and commodity production contradict the nature of a socialist state. He also felt that the peasants in the collective farms were not sufficiently dependent on the state. Stalin sees this, for instance, in the fact that the collective farms possess their own seed grain and sell their products to the state (albeit according to quotas and at a rate fixed by the state).

"But it would be unpardonable blindness not to see that these phenomena are already beginning to impede the powerful development of our productive forces, since they create an obstacle to the complete control of the entire national economy and, especially, of agriculture by state planning." (138: p. 68) Stalin proposes a new system for the organization of the economy, under which trade would be replaced by a "system of product exchange" and all economic life would come under even greater control by the state. "But this should be introduced steadfastly, without hesitation, step by step reducing the sphere of commodity circulation and extending the sphere of product exchange." (138: p. 94)

This program could not be undertaken, for purely practical reasons; in particular, it would have involved the risk of falling economically too far behind the U.S.A.

China's "Great Leap Forward" provides us with one more example. At the end of the fifties, a transition to communism in three to five years was proclaimed: "Three years of intense work and ten thousand years of happiness!" In several months time in 1958, "people's communes" sprang up all over the countryside; communes were introduced in cities as well. According to the plan, they were to become the basic form of the organization of agriculture, industry, administration, schools, the army. Militarized labor armies were created. People marched to work in formation. Everyday life was being socialized, and all equipment and household goods in the commune were being consolidated. Unpaid delivery of products was initiated.

We see the same picture in the attitude toward religion. All socialist states are fundamentally hostile toward religion, but the opportunities for expressing this attitude vary. Italian fascism at first came into sharp conflict with the Catholic Church, but was compelled to come to terms with it and refrain from serious oppression of religion. In other respects, too, it was the weakest socialist state of our century and had the least possibility for realizing its socialist tendencies. China, on the other hand, could permit itself to outlaw the Christian religion completely. Between these extremes, there is a whole spectrum of possible approaches toward religion—all of them basically hostile but only as harsh as given conditions permit.

Neither the abolition of the family nor communality of wives was fully realized in any known socialist state, but the rudiments of such an effort can be easily observed. For instance, in Nazi Germany there was an attempt to produce racially pure children out of wedlock. The organization *lebensborn,* founded by Himmler, selected Aryan sires for unmarried women. There were officially inspired suggestions about the desirability of extra wives for men of a racially suitable type. Bormann's wife propagandized these ideas and herself sanctioned another wife for her husband.

In all the examples cited, these undertakings were not carried to completion due to very specific external circumstances, but not because of ideological inconsistency. It seems that carrying through such transformations of life requires a definite level of agitation and the mobilization of a certain kind of spiritual energy. And this, in its turn, is dependent on the depth of the crisis that the society is undergoing at the given moment. In particular, the destruction of the traditional family and state control over family relations, which we introduced at the beginning of this section as an example of something peculiar to the doctrines of chiliastic socialism, may prove to be all too feasible under conditions of the approaching crisis of overpopulation. (Toynbee suggests this in 139.)

It therefore seems impossible to draw any firm theoretical distinction between the doctrines of chiliastic socialism and the practices of the socialist states. The only difference stems from the fact that in the first case we have a clearly formulated ideal, whereas the second presents a series of variants, stretching down through history, where no more than an attempt can be made to distinguish a certain trend. But this trend, if extrapolated to its logical conclusion, points toward the same ideal that is proclaimed by the socialist doctrines.

It is far easier to discern the distinctions between chiliastic and state socialism as they are revealed in history. To begin with, we encounter states of the socialist type thousands of years before the existence of any developed socialist doctrine. Second, socialist states appear in history in two quite different situations: in primitive cultural conditions at the very beginning of the state period of history (in the Mediterranean basin this occurred between the third and the second millennia B.C.) and in the industrial societies of the twentieth century. The development of socialist doctrines occurs during the interval between these two periods. Within chiliastic socialism it is also possible to distinguish two tendencies—one gives rise to abstract academic systems, elaborate plans for a future society; the other calls for the destruction of the existing world, for "liberation," revenge, and the reign of an elect. These two tendencies also undoubtedly manifest themselves during different epochs. Plato's *Republic* is most certainly the source of the first current: More, Campanella, Deschamps are under his obvious influence; even Marcuse in citing the myths of Narcissus and Orpheus to illustrate his concepts is clearly attempting to imitate Plato. The second current takes shape in the Middle Ages among the heretical sects. But if the history of these sects is traced, it is found that all of them (Cathars and the Brethren of the Free Spirit) originate in the gnostic sects of the early centuries A.D. In an admittedly undeveloped form, these earlier sects show some of the basic features that will appear later in the socialist doctrines.

Let us note, first of all, that socialist doctrines arose thousands of years later than socialist states. This compels us to reverse the usual axiom of socialist ideology: the doctrines of chiliastic socialism cannot be regarded as a prediction (scientific, mystical or rational) of a future social system. They are far more akin to *reaction*—i.e., to the desire to return mankind to a more primitive archaic condition.

However, this reaction is not simply aimed at restoring that which was; chiliastic theory goes far beyond the practice of early socialist states. The nature of this process will become clearer if we examine it in the light of a historical observation made by various authors, Karl Jaspers among them. It was Jaspers who suggested calling the phenomenon in question history's "axial time." (140) Jaspers has in mind those profound shifts which occurred in the period comprising approximately the first millennium B.C. During the two preceding millennia, the main force influencing the development of history were the powerful states organized in the manner of Oriental despotism, with entire populations under bureaucratic control, permitting them to undertake gigantic construction projects and to field huge armies. After a long interval, in the first millennium B.C., other, *spiritual* forces again began to have a decisive influence on the course of history. From Greece to China, there arose teachings that were directed to the soul of individual men, asserting individual man's responsibility before reason, before conscience or else before higher powers. These were: Greek philosophy, the preaching of the Israelite prophets, Buddhism, Confucianism. It is not the omnipotent state machine that is pronounced to be the force capable of determining the fate of mankind, but the human personality. A godlike despot before whom one could only bow down and obey loses his position as the creator of history. No less a role is now played by the teacher who calls on the people to believe in his message and to follow his example. Whatever approach one takes with regard to the origin of Christianity—whether "the Word became flesh" or whether mankind itself came to a new understanding of its fate— the process we have sketched finds here its highest expression. Jaspers believes that it is precisely in "axial time" that the conception of *history* appears. In his opinion, we consider historical those peoples who have either directly participated in this process or who subsequently came to share the values so created (the Germanic peoples, for example, or the Slavs).

There is no need for us to discuss here this vast and complex historical phenomenon. We shall only juxtapose it with the stages in the development of chiliastic socialism that we have noted earlier. Within the limits of the Mediterranean cultural circles, "axial time" was expressed in two basic phenomena—in the "Greek miracle," most vividly embodied in the personality of Socrates, and in the rise of Christianity. These two phenomena are very close in time to what we have indicated as the starting points of the two tendencies of chiliastic socialism. Plato's socialist utopia was promulgated several decades after Socrates' death, while the original gnostic sects appeared as early as the first century A.D. It is reasonable to suggest that we have here not only a temporal but also a causal relationship—i.e., the "utopian" chiliastic socialism of Plato, More, Campanella, Fourier, may perhaps be seen as a reaction to the vision of the world elaborated in Greek culture, while the "revolutionary" and "eschatological" socialism of the gnostic and medieval heresies, of Müntzer and of Marx, may be a reaction to the appearance of Christianity. Such a view is in fundamental agreement with the conclusions we came to concerning the general character of socialism. If socialism is a manifestation of a certain basic and constantly active force, it is natural that any obstacle to its action would call forth changes in the form of its manifestation. A profoundly spiritual understanding of human personality, an assertion of the central role that it plays in Greek culture and, in particular, in Christianity—these were the factors that shook the monolithic stability of the states based on socialist principles and showed mankind the possibility of another path.

The question of the affinities between primitive Eastern states of the socialist type and socialist states of the twentieth century is examined in the last chapter of Wittfogel's book. (89) The author believes that these are two variants of one and the same social structure. Primitive agrarian despotism "existed for millennia, until the time that it felt the impact of the growth of the industrial and commercial West." (89: p. 360) In the last sections of his book ("Whither Asia?" "Whither Western Society—Whither Mankind?") Wittfogel views the appearance of socialist states in the twentieth century as a return of Asiatic countries to the primitive structures that had existed for millennia. Yet he acknowledges that modern socialist states differ from their ancient predecessors by the fact that they undertake to control their citizens not only in economic but in social and intellectual terms. For that reason modern socialism is much more than an "Asiatic restoration." The lack of consistency may be explained, so it seems to us, by the fact that the author views socialism as an exclusively economic category and a definite form of state organization. Thus the development of chiliastic socialism (which required two and a half millennia) remains beyond his field of vision. Yet this is precisely the link joining the two types of socialist society. The distinguishing feature of twentieth-century socialist states is their dependence on an ideology that has been elaborated and forged over the course of thousands of years (and the better elaborated it is, the more stable they are). This is exactly what the Oriental despots lacked and what prevented them from retaining power over the world in the spiritual atmosphere created by "axial time." This ideology was created almost exclusively in the West, and this fact alone makes it impossible to regard socialism of the twentieth century as an "Asiatic restoration."

The contemporary socialist states could not have come into existence without the ideology created by chiliastic socialism. We have already described its basic features: the abolition of private property, hostility toward religion, destruction of the family, communality. This ideology is linked to the mythic concepts (expressed though they are in modern quasi-scientific terms) of the "golden age," "captivity," "liberation" and "the chosen people" destined to be the instrument of liberation, for which purpose the annihilation of an evil world will be required. Finally, there is the promise of a new world that will arise as a result of the catastrophe and where the ideals of chiliastic socialism will be realized.

It is evidently this system of views which must be examined in order to clarify the historic role of socialism.

# IX  Socialism and Individuality

It is natural enough to begin the analysis of this social ideal by elucidating the interrelationship of its various elements. It is immediately clear they do not play an equal role. For example, Plato argues for the necessity of communal property and wives, since only under these conditions will the citizens take joy in and grieve over the same things. In other words, he considers the communality of property and the abolition of the family as means for achieving *equality*. He regards equality, however, not in the usual sense of equality of rights or opportunities, but as identity of behavior, as the equalization of personalities. Both these traits—the abolition of private property and of the family as a means to achieve equality, and this special understanding of equality—run through the majority of socialist teachings.

The view that equality is the basic principle from which other socialist doctrines proceed played an especially large role in the gnostic sects. "God's justice consists of community and equality"—such a proposition was used to justify both the abolition of private property and the demand for communal wives. This theme can be traced in the medieval heresies and the doctrines of the Reformation. Niklaus Storch preached: "Everything should be common, for God sent all into the world equally naked." Müntzer taught: "No one should rise above others; every man must be free, and there should be community of property." Citing Plato, More asserted that those laws are best that provide for "distributing all the good things of life among all equally," and deduced the need for communality of property. Meslier writes that "all people are equal by nature" and also deduces the necessity

258

of abolishing private property. Representatives of the Enlightenment supplemented this argument with the notion of a "natural state" in which all people were equal and the disappearance of which gave rise to private property and all the vices of contemporary life. The only significant exception is "scientific socialism," which deduces the need to abolish private property from objective causes, such as the type of production. In so doing, Marx deduces the very notion of equality from the economic conditions of bourgeois society. (See 3: XVII: p. 68) But how, then, are we to deal with the just cited radical concepts of equality that were proclaimed in the early centuries A.D.? We have already shown why we cannot recognize "scientific socialism" as a genuinely scientific theory and why we must see it merely as a form or guise in which the socialist ideal appears (just as it can appear in mystic garb, for example). For the same reason, we cannot take on faith the assertion that the demand for abolishing private property is also a result of scientific analysis of the objective phenomena of social life. We shall soon return to the evaluation of the role which communality of property plays in "scientific socialism" and its connection with the concept of equality.

One of the most striking features of socialist ideology is that quite special sense which it attributes to the concept of equality. We have already pointed this out in connection with the rationale for communality of property, of wives and children proposed by Plato. And later, in the majority of socialist doctrines, we encounter a conception of equality which approaches that of *identity*. Dwelling lovingly on the details, authors have described the characteristic monotony and unification of life in the state of the future. Where More speaks about identical clothing, except for a difference between male and female attire, Campanella indicates that the dress of men and women is almost the same. In Utopia, everyone wears cloaks of the same color; in the City of the Sun a woman who attempts to alter her mode of dress will be punished by death. Solarians never have any privacy; they work and relax in detachments and share common sleeping and dining facilities. All the cities of Utopia are built according to one plan: "He who recognizes one will recognize all." The same ideal of life in absolutely identical cities consisting of identical houses is repeated by Morelly. His people also wear clothes made of the same material, and all children's clothing is absolutely identical. They all eat the same food and receive the same education. Babeuf and Buonarotti's circle, whose very title included the word "equality," understood this to include common obligatory meals, entertainment, etc. . . .

In the examples above, we see an external equalization of living conditions which symbolizes, as it were, the corresponding leveling of the inner world. Deschamps gives a more detailed description of the changes in human personality. Of the people of the future, he writes: "They would (much more than we) adhere to the same type of action and would not deduce from this, as we usually do with regard to animals, that to act thus is to reveal a lack of reason or understanding. Why do people who find perfection in nature's ever identical type of action consider this to be a defect in animals? Only because people are too far removed from this kind of action, and their haughtiness makes them interpret this very remoteness to their advantage." (53: p. 219)

More specifically, he foresees that people will begin to look alike: "Identical morals (and true morals can only be identical) would make, so to say, one man of all men and one woman of all women. I mean by this that ultimately they would resemble each other more than animals of the same species." (53: p. 176)

Deschamps proposes changes in language so as "to banish all terms presently used to express our good and bad qualities, even all terms unnecessarily distinguishing us from other things." (53: p. 503)

Finally, "scientific socialism" proclaims that the historical process is controlled by immanent laws which are independent of human will. An understanding of these laws makes history predictable. This conception was formed under the obvious influence of the advances of natural science in the seventeenth and eighteenth centuries, above all, the success of astronomy in predicting the discovery of planets, the return of comets, etc. Fourier asserts that mankind is ruled by the laws of "attraction of the passions," which are in his view precisely analogous to Newton's law of gravitation, whereby "the unity of the physical and the spiritual worlds is manifest." In terms of this analogy, individuals correspond to the elemental particles of matter, which must be identical (at least, from the standpoint of properties essential to the phenomenon under consideration—that is, *history*). As for Marxism, one thinks of an analogy with another physical theory. This is the kinetic theory of gases, according to which a gas is the aggregate of molecules that come into collision, with the result of each collision determined by the laws of mechanics. A very great number of molecules transform the statistical laws of their collision into the general laws of the physics of gases. The only form of social contact of the producers of goods in capitalist society is exchange (just as for gas molecules the only form of interaction is collision). The interaction of a great number of producers engenders that "social production" which, in its turn, determines their political, legal and religious notions, and the "social, political and spiritual processes of life in general." It is evident that such a conception makes sense only on the assumption that separate "molecules" (producers) are *identical*. Otherwise, instead of an explanation (or an "understanding," as Marx puts it), there would be only the individual properties of a huge number of people, and one enigma would be replaced by a mass of enigmas.

Proceeding from these examples, it is possible to attempt to formulate the specific concept of equality inherent in socialist ideology. The usual understanding of "equality," when applied to people, entails equality of *rights* and sometimes equality of *opportunity* (social welfare, pensions, grants, etc.). But what is meant in all these cases is the equalization of *external* conditions which do not touch the individuality of man. In socialist ideology, however, the understanding of equality is akin to that used in mathematics (when one speaks of equal numbers or equal triangles), i.e., this is in fact identity, the abolition of differences in behavior as well as in the inner world of the individuals constituting society. From this point of view, a puzzling and at first sight contradictory property of socialist doctrines becomes apparent. They proclaim the greatest possible equality, the destruction of hierarchy in society and at the same time (in most cases) a strict regimentation of all of life, which would be impossible without absolute control and an all-powerful bureaucracy which would engender an incomparably greater inequality. The contradiction disappears, however, if we note that the terms "equality" and "inequality" are understood in two different ways. The equality proclaimed in socialist ideology means identity of individualities. The hierarchy against which the doctrine fights is a hierarchy based on individual qualities—origin, wealth, education, talent and authority. But this does not contradict the establishment of a hierarchy of internally identical individuals who only occupy different positions in the social machine, just as identical parts can have different functions in a mechanism. The analogy between the socialist ideal of society and the machine is certainly not new. For example, speaking about the ancient states of Mesopotamia and Egypt (which, as we have seen, were to a considerable extent based on socialist principles), Lewis Mumford expresses the view that their social structure was the first to be based on the idea of a machine. He supports this idea by referring to the drawings of the time that show warriors and workers as completely identical, like the stereotyped details of a machine. (141: p. 150) Even more convincing is the evidence of a man who was clearly competent in this area: I. V. Stalin. He once expressed his social ideal by calling the inhabitants of the state ruled by him "nuts and bolts." He proposed a toast to them. And in contemporary China the papers glorify the hero Lei Fen, who wrote in his diary about his desire to be Chairman Mao's "stainless-steel cog."

The preceding considerations lead us to the conclusion that at least three components of the socialist ideal—the abolition of private property, the abolition of the family and socialist equality—may be deduced from a single principle: *the suppression of individuality*. There is also a large body of direct evidence that demonstrates the hostility of socialist ideology to individuality. Some examples:

Mazdak taught that the confusion of light and dark, as well as evil in general, derived from individuality and that the ideal condition cannot be achieved until people rid themselves of their individual qualities. Fourier believed that the "fundamental core of the passions" on which the future society will be founded is a passion called "unitheism." This force is not activated in conditions of civilization. The passion directly opposed to it is egoism or one's own "I." "This disgusting inclination has various names in the world of learning: moralists call it egoism; ideologues, the 'I,' a new term which, however, does not introduce anything new but is a useless paraphrase of egoism." (97: p. 105) It should be noted here that egoism in the usual sense is not at all excluded from Fourier's system. He held that the most useful people in the future society would be those who are inclined to enjoyment and who declare duty to be the invention of philosophers. Fourier offers a list of the most important passions for the new order: love of fine food, sensuality, a passion for diversity, competition, self-love. Evidently, "egoism" in the quotation above should be understood in a broader sense and the "I" in a direct sense.

In Marxism the idea is occasionally expressed that man has no existence as an individuality but only as a member of a definite class—individual man is the invention of philosophers. We come across attacks on the "corrupt" views that hold "instead of the interests of the proletariat, the interests of man, who does not belong to any class and, in general, exists not in reality but in the clouds of philosophic fantasy." (3: V: pp. 506–507) Marx says: "The essence of man is not an abstract quality inherent in a separate individual. In reality it is the aggregate of all social relations." (3: IV: p. 590) Marx was concerned with the question of why, under conditions of complete political emancipation, religion does not disappear. From his point of view, this testifies to the fact that a certain flaw remains in society, but the reason for this flaw should be sought in the very essence of the state. Religion is no longer presented as a cause but as a manifestation of general narrow-mindedness. The essence of this narrow-mindedness and limitation he sees in the following: "Political democracy is Christian in nature because man in it—not man in general but each man separately—is considered a sovereign and supreme being; and this is said of man in his uncultivated, non-social aspect, of man in a haphazard form of existence, man as he is in life, man as he is corrupted by the whole organization of our society, lost and alienated from himself; in a word, man who is not yet a genuine creature." (3: I: p. 368)

In the contemporary leftist movement, the theme of the struggle against individuality is particularly strong. The ideologists of this movement distinguish several aspects of revolution (or of a series of "revolutions," as they put it): social, racial, sexual, artistic, psychedelic. Among these, two especially are perceived as means for the annihilation of "bourgeois individuality"—the psychedelic revolution (collective use of hallucinogens and deafening rock music) and a particular aspect of the sexual revolution ("group sex," which goes much further than the group marriage of primitive tribes, since not only the personality but also the sex of the partners plays no role).

This tendency leads to attempts to overcome sex distinction. Thus we read in a contemporary leftist magazine: "Capitalism developed the ever more inhuman polarization of the sexes. The cult of making distinctions, which serves only for oppression, is now being swept away by awareness of resemblance and 'identity.' " The author quotes another representative of the same current: "Both sexes are moving toward general Humanity." (142: p. 25)

Marcuse foresees a society in which fantasy, now suppressed by reason, will open up a new approach to reality. In his understanding of the nature of fantasy Marcuse here follows Freud, citing, in particular, the latter's idea that fantasy "preserves the structure and tendencies of the psyche prior to its organization by the reality, prior to its becoming an 'individual' set off against other individuals. And by the same token, like the id, to which it remains committed, fantasy preserves a 'memory' of the subhistorical past, when the life of the individual was the life of the genus, the image of the immediate unity between the particular and the universal under the rule of the pleasure principle." (119: p. 142) It is precisely in the process of disintegration of this unity that there appears the "principium individuationis" hostile to fantasy. Marcuse believes that one of Freud's most important services was the destruction of "one of the strongest ideological fortifications of modern culture—namely, the notion of the autonomous individual." (119: p. 57)

Sartre's views in this connection are also of interest. He says, for example: "I believe that the thinking of the group is where the truth is. . . . I have thought this way since childhood. I always considered group thinking to be better than thinking alone. . . . I don't believe a separate individual to be capable of doing anything." (143: pp. 170–171) He feels particular antipathy for such individual action as sacrifice. "The sacrificial type is narrow-minded by nature. . . . This is a monstrous type. All my life I have fought against the spirit of sacrifice." (143: p. 183)

We meet with the very same features in the historical models of socialism. Discussing the influence of the Inca system on the Indians' psyche, Baudin writes: "Life itself was torn out of that geometrical and sad empire, where everything occurred with the inevitability of *fatum*. . . . The Indian lost his personality." (56: pp. 135–136)

The depth of the conflict between individuality as a category and socialist ideology is indicated by the fact that this conflict touches on the innermost core of individuality. As so much else in man, his individuality has two strata—one, the more ancient, is of prehuman origin and man shares it with many animals, while the newer stratum is specifically human.

Ethologists (scientists investigating the behavior of animals) see the moment when *individual bonding* appears as the first manifestation of individuality in the animal world (i.e., when there are relations in which one animal cannot be replaced by any other). This phenomenon may be observed experimentally by trying to substitute one animal for another. Certain types of fish, birds and mammals exhibit this type of bonding; a classic example of the phenomenon that has been thoroughly investigated is the bonding of the graylag goose. In this species, bonding is accomplished in a complicated ritual performed by parents and nestlings or by a pair or by two ganders. When one individual dies, the other calls him and looks for him everywhere, stops avoiding predators, becomes timid. Lorenz even assures us that in the eyes of such a creature there appears the same expression as in the eyes of an unhappy human. (144: Chap. 11)

The presence of individual bonds has great importance for the structure of animal societies, which are divided into *anonymous* societies, in which animals do not distinguish each other as individuals (for example, groups of herring or of rats), and *individualized* societies, in which animals are linked by individual relations (e.g., geese). Astonishingly, among the forces supporting the existence of individualized animal societies, according to the ethologists, are precisely those factors (seen in human society) with which socialism is in conflict: the upbringing of offspring by a family, individually bonded children and parents and, in general, individual bonds between members of society. (Deschamps foresees "life without separate bonds" in the future society.) Other individualized animal behavior includes animal hierarchies in which individuals have different importance, and where, for instance, older members can use their experience for the benefit of the whole group, while stronger individuals defend the weak. Finally, there is a phenomenon which may be regarded as a prehuman analogy of property: the notion of territory in animal society.

Socialism is equally hostile to those specifically human factors which account for the individuality of man, to those aspects of life in which man can participate only as an individuality and cannot be replaced by anyone else. Cultural creativity, particularly artistic creativity, is an example. We have seen how the most outstanding thinkers of the socialist trend (Plato, Deschamps) elaborate measures that provide for the complete disappearance of culture. And in periods when socialist movements are on the increase, the call for the destruction of culture is heard ever more distinctly. It is sufficient to recall the regular destruction of books in monastery libraries by the Taborites and the destruction of works of art by the Anabaptists in Münster. In the years of War Communism, an anti-culture trend was quite evident, as we have already indicated. The contemporary left radical socialist movements manifest the same attitude toward culture. Culture is understood by them to be "bourgeois" and "repressive"; the goal of art is understood as an "explosion" or the destruction of culture. The theoretical framework is derived from Freud, Adorno and Marcuse, with their notion of the uncompromising conflict between the instincts and oppressive culture. The prominent leftist H. M. Enzensberger, for instance, criticizes literacy and literature as typically bourgeois elements of culture. He considers literacy to possess "class character" and to be subordinated to numerous social "taboos." The rules of orthography are imposed by society as norms and their violation is punished or condemned. "Intimidation by means of a written text has remained a widespread phenomenon of class character even in developed industrial societies. It is impossible to remove these elements of alienation from written literature." (145: p. 181) Although the author does not foresee a complete destruction of literacy, literature and books, he assumes that they will be supplanted by such means of communication as radio and television (perfected to the point where each receiver will function simultaneously as a transmitter). In the new information system, the written word will be preserved only as an "extreme case."

One of the most significant features of spiritual life directly linked to the existence of individuality is a sense of individual (and not collective) responsibility for the fate of one's social group, city, nation, or of all mankind. With Plato being perhaps the only exception, all socialist ideologists are hostile to such an attitude. The medieval heretics, as we have seen, called either for a radical break with the world and life or for their destruction. This point of view was preserved in other socialist movements from the Reformation until our day. In recent centuries it has found support in the notion that history is governed by iron laws as precise as the laws of physics and that its basic direction could not be affected by human will. Fourier's position is typical. (Fourier is a forthright and honest writer whose philosophical views were not distorted by the exigencies of practical activity, by considerations of party politics or revolutionary struggle.) In answer to the question what one should do while awaiting the onset of the future order, he says: "Do not sacrifice the good of the present to the good of the future; enjoy the moment; avoid any matrimonial or other union which does not satisfy your passions—now. Why work for the sake of the future good? For this good will exceed your most treasured desires in any case, and in the combined social structure you will be threatened by only one trouble—the impossibility of making your life twice as long so as to exhaust the huge circle of pleasures awaiting you." (97: p. 293)

Finally, human individuality finds its greatest support and its highest appreciation in religion. Only as a personality can man turn to God and only through this dialogue does he realize himself as a person commensurate with the person of God. It is for this very reason that socialist ideology and religion are mutually exclusive. (Of course, if either of these world views is underdeveloped, they can coexist for a certain time.) It is natural to see here the cause of that hatred for religion which is typical of the overwhelming majority of socialist doctrines and states.

The same approach makes more comprehensible the curious traits we observed in the "Conspiracy of Equals" (see Part One, Chapter III, Section 4, above): the naïve adventurism, the arrogant boastfulness, the disposition to petty dishonesty and disruptive behavior, a certain inanity that gave the whole movement a somewhat comic and Gogolian flavor. These features are inherent in a majority of socialist movements in the initial period of their development. Among anarchistic and nihilistic currents in Russia, they found ultimate expression in "Nechayevism," so brilliantly described by Dostoyevsky in *The Possessed*. Early Marxism exhibits similar traits quite vividly. For example, there is the incredible history of the writing of the first critical reviews on Volume I of *Capital*—all composed anonymously by Engels. He offered Marx to write two, then four or five review articles "from different points of view" or "from a bourgeois point of view." Meanwhile Marx provided him with detailed instructions on what to praise and what to disagree with for the sake of authenticity. Marx writes: "In this way, I should think, it might be possible to hoodwink that Swabian Maier [the editor of a newspaper]. No matter how insignificant his paper is, it is still a popular oracle for all the federalists in Germany and is read abroad as well." "It's hilarious how both magazines have taken the bait," Engels informs Marx. In the first year after the appearance of the book seven reviews appeared—five of them by Engels, one each by his friends Kugelman and Siebel, who followed Engels' lead. As a result, Marx could say: "The conspiracy of silence in the bourgeois and reactionary press has been broken!" (Letter to Kugelman, February 11, 1869) He writes to Engels: "Jenny, a specialist in these matters, asserts that you have developed a great dramatic and even a comic

talent in this matter of 'different points of view' and various disguises."
(See 3: XXIII: pp. 406, 445, 453, 458, 465, 473, 483, 484; XXIV: pp.
3, 5, 26, 59, 65, 80, and the general survey in 146)*

Equally bizarre is the episode of the "portraits" of prominent revolutionary figures in emigration that were put together for twenty-five
pounds sterling for a certain Bann, who later proved to be an agent
of the Austrian and Prussian police. In response to Marx's proposal,
however, Engels immediately warns him that it would be regarded
as "assisting reaction," but concludes: "£25 valent bien un peu de
scandale." (3: XXI: p. 359) Or, finally, take the threats to blackmail
their comrades in arms: "Doesn't this brute understand that if only I
so desire, he would be up to his ears in a stinking swamp? I have
more than a hundred of his letters in my possession. Has he forgotten
that?" (Marx writing about Freiligrath, 3: XXII: p. 493)

The correspondence of the founders of the materialist approach
to history abounds in such passages. The same traits are evident in
today's more extreme left movements in America and Western Europe,
and often give these movements a rather frivolous character. (Cf. 147)

To get a better feeling for the characteristics of these phenomena,
it is worthwhile juxtaposing them with similar episodes from the sphere
of religion, or with nationalistic movements where completely unknown individuals or small groups first launch their ideas. Take, for
example, Captain Ilyin, the founder of the sect of "Forest Brethren"
or "Jehovists" at the end of the nineteenth century in Russia; he was
persecuted all his life and spent fourteen years in harsh confinement
in the Solovetsky Monastery. One can reject his religious ideas, but
it is impossible not to be struck by his profound dignity and moral
strength, which never left him in the course of his many ordeals. There
are thousands of such examples. It would seem that many people—
leaders of the movements in particular—do not derive from socialist
ideology the same sort of strength and self-confidence. This comes
only at the height of success when the movement attracts the broad
masses. Here, as elsewhere, Marx's words turn out to be to the point,
if we understand them as referring to himself: "*These* ideas do not
give strength of themselves but become a force when they hold sway
over the masses." The reasons are clear in the light of the above discus-

* In this connection, Engels' reproach to Loria appears in a different light: "The
importunate charlatanism of self-aggrandizement," "success achieved with the help of
clamorous friends." See p. 211n., above.

sion: an ideology that is hostile to human personality cannot serve as a point of support for it.

We can see that all elements of the socialist ideal—the abolition of private property, family, hierarchies; the hostility toward religion—could be regarded as a manifestation of one basic principle: the suppression of individuality. It is possible to demonstrate this graphically by listing the more typical features that keep appearing in socialist theory and practice over two and a half thousand years, from Plato to Berlin's "Commune No. 1," and then constructing a model of an "ideal" (albeit nonexistent) socialist society. People would wear the same clothing and even have similar faces; they would live in barracks. There would be compulsory labor followed by meals and leisure activities in the company of the same labor battalion. Passes would be required for going outside. Doctors and officials would supervise sexual relations, which would be subordinated to only two goals: the satisfaction of physiological needs and the production of healthy offspring. Children would be brought up from infancy in state nurseries and schools. Philosophy and art would be completely politicized and subordinated to the educational goals of the state. All this is inspired by one principle—the destruction of individuality or, at least, its suppression to the point where it would cease to be a social force. Dostoyevsky's comparisons to the ant hill and the bee hive turn out to be particularly apt in the light of ethological classifications of society: we have constructed a model of the *anonymous society.*

# x    The Goal
of Socialism

Difficulties in understanding socialist ideology arise when we try to correlate its doctrinal prescriptions for the organization of society with the actual forms of these principles as they are realized in history. For example, the picture of a society "in which the free development of each will be the precondition of the free development of all" contains no contradiction. But when the "leading theoretician" asserts that the creation of this harmonious man is achieved by shooting, we are face to face with a paradox. The view of socialism to which we have come encounters the same kind of difficulties and must be tested by this means for inconsistency. It is not enough to say that all the basic principles of socialist ideology derive from the urge to suppress individuality. It is necessary also to understand what this tendency portends for mankind and how it arises. We shall begin with the former question.

At the end of the preceding chapter we sketched the "ideal" socialist society as it appears in the classical writings of socialism. Of the features enumerated, we shall consider only one: state upbringing of children from infancy so that they do not know their parents. It is natural to begin with this aspect of the socialist ideal, if only because it would be the first thing that an individual born into this society would face. This measure is suggested with striking consistency from Plato to Liadov, a leading Soviet theoretician of the 1920s. In the 1970s, the Japanese police arrested members of the "Red Army," a Trotskyite organization, which was responsible for a number of murders. Although this group numbered only a few dozen people, it had all the attributes of a real socialist party—theoreticians, a split on the question of whether revolution should occur in one country or in the entire world at once, terror against dissidents. The group established itself in a lonely mountain region. And the same trait surfaced here: they took newborn children away from their mothers, entrusted them to other women for upbringing and fed them on powdered milk, despite difficulties in obtaining it.

Let us quote from a book by the modern ethologist Eibl-Eibesfeldt, which will help us evaluate the biological significance of this measure:

> It is especially in the second half of the first year of life that a child establishes personal ties with its mother or a person substituting for her (a nurse, a matron). This contact is the precondition for the development of "primary trust" (E. H. Erikson), the basis for the attitude toward oneself and the world. The child learns to trust his partner, and this positive basic orientation is the foundation of a healthy personality. If these contacts are broken, "primary distrust" develops. A prolonged stay in the hospital during the child's second year may, for example, lead to such results. Though the child will try even there to establish close contact with a mother substitute, no nurse will be able to devote herself intensively enough to an infant for a close personal tie to be established. Nurses constantly change, and so the contacts that arise are constantly broken. The child, deceived in his expectations of contact, falls into a state of apathy after a brief outburst of protest. During the first month of his stay in the hospital he whines and clings to anyone available. During the second month he usually cries and loses weight. During the third month such children only weep quietly and finally become thoroughly apathetic. If after three to four months' separation they are taken home, they return to normal. But if they stay in the hospital longer, the trauma becomes irreversible. . . . In one orphanage where R. Spitz studied ninety-one children who had been separated from their mothers in the third month of their lives, thirty-four died before they reached the age of two. The level of development of the survivors was only 45 percent of normal and the children were almost like idiots. Many of them could neither walk nor stand nor speak at age four. (148: p. 234)

This may be applied to the whole of a society built on the consistent implementation of socialist ideals. Not only people but even animals cannot exist if reduced to the level of the cogs of a mechanism. Even such a seemingly elementary act as eating is not reducible to the mere satiation of the organism. For an animal to eat, it is not enough that it be hungry and that food be available; the food must be enticing, "appetizing," as well. And in more complex actions involving several individuals, such as raising of young, the common defense of territory or hunting, animals establish relations that usually are ritualistic in nature and that elicit great excitement and undoubtedly provide deep satisfaction. For animals, these ties constitute "the meaning of life"; if they are broken, the animal becomes apathetic, does not take food, and becomes an easy victim for a predator. To a far greater extent, this applies to man. But for him, all the aspects of life that make it attractive and give it meaning are connected with manifestations of individuality. Therefore, a consistent implementation of the principles of socialism deprives human life of individuality and simultaneously deprives life of its meaning and attraction. As suggested by the example of the orphaned children, it would lead to the physical extinction of the group in which these principles are in force, and if they should triumph through the world—to the extinction of mankind.

But the conclusion that we have reached has yet to be tested by history because the socialist ideals have nowhere achieved complete implementation. The primitive states of the ancient Orient and pre-Columbian America had a very weakly developed socialist ideology. In keeping with Shang Yang's principle ("When the people are weak the state is strong; when the state is weak the people are strong"), particularly strong, conservative and long-lived state structures were created. In these states, however, the principle of the "weak people" was understood only in the sense of external, physical limitations—choice of work, place of residence, severe limitations on private property, the large number of official duties. These duties did not touch the life within the family or cut deeply into man's soul. They were not ideologically inspired, and it was apparently the same patriarchal quality that preserved these states from dying out but, on the other hand, left them defenseless in the face of new spiritual forces called forth by the abrupt shifts of the first millennium B.C.

The socialist states of the twentieth century are also far from being a model of the *complete* realization of socialist ideals. But one must note that when *survival* is at stake, it was achieved in these states precisely by giving up some fundamental socialist principle. This occurred with the introduction of the New Economic Policy in Soviet Russia and with the halt ordered by Stalin in the persecution of religion during World War II.

However, it is possible to point out a number of similar situations which may serve, though indirectly, to support our point of view.

It happens not infrequently that a nation or a social group dies out not because of economic reasons or due to destruction by enemies but because the spiritual conditions of its existence are destroyed. For example, H. G. Wells wrote the following after visiting Petrograd in 1920: "The mortality rate among the intellectually distinguished men in Russia has been terribly high. Much, no doubt, has been due to general hardship of life, but in many cases I believe that the sheer mortification of great gifts become futile has been the determining cause. They could no more live in the Russia of 1919 than they could have lived in a Kaffir kraal." (1: p. 57)

Another example of far greater scope involves the confrontation of primitive peoples with modern civilization. The majority of ethnographers now agree that the main cause of the dying out of these peoples was not physical destruction or exploitation by Europeans or contagious disease or alcohol but the destruction of their spiritual world, their religion and their rituals. For example, the prominent specialist in the culture of the Australian aborigines, A. Elkin, paints the following picture:

> What then is this secret life of the aborigines? It is the life apart—a life of ritual and mythology, of sacred rites and objects. It is the life in which man really finds his place in society and in nature, and in which he is brought in touch with the invisible things of the world of the past, present and future. Every now and then we find the tribe, or groups from more than one tribe, going apart from the workaday world. A special camp is arranged where the women remain unless some of them are called upon to play a subsidiary part in a ceremony. Then the men go on a mile or so to a secret site or to sites where they spend hours, or maybe days and weeks and even months, singing and performing rites, and in some cases even eating or sleeping there. When they return later to the world of secular affairs they are refreshed in mind and spirit. They now face the vicissitudes of everyday life with a new courage and a strength gained from the common participation in the rites, with a fresh appreciation of their social and moral ideals and patterns of life, and an assurance that having performed the rites well and truly, all will be well with themselves and with that part of nature with which their lives are so intimately linked. (149: pp. 162–163)
>
> . . . The missionary or civilizing agent may be successful in putting an end to initiation and other secret rites, or in getting such a grip over the rising generation that the old men make the initiation a mere form and not an entry into the full secret life of the tribe. But this implies a breakdown of tribal authority and a loss of the knowledge of, let alone the respect for, those ideals, sentiments and sanctions which are essential to tribal cohesion; and in Australia, such a condition is the accompaniment, and a cause of tribal extinction. (149: p. 161)

And G. Childe writes: "An ideology, however remote from obvious biological needs, is found in practice to be biologically useful, that is, favorable to the species' survival. Without such spiritual equipment, not only do societies tend to disintegrate, but the individuals composing them may just stop bothering to keep alive. The 'destruction of religion' among primitive peoples is always cited by experts as a major cause in their extinction in contact with white civilization. . . . Evidently societies of men cannot live by bread alone." (150: p. 8)

An example which partly refers to the same sort of phenomenon and, at the same time, brings us back to the main theme of our investigation is the fall in the birthrate among the Guaraní Indians in the Jesuit state. The Jesuits were compelled to resort to various means of pressure on the Indians in the hope of increasing the population. One can assume that the Draconian laws against abortion in the Inca state were also connected with a falling birthrate. Finally, should we not view in the same way the fact that the Russians, who were the most rapidly growing nation in Europe at the beginning of the century, now barely maintain their number?

We began with an example in which one can demonstrate experimentally the consequences of implementing only *one* principle in the socialist ideal, namely, the abolition of the family. Other examples illustrate the impact on society of the *partial* demolition of its spiritual structure (culture, religion, mythology). What, then, can be said of the possible situation where the socialist ideal would be embodied worldwide (since it evidently can reach its full potential only when it has overrun the entire world)? It is hardly possible to doubt that the same tendencies would then find their complete expression in the extinction of all of mankind.

This conclusion may be made more specific in two complementary ways. On the one hand, we may view our hypothetical case as a *limit situation* in the mathematical sense, as something that might never occur in reality. Just as in mathematics the concept of infinity clarifies the properties of constantly increasing sequences of numbers, so, too, this ultimate limit of historical development reveals the basic tendency of socialism: it is hostile toward human personality not only as a category, but ultimately to its very existence.

Or else we can assume that the complete victory of socialism is attainable. There is certainly nothing that suggests the existence of any kind of limit beyond which socialist principles cannot be applied. It would seem that everything depends only upon the depth of the crisis with which mankind may be faced. In this case, one could regard the death of mankind as the final *result* to which the development of socialism leads.

Here we touch on the most profound of all the many questions socialism evokes: How could a doctrine leading to such an end come into being and sway such tremendous masses of people over thousands of years? The answer to this question, to a large extent, depends on the view one takes of the interrelation of socialist ideology and the end point that we have postulated above. Are they quite independent of each other in the way that the improvement of living conditions and the resulting population crisis are, for instance? (However cruel and disastrous the effects of a demographic explosion might be, the factors that allow it to happen are the consequence of other, directly opposite motives.) Or perhaps there are essential features in socialist ideology that link it directly with what we have deduced to be the practical result of its rigorous implementation—the death of mankind? Several arguments incline us toward the second point of view.

To begin with, most socialist doctrines and movements are literally saturated with the mood of death, catastrophe and destruction. For the majority of them, it is this very mood that has constituted their basic inner motivation. The teaching of the Taborites is typical here: In the new age that was beginning, they asserted, Christ's law of charity would be abolished and each of the faithful must wash his hands in the blood of the godless. This is clearly expressed in a document that originated in Czech Picard circles but was known as far away as northern France. The text ends with the following exhortation:

> Let each gird himself with the sword and let brother not spare brother; father, son; son, father; neighbor, neighbor. Kill all one after the other so that German heretics should flee in mobs, and we destroy in this world the gain and the greediness of the clergy. So we fulfill God's seventh Commandment, for according to the Apostle Paul, greed is idolatry, and idols and idolators should be killed, so we can wash our hands in their accursed blood, as Moses taught through example and in his writing, for what is written there is written for our edification. (16: p. 140)

The same motifs are dominant in the Anabaptist revolution—in Müntzer's teaching and in Münster. In later years, they accompany the new upsurge in the activity of socialist movements and are manifest with equal clarity in the socialist-nihilist movement in the twentieth century. Thus Bakunin writes, in a proclamation entitled "The Principles of Revolution":

Therefore, in accordance with strict necessity and justice we must devote ourselves wholly and completely to unrestrained and relentless destruction, which must grow in a crescendo until there is nothing left of the existing social forms. . . . We say: the most complete destruction is incompatible with creation, therefore destruction must be absolute and exclusive. The present generation must begin with real revolutions. It must begin with a complete change of all social living conditions; this means that the present generation must blindly raze everything to the ground with only one thought: As fast and as much as possible. . . . (95: p. 361)

Though we do not recognize any other activity besides the task of destruction, we hold to the opinion that the form in which this activity manifests itself may be quite varied: poison, dagger, noose, and so forth. The revolution blesses everything in equal measure in this struggle. (95: 363)

It is striking that the mystique of destruction is here the only motivation; rapture in it is offered as the only reward, but one which must outweigh every sacrifice. And this is entirely consistent with a definition Bakunin and Nechayev constantly repeated: "A revolutionary is a doomed man." (151: p. 468) Death among universal destruction—this was subjectively the ultimate goal with which they lured their adherents. Higher feelings could not have fostered this activity, for they were utterly denied.

"All tender and gentle feelings of kinship, friendship, love, gratitude and even honor itself should be choked off in the revolutionary's breast by the single cold passion of his revolutionary task. He is not a revolutionary if he has pity for anything in the world. He knows only one science—the science of destruction. He lives in the world with a single aim—its total and swift destruction." (151: pp. 468–470)

Even dreams of the bright future for the sake of which all the destruction was to occur could not serve as a stimulus and were forbidden outright.

"Since our generation has itself been under the influence of the abominable conditions which it is now destroying, creation must not be its task but the task of those pure forces that will come into being in the days of renewal. The loathsomeness of modern civilization, in which we have grown up, has deprived us of the capability of building the paradise-like structures of the future life, of which we can have but the vaguest idea, and our thoughts are taken with diametrically opposite, unpleasant matters. For people who are ready to start the practical task of revolution, we consider it criminal to have these thoughts of the dim future, as they hinder the cause of destruction and delay the beginning of revolution. . . . For the practical task at hand, it is a pointless spiritual corruption." (95: p. 361)

It is often said that certain features so vividly expressed in nihilism—the goal of complete destruction, neglect of all moral principles, conspiracy, terror—are peculiar to this movement specifically, and that it is precisely these features that distinguish nihilism from its antipode, Marxist socialism. Sometimes this view is supplemented by the opinion that Bolshevism is a typically Russian phenomenon, the heritage of Nechayev and Bakunin and a perversion of Marxism. This view was expressed, for example, by Kautsky in his books (103 and 135) published in 1919 and 1921. (Kautsky notes that similar ideas had been expressed by Rosa Luxemburg as far back as 1904.) But what to do about the striking coincidence of Bolshevik ideology and practice with numerous statements by Marx and Engels? An attempt is usually made to explain these coincidences away by asserting that the particular statements of Marx and Engels are not characteristic and are at odds with their essential message. (Opinions, however, diverge about which part of their writing should be considered central. Kautsky believes that the later corpus of their writings, the works that appeared after the revolution of 1848, constitute the central core of Marxism, which was distorted by Bolshevism, while modern socialists—Fromm, Sartre—see the earlier works this way. Indeed, Sartre even speaks about those works by Marx that preceded his "ill-fated meeting with Engels.")

The facts hardly support such a view. Nihilism of the Bakunin type and Marxism developed from the same source. The differences between them (which explain, incidentally, why Bakunin has far less influence than Marx and Engels on history) lie not in the fact that Marxism renounced elements of nihilism but that it added to them some new and very significant elements. Marxism is based on the same psychological foundation as nihilism—a burning hatred for surrounding life that can be vented only through complete annihilation of that life. But Marxism finds a means of transferring this purely subjective perception of the world onto another, more objective plane. As with art, where passion is kept in check and transformed into creative works, Marxism accomplished a transformation of the elemental, destructive emotions that ruled Bakunin and Nechayev into a structure that seemed incomparably more objective and hence convincing—the concept of man's subordination to "immanent laws" or "the dialectics of production."

But the perception of the world on which the Marxist structure is founded is identical to that in Nechayev and Bakunin. This is particularly clear in the works of Marx and Engels written for a narrow circle of collaborators and, in particular, in their correspondence. (3: XXI–XXIV. It would seem that the full texts of these letters have been published only in Russian translation.) We encounter here the same feeling of disgust and seething hatred for the world, beginning with the writers' parents: "My old man will have to pay plenty for this, and in cash." (Engels to Marx, February 26, 1851) "Your old man is a pig." (Marx to Engels, November 1848) "Nothing to be done with my old woman until I myself sit on her neck." (Marx to Engels, September 13, 1854) The same feelings are vented on close friends: "The dog has a monstrous memory for all such muck." (About Heine, Marx to Engels, January 17, 1853.) The same holds for party comrades: Liebknecht is usually called an ass, a brute, a beast, and so on, even "it." (E.g., in a letter from Marx to Engels, August 10, 1869.) Their own party gets the same treatment: "What significance does a 'party' have, i.e., a gang of asses, blindly believing in us because they consider us equal to themselves. . . . In truth we would lose nothing if we were to be considered no longer 'a real and adequate' expression of these mediocre dogs with whom we have spent the last years." (Engels to Marx, February 13, 1851) The proletariat is not excluded: ". . . stupid nonsense regarding his being compelled to defend me from that great hatred the workers (i.e., fools) feel for me." (Marx to Engels, May 18, 1859) Neither is democracy: ". . . a pack of new democratic bastards." (Marx to Engels, February 10, 1851) ". . . democratic dogs and liberal scoundrels." (Marx to Engels, February 25, 1859) The people are sneered at: "Well, as for *loving* us, the democratic, the red, even the Communist mob never will." (Engels to Marx, May 9, 1851) And even the human race evokes disgust: "Not a *single* living soul visits me, and I am glad of that, for humanity here can go . . . The pigs! With regards. Yours, K. M." (To Engels, June 18, 1862)

The tactical devices that derived from this perception of life are very similar to those used by Nechayev of Bakunin. Kautsky, who accuses Bakunin of leading a party to which he had appointed himself head, might have recalled Marx's letter to Engels (May 18, 1859): "I declared to them point-blank: we have received our mandate as the representatives of the proletarian party from no one *but ourselves.* And it is confirmed as ours by the exceptional and universal hatred which all segments of the old world and all the parties harbor for us. You can imagine how these fools were taken aback." In criticizing Bakunin's penchant for conspiracy, Kautsky should have kept in mind a letter from Engels to Marx (September 16, 1868): "The method of engaging in trifles at public meetings and doing real business on the quiet justified itself brilliantly." And in claiming that the idea of terror and violence was an error of the *young* Marx and Engels, it would have been well to explain why Engels writes in *Anti-Dühring:* "It is only with sighs and groans that he [Dühring] admits the possibility that force will perhaps be necessary for the overthrow of the economic system of exploitation—unfortunately, don't you see, because any use of force demoralizes the person who uses it. And this in spite of the immense moral and spiritual impetus which has resulted from every victorious revolution!" (98: p. 185) And how is it that in the preface to *History of the Peasant War in Germany,* Engels advises contemporary Germans to follow the example of the "healthy vandalism" of the Peasant War? How can we explain his words in a letter to Bebel: "If, thanks to war, we should come to power prematurely, the technicians will become our special enemies, and will deceive and betray us wherever they can. We will have to resort to terror. . . ." (3: XXVIII: p. 365)

And at the same time it is impossible to deny that these ideas came into being at the very beginning of the activity of Marx and Engels. "This is at least the best thing that remains for us to do, while we are compelled to use the pen and cannot bring our ideas into life with the help of our hands or, if necessary, with our fists." (Engels to Marx, November 19, 1844) Kautsky undoubtedly knew all these passages and others like them, since he took part in the editing of the German edition of the Marx-Engels correspondence, from which most expressions of this type were eliminated by the editors. It is clear from his books what it was that evoked such dislike for Bolshevism and the desire to prove, at any cost, that it distorts Marxism: the astonishing contagiousness of Bolshevik ideas and their rapid diffusion in the Western socialist parties raised the old fears of "Russian dominance" in the International. (This misgiving was first voiced by Engels about Bakunin.)

The other link connecting socialist ideology with the idea of humanity's demise is the notion of mankind's inevitable death that is present in many socialist doctrines. We have seen, for instance, that the Cathars, whose teaching contained ideas of a socialist character, believed that after the fallen angels are freed from material captivity, the remaining people will die, and the entire material world will be plunged into primeval chaos.

As a second example, we take the views of the future of mankind held by three prominent ideologues of socialism: Saint-Simon, Fourier and Engels. In Saint-Simon's On Universal Gravitation there is a section on "The Future of the Human Race." Here, in detail and with great feeling, he describes the death of mankind—presented in reverse chronological order for effect, something like a film shown backward.

> Our planet has a tendency to desiccation. . . . On the basis of these observations, geologists arrive at the inevitable conclusion that a time will come when our planet will have dried up completely. It is clear that it will then become uninhabitable and, consequently, from a certain point onward the human race will gradually begin to dwindle. . . . Section Two: At the beginning of this section we shall describe the sensations of the last man, as he dies after having drunk the last drop of water on earth. We shall show that the sensation of death will be far more burdensome for him than for us because his own death will coincide with the death of the entire human race. Then, from the description of the moral state of the last man, we shall proceed backward to the investigation of the moral state of the remnants of mankind, until that point when it shall see the beginning of its destruction and become convinced that it is inevitable, a conviction that will paralyze all moral energy . . . the desires of these people will be the same as those of animals. (153: pp. 275–276)

It is curious that Saint-Simon begins his work with this depiction, apparently supposing thereby to create a background against which the meaning and spirit of his system will be clearer.

Engels not only depicts the death of every living thing, but regards death as the other side of life, or its goal. "It is already accepted that the kind of physiology which does not consider death an essential moment of life cannot be regarded as a science; this is the kind of physiology that does not understand that the *denial* of life is innate to life itself, so that life is always seen in relation to the inevitable result that is inevitably part of it from the beginning—death. This is the essence of the dialectical perception of life." (3: XIV: p. 399) And more succinctly: "To live means to die."

Engels' picture of the end is one of the most vivid pages of his writing:

> Everything that arises is worthy of death. Millions of years will pass, hundreds of thousands of generations will be born and go down into the grave, but inexorably the time will come when the weakening warmth

of the sun will not be able to melt the ice advancing from the poles; when mankind, crowded together at the equator, will cease to find the necessary warmth even there and the earth—a frozen dead sphere like the moon—will circle in profound darkness around a sun which is also dead and into which it will finally fall. The other planets will experience the same fate, some sooner, the others later than the earth, and instead of an orderly, bright and warm solar system there will remain a cold dead ball continuing on its lonely way in the universe. And the fate that will have befallen our solar system will sooner or later befall all other systems, even those whose light will never reach the earth while there is on it a human eye capable of perceiving it." (3: XIV: pp. 488–489)

Fourier, who in other cases seemed to show such a sincere attachment to life and its pleasures, also gave this idea its due. His "Table of Social Motion," encompassing the entire past and future of the earth, concludes thus: *"The end of the animal and vegetable kingdom, after approximately 80,000 years.* (The spiritual death of the earth, the stopping of rotation on its axis, the violent translocation of the poles to the equators, fixation on the sun, natural death, fall and disintegration in the Milky Way.)"

Although Engels foresaw the end of life on earth from material causes that differ greatly from those suggested by Fourier, the basic idea evoked his obvious approval: "Fourier, as we see, is just as masterful at dialectics as his contemporary Hegel. In the same dialectical fashion he asserts, in contrast to statements about man's capacity for unlimited perfection, that each historical phase has not only its ascending line but also its descending one, and he applies this method of perception to the future of mankind as a whole. Just as Kant introduced into natural science the idea of the future death of the earth, Fourier introduced into the perception of history the concept of the future death of mankind." (98: p. 264)

We note how different this notion of the death of mankind is from the conception of the "end of the world" in a number of religions, including Christianity. The religious idea of the end of the world presupposes, in essence, its translation, after human history has achieved its goal, into some other state. Socialist ideology puts forward the idea of the complete destruction of mankind, proceeding from an external cause and depriving history of any meaning.

A new synthesis of socialist ideology with the ideas of death and destruction appears in Marcuse's works, which have greatly influenced the contemporary leftist movements. Here, too, Marcuse follows Freud.

In the Freudian view (first expressed in the article "Beyond the Pleasure Principle"), the human psyche can be reduced to a manifestation of two main instincts: the life instinct or Eros and the death instinct or Thanatos (or the Nirvana principle). Both are general biological categories, fundamental properties of living things in general. The death instinct is a manifestation of general "inertia" or a tendency of organic life to return to a more elementary state from which it had been aroused by an external disturbing force. The role of the life instinct is essentially to prevent a living organism from returning to the inorganic state by any path other than that which is immanent in it.

Marcuse introduces a greater social factor into this scheme, asserting that the death instinct expresses itself in the desire to be liberated from tension, as an attempt to rid oneself of the suffering and discontent which are specifically engendered by social factors. In the Utopia proposed by him, these goals can be realized, Marcuse believes. He describes this new state in an extremely general way, making use of mythological analogies. Against Prometheus, the hero of repressive culture, he sets Narcissus and Orpheus—bearers of the principles upon which his Utopia is built. They symbolize "the redemption of pleasure, the halt of time, the absorption of death; silence, sleep, night, paradise—the Nirvana principle not as death but as life." (119: p. 164) "The Orphic-Narcissistic images do explode it [reality]; they do not convey a 'mode of living'; they are committed to the underworld and to death." (119: p. 165) About Narcissus he says: "If his erotic attitude is akin to death and brings death, then rest and sleep and death are not painfully separated and distinguished: the Nirvana principle rules throughout all these stages." (119: p. 167)

The less the difference between life and death is, the weaker will be the destructive manifestations of the death principle: "The death instinct operates under the Nirvana principle: it tends toward that state of 'constant gratification' where no tension is felt—a state without want. This trend of the instinct implies that its *destructive* manifestations would be minimized as it approached such a state." (119: p. 234) "In terms of the [death] instinct, the conflict between life and death is the more reduced, the closer life approximates the state of gratification." (119: p. 235)

This view has a more concrete interpretation: "Philosophy that does not work as the handmaiden of repression responds to the fact of death with the Great Refusal—the refusal of Orpheus the liberator.

Death can become a token of freedom. The necessity of death does not refute the possibility of final liberation. Like the other necessities, it can be made rational—painless. Men can die without anxiety if they know that what they love is protected from misery and oblivion. After a fulfilled life, they may take it upon themselves to die—at a moment of their own choosing." (119: pp. 236–237)

There is, finally, the case where the notion of the death of mankind combines with socialist ideology in such a way as to affect directly the fate of the individual members of socialist movements. In the Catharist movement, for example, obvious socialist tendencies were joined to the practice of ritual suicide. Runciman (11) believes that their ideal was the suicide of all mankind—either directly or by nonreproduction. We may place Abbé Meslier's suicide in the same category: so intimately was suicide linked to his general view of the world that he concludes his book *(Testament)* on this note: "The dead, with whom I intend to travel the same road, are troubled by nothing; they care for nothing. And with this nothing I shall finish here. I, myself, am now no more than nothing, and soon shall be in the full sense of the word nothing."

This frame of mind was particularly apparent in the Russian revolutionary movement. In the article "On Intellectual Youth" included in the collection *Landmarks* [*Vekhi*, 1909], A. S. Izgoev wrote: "No matter what the convictions held by the different groups of Russian intellectual youth were, in the final analysis, if we go deeper into their psychology, we see that they are inspired by one and the same ideal. . . . This is an ideal of deeply personal, intimate character, and it finds expression in the striving for death, in the desire to prove to oneself and to others the lack of fear of death and a readiness to accept it at any moment. This is, in essence, the only logical and moral substantiation of one's convictions that is accepted by the purest representatives of our revolutionary youth." (154: p. 116) Izgoev points out that the degree of "leftness" among political groups—Mensheviks, Bolsheviks, Social Revolutionaries, Anarchists and Maximalists—as this was evaluated by the intelligentsia, was not based on the political program of the given party. "It is clear that the criterion of 'leftness' lies elsewhere. 'Further left' is he who is closer to death, whose work is more 'dangerous'—not for the social system against which he is struggling, but for the activist himself, the individual in question." (154: p. 117)

He quotes a Maximalist pamphlet: " 'We repeat to the peasant and to the worker: when you go to fight and to die in the struggle, go and fight and die, but for your own rights, your own needs.' In this 'go and die' is the center of gravity of everything. . . . But this is nothing but suicide, and it is undeniable that for many years the Russian intelligentsia was an example of a peculiar monastic order of people who had doomed themselves to death, and the sooner the better." (154: pp. 117–118)

Indeed, the recollections of the terrorists of the day convey a strange sense of ecstasy persistently interfused with thoughts of death. Here are, for example, some excerpts from the recollections of Boris Savinkov (155), speaking about his collaborators in the attempt on Plehve's life: "Kaliaev loved the revolution as deeply and tenderly as only those who give up their lives for it can love. . . . He came to terror by his own peculiar and original route and saw in it not only the best form of political struggle but also a moral and, perhaps, a religious sacrifice." Kaliaev used to say that "a Social Revolutionary without a bomb is not a Social Revolutionary." Another participant, Sazonov, felt "strength beneath Kaliaev's expansiveness, burning faith beneath his inspired words, and beneath his love of life, a readiness to sacrifice this life and, even more, a passionate longing for such a sacrifice." And for Sazonov, too, "terrorist activity meant above all a personal sacrifice."

After the assassination, Sazonov wrote to his comrades from prison: "You gave me an opportunity to experience moral satisfaction incomparable to anything in the world. . . . I had hardly come to after the operation when I sighed with relief. Finally, it's over. I was ready to sing and shout with delight." A third participant was Dora Brilliant. For her, just as for the others, "terror . . . was colored, first of all, with the sacrifice that the terrorist makes. . . . Political questions did not interest her. Perhaps she had left all political activity with a certain degree of disenchantment; her days passed in silence, in silent and concentrated contemplation of the inner suffering with which she was filled. She seldom laughed, and even then, her eyes remained cold and sad. For her, terror personified the revolution; her whole world was enclosed within the militant organization." Savinkov recalls a conversation on the eve of the assassination attempt:

> Dora Brilliant arrived. She was silent for a long while, staring in front of her with her black, sad eyes.
> "Veniamin!" [Boris Savinkov's pseudonym]
> "What?"
> "I wanted to say . . ." She stopped, as if hesitating to finish the sentence.

"I wanted . . . I wanted to ask again that I be given the bomb."

"You? The bomb?"

"I want to take part in the attempt, too."

"Listen, Dora . . ."

"No, don't say anything . . . I also want to . . . I must die. . . ."*

A multitude of similar examples leads us to suppose that the dying and, ultimately, the complete extinction of mankind is not a chance external consequence of the embodiment of the socialist ideal but that this impulse is a fundamental and organic part of socialist ideology. To a greater or lesser degree it is consciously perceived as such by its partisans and even serves them as inspiration.

*The death of mankind is not only a conceivable result of the triumph of socialism—it constitutes the goal of socialism.*

One reader of my earlier essay on socialism (156) drew my attention to the fact that this thought had already been expressed in Dostoyevsky's "Legend of the Grand Inquisitor." It is true that Dostoyevsky's argument was directed at Catholicism, but he considered socialism to be a development of the Catholicism that had distorted Christ's teachings. (This view is elaborated in his articles that appeared in *The Diary of a Writer*.) Indeed, the picture of life presented as an ideal by the Grand Inquisitor closely resembles Plato or Campanella. "Oh, we shall persuade them that they will only become free when they renounce their freedom to us, and submit to us. . . . Yes, we shall set them to work, but in their leisure hours we shall make their life like a child's game, with children's songs and innocent dance. . . . And they will have no secrets from us. We shall allow or forbid them to live with their wives and mistresses, to have or not to have children, according to whether they have been obedient or disobedient, and they will submit to us gladly and cheerfully." And the Grand Inquisitor understands the ultimate goal for whose sake this life will be built:

"He sees that he must follow the counsel of the wise spirit, the dread spirit of death and destruction, and therefore accept lying and deception, and lead men consciously to death and destruction, and yet deceive them all the way so that they may not notice where they are being led." (157: pp. 325–327)†

* "I know that he was obsessed with the idea of death," says Sartre about the well-known leftist Nizan. "He had been in the U.S.S.R. and had spoken about it with his Soviet comrades, and he told me about this on his return. 'A revolution that does not make us obsessed with death is no revolution.' An interesting thought." (143: p. 81)

† In his letters, Dostoyevsky says that in "The Legend of the Grand Inquisitor" he wanted to show a "synthesis" of the fundamental ideas of contemporary socialism.

# XI   Conclusion

This paradoxical phenomenon may be understood only if we allow that the idea of the death of humanity can be attractive to man and that the impulse to self-destruction (even if it is only one of many tendencies) plays a role in human history. And there is in fact much evidence to support this hypothesis, particularly among phenomena that play an essential role in the spiritual life of mankind. Quite independently of socialism, each of these leads to the same conclusion. We can cite several examples.

We have in mind phenomena that relate to a vast and ancient religious and philosophical current: *pessimism* or *nihilism.* In the many variants of these doctrines, either the death of mankind and universal destruction are regarded as the desirable goal of the historical process, or else Nothingness is pronounced the essence of the world; the goal is then to understand that all reality is but a reflection of this essence. Vladimir Soloviev, who devoted an article to the notion of pessimism, singles out what he calls *absolute pessimism,* which corresponds to the tendency that interests us. (109: X: pp. 254–258) Its first complete expression is contained in Buddhism. Soloviev characterizes Buddhism as a doctrine of "the four noble truths: (1) Existence is *suffering;* (2) the cause of suffering is senseless *desire* which has neither basis nor aims; (3) deliverance from this suffering is possible through destruction of all desire, and (4) the path to deliverance leads through the *understanding* of the ties between phenomena and observation of the perfect moral commandments given by the Buddha; the goal of this path is Nirvana, the complete 'extinction' of existence." (109: X: p. 254)

Is Nirvana (literally, "extinction" as in the blowing out of a flame) actually a way to "Nothingness"? Buddha's views on this question have been interpreted differently. Max Müller, for example, thought that for Buddha himself Nirvana was the fulfillment and not the elimination of existence, assuming that a religion that offered *Nothingness* as an ultimate goal could never have existed. H. Oldenberg devotes a section in his book (158) to this question. He cites a number of episodes which characterize Buddha's attitude to the question whether the "I" exists and what the nature of Nirvana is. The import of these episodes is the same: Buddha refuses to answer such questions and by his authority forbids his disciples to consider them. But what is the meaning concealed here? The author believes that "if the Buddha avoids denying the existence of the 'I,' he does so only in order not to perplex the listeners who lack insight. In this denial of the question concerning the existence or nonexistence of the 'I,' an answer emerges in any case, something to which all the premises of the Buddha's teaching inevitably lead: the 'I' does not in truth exist. Or, what is one and the same thing: Nirvana is simply annihilation. . . . But it is clear that the thinkers who grasped and mastered this view did not want to promote it to the status of an official doctrine of the Buddhist community. . . . The official doctrine stopped short of questions on whether the 'I' exists, whether the perfect saint lives on or does not live on after death. The Great Buddha is said to have given no precept." (158: p. 227)

The fact that the Buddha left unanswered the questions of the existence of the 'I' and the nature of Nirvana naturally led to different interpretations of these problems within Buddhism. The two main Buddhist sects—Hīnayāna and Mahāyāna Buddhism—give opposite answers to the question of Nirvana. In Hīnayāna Buddhism, Nirvana is considered to be the cessation of the activity of consciousness. A contemporary Indian author characterizes the Hīnayāna teaching as follows: "In the Hīnayāna, Nirvana became interpreted negatively as the extinction of all being. . . . This view is an expression of weariness and disgust with the endless strife of becoming, and of the relief found in mere ceasing of effort. It is not a healthy-minded doctrine. A sort of world hatred is its inspiring motive." (159: pp. 590, 589) In Mahāyāna Buddhism, Nirvana is understood as a merging with the infinite, with the Great Soul of the universe, but it is not identified with the annihilation of existence.

However, it was to the Mahāyāna trend that Nāgārjuna belonged (he lived at a time around the beginning of the Christian era). His followers, the Mādhyamikas, are sometimes called nihilists.

Nāgārjuna proceeds on the assumption that that which is not understandable is not real. He then proves that the following are neither understandable nor explicable: motion and rest, time, causality, the notion of the part and the whole, the soul, the "I," Buddha, God and the universe. "There is no God apart from the universe, and there is no universe apart from God, and they both are equally appearances." (159: p. 655) "There is no death, no birth, no distinction, no persistence, no oneness, no manyness, no coming in, no going forth." (159: p. 655) "All things have the character of emptiness, they have no beginning, no end, they are faultless and not faultless, they are not imperfect and not perfect, therefore, O Sariputta, here in this emptiness there is no form, no perception, no name, no concept, no knowledge." (159: p. 656)

In China, the philosophy of Lao-tse (sixth century B.C.) may be seen as a part of the nihilist current. This is the teaching of the Tao, or "The Way." We find here a call for renunciation and quiescence that verges on the cessation of all activity:*

> One who is aware does not talk.
> One who talks is not aware.
> Ceasing verbal expressions,
> Stopping the entry of sensations,
> Dulling its sharpness,
> Releasing its entanglements,
> Tempering its brightness,
> And unifying with the earth:
> This is called the identity of Tao.
> Hence, no nearness can reach him nor
>     distance affect him.
> No gain can touch him nor loss disturb him.
> No esteem can move him nor shame distress him.
> Thus, he is the most valuable man in the world. . . .
>
> Much learning means little wisdom.
>
> . . . once the Way is lost,
> There comes then Virtue;
> Virtue lost, comes then compassion;
> After that morality;

* The texts are given in the translation of Chang Chung-yuan (*Tao: A New Way of Thinking*, N.Y., 1977) and Raymond B. Blakney (*Lao Tzu, The Way of Life*, N.Y., 1955).

And when that's lost, there's etiquette,
The husk of all good faith,
The rising point of anarchy. . . .

Let the people be free from discernment and
    relinquish intellection,
Then they will be many times better off.
Stop the teaching of benevolence and get rid of
    the claim of justice,
Then the people will love each other once more.
Cease the teaching of cleverness and give up profit,
Then there will be no more stealing and fraud. . . .

The Wise Man's policy, accordingly,
Will be to empty people's hearts and minds,
To fill their bellies, weaken their ambition,
Give them sturdy frames and always so,
To keep them uninformed, without desire,
And knowing ones not venturing to act. . . .

Ten thousand things in the universe are created
    from being.
Being is created from nonbeing. . . .

In Tao the only motion is returning;
The only useful quality, weakness. . . .

The Way is a void.

    "Absolute pessimism" is expressed in a different way in ancient Scandinavian mythology in the collection of songs known as the *Elder Edda*. (160) In this tradition (and especially in the "Prophecy of the Vala," the so-called "Voluspo"), we see a picture of a world ruled by gods personifying the forces of order and life and elemental destructive forces, embodied in the wolf Fenrir, son of Loki, held in check by a magic net. But at the appointed hour, the Wolf breaks loose and devours the sun; the world Serpent rises from the bottom of the ocean and gains victory over Thor. A ship built from the fingernails of the dead sails the sea, bringing giants who come to fight the gods. All people perish, heaven is cleft, the earth sinks into the sea, and the stars fall. (The concluding stanzas of the "Voluspo" describe the birth of a new world, but differ so sharply from the rest of the text that one tends to agree with the scholars who see this as a later interpolation, possibly reflecting the influence of Christianity.)

    Returning to Soloviev's article on pessimism, we find Schopenhauer and Hartmann presented as the major European representatives of this tendency. Schopenhauer considers the World Will to be that essence which cannot be reduced to anything else. But, at the same time, all will is desire—unsatisfied desire, since it has stimulated the manifestation of will; hence will is suffering. "The will now turns away from life. . . . Man attains to the state of voluntary renunciation, resignation, true composure and complete will-lessness. . . . His will turns about; it no longer affirms its own inner nature, mirrored in the phenomenon, but denies it." (*The World as Will and Representation*, I: section 68)

The aim of this process is Nothingness, achieved through the voluntary renunciation of will.

"No will: no representation, no world.

"Before us there is certainly left only nothing; but that which struggles against this flowing away into nothing, namely our nature, is indeed just the will-to-live which we ourselves are, just as it is our world. That we abhor nothingness so much is simply another way of saying that we will life so much, and that we are nothing but this will and know nothing but it alone. . . . That which remains after the complete abolition of the will is, for all who are still full of the will, assuredly nothing. But also conversely, to those in whom the will has turned and denied itself, this very real world of ours with all its suns and galaxies, is—nothing." (*op. cit.*, section 71)

To this system Hartmann adds the idea that the world process began through an initial irrational act of will and consists of the gradual preparation for the elimination of real existence. The aim is to return to nonexistence, implemented by the collective suicide of mankind and the destruction of the world, both of which are made possible by the development of technology.

The notion of Nothingness, which entered philosophy from theology through Hegel's system, plays an increasingly important role in the nineteenth century, until in the twentieth it becomes one of the dominant conceptions. For example, Max Stirner ends his famous book *The Ego and His Own* with the words: "I am the owner of my might and I am so when I know myself as *unique*. In the *unique one* the owner himself returns into his creative nothing, of which he is born. Every higher essence above me, be it God, be it man, weakens the feeling of my uniqueness, and pales only before the sun of this consciousness. If I found my affair on myself, the unique one, then my concern rests on its transitory, mortal creator, who consumes himself, and I may say:

I have founded my affair on nothing." (161: p. 246)

But it was within the framework of modern existentialism, especially in the works of Heidegger and Sartre, that Nothingness found its most important expression. Heidegger believes that man's individuality perishes in the leveling and the impulse toward mediocrity that is produced in society (something that is conveyed by the untranslatable German locution "man"). The only true individuality is death, which is always the death of a particular man and in which nothing links him to others. Therefore, a man can gain genuine existence only on the verge of death, only in what he calls "being-unto-death." (162: p. 144 f.) The being of every individuality is, from this point of view, merely *Noch-nicht* [not yet], a sort of period when death has not yet ripened. (162: p. 244) This concerns existence in general also: existence is Nothingness and Nothingness is—existence itself. (163: p. 104) Nothingness is the limit of existence determining its meaning. For Heidegger Nothingness is evidently an active force, for it functions—*Das Nicht nochtet.* It determines history's meaning, which is revealed in the attempts to overcome the senselessness of existence and to break through into Nothingness.

Nothingness is also the central category in Sartre's principal philosophic work, *Being and Nothingness.*

It is nothingness that connects consciousness and being. It is a fundamental property of consciousness; "Nothingness is putting into question of being by being—that is, precisely consciousness." (164: p. 121) Consciousness penetrates into the core of being as a worm into an apple and hollows it out. As it is only man who consciously strives for destruction, he is the bearer of Nothingness. "Man is the being through whom Nothingness comes to the world." (164: p. 60) Nothingness is so closely linked to man that, according to Sartre, human being-in-itself is also one of the manifestations of Nothingness. "The being by which Nothingness comes to the world must be its own Nothingness." (164: p. 59)

It is interesting to note that of these two best-known representatives of contemporary nihilism, Sartre adheres to Marxism, and Heidegger (until the end of World War II) inclined toward National Socialism. Heidegger, moreover, also views Communism (i.e., socialism of the Marxist brand) as a sort of incomplete nihilism. (165: pp. 145–395)

It seems to be no accident that the growth of influence of nihilistic philosophy coincided in Europe and in the U.S.A. with an extraordinary interest in Buddhism, particularly Zen Buddhism, which is a product of the interaction between the conceptions of Buddhism and Taoism. Zen typically stresses the illusory nature of life's problems, and their absurdity. For example, Gustav Mahler's "Kindertotenlieder" presents an image of a senseless all-consuming death, a black hole into which life collapses. Conscious of his approaching death, Mahler composed his "Das Lied von der Erde." This work begins with a poem of Li Po (a Chinese poet close to Zen) set to music, which is constantly interrupted by a refrain: "Life is darkness and death is darkness." But the spectacular spread of Zen occurred after World War II, especially in the U.S.A. It was propagated by such well-known modern writers as J. D. Salinger. The hero of a series of his stories dispenses Zen wisdom to those around him—and commits suicide, not as an act of despair, but for the sake of the overcoming of the seeming difference between life and death. Zen was also the favorite philosophy of the American beatniks, who frequently compared themselves to wandering monks.

Freud's world view is also pessimistic. He discerns a vicious circle in which society and human culture are locked: cultural activity is possible only at the expense of the suppression of sexuality, but this increases the role of aggressive and destructive forces in the psyche, and to keep them in check, still greater pressures on the part of social forces is needed. In this way, culture and society are not only organically tied to misfortune; they are also doomed to destruction. This is in conformity with Freud's view on the role of the "death instinct," a view that leaves to life only the choice of the "right path toward death." Freud's method, especially in establishing his basic concepts, is far from scientific. In general, Freud cannot be verified with concrete facts, so he must be accepted or rejected on the basis of one's inner feeling. In our day, when science is losing its role as an absolute authority, this characteristic of Freud's theories may not be regarded as a defect. In connection with Freud's anthropological and historical ideas, Marcuse writes: "The difficulties in scientific verification and even in logical consistency are obvious and perhaps insurmountable." (119: p. 59) "We use Freud's anthropological speculation only in this sense: for its *symbolic* value." (119: p. 60)

In just this way, we may regard Freud's conceptions not as indisputable scientific truth but as evidence of a certain perception of the world (the scope of whose influence may be judged by the success Freudianism has enjoyed).

Finally, the same tendency may be seen in theories according to which man (or animal) is regarded as a machine. All the aspects of life in man (or in animals) can be reduced in this way to the action of several simple forces. Thus Descartes expressed the opinion that an animal is an automaton incapable of thinking. The same idea was developed by La Mettrie in his book *L'homme machine.* He asserts that "the human body is a self-starting machine" and then extends this principle to the human psyche. Descartes's idea was later realized in Loeb's theory of tropisms, according to which the actions of organisms are determined by certain simple, physical factors (for example, the bending of a plant in the direction of the sun is explained by the fact that sunlight retards the growth on the side of the stem that it strikes). According to Dembowski, this theory regards the organism as "a puppet, whose every motion depends upon some outward factor pulling a corresponding string." (166: p. 55) Similar views became popular again in the second half of the twentieth century, in the wake of the invention of computers. Theories that hold that man (or animal) is a machine differ completely in their opinion as to what sort of machine is involved—mechanical, electric or electronic. And as all these explanations cannot be correct simultaneously, it is evident that the point of departure in each case is a similar a priori assumption, an impulse that derives from elsewhere, to prove that man is a machine.

The conclusions we have drawn as a result of our analysis of socialism are also confirmed, as we see, by a series of independent arguments. We may formulate these conclusions as follows:

a. *The idea of the death of mankind—not the death of specific people but literally the end of the human race—evokes a response in the human psyche. It arouses and attracts people, albeit with differing intensity in different epochs and in different individuals. The scope of influence of this idea causes us to suppose that every individual is affected by it to a greater or lesser degree and that it is a universal trait of the human psyche.*

b. *This idea is not only manifested in the individual experience of a great number of specific persons, but is also capable of uniting people (in contrast to delirium, for example) i.e., it is a social force. The impulse toward self-destruction may be regarded as an element in the psyche of mankind as a whole.*

c. *Socialism is one of the aspects of this impulse of mankind toward self-destruction and Nothingness, specifically its manifestation in the sphere of organizing society. The last words of Meslier's Testament (". . . with this nothing I shall end here") express the "final mystery" of socialism, to use Feuerbach's favorite expression.*

We have arrived at this view of socialism in attempting to account for the contradictions evident in the phenomenon at first glance. And now, looking back, we feel confident that our approach indeed accounts for many of socialism's peculiarities. Understanding socialism as one of the manifestations of the allure of death explains its hostility toward individuality, its desire to destroy those forces which support and strengthen human personality: religion, culture, family, individual property. It is consistent with the tendency to reduce man to the level of a cog in the state mechanism, as well as with the attempt to prove that man exists only as a manifestation of nonindividual features, such as production or class interest. The view of man as an instrument of other forces, in turn, makes it possible to understand the astonishing psychology of the leaders of the socialist movements: on the one hand, the readiness and even the striving to erase one's own personality, to submit it completely to the aims of the movement (so obvious in the statements of Piatakov and Trotsky cited earlier) and, on the other hand, the complete collapse of will, the renunciation of one's convictions in case of defeat (Müntzer and Johann of Leyden, Bakunin in his "Confession," the behavior of Zinoviev, Bukharin and others at the trials, etc.). In fact, if the instrument is no longer needed, all meaning for its existence is lost, and in man's soul the source of courage and spiritual strength runs dry. (Bakunin, for example, both before and after his imprisonment is quite a different person from the utterly broken and self-abasing author of the "Confession." And Bukharin, in his emotional "Testament," says that he has no differences with Stalin and that he has had none for a long time. He thereby dismisses his entire activity and even deprives himself of the right to protest against his own execution, since that would involve a disagreement.) This point of view is consistent with the calls to universal destruction, with the attractiveness of destructive forces like wars and crises, with the allure of death and the idea of Nothingness.

The same set of facts that has led us to the point of view expressed above allows us to discern the mechanism of the force of which socialism is the incarnation and to learn through what channels it acts on the individual.

It would seem, first of all, that this is an example of activity that is not guided by conscious intent. The proposition that a striving for self-destruction is the main impulse in socialism has been extracted from a multi-stage analysis of socialist ideology, and is not taken directly from the writings of socialist thinkers or the slogans of socialist movements. It seems that those in the grip of socialist ideology are as little governed by any conscious understanding of this goal as a singing nightingale is concerned with the future of its species. The ideology's impact is through the emotions, which render the ideology attractive to man and induce him to be ready for sacrifice on its behalf. Spiritual elation and inspiration are the kinds of emotions experienced by the participants in socialist movements. This accounts, too, for the behavior of the leaders of socialist movements in the thick of the fight, down through the ages—their seemingly inexhaustible reserves of energy as pamphleteers, agitators, and organizers.

For the very reason that the basic driving force of socialist ideology is subconscious and emotional, reason and rational discussion of facts have always played only a subordinate role in it. The socialist doctrines are reconciled with contradictions with an ease reminiscent of "prelogical," primitive thinking, which functions outside any framework of consistency, as described by Lévy-Bruhl. They are equally unconcerned with the fact that socialist conclusions are radically at odds with experience. Most astonishing of all is that these contradictions do not diminish the impact of the doctrine in the least.

Marxism reflects all these traits to a remarkable degree. Well-known thinkers have pointed out numerous fundamental contradictions, each of which would have been sufficient to demonstrate the groundlessness of a theory that lays claim to being *scientific*. For example, Berdiaev demonstrated that the concept of dialectical materialism is contradictory, since it attributes to matter a logical category—dialectics. Stammler (167) showed that the idea of historical determinism postulated by Marxism contradicts its own appeal to influence history, since it is equivalent to taking a conscious decision to turn with the earth around the sun. (Sergius Bulgakov paraphrased this thought as follows: "Marxism predicts the onset of socialism just as astronomy predicts the beginning of a lunar eclipse, and to bring about the eclipse it organizes a party.") The very heart of Marxist doctrine—the labor theory of value—was demolished by the work of the Austrian school (in particular by Böhm-Bawerk) and has been abandoned by political economy. Yet even without this heart, Marxism proved to be capable of survival.

Just as extraordinary is the reaction of Marxist thinkers to the experimental evidence of history over the last century. Take, for example, the article by Professor Rappoport of the University of Michigan. (168: pp. 30–59) He cites a number of Marxist predictions which history has disproved and asks whether it is possible "to declare the theory refuted." Such a conclusion, he declares, appeals to people who view with suspicion any theory based on general philosophical concepts (people like Berdiaev, Bulgakov, Max Weber or Karl Jaspers). As for the concrete projections, Rappoport acknowledges that the prognosis of a total impoverishment of capitalist countries did not come true. But if one considers poverty on a worldwide scale, then one sees that the gap between the rich and the poor countries has increased. It is true that "the confirmation of the Marxist conception of history does not necessarily follow from this. But there arises a certain possibility of a new understanding of the vital concepts of Marxist theory appropriate to our time." After these arguments, which are beyond logic, it remains unclear whether or not Marxist theory is correct in the light of historical verification. The author evades this question and, without benefit of proof, accepts that in some ways it is "viable," as if it were possible to retain part of a structured world view and throw away the rest.

Or consider Sartre, who declared, in the heyday of the Stalin epoch, that all information coming to the West about concentration camps in the Soviet Union should be ignored, even if true, as it might cause despair in the French proletariat (cited in *The Great Terror* by R. Conquest). Sartre now considers Soviet Marxism to be "repressive" and "bureaucratic," and of the French working class he says: "What is a proletariat if it is not revolutionary? And it is, indeed, not revolutionary." (143: p. 166) In what way were his judgments in the fifties incorrect? He does not inform us. No fundamentally new facts seem to have come to light in the interim. Therefore the change in his point of view cannot be attributed to a rational understanding of the situation, and his new infatuation with the "direct democracy" in China does not produce that impression either, for it leaves unanswered such elementary questions as why the details of this "direct democracy" should be so carefully concealed from foreigners? Why are foreign reporters forbidden even to read the wall posters?

All these characteristics prompt us to juxtapose the force displayed in socialism with *instinct*. Instinctive actions also have an emotional coloring, their fulfillment evokes a feeling of satisfaction, and the impossibility of fulfilling them (the absence of signals "switching on" an action) causes anxiety, the so-called appetitive behavior. Ethologists speak of the "state of enthusiasm" to describe a common instinctive action in man which is connected with the defense of what one considers most precious.

Furthermore, instincts combine badly with understanding and are even incompatible with it: if an animal can achieve a goal by virtue of its understanding, it will never attempt to achieve the same goal by instinct. Instinctive actions are not altered by the achievement of a goal, since they are not a result of training. In man, the influence of instinct is usually to lower critical abilities (for example, in the behavior of lovers), and arguments against the goal sought by instinct are not only disregarded but perceived as somehow base. For all these reasons, the term proposed by Freud—the "death instinct"—reflects many features of man's impulse toward self-destruction, which, as we have argued, is the driving force of socialism. (We use Freud's term but do not accept the meaning Freud ascribed to it; see the earlier discussion and the considerations offered below.) The term is applied with the reservation that it only partially describes the phenomenon; this is so for two reasons. First, the instinct in question is not that of separate people but of all mankind, which in this case is treated as a kind of individuality. It is evident that such an approach requires a sound substantiation. Second, instinct presupposes the achievement of a certain aim useful for the individual or at least for the species. This is extremely difficult to reconcile with the "death instinct," and until it can be shown that the striving for self-destruction plays some useful role for mankind, the analogy with instinct should be regarded as partial, illustrating only some aspect of this phenomenon.

Categories such as the striving for self-destruction or the "death instinct" are popularly associated with dualism, the conception of two equally powerful forces, the "life instinct" and the "death instinct," which determine the flow of history. It would be unfortunate if the views expressed here were interpreted as simply a variety of dualism, for dualism tends to be an unstable and fragmented world view. In the present study we examined two dualistic philosophies. One is the religion of the Manicheans and the Cathars, which undertakes to explain the phenomenon of evil by the existence of good and evil gods.

But by force of this religion's logic, the good God was expelled from the world, and hence the ground for the existence of good in the world also disappeared. S. Runciman, a student of this religion, believes that the Cathars, proceeding from the inexplicability of evil, arrived at the inexplicability of good. (11: p. 175)

Another dualistic theory, Freudianism, underwent a strikingly similar process of evolution. Freud began with an assertion of the universal role of sexuality, regarded as an elementary life force. The development of this view led him to a dualistic conception of the "life instinct" or Eros (coinciding with broadly understood sexuality) and the "death instinct" or Thanatos. But gradually the role of the "death instinct" (or "Nirvana principle") grew until, in "The Ego and the Id," Freud calls it "the dominant tendency of all mental life and, possibly, of all neural activity in general." Marcuse points out a passage in Freud's essay "Beyond the Pleasure Principle" where the pleasure principle is described as the "expression" of the "Nirvana principle." Freud also writes that "life is but a long detour to death." Marcuse's estimation of Freud's conception almost completely coincides with Runciman's views of the dualism of the Cathars. "The inability to uncover in the primary structure of the instincts anything that is not Eros, the monism of sexuality—an inability which, as we shall see, is the sure sign of truth—now seems to turn into its opposite: into a monism of death." (119: p. 28)

Evidently dualism is in general a transitional form from one monism to another, as we have seen in both examples here. But the same examples show that pure monism—the recognition of a single force which promotes improvement and development—also contains a contradiction. It leads eventually to the supposition of the existence of another equally powerful and active force moving in the opposite direction—i.e., toward dualism, then toward the monism of the second force. But it is also true that the idea of two forces acting in the opposite directions does not necessarily require the recognition of their equality—which would be fundamental for dualism. To show how the vicious circle of dualism may be avoided, we should like to point to Plato's splendid *Timaeus*. Plato here develops the notion of two souls—good and evil—innate in every living being. The whole cosmos is also a living being and also possesses two souls. Their influence alternates, and this is reflected in an alternation of cosmic catastrophes. But outside the cosmos and above it there is divinity—the incarnation of absolute good.

Returning to our specific theme, we see that the striving for self-destruction expressed in socialism not only is not analogous or "equivalent" to other forces acting in history, but is fundamentally distinct from them in character. For example, in contrast to a religious or a national ideology, which openly proclaims its goals, the "death instinct" that is embodied in socialism appears in the guise of religion, reason, social justice, national endeavors or science, and never shows its true face. Apparently its action is the stronger the more directly it is perceived by the subconscious part of the psyche, but only on condition that consciousness remains unaware.

We would like to propose, in a purely hypothetical manner and without insisting on this part of the argument, that the striving for self-destruction may perform a useful function in relation to other, creative, forces in history, and that humanity needs it in some way to achieve its goals. The only rational argument in favor of this supposition is the almost inexorable way, reminiscent of natural and scientific laws, with which different nations of the world, especially in our century, have been falling under the influence of socialist ideology. This could be an indication that it is an experience through which mankind must necessarily pass. The only question would then be the level on which this experience will run its course. Will it be on the spiritual plane? As the physical experience of certain peoples? Or of humanity as a whole? Soloviev, in his early works, developed an optimistic theory according to which mankind, in order to build life on religious principles, would first have to pass through an extreme phase of concern for individuality, to the point of hostility to God, finally coming to God by this route through a conscious act of this individuality. This is the reason for his interest in the pessimistic philosophies of Schopenhauer and Hartmann, which Soloviev regarded as a sign of the coming end of the individualistic epoch, as testimony of the spiritual death toward which the path of areligious development leads. However, this purely spiritual experience proved to be insufficient. Soloviev himself came to this realization, as is clear from his last and perhaps most profound works.

The last hundred years, particularly the twentieth century, have brought socialism unheard-of success. This has been primarily a success of socialism in its Marxist form, mostly because Marxism has been able to answer two questions that always stand before socialist movements: where to seek the "chosen people"—i.e., who is to destroy the old world—and what is the supreme authority sanctioning the movement?

The answer to the first question was *the proletariat;* to the second, *science.* At present both answers have become ineffective, at least for the West. "The proletariat has become a support for the system," Marcuse complains. "What is a proletariat if it is not revolutionary? And it is, indeed, not revolutionary," Sartre confirms. And science has lost its prestige and its role as unquestionable authority; it has become too popular and widespread, and ceased being the secret knowledge of a select few. Moreover, many of its gifts have recently proved to be far from beneficial. For this reason, Marcuse calls for replacing science with a utopia, for granting the role held by reason to fantasy. Until these fundamental questions find answers adequate to the new epoch, it will scarcely be possible to expect success for socialism commensurate with that of Marxism. Meanwhile there have been and continue to be attempts in this direction. For example, the search for the "chosen people" seems to be the real meaning behind the "problem of minorities" which so engages the Western leftist movements: students or homosexuals or American blacks or local nationalities in France. . . . There is no doubt that other answers will be found—the tendency toward socialism that grips the West speaks for this.

But if we suppose that the significance of socialism for mankind consists in the acquisition of specific experience, then much has been acquired on this path in the last hundred years. There is, first of all, the profound experience of Russia, the significance of which we are only now beginning to understand. The question therefore arises: will *this* experience be sufficient? Is it sufficient for the entire world and especially for the West? Indeed, is it sufficient for Russia? Shall we be able to comprehend its meaning? Or is mankind destined to pass through this experience on an immeasurably larger scale?

There is no doubt that if the ideals of Utopia are realized universally, mankind, even in the barracks of the universal City of the Sun, shall find the strength to regain its freedom and to preserve God's image and likeness—human individuality—once it has glanced into the yawning abyss. But will even *that* experience be sufficient? For it seems just as certain that the freedom of will granted to man and to mankind is *absolute,* that it includes the freedom to make the ultimate choice—between life and death.

# Bibliography

Russian-language entries are transcribed according to the Library of Congress system.

1. H. G. Wells. *Russia in the Shadows.* New York, 1921.
2. Aristophanes. *The Congresswomen (Ecclesiazusae).* Trans. Douglass Parker. Ann Arbor, 1967.
3. K. Marx and F. Engels. *Sochineniia (Works,* in Russian), vols. 1–15, 17–19, 21–29. Moscow-Leningrad, 1928–48.
4. H. Marcuse. *Psychoanalyse und Politik.* Vienna, 1968.
5. Plato. *Republic.* Trans. Paul Shorey. Cambridge, Mass., 1930.
6. R. Pöhlmann. *Geschichte des antiken Kommunismus und Sozialismus.* (Quotations refer to Russian translation, *Istoriia antichnogo kommunizma i sotsialisma,* St. Petersburg, 1910.)
7. W. Schultz. *Documente der Gnosis.* Jena, 1910.
8. A. Christensen. *Le Règne du roi Kawadh I et communisme mazdakite.* In: *Det. Kgl. Danske Videnskabernes Selskab: Historisk-filologiske middelelser* (Copenhagen), vol. IX, no. 6 (1925).
9. Ch. Hahn. *Geschichte der Ketzer im Mittelalter, besonders im 11, 12 und 13 Jahrhundert, nach Quellen bearbeitet,* 2 vols. Stuttgart, 1845–47.
10. J. Döllinger. *Beitrage zur Sektengeschichte des Mittelalters.* Erster Theil. *Geschichte der gnostisch-manichäischen Sekten.* Munich, 1890.
11. S. Runciman. *The Medieval Manichee.* Cambridge, Mass., 1955.
12. J. J. Herzog. *Abriss der gesamten Kirchengeschichte.* Bd. I, Abt. 2. *Die römisch-katholische Kirche des Mittelalters.* Erlangen, 1890.
13. M. Beer. *Allgemeine Geschichte des Sozialismus und der sozialen Kämpfe.* (Quotations refer to the Russian translation, *Vseobshchaia istoriia sotsializma i sotsial'noi bor'by,* Moscow-Leningrad, 1927.)
14. H. Grundmann. *Ketzergeschichte des Mittelalters.* Göttingen, 1963.
15. M. Erbstösser and E. E. Werner. *Ideologische Probleme des mittelalterlichen Plebejertums.* Berlin, 1960.

16. T. Büttner and E. Werner. *Circumcellionen und Adamiten.* Berlin, 1959.
17. M. Erbstösser. *Sozialreligiöse Strömungen im späten Mittelalter.* Berlin, 1970.
18. Herbert Grundmann. *Religiöse Bewegungen im Mittelalter.* Berlin, 1935.
19. J. Macek. *Tabor v gusitskom revoliutsionnom dvizhenii (Tabor in the Hussite Revolutionary Movement,* in Russian; original in Czech), vol. 2. Moscow, 1959.
20. M. M. Smirin. *Narodnaia reformatsiia Tomasa Miuntsera i velikaia krest'ianskaia voina (The Popular Reformation of Thomas Müntzer and the Great Peasant War,* in Russian). Moscow, 1955.
21. J. Macek. *Gusitskoe revoliutsionnoe dvizhenie (The Hussite Revolutionary Movement,* in Russian; original in Czech). Moscow, 1954.
22. L. Ranke. *Deutsche Geschichte im Zeitalter der Reformation.* Bd. II, Berlin, 1842.
23. F. Bezold. *Geschichte der deutschen Reformation.* Berlin, 1886.
24. L. Keller. *Die Reformation und die älteren Reformparteien.* Leipzig, 1885.
25. L. Keller. *Johann von Staupitz und die Anfänge der Reformation.* Leipzig, 1888.
26. L. Keller. *Die Anfänge der Reformation und die Ketzerschulen.* Berlin, 1897.
27. L. Müller. *Der Kommunismus der mährischen Wiedertäufer.* Leipzig, 1927.
28. *T. Müntzer. Sein Leben und seine Schriften.* Ed. Otto H. Brandt. Jena, 1933.
29. L. Keller. *Geschichte der Wiedertäufer und ihres Reichs zu Münster.* Münster, 1888.
30. R. Barclay. *The Inner Life of the Religious Societies of the Commonwealth.* London, 1879.
31. W. D. Morris. *The Christian Origins of Social Revolt.* London, 1949.
32. A. L. Morton. *The World of the Ranters.* London, 1970.
33. E. Bernstein. *Sozialismus und Demokratie in der grossen englischen Revolution.* (Quotations refer to the Russian translation, *Sotsializm i demokratiia v velikoi angliiskoi revoliutsii,* Leningrad, 1924.)
34. G. Weingarten. *Revolutionskirchen Englands.* (Quotations refer to the Russian translation, *Narodnaia reformatsiia v Anglii XVII v.,* Moscow, 1901.)
35. G. Winstanley. *The Law of Freedom and Other Writings.* Harmondsworth, England: Penguin, 1973.
36. H. Hollorenshaw. *The Levellers and the English Revolution.* (Quotations refer to the Russian translation, *Levellery i angliiskaia revoliutsiia,* Moscow, 1947.)
37. J. Krone. *Fra Dolcino und die Patarenen.* Leipzig, 1844.
38. A. Hausrat. *Die Weltverbesserer im Mittelalter.* Bd. III. *Die Arnoldisten.* Leipzig, 1885.

39. K. Kautsky. *Vorläufer des neueren Sozialismus,* 2 vols. Bd. II. *Der Kommunismus in der deutschen Reformation.* Stuttgart, 1913.
40. G. Adler. *Geschichte des Sozialismus und Kommunismus von Plato bis zur Gegenwart.* Bd. I. Leipzig, 1920.
41. J. Döllinger. *Kirche und Kirchen: Papstum und Kirchenstaat.* Munich, 1861.
42. T. More. *Utopia.* (Page references are to the Russian translation, *Zolotaia kniga, stol' zhe poleznaia, kak zabavnaia, o nailuchshem ustroistve gosudarstva i o novom ostrove Utopii.* In: *Utopicheskii roman XVI–XVII vekov,* Moscow, 1971.)
43. T. Campanella. *Civitas Solis.* (Quotations refer to the Russian translation, *Gorod Solntsa.* In: *Utopicheskii roman XVI–XVII vekov,* Moscow, 1971.)
44. D. Vairasse. *L'Histoire des Sévarambes.* (Quotations refer to the Russian translation, *Istoriia severambov.* In: *Utopicheskii roman XVI–XVII vekov,* Moscow, 1971.)
45. *Les Aventures de Jacques Sadeur.* In: *Bibliothèque des voyages imaginaires,* vol. XXIV. Paris, 1787–89.
46. Fénelon. *Les Aventures de Télémaque.* In: *Oeuvres complétes,* v. VI. Paris, 1851.
47. *La République des Philosophes ou l'histoire des Ajaoiens.* Ouvrage posthume de M. de Fontenelle. Geneva, 1768.
48. Restif de la Bretonne. *La Découverte australe par un homme volant ou le Dédale français: nouvelle trés philosophique.* (Quotations refer to the Russian translation, *Iuzhnoe otkrytie, sdelannoe letaiushchim chelovekom, ili Frantsuzskii Dedal: chresvychaino filosofskaia povest',* Moscow-Leningrad, 1936.)
49. Jean Meslier. *Testament.* (Quotations refer to the Russian translation, *Zaveshchanie,* 3 vols. Moscow, 1954.)
50. Morelly. *Le Code de la nature ou le Véritable Esprit de ses lois de tout temps négligé ou méconnu.* (Quotations refer to Russian translation, *Kodeks prirody ili dukh ee zakonov,* Moscow, 1947.)
51. V. P. Volgin. *Razvitie obshchestvennoi mysli vo Frantsii v XVIII veke* (*The Development of Social Thought in France in the XVIII Century,* in Russian). Moscow, 1958.
52. D. Diderot. *Sobranie sochinenii* (*Works,* in Russian), 10 vols. Moscow-Leningrad, 1935–47, vol. II.
53. Dom Léger Marie Deschamps. *La Vérité ou le Véritable Système.* (Quotations refer to the Russian translation, *Istina ili istinnaia sistema,* Moscow, 1973.)
54. S. Vasil'ev. "Vvedenie" ("Introduction," in Russian) to an earlier Russian edition of Deschamps' book. Baku, 1930.
55. P. Buonarroti. *Conspiration pour l'égalité.* (Quotations refer to the Russian translation, *Zagovor vo imia ravenstva,* 2 vols., Moscow, 1963.)
56. L. Baudin. *Les Incas du Pérou.* Paris, 1947.
57. R. Karsten. *Das Altperuanische Inkareich.* Leipzig, 1949.
58. Garcilaso de la Vega. *Comentarios reales de los Incas.* (Quotations refer

to the Russian translation, *Istoriia gosudarstva inkov,* Leningrad, 1974.)
59. H. Cunow. *Geschichte und Kultur des Inkareiches.* Amsterdam, 1937.
60. C. Lugon. *La République communiste chrétienne des Guaranis.* Paris, 1949.
61. G. Otruba. *Der Jesuitenstaat im Paraguay. Idee und Wirklichkeit.* Vienna, 1962.
62. P. Lafargue. *Der Jesuitenstaat im Paraguay.* (Quotations refer to the Russian translation, *Iezuitskie respubliki,* St. Petersburg, 1904.)
63. V. V. Sviatlovskii. *Kommunisticheskoe gosudarstvo iezuitov v Paragvae v XVII i XVIII st. (The Communist State of the Jesuits in Paraguay in the XVII–XVIII Centuries,* in Russian). Petrograd, 1924.
64. A. Kirchenheim. *Geschichte der Dichtung vom besten Staate.* (Quotations refer to the Russian translation, *Vechnaia utopiia,* St. Petersburg, 1902.)
65. A. I. Tiumenev. *Gosudarstvennoe khoziastvo drevnego Shumera (The Economy of Ancient Sumer,* in Russian). Moscow-Leningrad, 1956.
66. I. M. D'iakonov. *Obshchestvennyi i gosudarstvennyi stroi drevnego Dvurech'ia. Shumer (The Social and State System of Ancient Mesopotamia. Sumer,* in Russian). Moscow, 1959.
67. A. Deimel. *Sumerische Tempelwirtschaft zur Zeit Urukaginas und seiner Vorläufer.* Rome, 1931. (*Analecta Orientalia,* no. 2.)
68. R. McAdams. *The Evolution of Urban Society. Early Mesopotamia and Prehistoric Mexico.* Chicago, 1966.
69. I. J. Gelb. "From Freedom to Slavery. Gesellschaftsklassen im alten Zweistromland und in den angrenzenden Gebieten." In: *XVIII Recontre assyrologique internationale. München, 29 Juni–3 Juli 1970. Bayerische Akademie der Wisenschaften. Philosophisch-Historisch Klasse. Abhandlungen* (Neue Folge), Heft 75, pp. 81–92.
70. I. J. Gelb. "Prisoners of War in Early Mesopotamia." *Journal of Near Eastern Studies,* vol. 32, nos. 1–2 (January–April, 1973).
71. J. Pirenne. *Histoire des institutions et du droit privé de l'ancienne Egypte,* vols. I–III. Brussels, 1932–35.
72. Ed. Meyer. *Geschichte des Altertums.* Bd. I, Abt. II. Stuttgart-Berlin, 1926.
73. H. Kees. *Ägypten.* Munich, 1933.
74. S. Dairaines. *Un socialisme d'État quinze siècles avant Jésus-Christ.* Paris, 1934.
75. A. M. Hocart. *Kingship.* London, 1927.
76. J. Engnell. *Studies in Divine Kingship in the Ancient Near East.* Uppsala, 1943.
77. H. Maspero. *La Chine Antique.* Paris, 1927.
78. Kuo Mo-jo (Guo Mo-ruo). *Bronzovyi vek (The Bronze Age,* in Russian; original in Chinese). Moscow, 1959.
79. Kuo Mo-jo (Guo Mo-ruo). *Epokha rabovladel'cheskogo stroia (The Period of the Slave-Owning Social Structure,* in Russian; original in Chinese). Moscow, 1956.
80. M. Kokin and G. Papaian. *"Tsin' Tian'." Agranyi stroi drevnego Kitaia*

(*"Chün-T'ien."* The Agrarian Structure of Ancient China, in Russian). Leningrad, 1930.

81. L. I. Duman. *Ocherki drevnei istorii Kitaia* (*Essays on Ancient Chinese History*, in Russian). Leningrad, 1938.

82. L. S. Perelomov. *Imperiia Tsin'* (*The Ch'in Empire*, in Russian). Moscow, 1962.

83. H. Frankfort. *The Birth of Civilization in the Near East.* New York, 1956.

84. Shang Yang. *Kniga pravitelia oblasti Shan* (*Book of the Ruler of Shang*, in Russian; original in Chinese). Moscow, 1968.

85. *Ocherki po istorii Kitaia* (*Essays on Chinese History*, in Russian). Ed. by Shang Yü-erh. Moscow, 1959.

86. K. Marx. "Formy, predshestvuiushchie kapitalisticheskomu proizvodstvu" ("Forms Preceding Capitalist Production," in Russian). In: *Proletarskaia revoliutsiia*, 1939, no. 3.

87. *Vestnik drevnei istorii*, 1940, no. 1.

88. *Problemy dokapitalisticheskikh obshchestv v stranakh Vostoka* (*Problems of pre-Capitalist Societies in the Countries of the Orient*, in Russian). Moscow, 1971.

89. K. Wittfogel. *Oriental Despotism: A Comparative Study of Total Power.* New Haven, Conn., 1957.

90. F. Heichelheim. *An Ancient Economic History*, v. I. Leiden, 1958.

91. Ed. Meyer. *Kleine Schriften.* Bd. I. Halle, 1924.

92. F. Dostoevskii. *Polnoe sobranie sochinenii* (*Collected Works*, in Russian). 30 vols. Leningrad, 1972–.

93. M. V. Shchekin. *Kak zhit' po novomu* (*How to Live in the New Way*, in Russian). Kostroma, 1925.

94. D. Koigen. *Zur Vorgeschichte des modernen philosophischen Sozialismus in Deutschland.* Bern, 1901.

95. *Michail Bakunins sozial-politischer Briefwechsel mit Alexander Ivanovitsch Herzen.* Stuttgart, 1895.

96. M. Pokrovskii. *Ocherki po istorii revoliutsionnogo dvizheniia v Rossii XIX i XX v.v.* (*Essays on the History of the Revolutionary Movement in Russia in the Nineteenth and Twentieth Centuries*, in Russian). Moscow, 1924.

97. Charles Fourier. *La Théorie des quatre mouvements et des destinées générales.* (Quotations refer to the Russian translation, *Teoriia chetyrekh dvizhenii i vseobshchikh sudeb.* In: *Izbrannye sochineniia*, vol. I, Moscow, 1938.)

98. F. Engels. *Anti-Dühring.* (Quotations refer to the Russian translation, *Anti-Diuring*, Moscow, 1965.)

99. *Osnovy marksizma* (*The Foundations of Marxism*, in Russian). Samizdat, 1971.

100. S. Bulgakov. *Karl Marks kak religioznyi tip* (*Karl Marx as a Religious Type*, in Russian). Moscow, 1911.

101. K. Jaspers. *Möglichkeiten eines neuen Humanismus. Rechenschaft und Ausblick.* Munich, 1951.

102. N. Bukharin. *Ekonomika perekhodnogo perioda* (*The Economic Structure of the Transitional Period*, in Russian). Moscow, 1920.
103. K. Kautsky. *Von der Demokratie zu der Staats-Sklaverei. Eine Auseinandersetzung mit Trotzki.* (Quotations refer to Russian translation, *Ot demokratii k gosudarstvennomu rabstvu.* [*Otvet Trotskomu*].) Berlin, 1921.
104. W. S. Schlamm. *Die jungen Herren der alten Erde (Vom neuen Stil der Macht).* Stuttgart, 1962.
105. *XIII s"ezd RKP(b)* (The Thirteenth Congress of the Russian Communist Party). Moscow, 1924.
106. N. Valentinov. "Piatakov i bol'shevizm" ("Piatakov and Bolshevism," in Russian). In: *Novyi zhurnal* (New York), no. 52, 1958.
107. R. Chauvin. *De l'abeille au gorille.* (Quotations refer to Russian translation, *Ot pchely do gorilly,* Moscow, 1965.)
108. K. Jaspers. *Vom Ursprung und Ziel der Geschichte.* Zurich, 1949.
109. V. S. Solov'ev (Soloviev). *Sobranie sochinenii v desiati tomakh* (*Collected Works*, in Russian). 10 vols. St. Petersburg, 1911.
110. S. Bulgakov. *Khristianstvo i sotsializm* (*Christianity and Socialism*, in Russian). Moscow, 1917.
111. B. P. Koz'min. *Nechaev i nechaevtsy* (*Nechaev and the Nechaevists*, in Russian). Moscow-Leningrad, 1931.
112. D. Riazanov. "Marks i Engels o brake i sem'e" ("Marx and Engels on Marriage and the Family," in Russian). In: *Letopisi marksizma*, v. III, 1927.
113. V. I. Lenin. *Polnoe sobranie sochinenii* (*Collected Works*, in Russian), fifth edition. 55 vols. Moscow, 1958–65.
114. C. Hugo. *Der Sozialismus in Frankreich im XVII und XVIII Jahrhundert.* (Quotations refer to Russian translation, *Sotsializm vo Frantsii v XVII i XVIII stoletiiakh,* Ivanovo-Voznesensk, 1924.)
115. S. Bulgakov. *Pervokhristianstvo i noveishii sotsializm* (*Early Christianity and Modern Socialism*, in Russian). Moscow, 1911.
116. S. Frank. "Etika nigilizma" ("The Ethics of Nihilism," in Russian). In: *Vekhi (Landmarks),* Moscow, 1909.
117. G. Le Bon. *Psychologie du socialisme.* (Quotations refer to Russian translation, *Psikhologiia sotsializma,* St. Petersburg, 1908.)
118. W. Gurian. *Der Bolschewismus.* Freiburg, 1931.
119. H. Marcuse. *Eros and Civilization. A Philosophical Inquiry into Freud.* Boston, 1955.
120. *IX s"ezd RKP(b)* (Ninth Congress of the Russian Communist Party). Moscow, 1920.
121. L. Trotskii. *Terrorizm i kommunizm. Anti-Kautskii* (*Terrorism and Communism. Anti-Kautsky*, in Russian). 1920. (Quotations taken from 103, which is a response to 121.)
122. A. M. Kollontai. *Novaia moral' i rabochii klass* (*The New Morals and the Working Class*, in Russian). Moscow, 1919.
123. G. Grigorov and S. Shkotov. *Staryi i novyi byt* (*The Old and the New Way of Life*, in Russian). Moscow-Leningrad, 1927.

124. I. Il'inskii. *Pravo i byt* (*The Way of Life and the Law*, in Russian). Leningrad, 1925.

125. *Sem'ia i byt* (*The Family and the Way of Life*, in Russian). Collection of essays compiled by A. Adol'f, B. Boichevskii, V. Stroev, and M. Shishkevich. Moscow, 1927.

126. *Vserossiiskii Tsentral'nyi Ispolnitel'nyi Komitet XII sozyva. Vtoraia sessia (stenograficheskii otchet)* (*All-Russian Central Executive Committee. Second Session of the XII Congress.* [Stenographic record]). Moscow, 1925.

127. M. N. Liadov. *Voprosy byta* (*About the Way of Life*, in Russian). Moscow, 1925.

128. S. Ia. Vol'fson. *Sotsiologiia braka i sem'i* (*Sociology of Marriage and the Family*, in Russian). Minsk, 1929.

129. A. Borovoi. *Obshchestvennye idealy sovremennogo chelovechestva* (*Social Ideals of Contemporary Mankind*, in Russian). Moscow, 1927.

130. Brothers Gordin. *Sotsiologiia i sotsiotekhnika* (*Sociology and Sociotechnology*, in Russian). Petrograd, 1918.

131. E. Enchmen. *Vosemnadtsat' tezisov o teorii novoi biologii* (*Eighteen Theses on the Theory of the New Biology*, in Russian). Piatigorsk, 1920.

132. A. Stoliarov. *Dialekticheskii materializm i mekhanisty* (*Dialectical Materialism and the Mechanists*, in Russian). Leningrad, 1929.

133. B. Arvatov. *Iskusstvo i proizvodstvo* (*Art and Production*, in Russian). Moscow, 1926.

134. Rogovin. "Problema tvorcheskogo metoda v ideino-khudozhestvennoi bor'be 20-kh g.g." ("The Issue of Creative Method in the Ideological and Artistic Debates of the 1920s," in Russian.) In: *Voprosy estetiki*, Moscow, 1971, no. 9.

135. K. Kautsky. *Ein Brief über Marx und Mach. Der Kampf.* Vienna, 1909. Bd. 2.

136. S. Minin. "Filosofiiu za bort" ("Throwing Philosophy Overboard," in Russian). In: *Pod znamenem marksizma*, 1922, nos. 5–6.

137. P. Blonskii. *Sovremennaia filosofiia* (*Contemporary Philosophy*). Moscow, 1918.

138. I. V. Stalin. *Ekonomicheskie problemy sotsializma* (*Economic Problems of Socialism*, in Russian). Moscow, 1952.

139. A. Toynbee. *An Historian's Approach to Religion.* London, 1956.

140. K. Jaspers. *Vom Ursprung und Ziel der Geschichte.* Zurich, 1949.

141. L. Mumford. *The Myth of the Machine.* New York, 1962.

142. M. Walser. "Über die neusten Stimmungen im Westen." In: *Kursbuch*, Bd. 20, 1970, S. 19–41.

143. Ph. Gavi, J.-P. Sartre, P. Victor. *On a raison de se révolter.* Paris, 1974.

144. K. Lorenz. *Das sogenannte Böse.* Vienna, 1963.

145. H. M. Enzensberger. "Baukasten zu einer Theorie der Medien." In: *Kursbuch*, Bd. 20, 1970, S. 159–186.

146. *Letopisi marksizma* (*Annals of Marxism*, in Russian), v. III, 1927.

147. Jerry Rubin. *Do It!* (*Scenario of the Revolution*). New York, 1970.

148. J. Eibl-Eibesfeldt. *Grundriss der vergleichenden Verhaltensforschung.* Munich, 1967.

149. A. P. Elkin. *The Australian Aborigines*. Sydney-London, 1938. (Russian translation, Moscow, 1952.)
150. G. Childe. *What Happened in History*. London, 1942.
151. Iu. Steklov. *Mikhail Bakunin* (in Russian), v. III. Moscow-Leningrad, 1927.
152. K. Kautsky. *Terrorismus und Kommunismus*. (Quotations refer to the Russian translation, *Terrorizm i kommunizm*, Berlin, 1919.)
153. S.-H. Saint-Simon. *Izbrannye sochineniia* (*Selected Works*, in Russian), vol. I. Moscow-Leningrad, 1948.
154. A. S. Izgoev. "Ob intelligentnoi molodezhi" ("On the Youthful Intelligentsia," in Russian). In: *Vekhi (Landmarks)*, Moscow, 1909.
155. *Byloe*, no. I, July, 1917. (In Russian.)
156. I. R. Shafarevich. "Socialism in Our Past and Future." In: *From Under the Rubble*. Ed. Aleksandr Solzhenitsyn. Boston: Little, Brown, 1975. (Russian edition published in Paris, 1974.)
157. F. M. Dostoevskii. *Sobranie sochinenii* (*Works*, in Russian), 10 vols. Moscow, 1956–58, vol. IX.
158. H. Oldenberg. *Buddha, sein Leben, seine Lehre, seine Gemeinde*. (Quotations refer to the Russian translation, *Budda, ego zhizn', uchenie i obshchina*, Moscow, 1884.)
159. S. Radhakrishnan. *Indian Philosophy*, vol. I. New York and London, 1923.
160. *The Elder Edda*. (Russian translation, Moscow-Leningrad, 1963.)
161. M. Stirner. *Der Einzige und sein Eigenthum*. (Russian translation, St. Petersburg, 1909.)
162. M. Heidegger. *Sein und Zeit*. Halle an der Saale, 1929.
163. M. Heidegger. *Holzwege*. Frankfurt am Main, 1950.
164. J.-P. Sartre. *L'Être et le Néant*. Paris, 1943.
165. M. Heidegger. *Nietzsche*. Bd. II. Berlin, 1961.
166. J. Dembowski. *Psikhologiia zhivotnykh* (*Psychology of Animals*, in Russian; original in Polish). Moscow, 1959.
167. R. Stammler. *Wirtschaft und Recht nach der materialistischen Geschichtsauffassung*, 2nd ed. Berlin-Leipzig, 1906.
168. *Aggression und Anpassung in der Industriegesellschaft*. Frankfurt am Main, 1969.

# Index

Absolute pessimism concept, 286, 289
Adamite sect, 31–33, 67–68, 75
*Adventures of Telemachus, The* (Fénelon), 104
Agriculture: in Ch'in empire, 181; *Code of Nature*, 111; post-revolutionary Russia and, 239–241, 252; Shang-teaching, 176–178; in socialist novels, 104–105; in Sumer, 154–155, 157, 159; in *Utopia*, 83; Yin era, China, 168–171
Agrodespotic state, 192 *n.*
Ajaoiens, 104–105
Albigensian sect, 19, 67, 69, 73, 77
Altman, I., 251
Amalrician sect, 67, 78
Amalric of Bena, 25–26
American sects, 80, 197, 268
Anabaptist sect, 34–40; destructive elements, 275; as forerunner of socialism, 78, 197, 214; in Münster, 59–66; name and origin, 67, 69–71; violence and fanaticism, 37–40, 60–66, 73, 265
Anarchism, 215, 248–249, 267
Ancient Kingdom. *See* Egypt
Ancient Orient socialist states, 152–185, 196, 202; and ideology, 272; summary, 189–192, 255. *See also* "Asiatic Social Formation"
Animal societies, 264–265, 269, 271–272; and instinct, 297
Anonymous society, 265, 269
Anthropology of socialism, 227–234
Antichrist, 25, 27, 29, 46, 48
*Anti-Dühring* (Engels), 208–209, 212–213
Anti-cultural theme, 178, 184–185, 196–197, 233, 265–266; post-revolutionary Russia, 248–251

Antiquity: labor population, 190; and socialism, 3–18, 78. *See also* China, ancient; Egypt; Mesopotamia
Apostolic Brethren, 29, 46–50, 67, 71
Aristophanes, 3–4, 6, 14–15
Arts, 2; 18th-century novels, 105–106; Enlightenment literature, 111, 119, 121; in ideal socialist state, 269; of New Left, 233; in Plato's *Republic*, 9–10, 265; in post-revolutionary Russia, 248, 250–251; Utopians and, 85. *See also* Anti-cultural theme
Arvatov, B., 250
"Asiatic Social Formation," xi, 185–189, 207, 256–257; basic features, 187–188
Atheism: Deschamps and, 115–117; Levellers, 45–46; as "religion" of socialism, 130, 196, 225, 233–234; socialism as result of, 234–235
Australian aborigines, 205, 273
"Axial time," 255–257
Ayala, Guamán Poma de, 136, 139–140
Aztecs, 205

Babeuf, François Émile, 121, 124, 212
Bakunin, M., 186 *n.*, 203, 215, 219, 223; confession of, 294; destruction and terror theme, 212, 275–279
Baptism, 68–70, 75
Baptists, 70, 80
*Barilotto*, 27, 42
Batenburg, 40
Bau temple, 153–155, 155 *n.*
Baudin, L., 141–142, 264
Bazarov, V. A., 226
Beehive analogy, 218, 269

309

Violence and terror (*cont'd*)
ary youth and, 283–285; socialist party
concept of, 217–218. *See also* Medieval
heresies; Shang Yang
Vipper, R., 215
*Voice of Reason, The* (Deschamps), 116–
117
Voltaire, 106, 110, 151

Waldensians, 29, 36; beliefs, 73, 76–77; origins, 67, 69–71
Walwyn, William, 44
War Communism, 238–252, 265
Weber, Max, 296
Weitling, Wilhelm, 45 *n.*, 121
Wells, H. G., 2–3, 273
Western Europe: contemporary leftist movements, 268; meaning of Russian socialism, 300
Winstanley, Gerrard, 43–46, 95; concept of new society, 96–101, 219
"Withering away of the state" concept, 175, 206–207
Wittfogel, K., 191–192, 192 *n.*, 201, 207; ancient Eastern Socialism, 186–187, 186 *n.*; on state capitalism, 216
Wives, as common property: American sects, 80; Anabaptists, 36, 38–40; Apostolic Brethren, 29, 47–48; Cathars, 23–24; in Münster, 63–66; Plato on, 12, 258–259; as revolutionary slogan, 214; and socialism, 195, 236

Women: communality of, 4, 12, 15–17, 91–92, 95; Diggers and Winstanley against communality, 44, 100; Inca oppression and state regulation, 134, 136–138, 141–142; and men in Deschamps' paradise, 118–120; Meslier's complete freedom to, 109; in Mesopotamia, 153, 155, 158–159; Plato's equal rights to, 9; in post-revolutionary Russia, 245; Solarian regulations, 91–92. *See also* Family, Marriage customs; Wives, as common property
Work and workers: liberation from, Marcuse thesis, 6, 231–232; and revolution, 203; socialist goal of social justice and, 223–224. *See also* Compulsory labor
World empire concept, 161–162
World view: of Deschamps, 120; dualism, 297–298; of "Equals," 130; of Freud, 292, 297; inevitable death theme, 280–285; Marxism and nihilism, 278–279; of religion, 267; of socialism, xv, 226–227, 231, 237
Writing and recording systems: ancient China, 168, 172; ancient Mesopotamia, 153–157, 161; Deschamps prohibition, 119; Egyptian scribes, 162–165; Incas, 134, 134 *n.*, 138–139; Jesuit state, 144

Zen Buddhism, 291–292
Zinoviev, G. E., 294
Zulus, 141
Zwickau Prophets, 37
Zwingli, Ulrich, 34, 37, 71, 73

## About the Author

Igor Rostislavovich Shafarevich was born in 1923. In 1940, at the age of 17, he graduated from Moscow University (Faculty of Mechanics and Mathematics). He was employed in the Steklov Mathematics Institute of the Academy of Sciences and simultaneously held a teaching position in mathematics at Moscow University 1944–49 and 1953–76. The university connection was terminated after the publication abroad of his essays in the collection *From Under the Rubble.*

Shafarevich is a mathematician of world-wide repute. Among the awards he has received in recognition of his achievements in this field are the Lenin Prize (1959) and the Heineman Prize of the Göttingen Academy of Sciences (1973). He is a corresponding member of the Academy of Sciences of the USSR, a foreign associate of several Western learned societies (including the National Academy of Sciences [USA] and the London Mathematical Society), and has had an honorary doctorate conferred upon him by the University of Paris.

Igor Shafarevich is the author of *The General Law of Reciprocity* (195), and is credited in the American Directory of Science as having discovered the law of reciprocity. One American mathematician who had occasion to have first-hand knowledge of Shafarevich's achievements describes them as being breakthroughs of the highest rank. Shafarevich, himself, has been described as a great mathematical statesman and leader, as well as a creative mathematician of the first order.

Shafarevich currently resides in Moscow. He is married and has two children.